Mills College Library
from

Boston
December
1951

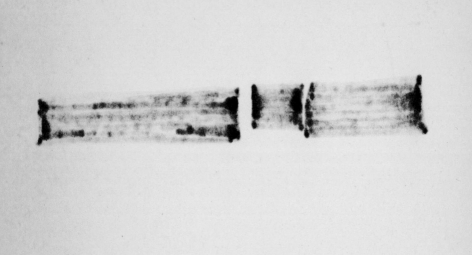

BY SAMUEL SHELLABARGER

Biography

THE CHEVALIER BAYARD
LORD CHESTERFIELD AND HIS WORLD

Fiction

THE BLACK GALE
CAPTAIN FROM CASTILE
PRINCE OF FOXES
THE KING'S CAVALIER

LORD CHESTERFIELD
AND HIS WORLD

Philip Dormer Stanhope, 4th Earl of Chesterfield
From the original painting by Gainsborough

Lord Chesterfield
and His World

by
SAMUEL SHELLABARGER

*Quia filii hujus saeculi prudentiores
filiis lucis in generatione sua sunt*

Little, Brown and Company · Boston
1 9 5 1

Published simultaneously
in Canada by McClelland and Stewart Limited

PRINTED IN THE UNITED STATES OF AMERICA

TO
PHILIP MARSHALL BROWN
AND
JANE BROWN
WITH DEEPEST AFFECTION

Contents

Contents

LORD CHESTERFIELD
AND HIS WORLD

Introduction

THE SUPREME DISTINCTION of Philip Dormer Stanhope, fourth Earl of Chesterfield, is that he wrote a series of letters which has become one of the world's permanent books. It became so independent of his desire and will; indeed, had he been alive at the moment of its publication he would unquestionably have done everything in his power to prevent it. Yet none of his other titles to memory — his rank, political career, social eminence, talent as an essayist — none of these will be considered nowadays as comparable in importance to the authorship of the *Letters to his Son;* indeed, were it not for the *Letters* none of them would be remembered at all except by those interested in the general subject of eighteenth-century history and manners. His significance to most of us will almost exclusively consist in this accidental, unsought achievement.

For the *Letters to his Son,* though composed in eighteenth-century England and aromatic of their age, belong primarily neither to England nor to the eighteenth century. Translated into all the considerable languages of the world, familiar to Japan as to France, they possess obviously a timeless, placeless quality adaptable to civilized mankind as a whole, and not greatly affected by change of fashion or environment. They are an exquisite flower of civilization, and depend more upon the persistence of culture than upon the element of time. We may safely predict (unless civilization itself, as we know it, perishes) that three centuries hence the *Letters* will be still read with the same degree of praise or censure which has been accorded them during the last hundred and fifty years.

Apart from the charm of grace, vigor, suppleness, and pungency, the distinction of style that characterizes them and gives classic finish to their content, the reason for this perennial value is that they describe, with singular assurance and felicity, one of the arts of life which will always interest the major portion of mankind. It is the art of worldly success, of getting on, of achieving power and place among one's fellow men; the art of gauging and manipulating human nature, the cardinal factor of success, to one's own profit. It will be a long time before so useful a thesis fails to attract, to convince, and to enlighten. The *Letters* are without question the premier textbook on this alluring subject. Or, to put it in other words, they are the classical expression of worldly wisdom.

It is no small thing to have written a book of this enduring quality. That fact alone gives interest to the life of its author. But with a pedagogical work such as the *Letters*, a question of competence arises. Was the teacher himself a practitioner? Are his precepts delivered at second hand or out of personal experience? No one can write more fluently of life than one who has never lived, of success than a failure. If Chesterfield's letters on the technique of getting on in the world are to be fully relished, it is important to determine whether they were written by a man who fully knew the world.

But there is a still more important connection in this instance between the author and his work. Letters are peculiarly the expression of a personality, of a personal attitude, a personal philosophy. They are (in a sense applicable only to memoirs among other literary species) the man himself. Thus, in the case of these particular letters, one is led inevitably back to Chesterfield's life for their sanction and commentary, and again from him to the *Letters* for the quintessence of his thought and character. Briefly then, worldly success is a matter of such perennial interest that its leading exposition is of importance; but as this last is in the form of letters, it cannot be separated from the expositor himself.

Great men are of two kinds. There are those who excel by virtue of an original, an originating quality of thought, act, or emotion, who are the founders of schools, systems, and traditions, or lone stars of unique achievement. They are perhaps the greatest, they are at least the most arresting, names. Newton, Locke, Dryden, and Swift may serve as examples of this class. Then there are men whose excellence is of an interpretative order. They mirror and embellish; they give perfect expression to enduring tendencies of thought, and, though conventional in the sense that they originate nothing, they are still frequently the protagonists and exponents of widespread and persistent human types. Of this order were Fontenelle, Addison, Pope, and Chesterfield. They are the truly *representative* men.

It is characteristic of this class that any given member of it belongs to a family and shares a family likeness. To some, Chesterfield will recall the younger Pliny; to Cowper he suggested Petronius Arbiter; there is a touch of Maecenas, a touch of Cicero, a touch of Pandarus about him; he becomes easily a composite of the diplomats, men of affairs, cosmopolitans whom we have known or of whom we have read. This does not mean that his personality is vague or featureless, but it does mean that to an unusual degree he displays those traits which have characterized the patrician man of the world in every age. While speaking the idiom and reflecting the color of his century, there was still something in him which belongs to all centuries; and it is this timeless quality which gives him a rank among great men.

Every human type is such by virtue of a unifying attitude, a common allegiance to certain values. Distinguishing the man of the world of all ages is a philosophy at times implicit, but in general avowed, which perhaps is most conveniently expressed by the indefinite term worldliness. It is an alliance of rationalism with materialism in the practical exercise of social life. Less formally stated, it is a belief in the supreme desirability of what most men strive for — power, position, wealth, the esteem of one's associates, the pleasures of the senses — the pursuit and enjoyment of all this to be regulated partly by some code of good form and partly by common sense, which is rationalism *en négligé*. The objectives of worldliness will always commend themselves to that legal fiction, the ordinary prudent man; its values will always seem valuable to 99 per cent of the population; it is the most plausible form of selfishness.

The true man of the world is no doctrinaire and would warmly disclaim the title of worldly. It may often serve his purpose to be considered or consider himself an idealist. But his distinguishing features are the same: he is the adept of compromise, expediency, the unburned bridge, the secret reservation, the ultimate confidence in Mammon. It matters not whether or no he admits these tendencies to himself; they remain characteristic of him. It is unnecessary to point out how large a section of the great and fair in all generations belong to this persuasion. It is one of the most distinguished human categories.

The claims of worldliness in any manual of worldly wisdom are manifold and compelling. Its rules and recipes assure the heart's desire. Unconcerned with any other existence, they guarantee in this, at least, as much success in terms of wealth and fame as the accidents of life permit. Their boast it is to be practical, to lay bare the heart, to expose the springs and pulleys of behavior, to show men how they may govern themselves and others, to foretell the future, and, in brief, to provide the best possible tool for opening the world oyster. From the standpoint of worldliness any other system is merely pathetic or absurd, nor can it be taken seriously. Such are the claims of this imposing faith.

We have pointed out that Chesterfield's *Letters* are its most perfect exposition. And this is true because their author, a supreme representative of his class, happened also to be a distinguished literary man. But the *Letters* and Chesterfield himself are indebted for their peculiar authority to still another factor. It is nothing else than the age in which they were written, when the cult of worldliness attained its more refined, its most gracious development. The *ancien régime* lent the charm of sophistication, the splendor of an aristocratic caste with its pride of bearing and manners, to the worship of success in a somewhat limited society. It was the heyday of the beau monde, of Vanity Fair in its most beguiling aspect. And the eighteenth century, the meridian of reason, common sense, and the social arts, contributes a fitting background for Chesterfield, who was one of its most eloquent interpreters.

There is a perfection and completeness in him that one finds but seldom in actual life. As representative of the worldly tradition at its best, we can suggest no change or improvement. He was a great nobleman of the great age of noblemen; by birth, by training, by natural aptitude and long experience he fitted his role; he was wealthy, prominent, and admired; he was learned, witty, versatile, cosmopolitan; he lived to an advanced age, and hence reviewed the whole of life. He wrote as one would expect him to write; he lived as one would expect him to live.

A biography of Chesterfield, if it is to be more than a chronicle, if it is to have vital significance for our time, becomes inevitably a study not only of the man himself but of the man in relation to the book which has ensured his fame, or rather to that philosophy of which the book is a monumental expression. It involves necessarily the examination of what he stood for — an attitude of mind and heart no less prevalent now than then, the attitude of worldly rationalism. The man and his philosophy are mutually illustrative and inseparable.

It is the failure to grasp this fact, a failure likewise in determining exactly what is the reason for Chesterfield's perennial importance, which accounts, I believe, for so much unnecessary criticism and defense of him since the publication of the *Letters*. He has been exceedingly vilified and extensively whitewashed, whereas the truth is that he was ethically like thousands of his own and of other generations who have had the sense or good fortune to keep their frank opinions from the public, and have therefore escaped with undamaged reputations. It is but a pettifogging business to excuse or accuse him in regard to details which are the result of a general conception of life, shared, though not necessarily avowed, by most of his class. Why cavil as to the degree of his honesty, the degree of his altruism or egoism? Why defend or denounce his attitude toward women? Why be concerned at the implication that he desired to know human nature so that he might exploit it? These are not important points; the main issue is to accept or reject that way of the world which he so bluntly expressed. Once admit the major position and there is no use protesting against consequences. The problem is really not Chesterfield's but his critics' — whether they will be equally sincere, consistent, and definite. Do they or do they not live by, or at least admire, the standards, the strategy, and rewards of worldliness?

Such are the considerations that justify the following pages. Merely to review once more the facts of Lord Chesterfield's life, to present one more estimate of his character, would be at this late date a pointless duplication. It may be confidently stated that although an occasional piece of mosaic may be discovered — some unknown episode, some letter or collection of letters, hitherto mislaid or withheld — nothing will be found to alter the now established outlines of his life and thought. In the study we shall make of him a few crumbs of information will be added to the previous store, and the chief events of his career will, of course, be presented; but our concern is only with these insofar as they are germane to the conception we have already indicated. It is this *interpenetration*, if we may call it so, of a book, a man, an age, and a philosophy, which will be our theme; and it is this conception which brings Chesterfield's life into a new and, I believe, the only proper focus.

Curiously enough, it has hitherto never been attempted. The *Letters* themselves, the relationship with his son, which, it must be repeated, is for us the most important passage of his life, have been invariably accorded no more than a summary attention. It is as if his performance in parliament, his conduct as a diplomat, his contributions to periodicals, were of equal or even greater significance. But, to our way of thinking, not only the *Letters* and the education of Philip Stanhope but friendships, correspondents, the *mise en scène* of his life, are more illuminating than his public actions. The building of Chesterfield House is biographically of greater import than his second embassy to The Hague. His life at the watering places, his passion for Ranelagh, reveal more of his personality than do the speeches in opposition to Walpole. It is unnecessary to labor this point, which is simply that biographical data should be ordered so as to explain and emphasize the phase or phases of a man's life which are of lasting importance, and that this has never been done in the case of Lord Chesterfield. Not that any facts are negligible but that in a complete biography some gradation of values must be established. In this belief, the present writer has edited a very considerable mass of details.

Thus no attempt has been made to trace step by step the negotiations in Holland which brought the United Provinces into accord with the Second Treaty of Vienna. Chesterfield's performance in parliament or as ambassador a second time to Holland in 1745 or as Lord Lieutenant of Ireland has been described but not itemized. The minutiae of his participation in politics, diplomacy, and administration belong to special studies. It is believed that enough has been included to contribute to a well-balanced appraisal of his character and achievements; but more than this would be extraneous to our purpose. The reader who is specifically interested in these aspects of his life should consult the appropriate works listed in the bibliography.

Therefore, in the following investigation we shall seek first of all to know more of Chesterfield the individual, the wit, politician, and pedagogue of the eighteenth century, but in him we shall also study under the most favorable light, during its most illustrious period, a certain imperishable human type. And the final result should be an enrichment not only of knowledge but of understanding – a wider philosophic experience.

PART ONE
1694 - 1715

CHAPTER I
Savile and Stanhope

AT THE CLOSE of the seventeenth century, London, externally at least, was not much more than thirty years old. The great fire of 1666 had erased the Gothic past and cleared the ground for sensible modern architecture. Gone were gables and overhanging house fronts, oak beams, undulating walls, and round-bellied windows, the whole rabbit warren of courts and alleyways. St. Paul's and other churches were gone with faith, legend, and memory; the very churchyards were consumed. In place of this, new house fronts, conventional, neat, and sober, stood rigidly in line along wider and better-paved streets. Miles of red brick,[1] leagues of cobblestones, stretched out between colonnaded and stone-faced public buildings and noblemen's mansions. New St. Paul's arose, no longer spired, but domed — everything orderly and correct, a brand-new, up-to-date city. The poet Dryden burst into raptures over it. He sang:

> More great than human now, and more august,
> Now deify'd she from her fires does rise:
> Her widening streets on new foundations trust,
> And opening into larger parts she flies.[2]

But as we study the prints, now more than two centuries old, of this revived and modern London, a cold smell of new mortar and masonry seems to cling to them; it is all a little stiff and chilly, gaunt and hard.

The city was not only up-to-date materially, but spiritually. Puritan zeal and Cavalier loyalty having been equally discarded, common sense had once more come into her own. Locke and Newton, Butler and Dryden, were all promoting in one way or another the new cult of rationalism. Virtue had become conventionality; religion had been pigeonholed as theology; the reaction to Puritanism did not restore mirth or sensuousness or *joie de vivre*, but it established wit, sensualism, and worldliness. Of this indwelling spirit, the distinct, angular architecture was a reflection.

Upon such a stage, in such an atmosphere, Philip Dormer Stanhope, the future Chesterfield, was born on September 22, 1694.

The newness of London and what that newness represented will account for many phenomena of the period. It should be remembered as the background of Chesterfield's life. He would grow up in a city more spick-and-span and staringly modern than any metropolis of the present day — the setting within which a new epoch, freed from the superstitions and prejudices of the past, had recently begun.

His parents were Lord Philip and Lady Elizabeth Stanhope. His paternal grandfather, who lived nineteen years after his birth, was likewise Philip Stanhope, second Earl of Chesterfield, a picturesque survival of Restoration days, a duelist, a Jacobite, an old fire-eater who did not belong to the new age.* But the Stanhope inheritance would play no role spiritually or intellectually in the life of the most distinguished of the Stanhopes.† It was his mother's father to

---

* He had been naïve enough to show jealousy of the Duke of York in Charles II's time and to remove his wife from that prince's attentions; he had been loyal enough to hold by King James and refuse all allegiance to King William. He was a sturdy sentimentalist of the romantic order. In his comments on Macky's *Characters* (*Works*, Bohn edition, vol. x, p. 279) Swift writes of him unjustly that he had heard he was the greatest knave in England. Certainly he had had a checkered career — exile, squire of dames, and very minor statesman. He was typically of the Restoration in appearance, morals, manners, and interests. He beautified his estates, wrote entertaining letters, and patronized Dryden. The latter dedicated his translation of the *Georgics* to him, after flattering letters to which the Earl returned a "noble present" (*Letters of Philip, 2nd Earl of Chesterfield*, London, 1829: Dryden to Chesterfield, Aug. 18, 1697). To the end, in spite of the gout, he enjoyed "a mate at chess, a bottle of Burgundy, and a friend by the fireside." He differed from many of his rank and age in maintaining a steady loyalty to the House of Stuart. He was also a man of strict honor according to the code of the time, had never sold himself or groveled to anyone, and died a notable, if not an eminent, person. On almost every count, except that of political probity, no two people could be more unlike than this nobleman and his grandson. As the latter seems to have seen practically nothing of his grandfather, who in latter years remained almost entirely on his Derbyshire estate, and as the second Earl presumably had not the slightest influence on Philip Stanhope's career, any account of him beyond the briefest mention appears unnecessary.

† "We believe, taking the blood all together, not one race in Great Britain has produced within the last two hundred and fifty years so many persons of

whom he would remain indebted to an almost uncanny degree.*
There can be no better approach to Chesterfieldianism than by way
of this grandparent, of whom the grandson seems rather a reincarna-
tion than the offspring. He was George Savile, Marquis of Halifax.
Let us consider him briefly.

From the throng of smiling, cold-eyed courtiers which surrounded
the last two Stuarts, he stands forth as a model and beau ideal. He
had been Privy Councilor and an intimate of three kings, Lord Privy
Seal, President of the Council, Speaker of the House of Peers. For
a while, in parliament and at court, he had been supremely powerful.
He was wise, witty, rich, and fortunate, a favorite in society, a patron
of letters, and oddly enough both patriotic † and incorruptible. He
set the golden mean at the center of his philosophy, temperate in
good and evil, personally fearless, but seldom so much involved with
any loyalty as to burn his bridges for it, prudent in safeguarding retreat, proud to style himself a trimmer, the "skillful pilot" of
Dryden's eulogy.[3]

He was a man of the world in the greatest sense, a politician in
the greatest sense, schooled by the intrigues of three courts, adroit
in parliamentary management. But, more than this, he achieved
finally a permanent rank among statesmen by giving direction to a
new political epoch. The Revolution of 1688 was not only supported
and in large measure presided over by Halifax, but it and the subsequent constitutional trend remain forever identified with his stubborn
Protestantism and his hatred for autocracy. His thought, coloring it
at the source, became integral with the Whig Party.

There is something Januslike about him. His appearance, as we
study it in the engraving by Houbraken or on the mortuary bust in

---

real and deserved eminence; but still for the brilliant variety of his talents and
attainments, the general splendour of his career, influence, and fame, the fourth
Earl of Chesterfield remains the *facile princeps* of his house and name." Lord
Brougham, *Quarterly Review*, 1845, vol. 76, p. 459.

* There is, of course, nothing new in pointing this out. It impressed contemporaries such as Lord Hervey and Dr. Maty (Hervey, *Memoirs*, 1931, vol. i,
p. 7; Maty, ed., *Miscellaneous Works of Chesterfield*, 1777, vol. i, pp. 268–269)
and has since been often repeated, though it seems to me insufficiently emphasized.

† Though fashionably hard, thoughts of his country would sometimes tempt
him to a warmth of sentiment. "The earth of England," he exclaimed, ". . .
there is divinity in it!"; or with hearty gusto, "There is a smell in our native
earth, better than all the perfumes of the East." Halifax, *Miscellanies*, 1704,
pp. 151, 176, "Character of a Trimmer."

Westminster Abbey, recalls, in spite of its peruke, the stout, jack-booted Cavaliers of the sixteen-thirties; and Burnet reports of him that "he was a man of a great and ready wit, full of life and very pleasant." But his writings bear a curious discrepancy to this appearance. They announce rather the eighteenth than the seventeenth century. We would expect, as more appropriate to them, the passionless face of a Marlborough or an Addison. The judicial quality of his mind, its freedom from emotion, his emphasis on common sense, his religious skepticism, were all prophetic of the oncoming time.

While hating France in a traditional manner as the arch foe of England,[4] it was in French culture that he found himself at home; it was French clarity and realism that best suited his own attitude. He would cavil on the ninth part of a hair for the advantage of England; but he dispatched his sons for their training to Switzerland and Paris. In his opinion it was Montaigne who had written the most entertaining book in the world,[5] and he and the great French skeptic would have seen eye to eye in religious matters. Regarding the latter, he asserted "that he believed as much as he could, and hoped that God would not lay it to his charge if he could not digest iron as an ostrich did." [6] But with reference to Popery, he was a zealous Protestant, not from conviction, but from politics.

His wit, too, was Latin. He could not resist the temptation of an epigram, whatever the recoil of it upon himself might be. Lord Hervey, writing forty years later of Chesterfield's passion for raillery, declared that "no sex, no relation, no rank, no power, no profession, no friendship, no obligation, was a shield from those pointed, glittering weapons, that seemed to shine only to a stander-by, but cut deep in those they touched." [7] And the same might equally have been affirmed of Halifax. He was quite aware of the danger of this, and advised others against it,* but in his own case the thirst for satire prevailed.

As they grow older, men of the world and of great experience sometimes yield to the subtle form of self-indulgence which con-

---

* He lost his place on the council in Lord Danby's time because of an alluring quip at that minister which he was unable to repress. It had been said that Danby had been offered a huge bribe for the farm of the taxes, and had courteously declined it though not so as to discourage a second attempt. It was exactly, remarked Halifax, as if a man should ask another for the use of his wife, and should be refused, "but with great civility." Bishop Burnet, *History of My Own Time*, 1818, vol. i, p. 448.

sists in parading their age and the results of their long observation
of life before other people — usually young people. They abound in
maxims or instructive reminiscences, or they write admonitory
essays or letters. These are at times so charming and valuable that
they eclipse all other achievements of their authors, who live for
posterity largely on the score of them. In the case of Halifax, it
was his daughter Elizabeth, the future mother of Chesterfield, who
enjoyed the fruit of his wisdom. For her he composed a little treatise
called *Advice to a Daughter*, of which he thought highly enough to
publish it. Within a century it had gone through sixteen editions,
and long after his political triumphs had been forgotten he remained a mentor of young ladies.

In this pamphlet may be found the quintessence of Halifax's
philosophy — his emphasis on reputation, his cynical opinion of
human nature, his praise of calculation and reserve.* The Marquis's
standard of morality stood high relative to that of his political
cronies or rivals, the Rochesters, Buckinghams, Danbys, Montagus,
and Sunderlands, but it was comfortable rather than exacting. His
advice to Lady Betty adequately expresses it. He pointed out that
adultery and drunkenness had become so common that a good wife
should overlook them in her husband, and indeed, my dear, should
thank God for such faults as these which would blind him to hers,
and gradually give her an advantage over him. "For nothing," continued the Marquis, "softneth the arrogance of a man like a mixture
of some frailties . . . so that when the errors of the masculine sex
make up for the inferiority of yours, it is more your part to make use
of the benefit, than to quarrel at the fault." [8]

During the few years of retirement before his death he had every
reason to look back over his life with satisfaction. Baronet, earl, and
marquis, he had had his finger in all the important pies, had acquired
a fortune outrivaling the King's, had trimmed his sails to every
popular gale, and finally, reefing them still more, had run victorious
into port — his splendid Halifax House [9] on the new "piazza" of
St. James. He had buried his first wife and two sons; but he had still
an heir to his title, and no one could excel Lady Gertrude, the

---

* His daughter should abandon a friend who has incurred the censure of
society rather than share that censure. She should avoid intimacies for fear that
they would be betrayed. She must be eager to surpass others in virtue and all
such other things so as to gain a greater share of the good opinion of the
world. Halifax, *Miscellanies*, pp. 60, 62, 78, "Advice to a Daughter."

present Marchioness, in charm and *savoir-faire*. A number of his friends were dead, and others had dropped away; but old age at best is apt to be lonely.

It was the Stanhope alliance which may well have been his only vexation at the end. His former intimate, the old Earl of Chesterfield, with whom he had dined, wined, and talked bawdry and politics so often,* having at length been unable to follow his political veerings, had told him to his face that he would "rather be a plain, honest country gentleman, than a cunning, false, court knave," and had broken with him. The ancient ruffler had actually forbidden his son and daughter-in-law to have dealings with the Marquis. Lady Betty, who was something of a scold and had benefited no whit by the sage pamphlet which had been dedicated to her, was on strained terms with her husband. Her father-in-law, old Chesterfield, had derisively scribbled "labour in vain" on her copy of the famous treatise. Her husband, Lord Stanhope, begged the Marquis to help him manage her, persuade her to leave town for the winter, complained of her coldness.[10] He was a sour, moody fellow, a Jacobite like his father, and completely overshadowed by him. He was certainly not to the taste of Halifax, who sided with dear Betty.†

Labor in vain? Was it all labor in vain — his title and wealth, ambition, renown, the endless days and ways up and down court stairs, attending levees, whispering in alcoves, debating at council boards, speaking in parliament, changing from side to side, juggling, scheming? We may imagine him sometimes standing at his windows

* *Letters of Philip, 2nd Earl of Chesterfield*, London, 1829. Halifax seems for years to have been the Earl's most intimate and trusted friend. Their correspondence forms a considerable part of the extant letters. The following may be regarded as an instance of Halifax's vein: "Your birds," he writes to Chesterfield in the country, "have, no doubt, made a new tune to bid you welcome, and your flowers strew you with their perfumes, to cleans you from any remainder of London ayre, which may yet hang about you. I must not forget the tame creature with black eyes, who maketh such an essential part of your lordship's entertainment, that I wish you may, in some reasonable measure, contribute to hers." — Oct. 1685. The second Earl appears at times to have condescended to his maidservants. See his letter to Bates, Jan. 7 [1673].

† In February [1695?] Lord Stanhope seems to have been away from England. Perhaps he was not even present at the birth of his son. At any rate, the Marquis refers to him as being abroad. *Historical Manuscripts Commission*, MSS. of the Marquess of Downshire, vol. i, p. 461, Halifax to Sir William Trumbull. See also, with regard to the strained relations between Lord Stanhope and his wife, the richly documented opening chapters of Willard Connely's *The True Chesterfield*, London, 1939.

and looking out at the new, fine, bleak London; and it would be strange if the mood of Ecclesiastes did not occasionally descend upon him. But after all, what more could he want who had everything? . . . Youth, perhaps? The old faces? Or something else — something inexpressible? Years later his grandson would in his turn stand looking out upon the emptiness of age, and would watch the falling leaves, and sigh over the dust and ashes of past illusions.[11]

Shortly before Halifax died, there was published a booklet called *A Proposal for a National Reformation of Manners*. "Our light," it declared, "looks like the evening of the world." [12] Realistic, superficial, hard, England was approaching the new century. The trim, angular city expressed her soul. "Our light looks like the evening of the world. . . ."

But there was no trace of heaviness even at this period in the Marquis's essays, which were as forceful as ever. He was not concerned with a reformation, ethical or religious, but left that to fanatics. What interested him was British naval strength and the channel. "It may be said now to England," he wrote, " 'Martha, Martha, thou art busy about many things, but one thing is necessary to the question, What shall we do to be saved in this world? There is no answer but this, Look to your moat.' " [13]

He had neglected an old hernia; gangrene set in. They told him he could not recover. For once no trimming would solve the problem, no wealth nor title nor any other thing. But he died as he lived, conventional and prudent, calmly receiving the Sacrament in which he did not greatly trust. Still, who could tell? Burn no bridges. And at least it was a polite gesture. They buried him with considerable éclat in Westminster Abbey.

It was under the shadow of this great name that the future Chesterfield began life. At the time of the Marquis's death, on April 5, 1695, his son-in-law, Lord Stanhope, occupied a house [14] nearby on St. James's Square, so that, from the very day of his birth six months earlier, Philip Stanhope had belonged to the Halifax circle. It was to him that the dying statesman bequeathed his richest properties, not of title and wealth, indeed, but more valuable gifts — a strong will, a retentive memory, a cool head and docile heart, wit, grace, eloquence, the most exquisite sense of propriety — a splendid inheritance, of which his father's family would fill up the measure by contributing the externals of rank and lands.

But Philip Stanhope was not only born in St. James's Square under the Halifax aegis; he was brought up there or in the neighborhood, and environment completed heredity. His grandmother, Lady Halifax, took charge of his education. He remained with her until he left for the university; and it was, therefore, steeped in the Savile tradition, democratic and liberal, in a house haunted by the memory of Lord Halifax's urbanity and skepticism, that the formative period of his life was passed.

These are the positive elements that determined his youth; a negative element no less important has been indicated. That he was brought up by Lady Halifax, separated from his parents,* deserves far more attention than it has hitherto received; for the absence of one of life's normal influences must have, and certainly had in his case, a distinctive effect upon character.

The reason for this separation remains obscure. Early biographers have evaded the point by incorrectly affirming that Lady Betty died in her son's early childhood. But this is obviously untrue; he was fourteen years old at the time of her death in 1708. Originally, no doubt, Philip Stanhope was kept by his grandmother to avoid his being moved from place to place; for his father seems never to have been long contented anywhere. But his sister Gertrude, afterwards Lady Hotham, who was three years younger, was also educated together with him by Lady Halifax. On the other hand his brother William, born in 1702, and his sister Elizabeth, born in 1703, remained with their parents in the country. Family friction had certainly a part in it, Savile disputing with Stanhope,† Lady Halifax and her daughter on one side, the old Earl of Chesterfield and his son on the other — all the venom of an unhappy marriage. Although, after the Marquis's death, a *rapprochement* apparently took place between his widow and Lord Chesterfield,[15] relations were never very cordial, for the fundamental antipathy between Lady Betty and her husband remained. Lord Stanhope was an ill-tempered, defeated man, cut off at thirty by deafness and ill-health from any active life, though valuing himself as a patron and critic of letters. Low-spirited, pedantic, and at times dissipated, he was given to classical allusions and

---

* On Lady Betty's occasional visits to her mother and equally occasional supervision of her son's education, see Connely, *op. cit.*, chap. I.

† The second Earl refers to Lady Betty's dowry as a great fortune; the desires of the Saviles would receive a certain amount of consideration.

to girding at "degenerated Britons." * He disliked London and preferred the country, where, at his house in Lichfield or at Brisancoate, Bretby or another of the many Stanhope holdings,[16] he led a featureless life to the end of the chapter. On the other hand, Lady Betty was the spoiled and spirited daughter of a great man, was devoted to the city, but condemned, after her father's death at least,[17] to exile in Derbyshire,[18] to isolation and childbearing,† and to smolder out in domestic monotony. It was perhaps to save Philip and her namesake, Gertrude, from the miasma of such a relationship that Lady Halifax kept them in London.

Whether because of Philip's education in the Savile camp, or by reason of a natural dislike, Lord Stanhope seems early to have felt an aversion for his eldest son. Not only was the boy a virtual orphan, but his absent father hated him into the bargain. Writing in 1703 to Dr. Atterbury, the subsequent Bishop of Rochester, his lordship, rancorous as usual, could not resist jeering at the eight-year-old boy then under the roof of his grandmother, who in 1698 had moved from St. James's Square to a large house in Park Place, several blocks distant, off St. James's Street.‡ The Doctor had apparently offered his services to smooth over some domestic difficulty. "I am very much obliged to you," wrote Stanhope, "for the service you offer

---

* Recalling once that Caesar had inquired regarding some Roman matrons, who were fond of lap dogs, whether they were past childbearing, he felt inspired by such an example to ask a fine and pet-loving lady of his acquaintance the same question, and seems to have been surprised at her resentment. Francis Bickley, *An English Letter Book*, two letters from the third Earl of Chesterfield to Matthew Prior. The Earl sent money to Prior in return for some verses and a portrait. Prior, however, was not his only literary friend. He made a point of mentioning to the latter his friendship for Dryden. Other letters from the Earl to Prior are to be found in *Hist. MSS. Comm.*, MSS. of the Marquis of Bath, vol. iii, pp. 447, 465, 474, 480, 494, 497.

† There were six children who lived: Philip, *b.* 1694; Gertrude, *b.* 1697; William, *b.* 1702; Elizabeth, *b.* 1703; John, *b.* 1704; Charles, *b.* 1708. There were also two miscarriages and a son who lived only a week. Lady Betty died following the birth of Charles in 1708.

‡ Upon the death of Halifax in 1695, his mansion was inherited by his son William, the second Marquis, who in his turn died in 1700, and with whom the title became extinct. The Dowager Lady Halifax occupied the former house of her stepson, William, on the south part of the square until 1697. It is to be noted that after Halifax House was pulled down Chesterfield acquired in 1727 one of the two houses (No. 18) erected on its site, and continued to live there until his marriage in 1733, when he moved to Grosvenor Square. If this means anything, it might indicate an attachment to a neighborhood with which he was long familiar. See Chancellor, *History of the Squares of London*.

to do for me at St. James's; but in that undertaking I do really think you will only lose your time to no purpose; for I expect nothing from the gentleman that is there, but to see him bred up an ignorant, worthless, amorous fop." [19] With this paternal benediction the future Chesterfield is first encountered. But Lord Stanhope's ill will did not stop at words. When he came to his title in 1713 it was upon his second son, William, that he showered his favors, deeding him for life his Buckinghamshire estate with its income of eight thousand pounds, while he restricted his eldest son to a bare five hundred.[20]

His dislike was reciprocated. Years later Chesterfield declared that his father neither desired nor was able to advise him; [21] and at the time of the latter's death, while he waited, kicking his heels at Bretby, and filling in time with graceful letters to the Prince of Wales's mistress, he observed that when pious Aeneas took such care of his father, that old gentleman was "turned of fourscore, and not likely to trouble him long," but if he had been "of the same age as mine, he would not have been quite so well looked after." [22]

Probably the account was balanced in the end.

This lack of parental influence, of the normal filial ties, is important to an estimate of Chesterfield. His contempt for women, his aversion to matrimony, his emotional skepticism, may well have been owing in part to this early privation. Lady Halifax could not wholly replace what under happier circumstances might have been. The times at best did not favor the gentler relationships of a home, but still for many the memory of a father's solicitude, a mother's love, must have softened and colored experience. It would not be so with him.

From the outset, a curious isolation marks him. Just as his only son would be illegitimate, and his marriage a mere social bargain, so that in terms of ordinary family life he may be said to have had neither wife nor child, in the same fashion he had no parents. He stood always alone; nor would it have occurred to him to repine. Any domestic bonds would have been inappropriate to his personality.

CHAPTER II
St. James's Square

LORD STANHOPE's expectation that his eldest son would be brought up an "ignorant, worthless, amorous fop" had, from his standpoint, a good deal more to justify it than chronic ill-humor. It expressed the attitude of a conservative toward progressive education. It was the contempt of a Westminster School alumnus, who had been properly birched by the great Dr. Busby,[1] for the Montessori system of his age; the contempt of a public school man for a Miss Nancy attached to his grandmother's apron strings and waited upon by private tutors.

We can partly sympathize with him, for though essentially an orphan, young Philip was a coddled orphan. Of his grandmother, Lady Halifax, we know little, except for a charming portrait by Sir Peter Lely, which shows her, possibly as a bride, with a delicate, eager, typically English face, not that of a court beauty, but brave and vivid and intelligent, a face which would retain something of its youth even in old age. She was a daughter of "Wise" William Pierrepoint, popular leader and friend of Cromwell's during the rebellion, and of a background congenial to the Whiggish principles of the late Marquis — apparently an alert, vital woman in her fifties, a woman of the world, but devoted to her eldest grandchild. The fact of her devotion, or perhaps of her indulgence, is preserved by Matthew Maty, Chesterfield's physician and first biographer, who asserts that "Lady Halifax's understanding and wit were still exceeded by the goodness of her heart."[2] Without Lord Stanhope's rancor, we might still agree with him that an indulgent grandmother, however exemplary, was not the best supervisor of a boy's education.

But bad as this was, an old-fashioned Briton, such as Lord Stanhope liked to fancy himself, would have considered the other features of Philip's training as even worse. True to the Savile preferences, Philip was not being brought up as an Englishman at all. In that environment, the first influence would be French, which represented the modern and progressive in education. The "ignorant, worthless, amorous fop" remark had probably to do with that aspect of the case.

About that time the medieval tradition of the English public schools had been attacked on various counts: barbarity of manners, the system of flogging, too mixed a personnel, insistence on the classics as the chief end of learning, exercise of the memory rather than of the reason as the primary method of instruction. Increasingly men of wealth and position had been withdrawing their sons from these schools and bringing them up at home under the charge of tutors and special teachers, a training completed by foreign travel and attendance at one of the finishing academies in Paris, though sometimes a year or two at one of the universities was added as a concession to national prejudice. This was the training sponsored by John Locke, approved of by Halifax, and to which, as a matter of course, the young Stanhope stood committed.

> How anyone's being put into a mixed herd of unruly boys, [wrote Locke] and then learning to wrangle at trap, or rook * at spanfarthing, fits him for civil conversation or business I do not see. And what qualities are ordinarily to be got from such a troop of play-fellows as schools usually assemble together, from parents of all kinds, that a father should so much covet it, is hard to divine. I am sure, he who is able to be at the charge of a tutor at home, may there give his son a more genteel carriage, more manly thoughts, and a sense of what is worthy and becoming, with a greater proficiency of learning into the bargain, and ripen him sooner into a man, than any at school can do. . . . It is not the waggeries or cheats practised among school-boys, it is not their roughness one to another, nor the well-laid plots of robbing an orchard together, that make an able man; but the principles of justice, generosity and sobriety, joined with observation and industry, qualities which I judge schoolboys do not learn much of one another.[3]

Accordingly young Philip had first a French nursemaid and then a French tutor. "He was not sent to any of the public schools,"

* I.e., Cheat.

Dr. Maty explains. "His sentiments, manners, and taste, were all formed upon the model he found at home. The best masters were chosen to render his accomplishments suitable to his birth. They hit upon the art of adapting their instructions to his disposition, and by this method improved his mind, while they gained his affection." [4] At nine he could write a good hand, understood arithmetic, talked French perfectly, and had read Cordier, Eutropius, Justin, and Cornelius Nepos in Latin.[5] All of this had been gently, diplomatically instilled; it was, as we have pointed out, the Montessori system at the beginning of the eighteenth century.

Of course it must be allowed that there are evidences of shallowness in his learning such as might be expected under lenient masters. He had only a smattering of Greek, and his Latin misquotations have shocked the sensitive ears of Etonian Englishmen.[6] He admitted himself, indeed, that he had learned Latin in the French way, which meant knowing by heart a number of words and phrases, and that it was not until he went to Cambridge that he busied himself with grammar and parsing.[7] Even in French, which he spoke and wrote with consummate ease, the grammatically alert can spy out mistakes of syntax.[8] It might be urged, moreover, that a boy educated at home by his grandmother in company with his sister, and under indulgent tutors, would lack a certain rough-and-tumble quality in the melees of life; and indeed Chesterfield, however courageous in support of his opinions, at no time gives the impression of physical hardihood.

But such criticism is beside the point. The system was not framed to produce a pedant or a paladin, but an expert in human nature equipped with all the attributes, physical and intellectual, which enable a man to please, impress, and therefore to govern his fellow men. From the cradle, it was a training not in books or sports, but in address. It was an early specialization in the social arts.

Great names were opposed to it. If John Locke advocated the New Education, no less a person than Dean Swift attacked it with all the force of his satire.

"The current opinion," he says, "prevails, that the study of Greek and Latin is loss of time; that public schools, by mingling the sons of noblemen with those of the vulgar, engage the former in bad company; that whipping breaks the spirits of lads well born; that universities make young men pedants; that to dance, fence, speak French, and know how to behave yourself among great persons of both sexes, comprehends the whole duty of a gentleman." This he ridicules, and adds that a "hindrance to good education, and I think the greatest of any, is that pernicious custom in rich and noble families, of entertaining French tutors in their houses. These wretched pedagogues are enjoined by the father, to take special care that the boy shall be perfect in his French; by the mother, that master must not walk till he is hot, nor be suffered to play with other boys, nor be wet in his feet, nor daub his clothes, and to see the dancing master attends constantly, and does his duty; she farther insists, that he be not kept too long poring on his book, because he is subject to sore eyes, and of a weakly constitution. By these methods, the young gentleman is in every article, as fully accomplished at eight years old, as at eight and twenty, age adding only to the growth of his person and his vice." [9]

There is something very familiar and modern about this controversy, which is still being debated after two centuries. The truth on both sides of it is that youth cannot be regimented, that the poison of one is the meat of the other, that not even Busby could birch Lord Stanhope into distinction, and that if the New Education succeeded with Chesterfield, it failed utterly with his son.

But whatever the general aspects, it will be readily conceded that a boy brought up in a great house, in the fashionable section of the metropolis, would acquire the adult point of view at an earlier age than if he had been kept in school, especially as one of the chief points of his education was that he should acquire it as soon as possible. Kept in the background and seen rather than heard, Philip Stanhope even as a child would still make his bow to Lady Halifax's friends. Taken out to walk in St. James's Park by his Norman nurse, or later by Monsieur Jouneau, he would be conscious from infancy of that beau monde in which his entire life would be passed: the court ladies strolling in the Mall with their gallants, or along Duke Humphrey's Walk beneath the lime trees; the glow and glitter of brocade or buckle along the Canal, under the elms by the Pond around the pedestal of the Gladiator; [10] a twinkling of high red heels and amber canes, drifting of laced hats, majesty of Ramillies wigs; the toasts, and wits, and notables of the age. He would be taken upon the laps of great ladies and patted by great lords. Unconsciously he would absorb the gossip, would understand the smirks and allusions, would become precociously knowing and sophisticated. It was the process of developing an attitude, an invisible armor, colder and less penetrable than Milan steel. Except for servants, all that was low, all that was middle-class would be rigorously excluded; he would be confined to the intelligent, the noble, and well-bred.

Actually they were a brutal lot. When every allowance has been made for the distortion of contemporary epigram and slander, these noble relics of the last forty years of the seventeenth century were a most terrible company. The moralists of Queen Anne could put up screens and spray the air with rose water, but they could not change the lustful, greedy hearts of that generation. And at Anne's death, the old license broke out. We must remember the shining exceptions of this elite, but we cannot forget the rank and file of peculators, debauchees, and mercenaries. The worst of it is that many of them were so accomplished and clever. For one thing, it was an age intelligent enough to be aware of its own brutality. Was ever satire so gross? Has ever caricature portrayed humanity as so completely animal?

The cause for this, naturally, was a religious, or rather spiritual, nihilism. If men and women insist that they are only clay, clay only will they be. Codes are not enough, reason fails, ethics are inadequate to preserve society from the corruption which attends the various forms of self-sufficiency. At this period, between the middle of the seventeenth and eighteenth centuries, humanity was more deeply sunk in its own mire than usual. We have no need to discuss the ferocity of the laws, the physical and moral degradation of the people. We have only to consider the patricians of the West End with their satellites.

London was a small city of five hundred thousand in the days of Queen Anne; but fashionable London was a very restricted area indeed. Everybody had some acquaintance with everybody else either personally or by hearsay. There was an enormous amount of interrelationship between the various families. Gossip was a passion, and minding the business of others a habit. In an age where conversation and cards were the chief amusements, when a retinue of tale-bearing flunkeys was attached to each family, when the court was still the hub of the English wheel, when the recently invented newspapers confined themselves chiefly to personalities, the celebrities of the West End lived in glass houses. By the time he was fifteen, Philip Stanhope, heir to an earldom, the grandson of two distin-

guished men, and brought up in the St. James region, knew a great
deal about his world.

Consider a few of them, these figures of his boyhood, as they
pass through the salon of Lady Halifax, or linger there at basset or
omber, or drift in coach or sedan or on foot over the cobblestones
outside. And remembering that "as the twig is bent, the tree's
inclin'd," we recognize that these were young Philip's earliest specimens in that science of human nature to which he afterwards contributed such brilliant chapters. For a survey of worldly values and
the various types of success no better school could have been devised.

The Duchess of Cleveland, for instance, his grandmother's old acquaintance, his Grandfather Chesterfield's old mistress,[11] more famous
in Restoration days as Lady Castlemaine, chief concubine of the
Merry Monarch, queen of the seraglio. Surely he was familiar with
that rich and ghastly beldame. She had bullied a queen and led a
king by the nose, she had battened on the national treasury, had
destroyed great statesmen and sold their places to scoundrels, had
borne a number of bastards, had devoted her life to bawdry and
avarice, could outswear a fishwife or outogle a prostitute, until in
the end, at the age of sixty, she purchased in marriage a fashionable
young beau named Feilding, who wrung money out of her by
violence and from whom she freed herself by proving him a biga-
mist, then crawled off to die, a palsy-stricken hag, at Chiswick.

Or the Duchess of Richmond, *la belle* Stuart, another flame of
Charles II's — perhaps, as a child, he shrank from her smallpox-
ravaged face and blind eye, as she played her eternal cards. Or perhaps she amused him with one of the multitudinous cats who formed
her chief devotion and to whom she left legacies.

Or Mrs. Godfrey, whom he certainly knew, the sister and first
patroness of Marlborough, mistress of King James, mother of the
Duke of Berwick, and of less notable Fitzjameses. Or the French
courtesan, Louise de Kéroualle, Duchess of Portsmouth, still at
seventy with a fine figure admired by Voltaire. She had been an
agent of Louis and had managed King Charles for him. She was
mother by that versatile sovereign of the Duke of Richmond. She
lived in France, but came visiting at times.

These great ladies represented a certain kind of success. They
represented also a system by which obscure men could climb to

rank and wealth, and by which the secret policies of state could be discovered or manipulated or betrayed. They were hulks out of commission, but valuable specimens of their class. From the standpoint of worldly practice much more could be learned from them than from demurer, more respectable survivals, like the Duchesses of Devonshire and Somerset, the Countess of Sunderland, or Lady Belasyse. There were also the present reigning beauties, toasts of the Kit-Cat and other clubs, to fill up the stage, the Duchesses of St. Albans and Beaufort, the young Duchess of Richmond, the young Countess of Sunderland, Lady Mary Churchill, and Mademoiselle Spanheim among others.[12]

But it was not women, those "agreeable trifles," [13] who would most impress an ambitious youth. It would be early borne in on him (in any case by his middle teens) that women were uneducated, domestic creatures, or decorative toys, that they were household and social necessities, placed by convention on a fictitious pedestal, but actually on a lower plane than men. The vacancy of their minds, the triviality of their interests, their vanities and affectations, their physical dependence, consigned them to a different order. It would be the statesmen, wits, soldiers, beaux, and ecclesiastics, men with big names and wigs and equipages, who would attract and inspire him. At ten he was already consumed with ambition, a thirst for praise and notoriety,[14] already he longed to glitter in the world, had resolved to attain some great position of state; already, as he confessed long afterward, the blue ribbon and blazing star of the Order of the Garter dazzled him.[15] Traits like these delighted his grandfather's old cronies.

They caught the attention of a gallant old soldier, Lord Galway, who condescended to give him a piece of advice couched in flattery. "Rise early," said Galway. "In the distinguished posts your parts, rank, and fortune will enable you to fill, you will be liable to have visitors at every hour of the day, and unless you will rise constantly at an early hour, you will never have any leisure to yourself." [16] Words like this from such a person fired him. The distinguished posts which his parts, rank, and fortune would enable him to fill glimmered miragelike on the horizon. He adopted the advice; it became a permanent feature of his self-discipline.

The Huguenot nobleman and English general, Henri de Massue de Ruvigny, Earl of Galway, is an imposing figure in that drawing room of Lady Halifax's. No doubt Philip's Huguenot tutor, Monsieur Jouneau, greatly respected him. In young Stanhope's eyes, he would enhance still further the French influence. An atmosphere of seventeenth-century France with its more virile gallantry attends this scarred, soldierly person. He was one of the finest gentlemen in the army, declared an admirer about 1700, he was modest, vigilant, and sincere; a man of honor and honesty, without pride or affectation; he even wore his own hair, and was plain in dress and manners.[17]

But there was another caller at Lady Halifax's, of whom nothing of this could be said, and who belonged more appropriately to that age. Sir Thomas Osborne,[18] Earl of Danby, Marquis of Carmarthen, Duke of Leeds — to record the rungs of the ladder he had climbed — abounded in nicknames, which reflected his prominence. He was a fungus-pale, thin man, called by some people the White Marquis from his ghastly complexion. He was jealous and corrupt, had connived with King Charles to sell British neutrality to France in return for a bribe, and had then double-crossed the French. As Lord Treasurer he had emptied the treasury. He had been twice impeached and had spent five years behind bars in the Tower; but for all that had safely reached his goal. He had served as chief minister to two kings and had been rewarded both with a dukedom and the whole of his ill-gotten plunder. A venerable old man, who had outdistanced nearly all his contemporaries. Nicknames broke no bones. The Whigs might call him "King Thomas" or "Tom the Tyrant," or speak of him as "the thin, ill-natured ghost that haunted the king"; or Lord Mulgrave might poetically describe him as "a great, false jewel," and rhyme wise with lies; or low lampooners might scoff at his years in prison; he cared nothing, but went on prudently peculating — a racketeer of the first magnitude. At Oxford he was made a Doctor of Common Law.

The squib of an anonymous rhymester gives a more living portrait of Osborne than the one in all his regalia by Van Vaart.[19]

> He is as stiff as any stake,
> And leaner, Dick, than any rake;
>   Envy is not so pale.
> And though by selling of us all,
> He has wrought himself into Whitehall,
>   He looks like bird of gaol.[20]

The most solid achievement of his life was to have effected the marriage of the Duke of York's daughter, Mary, with William of Orange, thus securing a Protestant successor to the throne. He may well have described the finesses of this important measure within young Philip's hearing. By a singular coincidence, one of Chesterfield's most brilliant diplomatic triumphs would consist in negotiating a similar marriage between another Princess Royal and another Prince of Orange.

The suave Maty draws a touching picture of this old rascal hobnobbing at Lady Halifax's with a similar scamp, his former enemy, the Duke of Montagu — "as arrant a knave," says Swift, "as any in his time," [21] and a friend of Grandfather Chesterfield's.[22] "Free from those tumultuous passions," wrote Dr. Maty, "which had so long kept them at variance, they daily met, like friends, at the house of Lady Halifax; as the elder African's brother, and old Cato, may be supposed to have done at the house of the mother of the Gracchi." [23] What profane anecdotes and leering confidences such veterans as these would exchange over their snuff!

If the Duke of Leeds may be taken as the elder African's brother, then "Cato" Montagu was a still meaner blackguard, in the sense that a petticoat parasite is mean. From the embraces of the languorous Mrs. Myddelton to an intimacy with Lady Castlemaine (they betrayed each other in the coolest fashion), a marriage with the Countess of Northumberland and six thousand pounds a year to a second marriage with the Duchess of Albemarle and seven thousand pounds a year, he chambered his way up. He was fat, stocky, and dark. He had unlimited nerve. In the good cause of money, he was prepared to swallow a camel. The Duchess of Albemarle, who was quite insane, had refused to marry anyone but royalty. Montagu, undaunted, proposed to her as the Emperor of China; and, having married and locked her up, appropriated her fortune. This was a good business stroke. His public life abounded in treacheries and treasons. He betrayed his country as casually as his king; and, fishing in the troubled waters of intrigue, had hooked an earldom and a marquisate. Less clever than Osborne, he might have failed of his dukedom, had not the favoring petticoat once more supplied him by a marriage between his son and Lady Mary Churchill, daughter of the omnipotent Marlborough. He had magnificent tastes and was an amateur of palatial residences. Boughton House in the country and Montagu House in town memorialized him. It takes a number of heiresses for such creations.

Forming a trinity with these statesmen appears the Right Honorable Robert Spencer, Earl of Sunderland. He too lived in St. James's Square, and must have been a familiar figure to young Stanhope, though whether his quarrels with the late Marquis permitted him to call on Lady Halifax may be questioned.* His presence, however, would belong to Philip's childhood memories.

Bad as were Osborne and Montagu, they were inferior devils to this political Beelzebub, who towers monumentally among corrupt ministers of state.

> A Proteus, ever acting in disguise,

says a contemporary and almost reverential lampoon,

> A finished statesman, intricately wise,
> A second Machiavel, who soar'd above
> The little ties of gratitude and love.[24]

"The art in which he surpassed all men was the art of whispering," declared another. He had a dark, handsome, faun face which did not betray him on that occasion when his witches' kettle boiled over, and he fled from England disguised as a woman. He was the son of Waller's Sacharissa and the husband of Lady Anne Digby, whose immorality and cleverness equaled his own. He outdid Montagu in courting the royal mistresses; he outdid Osborne in hunger for place; and, if possible, he outdid them both in treachery. But England owes him an invention upon which her entire form of government rests, that is, a ministry responsible to the dominant party in parliament. As a convenient, sensitive device of representation, no other democratic instrument has ever equaled it.

It would be tedious to chronicle Sunderland's tricks and betrayals. Like Osborne and Montagu, he lived till well past middle life, and enjoyed a great estate and public pensions. Like Montagu, he married his son to a daughter of Marlborough's and would have ended as a duke himself had not envious death prevented it.

Around these three antiquated Solons, less notorious and sometimes better men gathered, but a family resemblance attaches to most of them. They all seem, in one way or another, to have suffered an

---

* Robert Spencer's sister, Dorothy, had been Savile's first wife. His mother was an old friend of Halifax's.

invisible blight. They have discounted everything; they have taken a pinch of snuff over virtue and purity and faith; they think in terms of satire and express themselves in lampoons. They have known too much evil to believe very much good. Their horizon is narrow and definite and hard. As in Shakespeare's *King Lear*, we are constantly reminded of animal prototypes, the fox and the peacock, the swine and the wolf, behind so much splendor of stately façades.

Consider, for example, the best of Osborne's or Savile's coterie: William Cavendish, first Duke of Devonshire. He is the perfect illustration of a magnificent patrician: the face of an Apollo, but with an aquiline firmness that saves it from mere beauty; tall, courteous, something of a poet, with a fine taste for architecture (which he indulged in the building of Chatsworth); munificent, dissolute. Like Tybalt, he was a duelist, a gentleman of the very first house. He served with the fleet and in the army. He loved horse racing and cockfighting, art and music. He lavished his money on splendid entertainments. He left behind him a troop of illegitimate children, and died lamented by the sex. But behind the pomp and glitter, what real greatness was there? What motive for his displays except the pride of name and rank? What the source of his fisticuffs, challenges, and duels except the ferocity of an Iroquois?

Or Charles Talbot, Duke of Shrewsbury, a Hamletlike figure, whose father and brother had each been slain in a duel — his father in a quarrel with Buckingham about his mother, while that lady, dressed as a page, held her lover's horse. He passes across the stage of that time, timid, irresolute, pursued with royal favor which he does not want, forced into high positions from which he yearned to escape, married to a dubious foreign wife, converted from Roman Catholicism to a faith which gave him no comfort; and yet a charming, gentle person, whom even Swift could praise and the cold William of Orange love. But across two centuries he gives the impression of bewilderment and desolation.

Or James Butler, Duke of Ormonde, the popular, generous, and magnificent, living nearby on St. James's Square in his great house. A very noble duke but, like others, tangled in the equivocal politics of the times, in spite of himself not altogether loyal, a little stupid, a little bewildered; and, unlike others, too proud or too inept to retrieve his blunders. It would be against him that Philip Stanhope with much apparent fury and actual indifference would deliver his maiden speech in parliament. Years afterward, it would be at his house in Avignon, the Jacobite headquarters, that the same Philip, now Earl of Chesterfield, would be entertained. His estates confiscated, his honors extinguished, himself attainted, Ormonde would escape into perpetual exile; the great mansion in St. James's Square would come under the Crown auctioneer's hammer; nothing of him would remain except his memory as an example (to be regarded with a sigh and a shrug) of the treachery of fortune. But during these earlier years, magnified by the background of his Irish wealth and many titles, how great and splendid a simulacrum!

Or Henry Compton, Bishop of London, who, zealous Whig as he was, would be often a guest at Halifax House. He might be called the last of medieval prelates, more soldier and nobleman than ecclesiastic. He was a trooper till thirty and talked like a colonel of horse. He was the religious supervisor of the Princesses Mary and Anne. He stripped off his canonicals and donned a uniform to escort the latter with forty horsemen up to Nottingham in the troubled days of the Revolution. Then, at the head of two hundred more, unfurling his banner of *Nolumus leges Angliae mutari*, he marched into Oxford in a blue coat and carrying a naked sword. A great, hard-riding gentleman. But it would not be from him that Philip Stanhope would gather a very accurate notion of the Christian faith.

Or Thomas, Marquis of Wharton, who maintained that "a lie well-believed is as good as if it were true," whose policy it was never to give nor refuse a challenge, and as his enemies put it, never to refuse nor keep an oath; who composed "Lilliburlero, bullen-a-la," the song that hummed King James out of England; who owned the most famous horses of his time — Snail, Colchester, Jacob, Pepper, Careless, and Chance; who loved to win plates from Tories and High-churchmen; who as Lord Lieutenant of Ireland would recommend one of his henchmen for ecclesiastical preferment as "a character practically faultless except for his damned bad morals." He patronized Addison. He developed the system later perfected by Walpole of bribery at elections, soused his constituents in the strongest ale, and learned the names of all their children. Swift remarks of him that "he was wholly occupied by vice and politics, so that bawdy, profaneness, and business filled up his whole conversation — the most universal villain," adds the satirist despairingly, "that I ever knew."

Or Charles Mordaunt, Earl of Peterborough, whom we will be meeting again, the most amazing Don Caesar de Bazan in England. His adventures as admiral in Spain, his victories won by others, his inefficiency and pleasure-seeking, read like *opéra bouffe*. Indeed, he remained always a comic hero — at one time exalted on a puff of political jingoism to a plane even above Marlborough, at another dismissed from public office, save for a fictitious post of general of the marine forces which had never been enlisted. A Maecenas to literary men. A philanderer till his death. "The ramblingest lying rogue on earth," observes Swift affectionately.

Or Sidney, Earl of Godolphin, Lord High Treasurer under Anne, singular in his impolitic fidelity to the Stuarts, the loyal friend of Marlborough, an honest, able man, a gambler and horse racer.

Or, finally, the Great Duke himself. What a tremendous impression Marlborough made on Philip Stanhope! Courteous, majestic, invariably serene! — it was upon that splendid model that the future Chesterfield began early to fashion himself. When the Duke had withdrawn in a self-imposed exile to Antwerp, it was at his house, and affectionately entertained by him, that young Philip, fresh from Cambridge, spent the first stage of his continental experience.[25] The Duchess, the formidable Atossa, remained his friend to her death and left him a legacy of twenty thousand pounds. We will have occasion later on to consider Chesterfield's estimate of Marlborough and his debt to him. Suffice it that he studied him with an enthusiastic though critical eye, noted his defective education ("he was eminently illiterate; wrote bad English and spelled it still worse"),[26] his somewhat humdrum mentality, the avarice that dominated him. Yes, all this — but then what grace! It secured him the favor of Lady Castlemaine and a tip of five thousand pounds. "His figure was beautiful," wrote Chesterfield, "but his manner was irresistible by either man or woman." [27] As paragon for his ambition, Stanhope could not have chosen better.

These were the older men, the Restoration men, the setting stars, during Philip Stanhope's early years. Some, like Marlborough, were still in the ascendant; but, generally speaking, a newer galaxy had risen.

As a whole the latter showed progress in honesty, decency, and decorum; perhaps, too, in patriotism. They were not so picturesque, but they accomplished something for England. They were the first flight of a political era that has continued ever since. There followed them at least seven decades during which a wholehearted Epicureanism, undisgraced by the previous excesses, reached its most exquisite development. In England the commons ruled, but a lingering aristocracy lent a sunset splendor to the age. They were the decades when, if ever, the cult of the material and the rational softened by elegance, etherealized by wit, has justified itself. They are the Golden Age of this cult, its highest reference, and most attractive illustration.

But if the newer men were more circumspect than their fathers, one looks in vain for an essential difference. Their selfishness was more enlightened; it was not less engrossing. They might not rob the Exchequer on as grand a scale as Osborne, for the simple reason that it was now impossible to do so. They might not rise, like Montagu or Churchill, by the favor of royal mistresses, because by the Glorious Revolution of 1688 the English people had refused to be pillaged any longer in that fashion. But by the accession of Anne and the moral essayists, the blight, which we have already noticed, had not been eliminated.

There are certain exceptions. It is pleasant, after so much heraldry and vice, to glance at the shrewd, plebeian face and strenuous career of Lord Chancellor Somers, chief author of that Declaration of Rights which ushered in constitutional government and formed the model of later "declarations" such as that of Independence; or at another lawyer and Lord Chancellor, William, Earl Cowper, whose charm of style and elegance of oratory Chesterfield loved to remember; or at James Stanhope, afterwards Earl Stanhope, a kinsman of Philip's, handsome and dark-complexioned, brought up in camps and with something of the camp about him — frank, highminded, liberal, a good man and an able statesman. He also was an exception, he and Viscount Townshend, subsequently Secretary of State during Chesterfield's first diplomatic mission, burly, brusque, hot-tempered, and loyal.

But Charles Spencer, third Earl of Sunderland, was a Queen Anne edition of his father, an expert in intrigue and court maneuvering, the promoter of the South Sea Company, who pocketed *sub* *rosa* £50,000 in stock for launching it. Nor can much good be said of his political adversary, Robert Harley, Earl of Oxford, a great figure at the close of Queen Anne's reign, a master of subtlety; * nor of Henry St. John, Viscount Bolingbroke.

Dazzling, profligate, fascinating, Bolingbroke seems always to have commanded Chesterfield's admiration. Here, again, it was a question of charm in speech and behavior and literary style. As a young man during Philip's boyhood, he had already reached the height of his popularity.[28] We shall meet him often enough again and need not pause here longer than to point him out — the wit, statesman, and philosopher, essentially shallow, but infinitely pleasing — one of Chesterfield's few heroes.

And, still more characteristic of the newer age, we must not forget that group of wits who were also men of the world: the sedate Addison recently home from his foreign travels; the impulsive Steele delighting the town with his *Tatler;* "Gentleman" Congreve ashamed to be thought a writer; Sir John Vanbrugh, the architect of Blenheim and other Brobdingnagian palaces, whose comedies once had shared with Congreve's the applause of the public and the wrath of Collier; or Matthew Prior, diplomat and poet; or Sir Godfrey Kneller, the Fortunatus of portrait-painters; or Dr. Arbuthnot, the Queen's physician. All these were in the radius of Halifax House. They were familiar to the small, fashionable London around St. James's Square.

And lastly, one of them and yet beyond them, uniting in himself the varied phases of his generation, Charles Montagu, Earl of Halifax, who wrote epigrams and poems, funded the national debt and established the Bank of England; remedied, together with Somers, the depreciation of the currency; was the patron of Addison, Congreve, Newton, Prior, and Stepney; was the friend and perhaps the husband of gay and witty Catherine Barton, Sir Isaac Newton's niece. Pope condescended to borrow from him for the "Rape of the Lock." [29] Matthew Prior addressed him in a poem

---

* His earlier Presbyterianism, exchanged for the High Church, still expressed itself in homely, Biblical expressions. His middle-class wife used to talk about the Lord Jehovah. "Oh, dear Madam," once exclaimed the Duchess of Shrewsbury, "who is that? I believe 'tis one of the new titles, for I never heard of him before." W. S. Sichel, *Bolingbroke and His Times,* vol. i, p. 74 — a deeply illustrative remark.

which, with some verses of his own, may fittingly serve as post-
script to this section.

> Seeing aright, we see our woes:
>   Then what avails it to have eyes?
> From ignorance our comfort flows,
>   The only wretched are the wise.
>
> We wearied should lie down in death,
>   This cheat of life would take no more,
> If you thought fame but stinking breath,
>   I, Phillis, but a perjured whore.[30]

And Montagu warbling on the eternal theme of the coy mistress:

> Ah, Celia, then be not so nice,
> For that betrays thy thoughts and thee;
> There's not a feature or a grace
> Bedecks thy body or thy face,
> But pimps within for me.[31]

These were some of the faces in the fashionable great world of
London at the end of the seventeenth and the beginning of the
eighteenth centuries. They represented the only world that Philip
Stanhope could know. There were reasons for his father's prophecy
that he would become no more than a fop. Most boys in such surroundings have become no more than that. But it would not be so
with him. By nature, he belonged to this milieu, inoculated at
birth with germs which would have withered a less native personality. He had too good and too hard a mind for mere trifling.
With him there was no question of thwarting a natural bent; his
spirit flowed easily into the mold prepared for it.

And yet it was a mold, a very narrow and rigid one. The range
of choice was not great. He could become a fop, or he could train
himself "for the distinguished posts which his parts, rank, and fortune would enable him to fill." He could play a subaltern or a leading part in that caricature of life represented by St. James's Square.
Nothing else was possible. The spiritual amenities, the love of God
and man, home, friendship, leisure, would have small space in these
distinguished posts; but, on the other hand, fashionable prominence
would be assured. He chose early to become a leader, accepted the
limitations and discipline of the role, achieved a share of success in
it, spent his strength and health in the process, and, far from re-
pining, forced his son later on into the same glittering groove.

What other standards of living were possible for him than those of St. James's Square? As it was, he made the best of them. Note his preferences among that throng of distinguished men: they were Marlborough and Bolingbroke. He might have selected Sunderland and Wharton. But these beau ideals of his give the measure of what he loved: success, ambition, polish, and brilliance.

Thus early, the twig was bent. Maty relates that when very young, Philip Stanhope schooled his temper to such good effect that "for the remainder of his life he was never known to be discomposed by any emotion of his mind." [32] It was a useful quality and very precocious! Emulation, self-control, a good intellect, the best teachers, unlimited opportunity, a splendid but definite goal — what youth has ever begun life with more flattering prospects of success?

The West End. Without hesitation an Englishman of the time would have considered it the rendezvous of the great. As London to England, so were St. James's Palace and Square, Berkeley and Grosvenor Squares, with their purlieus, to all that was noble and eminent. The political, military, and ecclesiastical leaders, the great names, are here or at least are honorary members. With generous condescension, an occasional man of letters or of science, a Locke or Bentley or Newton, an Addison or Congreve, is accorded an almost plenary entree.[33] But beyond this center with its fringes — nothing; the great are only here. What a blaze of splendor! What deep political secrets go the rounds in anteroom and salon! What portentous changes of ministry are bruited here and there! What a to-do about the marriage of Villaria and Orlando! [34] What a rattling of coaches, scuffling of sedans, visiting back and forth, scraping of violins in glimmering ballrooms! What an expenditure for *commodes*, jeweled fans, scarlet cloaks, point ruffles, and jasmine water!

The whole of England realizes that these are the Great; above all the Great realize it themselves, are exclusively absorbed in themselves as arbiters of the national destiny.

In Dartmouth, on Lower Street, a very low fellow, indeed a microscopic fellow from the standpoint of St. James's, was tinkering in those days on a mad device for pumping water by fire out of mine pits. It was a blacksmith called Newcomen. But the device he forged was to prove an Aladdin's Lamp that would raise genii to change the face of England. It needed merely the insight of Watt to develop and apply it. At a breath new hordes of men, new cities, new industries, new classes, would rise to overshadow the St. James's puppet play. In the smoke of it a new nation would emerge. But there was no hint of this at the moment. His Grace and his lordship were buried one by one in Westminster Abbey. No one knows where Thomas Newcomen was buried.

About this time too was born at a poverty-stricken rectory in Lincolnshire a boy who had as few and as poor expectations as Philip Stanhope had great ones. The last of fifteen children, his father imprisoned for debt, his family harassed by want, his mother at her wits' end to provide the most meager fare — what could he do in the world, utterly negligible child, as compared with the scion of the Earls of Chesterfield? And yet he would deeply affect the course of English history; he would save England from revolution by a more subtle revolution; through him the slave would be freed, the laws reformed, the vast suffering of the poor, the helpless, and unfortunate relieved. Through him a new spiritual dawn would break upon England, and what the graceful essayists of Queen Anne had been unable to effect would through him become reality. The obscure rector's son would change the manners and customs, nay, the entire social attitude. He would prove the solvent of the old ways. But far greater than this, through him there would flood anew into the human heart the power of a forgotten dream and a forgotten faith.

However, this day was not yet. Queen Anne, changing dresses while her chaplain conducted prayers, and deeming it more modest to close the door between, asked why he stopped. Because, explained the courtly worm, daring to turn, because he would not whistle the word of God through the keyhole.[35] Christianity had become a fiction set up as a subject of ridicule.[36] Churches were empty, religion had withered to a form. Faith in anything had reached an unequaled ebb.

Correlative with this there was decorum, but scant morality; there were laws, but little mercy; there was much common sense, but small common feeling. Drabs were still lashed publicly at Bridewell; lunatics were displayed at Bedlam for the amusement of the crowd; the pillory and whipping post and gallows were seldom idle. The weak, the poor, and the wretched went to the wall. John Wesley was still a child at Epworth.

CHAPTER III
Higher Education

AT THE BEGINNING of the eighteenth century, Oxford and Cambridge had lost some of the earlier prestige which they have since regained. During the previous hundred years, it had become a commonplace to ridicule the conservatism which would not yield one iota to modern needs and a changing order, to ridicule also the unmannerly pedants fashioned by so archaic a system. John Earl in 1628 derided the scholar of his day in terms about the same as those used by Richard Steele a century later. "His scrape," * says Earl, "is homely and his nod worse. He cannot kisse his hand and cry Madame, nor talk idly enough to beare her company. His smacking † of a Gentlewoman is somewhat too savoury, and he mistakes her nose for her lippe. A very wood-cocke would puzzle him in carving, ‡ and he wants the logicke of a Capon." [1] In 1713 Steele observes that "the most established error of our university education is the general neglect of all the little qualifications and accomplishments which make up the character of a well-bred man." [2] The tradition of the sword, which had once segregated the nobility, was now yielding to a tradition of the world equally remote from academic preoccupations. Young aristocrats destined to the court, parliament, or foreign affairs were apt to leave the universities altogether on one side, and finish their education by a long period of continental travel.

But these, after all, were exceptions rather than the rule. There lingered on into the utilitarian, pragmatical present a memory and a reputation that was in itself a useful asset. Identified with cen-

* I.e., bow.
† I.e., kissing.
‡ An indispensable accomplishment at the time.

turies of English history, the universities had become an institution too venerable to be daffed aside by callow fashion. They demanded homage, however perfunctory, even from rationalists, even from patricians. And while providing a not unpleasant sojourn for the period of transition between a London academy and the pleasures of Paris, residence there supplied valuable connections, gave a classical flavor to education, and conferred the vague distinction of age and custom. It is therefore not surprising that Philip Stanhope, having finished with his grandmother's and Monsieur Jouneau's tutelage, should have taken the highroad to Cambridge a month before turning eighteen.* But a student less adapted by nature or upbringing to relish the charms of his college can seldom have entered those historic walls.

In most lives there occur inappropriatenesses and discordances that provoke a smile, and surely the mental picture of young Stanhope approaching Cambridge on a late August afternoon belongs to the humorous category. As he jolts over the rutted road in the Halifax family coach, or perhaps in a chariot- or post-chaise-and-four,† he is worth considering in some detail. He has probably broken the long journey of fifty-six miles between London and Cambridge by stopping overnight at Hockerill or Bishop's Stortford. Otherwise he must have started at dawn and traveled hard to be catching a glimpse of the university towers before dark. He is a dumpy, unprepossessing youth, very short and with a very big head. His broad, irregular face is relieved by the beauty of the eyes, which are keen and almond-shaped, of the French rather than the English type. His lips form a thin line. There is something alert, vital, and concentrated about him, as of a mind continually active and interested, nothing of the dreamer, a personality forever abreast of the present and unconcerned with the past.

He wears his hat cocked and laced, as a gentleman should. He will continue to wear a hat cocked and laced, if he pleases, even at Cambridge, which relaxes its sumptuary rules in favor of noblemen; or if he condescends to the student's cap, it will be of velvet

---

* He was admitted to Trinity Hall, August 1712. Maty, *op. cit.*, vol. i, p. 272. From the dates of letters, it is certain that he had left it by the spring of 1714, contrary to Maty's assertion that it was in December of that year.

† The chariot-and-four was used by Horace Walpole from London to Cambridge in 1735. See his letter of that year to Thomas Gray.

with a golden tuft. His clothes are of the latest Paris fashion. He is the Honorable Philip Stanhope, whose name the humblest inn-keeper will have heard, the heir apparent to broad estates, who will be ushered deferentially into the private parlors of taverns and treated with the best, whose servants will swagger and be gaped at by the county yokels. At eighteen, if not a lord, he is at least a lordling, and takes the fact as much for granted as the air he breathes, so much for granted that he rarely thinks of it.

The journey from London has been his first experience of travel, and since leaving Bishopsgate he has seen more of the English countryside than in all his life hitherto.[3] Probably its beauty does not impress him. The roads were bad and the population barbarous. If it were not for an occasional fine house, like Audley Inn, the seat of the Earls of Suffolk, or Lord Godolphin's mansion on the Gogmagog Hills, he would feel cut off from every familiar, repu-table thing. No, it is London he will always love, to which he will always turn with a well-nigh lyric delight, not this sort of earthy emptiness. Perhaps he designs elegiacs in the style of Ovid at Pontus.

The carriage rattles on at a brisk pace of seven or eight miles an hour, passing the slower public vehicles; but he has leisure to con-template for some time the village of Cambridge sketched against the horizon. It was Cambridge he approached because, in spite of his Tory father, he had been dedicated from birth to the Whig Party. If the Halifax politics had been different, it would have been Oxford. The choice, however, was unimportant. To a young man of Stanhope's attitude, either university would be equally accept-able or distasteful. To be sure, everything that birth, influence, or money could do to shut him off from the grubby undergraduate mob would be available. His college, Trinity Hall, was the law college of the university and therefore attended by a more sophisti-cated class than the grammatical drudges. He would be a fellow commoner, one of the *generosorum, nobilium, et magnatum liberi*, sharing the privileges of the fellows, waited on by sizars, that is, poorer students, instructed by submissive tutors hungry for a future preferment, dressed in a rich embroidered gown, excused from any exercises he chose to omit, associating only with those of his own class, slightly patronizing even the college heads. Around him would gather, prophetic of days to come, the "tuft-hunters"[4] or college parasites, the would-be "smarts," basking in his company, heedful of his moods. He would "bosh" it about town, and dazzle the eye of plebeian youth with his lace ruffles and flaxen tyewig.[5] For him the hearts of Cambridge toasts would flutter, and he might seduce a wench of the poorer sort before leaving college. He would be running up to London from time to time; and besides to him Cambridge was not a privilege, a dearly purchased Mecca, but a gesture, an interim of at most two years.

Yet Philip Stanhope would suffer at Cambridge. He had never known and would never know or understand unconventional, boisterous youth. His sense of urbanity would suffer. What had he in common with bullbaiting, cockfighting striplings of mean extraction and no manners? How he would scorn and how his head would ache at the constant bell ringing that formed the athletic exercise of many collegians! This tugging at bell ropes and skillful ringing of chimes was no doubt a muscle-making sport; but imagine the future Chesterfield fresh from the West End invited by some bell-ringing enthusiast to take part in the amusement. Or picture his first dinner in the hall after the *Quicquid appositum est, aut apponetur, Christus benedicere dignetur, In Nomine Patris et Filii, et Spiritus Sancti, Amen,* had been gabbled,[6] scooping his victuals from a wooden trencher, and asphyxiated by the stench of stale bread and meat, rancid enough to have turned the stomach of the German traveler Uffenbach two years before.[7] Picture him, trained to the cuisine of Lady Halifax, absorbing the apple dumplings and rotgut small beer that even the humble Nicholas Amhurst deplored.[8] Yes, he would suffer at Cambridge, "that illiberal seminary," as he dubbed it years later.[9]

But now, probably expecting to suffer, perhaps mildly interested, but as always intent and alert, he rattles down Trinity Street and observes that it is unpaved and with a gutter in the center.[10]

The records of Stanhope's Cambridge sojourn are few, but such as they are and with the help of contemporary marginalia, it is possible to reconstruct his life at the university with tolerable precision. Indeed, the four or five extant letters of this period contain, I think, far more valuable biographical material than has hitherto been drawn from them. They show vividly certain dominant traits of character, and serve as checks and comments on Chesterfield's later correspondence, which was written long after these youthful jottings had been forgotten. Consider, for instance, the portrait of his Cambridge self which he drew for his son forty years later and which successive biographers have taken at its face value. "I was," he writes, "an absolute pedant: when I talked my best, I quoted Horace; when I aimed at being facetious, I quoted Martial; and when I had a mind to be a fine gentleman, I talked Ovid. I was convinced that none but the ancients had common sense; that the classics contained everything that was either necessary, useful, or ornamental to men; and I was not without thoughts of wearing the *toga virilis* of the Romans, instead of the vulgar and illiberal dress of the moderns." [11]

There is not a trace of this to be found in the letters of the Cambridge period. Indeed most of what has been preserved points to a character just the reverse of pedantic or even studious. Having reached Cambridge in the early days of August, he left it at once to spend a week at the episcopal palace in Ely as guest of the bibliophile bishop John Moore.[12] Thence back to Cambridge, where he put in a few days at Greek and Latin before the opening of Stirbridge Fair, a festival which interrupted all studies for the next month — at the end of which time we find him returned to London on a jaunt, a not inconsiderable journey of at least twelve hours. Thence to Cambridge, once more, where it might be imagined that work could now begin; but the Newmarket races opened about that time and he attended them for three or four days. In this fashion were spent the first two months of his university career. It will be admitted that nothing of the studious pedant appears so far. But it is not only what he did: his manner of writing displays an already advanced sophistication. That note which will be incessantly reiterated throughout his life, the worship of *savoir-faire*, makes itself audible in the first of his letters which has been preserved.

Writing in French to his old London tutor, Monsieur Jouneau, he observes, "I find this college to which I belong infinitely the best in the entire university, for it is the smallest * and is filled with lawyers who have been in the world and who know how to live. We have only one clergyman with us, who is also the only drunkard in

* There were at the time about fifty members of Trinity Hall. *Cf. Warren's Book* (ed. A. W. W. Dale), 1911.

the college. Whatever the rumours, there is very little debauchery in this university, and above all not among people of birth, for one must have the tastes of a porter to engage in it here." (A pinch of salt must be taken with this last remark. He was writing to Monsieur Jouneau.)

There is a startling dearth of Latin quotations in these letters, which for a contrast at this point should be compared with the student correspondence of Horace Walpole. Their manner throughout is light and as cynically worldly as eighteen years can achieve. If this was his attitude upon entering Cambridge, there appears to have been no change toward pedantry a year later. On June 25, 1713, he wrote his friend George Berkeley a letter wholly devoted to describing the various pleasures, some of them none too refined, in which he had been indulging. Let the reader bear in mind that picture of a youthful high-brow which his lordship subsequently chose to present to his son as authentic.

> MY DEAR GEORGE [he wrote],
>
> I would have written to you before I received your last letter, but I found by your first that you were so expeditious in moving from place to place that I thought my former directions would not serve. You do not know what you ask when you would have me write long letters; you would quickly be aweary on it, should I obey you: what a number of insignificant trifles must I put together to fill up this sheet of paper, and how tiresome it would be to you to have a true and faithful history of Midsummer fair, which is our present diversion! * But since you will — faith, you shall have enough on it; but I give you free leave to throw this letter by as soon as ever you are tired on it.
>
> I came down from London † a week ago, which place afforded me little diversion. Plays and operas were left off, and I fell short of the pleasure I proposed to myself from the French Ambassador's masquerades; ‡ for our good Queen, thinking them encouragements to vice, discountenanced them so much, that he, out of complaisance, gave them over. The truth of it was, that there was not a gentleman of any tolerable dimensions that did not take care to make a good many ladies of a night sensible of them; I leave you

---

* He is attending the Fair again! *Cf.* with letter to Jouneau, Aug. 22, 1712.

† London again! *Cf.* with letter to Jouneau, Sept. 21, 1712.

‡ At eighteen, as might have been expected from the St. James's training, he is already apparently initiated into fashionable society.

to judge whether the ladies flocked to it or no, when they could meet with such good diversions as not many other places will admit of.

But now to come to Cambridge: I must first tell you that I have not yet seen Miss Neville, but it will not be long first, for her sagacious father is at London; so, if the daughter and the greyhound be not locked up, I will take this opportunity of tête-à-tête, where I will endeavour, if possible, by talking very much of you to her, to work her up to such a pitch as I could wish. The Tippins appeared last night at the fair, where Pat and I, after a damned quarrel we have had these two months, were reconciled. She's a fine girl, faith, and seems to have good dispositions. Oh! how I could! *sed me reprimo*, I consider the sin of fornication, and won't so much as indulge myself in the thought of it. Jack Cowper * is more and more in love every day, passes three parts in four of his life with the nymph, and is gay or sad just as it pleases her Ladyship to frown or smile. Our old buggering Heads † would not let us have a public *commencement*, ‡ to the great disappointment of all our young folks, whether male or female.

Your departure, dear George, has been very unsuccessful to us, for as soon as you went away we immediately lost the name of the Witty Club, and I am afraid we shall soon dwindle into no club at all, for Exton Sayer § is gone to London, and George Stanley § goes this week; the *Bonny* § goes in a fortnight into Staffordshire; so do but think what a poor solitary remnant we shall be. Prithee comfort us as often as you can with a letter, which we will retail at proper times, as our own wit, to retrieve as much of our character as we can. None of our Cambridge verses ** are worth sending

* Perhaps John Cowper, the father of the poet, himself a man of some poetical talent. He died in 1756, rector of Great Berkhampstead. *Suffolk Correspondence* (ed. Croker), Croker's notes, p. 3.

† The Heads of Houses.

‡ An occasion for much parade on the part of the fair inhabitants of Cambridge. See Christopher Wordsworth and R. Brimley Johnson, *The Undergraduate*, p. 272, quoting the Music Speech of Roger Long, M.A., at the Public Commencement in Cambridge, July 6, 1714.

§ Exton Sayer — probably the son of Mr. George Sayer, who, in 1718, succeeded Mr. Exton as King's proctor. Mr. Exton Sayer was afterwards an eminent civilian, filled several offices in the ecclesiastical courts, and was a member of parliament. George Stanley, probably the Mr. George Stanley who afterwards married Sir Hans Sloane's eldest daughter, and was the father of Hans Stanley. The *Bonny* remains unidentified. *Suffolk Correspondence*, Croker's notes, p. 3.

** In praise of the Peace of Utrecht.

you; a great many of them are egregiously silly; mine are some of
the prettiest in the book; the *Bonny* made them for me; we are
now burlesquing them as fast as ever we can. I rejoice much that
your nut-brown girl * offered you such good sport; I should
be glad to be with you to partake of those innocent amusements
to which you dedicate your *horas subsecivas;* but pray set one or
two of them apart sometimes, to oblige with a letter, my dear
George,

> Thy most sincere friend . . .

There is no vestige of the laborious student in this letter. † He
was playing a role either with George Berkeley or his son — perhaps,
indeed, with both — but at least his college friend would be in a
better position to judge whether or not it was appropriate. No, the
youthful pedant was a good deal of a fiction. When convenient, he
forgets it, and on one occasion observes, no doubt more accurately,
"that when I first went to the university, I drank and smoked, notwithstanding the aversion I had to wine and tobacco, only because
I thought it genteel, and that it made me look like a man." [13]

Why, then, did he paint a false portrait of himself — particularly
since he held it up to his son as something to be avoided? We shall
have occasion to touch on this point later when we discuss Chesterfield's technique as a pedagogue; but it may be suggested here that
it was simply a palatable form of instruction. It was not his own
boyhood portrait, but that of his son, the classically well-crammed
Philip Stanhope, Jr., that he was painting. Fictitious self-criticism
is often the most subtle and effective means of criticizing another.

But if the pedant was a lay figure, it is likely enough that the
playboy, the rakish trifler exhibited in the Berkeley letter, is almost equally suspect. It gives the impression of strain and gush, of
the desire to be thought a "smart." And if this is true, it reveals at
the outset of his career one of Chesterfield's dominant passions, the
one, indeed, which he most often took pride in confessing and
which is frequently the obsession of short, physically inferior men:
his hunger for admiration and applause, his fever to impress others.
At Cambridge, the fashionable, glittering thing was to be a man

* George Berkeley was probably traveling on the Continent at this time.
† Nor any justification, as far as I can see, for the remark of Dr. Maty's
informant that "when Lord Chesterfield was at the university, he used to
study in his apartment, without stirring out of it till 6 o'clock in the evening." Maty, *op. cit.,* vol. i, p. 271.

of pleasure. He adopted the attitude and lingua franca of that type. But his eroticism strikes a chill and his coarseness is anemic. Compare this with the strong pulse beat of a Fielding and the salt of a Rabelais; compare it even with the frank lechery of his Grandfather Chesterfield, the second Earl [14] — what a tin-foil sensualism it is! He was not in amorous encounters a very potent man, but he liked to talk as if he were. One is sometimes tempted to feel that the delight he took in his only child, the illegitimate Philip Stanhope, was heightened by his satisfaction at displaying before the eyes of the world a proof of his vigor. As it was chic to have a mistress, it was chic also to have a bastard. So much transpires from the letters themselves without corroborative witness — an illustration, even in so trivial an instance, of the unconvincingness of pretense. But there is additional witness. Lord Hervey, whose references to Chesterfield are always questionable because of their rancor, gives an impression of truth in this remark that "he [i.e., Stanhope] affected following many women of the first beauty and the most in fashion, and, if you would have taken his word for it, not without success; whilst in fact and in truth he never gained anyone above the venal rank of those whom an Adonis or a Vulcan might be equally well with for an equal sum of money." [15] In support of this it should be noted that scandal, usually prompt to link two names together in that gossipy world, remained languid regarding him. Hervey was right in suggesting that he liked the name of a man of pleasure; but with one or two exceptions, he deserved the reputation rather of a philanderer than a Don Juan. The truth appears to be that on this side of his nature, he was prurient rather than passionate, and loose rather than coarse. The desires of a frail constitution were not so imperious as vanity led him to suggest. In matters of sex, he was guilty often enough of that fashionable form of hypocrisy against which, perhaps in a moment of self-knowledge, he warned his son: that of popularity-hunting by appearing more immoral than one really is.[16]

If the rake and the pedant should be in large measure dismissed, what kind of youth then was it who struts so bravely in these college letters? In the first place, there can be no reason to doubt that ambition for prominence of one sort or another focused the greater part of his active life. He asserts and reasserts it himself; [17] he praises and parades and analyzes the means of attaining it; it

explains numerous episodes of his career. When he declares that
from youth up he strove to excel and, among other means, invariably rose early in the morning to gain time for serious reading,
there is no excuse for questioning it. It throws an instructive light
on the young student at Trinity Hall. When he records that at Cambridge pieces of eloquence were his chief study, and that in order
to form his style he took infinite pains in translating the shining
passages of Latin and French into English or English into French,[18]
it was probably true.

The point is that the letters to Monsieur Jouneau and to George
Berkeley do not reveal, except by implication, the real character of
their author: that cold, passionless intellect which, in spite of
trivial vanity and unpleasant lapses, raised him to a plane of real
greatness and of permanent significance. For in the ill-favored
lordling at Cambridge we have the comparatively rare case of a
young man who knows his own mind, who has selected his goal
and is pursuing it steadily. It was the goal that most men follow
according to their several opportunities, and may be vaguely described as success — i.e., objective success in material or social terms.
With him, it meant admiration, power, prominence; and beneath
the mask of an Epicurean elegance, he subjected himself to the
requisite discipline and toiled with an almost ascetic fervor. Whatever the limitations of Chesterfield, he was from youth to age the
captain of his own soul. Whether or not the harbor he sought and
the course he shaped were worthy, he at least knew where he was
going and kept his hand on the wheel.

So he cultivated and perhaps seduced the lowly Pat Tippins as
an infinitesimal mosaic in the pattern of a fine gentleman, diverted
himself at Stirbridge Fair and Newmarket, appeared at the opera
and in brilliant assemblies, visited the Bishop of Ely, belonged to
the elite of Cambridge, had already dabbled in letters * and achieved
a reputation for wit † — while, gazing out through these serene, almond-shaped eyes that so cleverly disguised it, was something that
weighed and calculated and willed, something that did not let him
sleep on cold gray mornings, but roused him to the unfashionable,
secret task of study, set him exacting exercises, tamed his emotions
to a cool passivity. If there is nothing lovable in this, if there is

---

* *Cf.* "Cambridge verses" on the Treaty of Utrecht mentioned above.
† *Cf.* Witty Club above.

eventually something sinister, there is also something admirable.

His tutor at Trinity Hall was the Reverend William Crowe, who had the distinction at one time of lending some classical notes and observations to the great Dr. Bentley, at that time Master of Trinity College, who never returned them. Crowe illustrates the smallness of the English world at that time. Stanhope would meet him again later on as chaplain of the Bishop of London and chaplain at the court of George II. He refers to him patronizingly as a living grammar, who saved him the trouble of learning Greek rules of syntax, but supplied him with them as they went along, reading Xenophon and Lucian together.[19] One gathers that Crowe was an amiable, perhaps even an obsequious, teacher, and no wonder, when it is recalled that the college tutor of that day received "but little above half as much as a footman." [20]

Besides the classics, Stanhope studied mathematics (presumably algebra) under the blind Nicholas Saunderson, at that time a young man of thirty,[21] and dabbled also in anatomy. He devoted an hour a day each to philosophy and civil law. In general he was a smatterer rather than a delver. He had a mind quick to learn, shrewd to apply, and a very retentive memory. But he never became, nor desired to become, a learned man. What knowledge he had could be paraded in full dress at a moment's notice, and the range of it was wide. He could outshine an academy of scholars. As a man of the world destined for foreign affairs and parliament, he quite properly learned much about many things, and exhaustively about none. But let no modern statesman or diplomat despise the dabbling of Philip Stanhope. In the eyes of that young gentleman, he would himself appear no better than illiterate. What does 1951 know of Lucian with or without rules? Or of Cicero? Or of Grotius? What kind of Latin or French style has 1951? Somehow the reading and teaching of that time stuck and retained sharp edges in contrast to the present blur. We shall have a more appropriate occasion later to discuss the scope of Chesterfield's reading.

But Cambridge consisted not only, on one hand, of the Devil's Ditch, the Choke-Jade, and jockeys of Newmarket,[22] or the booths and tumult of Stirbridge Fair, or the callow philandering with tradesmen's daughters, nor, on the other hand, of Crowe's tutoring and the university lectures. It was the day of Greek's Coffee-house,[23] where the college dons and more opulent undergraduates refreshed themselves with Bohea and sharpened their wits on current topics. "At times," observes Stanhope to Monsieur Jouneau, "I enjoy watching the pitched battles at the coffee-house between heroes of each political party, which are fought with inconceivable courage, and end only with the utter defeat of some tea-cups on either side." [24] In addition to tea, one could partake here of delicacies ordered beforehand from the cookshop or tavern — venison and salmon, Burgundy, champagne, and rack-punch — to break the deadly monotony of college fare.[25]

It was here, no doubt, that the self-styled Witty Club assembled now and then — the Cambridge Olympians, of whom, except for Berkeley, little is known. Who were the *Bonny* and Exton Sayer and George Stanley? What were they like? Rattling swells, of course, once upon a time and now mere names. It was among them that Stanhope exercised that "sauciness of literature, a turn to satire and contempt" [26] of which he warns his son, and which, indeed, served him many an ill turn. Did they, flown all together at last with rack-punch, issue forth like the Oxford "smarts" of Amhurst's *Terrae Filius* to bullyrag the town?[27] No, not that. Stanhope would never have risked a brawl. More sensibly he played tennis with them for the sake of the *mens sana in corpore sano*, because, as he sagely informed his London tutor, the one was not much good without the other.

College friendships are apt to be lasting ones. Two or three usually linger on, maturing and deepening with the years. But in college no more than in later life does Stanhope appear to have formed strong attachments. The *Bonny*, Exton Sayer, and George Stanley vanish, as far as we are concerned, from his history, though perhaps, like George Berkeley, they continued to play a role in the fashionable come-and-go of that time. Berkeley, for instance, served in parliament for many years and joined the opposition to Walpole. He and Chesterfield are mentioned together by Hervey as intimates of Pulteney.* In the end, gouty and middle-aged, he married the equally veteran Countess of Suffolk, retired mistress of the king and one of Chesterfield's courtly correspondents.

---

* Lord Hervey, *op. cit.*, vol. i, p. 8. It should be noted also that Berkeley was probably a childhood friend or acquaintance, for we find his father, the second Earl of Berkeley, occupying a house in St. James's Square from 1697 to 1699. Chancellor, *History of the Squares of London*, p. 84.

Casually preserved in the letters of that amiable lady and in this connection mentioned by others, he enjoys a modest and reflected immortality. But even he does not seem to have been, in the deeper sense of the word, a friend of Chesterfield's. The latter had countless acquaintances, many of them close and well disposed, but, if we except Scarborough and the two protégés, Dayrolles and Chenevix, it would be hard to point out a friend.[28] There is a certain opaque quality even in his most intimate letters, which in spite of their graciousness reveal less of his essential self than would at first appear. He is never to be encountered undressed and ungroomed, but only in the most appropriate costume for the occasion, whether formal or informal, turned out with an easy elegance, and receiving in the salon or library. But as friendship springs rather from the heart than the head, it must find at least a corner of a heart to spring from. In the correspondence and memoirs of the period, references to Chesterfield are often admiring, sometimes indifferent, often hostile, but never affectionate. He could inspire respect, gratitude, fear, hatred, and contempt, but not love. Perhaps this much sufficed him; but when we consider the emphasis he laid on winning the hearts of men and women in order to control their minds, it is surprising to note how few he won. We have had occasion earlier to point out that as, in a normal, usual sense, Chesterfield had neither parents nor wife nor child, so it appears also that he had few friends. But in a world which is governed by the laws of compensation, and where every disadvantage is remedied by a corresponding gain, his isolation procured him independence, privacy, and all the amenities (such as they are) of reserve.

At about the first of February, 1714, the Witty Club probably celebrated the accession of Philip Stanhope to a title, for his grandfather, the second Earl of Chesterfield, died at the age of eighty on the twenty-eighth of January in that year. At his death the sour lord, his son, moved up to an earldom, and the Cambridge Freshman in turn moved up to the courtesy title, Lord Stanhope of Shelford. It was only a courtesy title, but none the less a plume in the hat of a fellow commoner. Mr. Crowe probably enjoyed calling him "my lord."

A few months later the Cambridge interlude came to an end. It had not been altogether unprofitable or unpleasant. But in his own mind, without question, the most important part of his education remained to follow: the great world of the Continent, its capitals and courts, its more cosmopolitan and debonair society, in a word, the Grand Tour culminating at the climax of Paris. How mean, as compared with this, were the unpaved streets and Gothic colleges, the frostbitten nymphs and lubberly pedants of Cambridge! It left no pleasant impression with him. He sniffs (if so courtly a writer may be said to sniff) at the memory of it. That illiberal seminary! *

* In the *World*, No. 18, May 3, 1753, Chesterfield, impersonating a distressed English parent, wrote as follows: "My son passed nine years at Westminster school, in learning the words of two languages, long since dead, and not yet above half revived. When I took him away from school, I resolved to send him directly abroad, having been at Oxford myself." And to Newcastle, Feb. 25, 1764: "Though I have a very indifferent opinion of my Alma Mater, etc." Also to Madden, 1749.

CHAPTER IV

Continental Intermezzo

See how we trifle! but one can't pass one's youth too
amusingly; for one must grow old, and that in England; two
most serious circumstances, either of which makes people
grey in the twinkling of a bedstaff; for know you, there is
not a country upon earth where there are so many old fools
and so few young ones. — HORACE WALPOLE TO RICHARD
WEST.

THE GRAND TOUR consisted usually of France and Italy, with a
connective, shivering view from the crags of the Mount Cenis.
It represented a misery of inns and post chaises, broken by prolonged stays at such favorite places as Lyons, Turin, Milan, Venice,
Parma, Reggio (for the opera), Florence, Rome (with a dash to
Naples), then back, perhaps via Genoa to France, Montpellier, and
at last the supreme windup in Paris.[1] It took upwards of a year and
supposedly imbued young gentlemen with that final polish and accent of the world which could never be achieved in England. Another feature of the Grand Tour was the male duenna, or cicerone
from one of the universities, hired to point out the antiquities of
towns visited, to read Latin with young master, chaperon him, keep
him out of mischief, and in general counterbalance him during the
course of their travels. He was guide and philosopher, but often more
nuisance than friend.

In respect both to route and companionship, Lord Stanhope of
Shelford, having consigned his tufted cap and embroidered student's
gown to the limbo of outworn costumes, followed a less conventional plan. He crossed to Flanders and Holland, and except for a
valet de chambre and a footman,[2] he traveled alone. This was in
the early spring of 1714, for we find him writing to George Berke-

ley from The Hague on May 29 and he had already spent some time in Antwerp.

There is, of course, no reason why he should not have visited the Low Countries before traveling south. A Dutch King of England, the Dutch alliance, and the ensuing wars, had produced a lively interchange between Holland and Great Britain, and had brought both countries closer together than they are at present. English titles had been conferred on Dutch noblemen,* and hosts of Englishmen had campaigned through Flanders. Indeed, English itself was a language generally understood in those parts. The cities — Bruges, Ghent, and Antwerp to the south; The Hague, Amsterdam, Leyden, and Utrecht to the north — were worth visiting on account both of their ancient splendor in one case, and their present affluence in the other.[3]

But for all that, one is tempted to find something more than the indifference of a careless tourist in Stanhope's hurried passage through Flanders[4] and his sojourn in Antwerp; for it was the year of Queen Anne's death, the year when the Stuart fortunes looked brightest, and when Whig noblemen conspired to take arms in defense of the Constitution. Antwerp, at the time, was chiefly famous not for its cathedral and Bourse, but as the residence of the exiled Mars of the Whig party, none other than Marlborough himself. Could it have been primarily not as traveler but as messenger that young Stanhope passed that way? And were the attentions of the ducal couple, which monopolized his time there, prompted solely by liking for the grandson of an old friend?[5]

The probability is that the Duke's presence accounted for Stanhope's visit to that city. It is probable too that he carried letters, and was thoroughly pumped for English news by the Duke and Duchess, who were biding their time none too patiently. In any case, whether he learned it then or later, he was thoroughly cognizant of the plot whereby, if the Queen's life had been prolonged, the Whigs would have taken arms under his kinsman, General Stanhope,[6] while Marlborough would have been summoned back from Flanders as generalissimo. Indeed, there were plots on both sides, and the air must have seemed charged with them that year.

Thus, presumably, it was not the cathedral with its spire and

* For example, on William Bentinck, who had been made Earl of Portland.

chimes, nor Rubens's "Descent from the Cross," nor the Gothic Exchange with its deserted piazzas, nor the Jesuit church, nor St. Jacques with its twenty-eight chapels that absorbed him here, but English politics and two imposing English personalities. No doubt it would flatter a youth from college to attend such a host and hostess in their coach on the Place de la Meir among other "moveable gallantries" of the city, and partake of Marlborough's universal distinction; or stroll respectfully with the Duke upon the tree-lined ramparts.[7] It would flatter him, who as a child must have admired them from a distance, to be now on intimate social terms with such tremendous grandees. There is a distinct note of elation in his letter to Berkeley; and years afterwards, he was proud to recall that he knew the Duke of Marlborough extremely well.[8] With the exception of Bolingbroke, no one in the letters was praised more often or more unreservedly as a pattern of worldly address. It was a reasoned, pondered praise, the evident fruit of much reflection. "He had wound up and turned his whole machine to please and engage," wrote Chesterfield. "He had an inimitable sweetness and gentleness in his countenance, a tenderness in his manner of speaking, a graceful dignity in every motion, and a universal and minute attention to the least things that could possibly please the least person. This was all art in him; art of which he well knew and enjoyed the advantages; for no man ever had more interior ambition, pride, and avarice, than he had." [9] What a dazzlement, what a mentor and paragon for an ambitious young man! We can picture them on those ramparts, which surpassed any others in the world: the tall Duke and the diminutive youth, Marlborough so famous, so affable and responsive even to the poorest salutation, and Stanhope, admiring, studying, imitating him. Then home through the winding streets of the city between the high brick houses with their steep roofs.

But Marlborough, who died a few years later, would remain rather a glamorous memory of youth than a continuing factor in Chesterfield's life. It was the Duchess (as formidable a duchess as ever drew breath outside of Carroll's pages) who, up to his middle age, at least, maintained her place on the fashionable stage and figured as one of his more intimate older friends.

Sarah Jennings Churchill was at that time fifty-four years old. If she had failed in beauty from the piquante belle of King James's court, there was no failure in spirit and bad temper, though Stanhope seems to have been one of the few who never suffered from it. Always faithful to her handsome lord, she is one of the strangest constant nymphs in history, a volcanic, rattlebrained constant nymph, who swore so horribly that even the poor lawyer's clerk, who did not know her, realized that she must be a *grandissime* lady. Yet she was capable of a sharp thrust of wit now and then, as in that famous epigram concerning King James, who, she affirmed, sacrificed his country to his desire for dragging it to heaven with him.[10] She railed at religion, railed at the Queen, railed at three quarters of the world, and spent her eighty-four years in a glorious feud. Pope would immortalize her in one of his most telling caricatures:

> Full sixty years the world has been her trade,
> The wisest fool much time has ever made.
> From loveless youth to unrespected age,
> No passion gratify'd except her Rage.
>
> .   .   .   .   .
>
> Offend her, and she knows not to forgive;
> Oblige her, and she'll hate you while you live:
>
> .   .   .   .   .
>
> Strange! by the Means defeated of the Ends,
> By Spirit robb'd of Pow'r, by Warmth of Friends,
> By Wealth of Follow'rs! without one distress
> Sick of herself thro' very selfishness!
> Atossa, curs'd with ev'ry granted pray'r — [11]

The young Lord Stanhope was not important enough to provoke her ire. Perhaps her friendship after he had become Earl of Chesterfield is explained less by her liking for the man himself than by their mutual hostility to Sir Robert Walpole.

There were urgent subjects discussed that spring in the Duke's house at Antwerp. Bolingbroke and the Tories had reached the zenith of their power; Lady Masham, the Duchess of Marlborough's successor in the Queen's favor, enjoyed undisputed influence; the Duke, in constant touch with Robethon, confidential secretary at Hanover, was explaining (perhaps unjustly)[12] how the British ministers were betraying England to the Pretender.[13] It was a question of the disgruntled Whigs, the party out of power, conspiring to get in — by armed force, if necessary. The Peace of

Utrecht, which, though saving Britain from an almost intolerable burden of war, had deprived Marlborough of further glory; the schemes of Bolingbroke and counterschemes; the dangers of a disputed succession, which by jeopardizing the fruits of the Revolution of 1688 might result in a return to absolutism — such were the matters undoubtedly discussed at the Churchills' table or of an evening during the intervals of omber or basset.

But the real issues involved something less obvious than political personalities or the change of a dynasty. They were issues obscure to the participants themselves or at best vaguely apprehended by them, for of all historical periods the one nearest at hand is the hardest to evaluate. A good argument could be made in support of the thesis that what Pope, Prior, Swift, Arbuthnot, Atterbury, and others of their circle felt at the triumph of Whiggism, the Hanoverians, and Walpole — what they felt, and what, indeed, they expressed in one fashion or another, was the disappearance of finer loyalties and values. To them the High Church and the old monarchy represented those elegancies of the spirit which elude description, which commend themselves to the heart rather than the head, and which, as compared with the excellent good sense of grosser reason, must ever appear trivial and fine spun. The beggarly Jacobite, drinking to his king over the water, caught at least a glimpse of altitudes denied to the prosperous courtiers of King George. Brimley Johnson observes that "the Hanoverian dynasty seems to have brought in, along with certain good things, a sort of triumph of pudding, turnips, and muddy ale, over the lace, maypoles, champagne, and burgundy of the preceding period," [14] and this expresses a nuance pertinent to many phases of life.

The trouble is that Whiggism was so oppressively plausible. It marshaled the most seductive of ideals: liberty, tolerance, the rights of man, commerce, common sense, and enlightenment. It could at once show tangible fruits: a revolution that produced the Bill of Rights, a more efficient fiscal system, a more balanced government, wars mainly supported by the Whigs and conducted by a Whig general, which at Ramillies, Oudenarde, and Blenheim reestablished the prestige of England. Following an eclipse of two years from the Treaty of Utrecht to the death of Anne in 1714, its steam-roller resumed for another half century that witnessed, under Walpole, the foundation of British wealth, and, under Pitt, the foundation of the British Empire. Moreover, from the historical standpoint, of even greater importance than its achievements have been the number of brilliant pens which have glorified it. Practically all English historians have upheld that party and magnified its leaders, while at the same time they censured the malice or obscurantism of its opponents.

Can there be another side to the question, when every humane, every reasonable argument supports this one? What can be urged against Whiggism except that millions of illogical people remained passionately Tory? What can be urged except that Whiggism, so glorified, so triumphant, so convincing, sounds almost too good to be true? Pudding, turnips, and muddy ale were unquestionably more sensible and democratic than burgundy or champagne — but, ah, the delight and glory of useless, extravagant things!

It is not surprising that Philip Stanhope belonged to the Whig tradition. Indeed, hardly anyone has more consistently embodied or more emphatically expressed it. His virtues and defects alike were of that school. He accepted each of its tenets with the most unquestioning sincerity. The latitudinarian character of its Protestantism, which had declined into deism, perfectly fitted his religious indifference. Its practicality appealed to his common sense. Its rationalism viewed the world in a so-called white light, which was the only light he himself approved, nor had he an inkling that it might be as fallacious as any. Its emphasis, he realized, was on fact, the ultimate pilot star of such a mind as his; but he failed to perceive that of all bigotries, the cult of fact is the most intolerant.

We are not concerned here, of course, with mere names. If, during the long years of opposition to Walpole, he consorted with Bolingbroke and voted at times against the rank and file of the Whig party, he was no less a Whig. And even in the retirement and invalidism of his old age, when the finer qualities of the man became manifest, he appeared then more than ever essentially a Whig.[15]

From Antwerp he continued north into Holland and spent the summer at The Hague. Even at that time the dominant interest of his life (the dominant interest of any true man of the world) was becoming manifest. Not picture galleries, nor cathedrals, nor cities, nor landscapes, except as an index and setting for human nature; not things, but people. From first to last, the study of mankind would absorb him. "In regard to reflections [on the tour through Flanders]," he wrote Jouneau, "I was unable to make any, for you know that they ought to concern people rather than things, and, as I only passed through, I had no time to form any acquaintance there." [16]

But if he had already begun his study of men and women, it will be remembered that he confined himself then and always to a special group. In the letter we have just quoted, he remarked that society at The Hague was exceedingly good, on account of the number of foreigners there — the cosmopolitan, diplomatic set. As far as the natives went, he continued, it was obvious that they did not belong to the best circles. They were worthy enough people, but unconcerned with polite intercourse. Here as elsewhere, he found himself in the society to which he was born and from which there is not the slightest indication that he at any time ventured forth: that strange, gossipy, international beau monde of the eighteenth century, with its patter of French and common ground of manners, with its cult of wit and its philosophy of *savoir-vivre*. His Continental travels would enrich his experience, but upon no different plane than that he had already known. Indeed, it would hardly have occurred to him that there was any other worth his knowing.

Even to-day The Hague conserves much of its earlier grace. There is a charm about the small, neat capitals of the north, a quality of light, which is particularly evident here, especially on long summer evenings haunted by a sense of the neighboring ocean and by the redolence of trees and gardens. Then, undisturbed by any discord of modern machines, a town of thirty or forty thousand, dedicated to the uses of government, diplomacy, and leisure, it ranked as one of the most fashionable European cities.[17] Sixty years later the encyclopedist, Denis Diderot, visited Holland and wrote a description of it which applies as well to 1714 as to 1773. Of The Hague he reported that "it was perhaps the most beautiful village in the world"; * that "the residence of foreign ministers there had made it a centre of espionage, and the idleness

* In 1716 Lady Mary Wortley Montagu called it "the finest village in the world." *Letters*, ed. Wharncliffe-Thomas, vol. i, p. 227. It seems to have been a more or less conventional phrase.

of its population a centre of gossip." "There are no end of royal
ambassadors and representatives of the United Provinces here," he
went on, "all of them people who scrutinize each other incessantly and see each other seldom." [18] And long afterward Chesterfield, looking back from middle age and London March weather,
advised his son to spend May and June at The Hague, which he
considered at that season of the year "the most agreeable, smiling
scene in Europe." [19]

Then, even more than now, it was a place of parks and villas.
Along the Voorhout, or promenade, flanked by its rows of trees and
refreshment shops, people of quality took the air in their coaches or
on foot; or they rumbled along the arrow-straight avenue to
Scheveningen. In an age of cobblestones and mire, this famous
road was paved with small yellow bricks, a glory in itself, not to
speak of the four rows of lofty trees bordering it on either hand and
forming a vista that ended two miles off in the Scheveningen
church spire. They pass along the golden, tree-arched boulevard:
coaches, chariots, chaises, equestrians, stars and ribbons, divers
colored hoods (blue, yellow, and filemot), Mantua silk and
Geneva velvet, laced hats and stately periwigs. Invisible puffs of
Eau sans Pareil and Eau de Carm drift by each other in the summer
air.[20] And on either side lay the villa gardens of great noblemen,
especially Lord Portland's, with its yews and sycamores, hedges
and grass walks, its splendid greenhouse, its grottoes of shells, coral,
mirrors, and fountains.[21]

"In Holland," wrote Diderot, "luxury consists in pleasure houses,
in spacious, orderly gardens, in flowers. . . . The Dutch love paintings, engravings, and designs; they throw themselves furiously on
all the merchandise of the Indies and of Asia. Their houses over-
flow with porcelains, with trinkets of gold and silver, with diamonds,
furniture, and costly fabrics. . . . They are the human ants who
spread through every country on earth and garner all that they find
of rare and useful and rich." [22]

There were pleasant walks on every side: along the brick-
paved road to Delft, or in the splendid park of the Huis ten Bosch,
a royal villa. Here there was another promenade or mall and many
shaded paths between the oaks and elms. Here too were formal
gardens fenced around by a brick wall, a space of arbors and
hedges and sandy walks.[23]

As sights in The Hague itself stood the Great Church of Saint James (the Groote Kerk), and especially the palace, or Binnenhof, where then as now the States General met. But it was chiefly the social round itself, the dining room or salon, the card tables of marquis, count, or *abbé*, princess, madame, or countess, which would engross the genteel visitor such as young Lord Stanhope. It was at these card tables, youthfully proud of his admission to them, that he contracted that passion for gaming which was perhaps his only vice, but which dominated him during the greater part of his life.[24]

The company disbands; a flitting through silent streets from stately house to stately house; a hint of dawn; sleepy footmen snuff the candles; off with wig and on with nightcap; a drifting through the mind of ace or knave, jeweled fingers and golden coins. . . .

This sketch of The Hague is not inappropriate, for second only to London or Bath it was the town most closely associated with Chesterfield's later life. It was to The Hague fourteen years later that he was sent as British ambassador. It was there again in 1745 that he was once more dispatched on a second embassy. It was here that he achieved his modest, but creditable, diplomatic successes and formed some of his most interesting associations. Romantic biography would also no doubt portray The Hague as the *mise en scène* of the tender passion; nightingales would be set to singing in the park of the Huis ten Bosch; for it was here, to use the proper phrase, that he would make a conquest of that poor governess, Elizabeth du Bouchet, the future mother of his son. Possibly there were others equally frail or mercenary and with the usual accompaniment of trysts and billets-doux. But if there is anything worse than the prudish, it is the sentimental violin turned up on this hackneyed theme — especially with Chesterfield as the hero. He could be the witty and well-liked companion of women, but in more amorous roles a wit and satirist is not convincing.

There were two other young Englishmen at The Hague that summer. One was Richard Boyle, Earl of Burlington, fresh from Italy with his tutor, Mr. Gervais.[25] He would later distinguish himself as an architect and patron of art and letters, a generous, patriotic, beloved man, of whom even the waspish Horace Walpole reported that he had every quality of a genius and artist except envy, and to whom Pope dedicated his moral *Essay on the Use of Riches*. He married Chesterfield's cousin, the Lady Dorothy Savile, and remained an intimate acquaintance at court and in London for forty years. Stanhope ridiculed his too professional interest in architecture as that of a mason or bricklayer. Minute, mechanical things were beneath the dignity of a nobleman.[26]

In contrast to him at every point was another youth similarly engaged in making his debut, one of the strangest, most notorious figures of the time. This was George Bubb, later Dodington, and at last Baron Melcombe of Melcombe Regis. A hulking, awkward man, well enough born on the distaff side (though Chesterfield sneers at his paternity),[27] exceedingly rich by the death of an uncle, utterly unscrupulous, the spaniel of one patron after another whom he deserted with equal indifference, never quite successful, but at length, just before death, climbing into a peerage. Such, from one angle, was George Bubb, the Bubo of Pope's satires.[28] But he had another side: that of the distinguished wit, sound scholar, and graceful poet,* a friend too of literary men, such as Young, Thomson, Fielding. And all this he crowned with a nimbus of conceit. "There was never," says Walpole, "such a composition of vanity, versatility, and servility."[29] Chesterfield would take the trouble to court his political aid,[30] but entertained himself with dissecting him. He served, no doubt, as the model of Fatuus in the essays,[31] and elsewhere appears a brief sketch of him by the archanalyzer. "God made Dodington the coxcomb he is; mere human means could never have brought it about. He is a coxcomb superior to his parts, though his parts are superior to almost anybody's."[32]

The English ambassador at The Hague was at that time Thomas Wentworth, Earl of Strafford, a proud, hot-tempered Tory, one of the negotiators of the Treaty of Utrecht, and who would be impeached for it the following year. Lord Hervey, with his usual mildness, describes him later as "a loquacious, rich, illiterate, cold, tedious, constant haranguer in the House of Lords, who neither spoke sense nor English."[33] He was a bête noire of Stanhope's father, the sour Earl, who agreed with his friend Prior in roundly

---

* For example, the lines "Love thy country, wish it well," etc., included in such an anthology as *The Oxford Book of English Verse*.

damning him.* In the circumstances, Philip could not have been particularly welcome at the embassy. Mr. Gervais, the tutor of Lord Burlington, recalled years afterward when Dean of Tuam that his noble pupil, together with Lord Stanhope and Mr. Bubb, used to smoke the arrogant ambassador about Tory versus Whig politics.[34] But considering the age of the young gentlemen, such chaff must have been demure and well disguised.

From The Hague there were excursions to various points of interest. Lord Stanhope visited Amsterdam, Leyden, and Utrecht.[35] But it was not sight-seeing that would absorb him, nor was he summering at The Hague with that in view. Since his paramount interest, as we have seen, was people rather than things, and important or fashionable people rather than others, he may be regarded as specializing still further at that time and focusing his attention on a single point — that is, on ways and means: how in a society made up of conflicting personalities, interests, and passions, success could be achieved, human egoism harnessed to his uses, and human vanity correctly played upon. In a word, he was learning his tools, and these tools were manners.

The Hague supplied an excellent clinic for the purpose, a microcosm more easily grasped than the diffusion of Vienna or Paris. The importance of the United Provinces to the balance of power in Europe against the might of France had greatly exalted them in proportion to their size and population, and the post at The Hague was coveted by ambitious diplomats. Here, then, in small compass would meet the experts in finesse and *savoir-faire*. Their technique could be studied and compared. The most finished masters could be copied.

We shall have occasion later, when reviewing the education of Chesterfield's son, to consider and appraise the philosophy of manners; but let it be noted here that, now vanishing, it was then a fine art beyond any modern conception. It expressed infinite nuances; it reflected countless traditions; it gave a warp and woof to social intercourse and therefore implied standards which exacted obedience. It represented the mandarin culture of a mature aristoc-

---

* Francis Bickley, *An English Letter Book*, the third Earl to Prior, June 15, 1717. Strafford had been too proud to be associated with such a commoner as Prior in the Utrecht negotiations.

racy that disappeared with the nineteenth century, and of which the now rising generation can form no adequate notion. Some of us who are of middle age can recall from our extreme youth figures of aged gentlemen or ladies who were themselves brought up in the memory of that system. We will recall in them a delicate formality that preserved their own and implied the dignity of everyone, that implied also differences in age and sex and rank and gave the glamour of diversity to life. We will recall a grace of movement, a certain fastidiousness of thought and language. We can imagine dimly, therefore, what may have been the cult of manners in those Parisian salons that set the tone for eighteenth-century Europe. With the disappearance of all this, there faded from human conduct an inestimable beauty. The fact that we not only no longer have time for manners, but even ignore what they are, is in itself a sufficient commentary on the change of civilization. Artificial, over-elaborate, they were still a product of those faculties which have raised mankind from the mire.

It required more than good will and a good heart to learn the code of that time. It demanded talent and intelligence. From his youth up, Stanhope seems to have been unusually interested in this question, although it was present in the consciousness of nearly everyone. He discerned in it the key to all he wished for in the world. Behind the sight-seeing, gaming, and idling of that summer, behind the studied smile and unrevealing eyes, burned constantly, alertly, the flame of his purpose. He had, as he called it, "an uphill game." [36] With his small stature and plain features, he possessed none of that physical impressiveness which smoothed the way for others; but he possessed a shrewd, logical mind and nearly perfect self-control.

Rules are useful enough, but an art such as manners demands infinite practice. He followed the method of imitation and played sedulous ape to experts. It became afterwards a cardinal point in his method to advise the careful study of those distinguished by their good breeding. "Imitate," he would urge, "nay, endeavour to excel that you may at last reach them." [37]

He won his uphill game according to that law of seeking and finding which applies to almost every aim in life. Among the tactful, most tactful; among the adroit, most adroit; among the gracious,

most gracious. A critical age acknowledged his mastery.* If, as he
might have wished, he did not succeed in winning the love of men,
he at any rate elicited their applause.

But The Hague was merely one stop on the Grand Tour. He
planned to continue his studies at the Court of Savoy in Turin until
carnival time, then cross Italy to Venice, have a fling at the masquerades, ridottos, and operas there, and then continue down to
Rome. On August 10 (New Style) he was preparing for his departure, and expected to leave the following week. That same day,
Queen Anne was stricken with the final attack of her illness; two
days later she died.†

Dispatches had already been sent to the Elector at Hanover, advising him of the next step "in case it pleased God to call the Queen
to His mercy." Trumpets and proclamations sounded through the
streets of London; heralds and Life Guards paraded. "The Queen
is dead; long live the King!" But it was not the King of the Jacobites, of Ormonde or Atterbury, that was proclaimed, not a Stuart,
but a Guelph. The Tories were down. A Whig lord, the Earl of
Berkeley, brother of Stanhope's college friend, was in command of
the fleet. Whig generals were in Scotland to stifle any attempt by the
Pretender. Several days after the Queen's death, Marlborough and
the Duchess entered London in triumph with horse and foot and
fifty coaches.[38] The Whig era was at hand.

In these circumstances, the Grand Tour had to be curtailed. If
court plums were to be handed out, they would be conferred on
courtiers within reach. Philip's kinsman, General Stanhope, stood
high in the favor of the new King; within a year, Philip himself
could take his seat in parliament. The situation provided opportunities that had to be watched. Italy, therefore, dropped out of the
Grand Tour, and Lord Stanhope seems to have spent the autumn
in Paris. He was at home there both by his mental attitude and by
his knowledge of the language. "I am often taken for a Frenchman,"
he wrote Jouneau, "and more than one has paid me the greatest

---

*Lady Hervey, a veteran *grande dame* and woman of fashion, ranked
him with Lord Bolingbroke among the politest people of the age. *Letters
of Lady Hervey*, London, 1821. To the Rev. Edmund Morris, April 2, 1748.

† On August 1 (Old Style); Aug. 12 (New Style), 1714.

compliment in their power, to wit: 'Sir, you are altogether like one of us.' . . . I am insolent; I talk a great deal in loud, masterful tones; I sing and dance, as I walk; and finally I spend an outrageous sum on powder, plumes, white gloves, etc." [39]

Watch his short figure go swaggering down one of the winding streets of the Faubourg St. Germain: feathered hat, clouded cane, high red heels, a complete little marquis, adaptable as ever to the proper role. He has not yet acquired that supreme art which conceals art, but he has made good progress since Cambridge. His youthful education is almost complete.

Meanwhile, friends have been active for him. He returned to England early in 1715 to be elected (though under age) member of parliament for St. Germains in Cornwall, and to be appointed Gentleman of the Bedchamber to the Prince of Wales. He found the young Earl of Burlington in the Privy Council,* George Bubb with a seat in the Commons and slated for a diplomatic mission.† The *cursus honorum* of their generation had begun.

But before continuing the survey of Stanhope's early career in London, it will be well to examine at greater length his debt to France and to French culture. It is too important an element in his life to be dismissed with a few paragraphs. We have considered the factors of heredity, early environment, and youthful tendencies; the influence of France in a sense re-emphasizes and resumes them; for perhaps more than any other Englishman, it is difficult to interpret Chesterfield in purely English terms. Something essential in him, something inborn and profound as personality itself, identifies him with the French tradition.

Moreover, though bravely begun, his attendance at court and in parliament suffered a temporary interruption. By the middle of August, 1715, he was back in Paris.

* Appointed Oct. 9, 1714.
† A member for Winchelsea, a family borough. In May 1715, he was sent as envoy extraordinary to Spain, where he remained for two years.

CHAPTER V
Paris

STANHOPE's return to Paris after so brief a parliamentary experience was not altogether voluntary. He began his political life naturally enough as a Whig henchman, and the Whigs were no sooner in office than they launched out upon a rancorous investigation of their predecessors, especially in regard to what they chose to consider as the pusillanimous Treaty of Utrecht. Robert Harley, Earl of Oxford, was sent to the Tower; * Bolingbroke and Ormonde took refuge in France. It was in regard to these fugitives that on August 5, 1715, Lord Stanhope rose in his seat to declare that though "he never wished to spill the blood of any of his countrymen, much less the blood of any noblemen, yet he was persuaded that the safety of his country required that example should be made of those who had betrayed it in so infamous a manner." [1] He referred here, of course, to the Treaty of Utrecht, in honor of which he had composed verses three years before; † but this had been long since forgotten.

The speech, he admitted later, was "strong and indiscreet, but it passed tolerably, in favour of the spirit with which he uttered it." He had thought of nothing else since his election. It represented his first essay in that art of the forum where he finally succeeded in obtaining an honorable rank. But though it passed the indulgent Whigs, it did not escape challenge by the Tories. One of them detained the young orator afterwards, courteously disclaimed any wish to prosecute the matter, but declared that if his lordship, being still under age, took part in the voting, he must face the consequences. Philip executed his best bow, considered that a second

* This was on July 16, 1715.
† The "Cambridge verses," *supra*, p. 45.

visit to Paris would be more entertaining than a fine of £500 and a voided election, and withdrew temporarily from Westminster.[2]

It was first suggested by Dr. Maty, and has been repeated by subsequent biographers, that Stanhope's departure for Paris at this time had a diplomatic significance. Bolingbroke was busy at the French court intriguing for the Pretender, and Lord Stair, the British minister, was equally busy with counterespionage. The services of an adroit young gentleman may very well have been valuable at such a time. But this is no more than a probability about which nothing definite is known. Meanwhile, it is of greater importance to determine what France would give and what her culture first and last would mean to him. His debt to her is well-nigh incalculable; she remained the native country of his mind. The compliment paid him by French acquaintances and reported not without elation in one of his early letters was, for once, more than a flourish: *Monsieur, vous êtes tout comme nous.*

How often and for how long at a time he visited France during the course of his life, we cannot be entirely certain. We know that he was in Paris in 1714, 1715, 1720,[3] and 1741. There were probably other visits, especially during the obscure years prior to his appointment as ambassador to The Hague in 1728. But on the whole, he does not seem to have spent an unusual amount of time in France. He was brought up speaking French and by a French tutor whom he respected; but other English boys, his own son for instance, had a similar education, and emerged entirely English. With him it went deeper than residence or education to an inherent identity with the French attitude. This did not affect his loyalty to England nor his national pride; it did not expatriate him nor provoke a chronic nostalgia for Paris; it simply represented his entire point of view.

To speak of the French attitude is perhaps a misnomer when at that time so small a part of France was articulate. In the last chapter, we pointed out that Stanhope's experience with men and women was confined almost entirely to the beau monde, and it is this, of course, which we are still concerned with: the voice of eighteenth-century France, the voice of the salon with its highborn hostesses and great lords, its wits, philosophers, and statesmen, the republic of thought which could be democratic because it was so rigidly exclusive.

When Stanhope returned to Paris in 1715, the King was dying
and the court was dull; but the leading salon, which perhaps replaced it, was that of Madame de Lambert in the Palais Mazarin. It
was attended by Fontenelle, who then or later became Chesterfield's
lifelong acquaintance, and it is possible that the young Englishman
may have appeared at some of the Wednesdays of the famous
Marquise.* It is significant, for example, that in his will the reference
to his servants as "unfortunate friends," a phrase which has been
generally considered his own, is simply a translation of one of
Madame de Lambert's epigrams.† But whether or not he was accepted here or attended the salon of Madame de Verrue, Madame
de Villars, or Madame de Matignon, makes little difference. The
Hôtel Lambert may be taken as typical of the transition between
the conservatism of the Hôtel de Rambouillet thirty years earlier
and the progressive salon of Madame de Tencin, which we know
that Chesterfield did attend later on.

At the suppers of the Marquise appeared the intelligentsia of the
time — Mesdames de Caylus, de Fontaines, de Sainctonge, Mademoiselle de Launey, and Fontenelle, La Motte, de Choisy, the
Marquis de Lassay, Adrienne Lecouvreur, Marivaux, Watteau,
among many others. "To be invited to the Palais Mazarin was to be
breveted a wit." [4] No gaming here, no license. Whether in the
graver receptions of the afternoon or at the gayer evening parties,
there was no relaxation of good manners or good taste. For the
salon was more than a social diversion; it became in a sense the
temple of the French spirit, the expression of the national mind at
its most living, its most glowing point. Here public opinion began,
was trained and received its direction. Here was to be found the
cradle of that enlightener and destroyer: thought.

A strange wind had begun to breathe through the ruelles of
those days, a wind as yet playful and merely refreshing, but for all
that uncanny and with a vague foreboding of the still distant hurri-
cane. It was modernism. The battle between Ancients and Moderns,
which provoked a flood of ink about that time and served to
animate conversation, had at least so much importance that, like

---

* She had two days a week: Tuesdays for the literary set and Wednesdays for people of society. V. du Bled, *Société française*, 5ᵉ Série, pp. 172–
173.

† *Il faut traiter ses domestiques comme des amis malheureux. Ibid.*, p. 170.

a straw, it showed the direction of this wind. And the Hôtel Lambert sided with the Moderns. Madame de Lambert detested Homer. It was not the thought or the authors of the past, but those of the present, that absorbed her coterie. The past was being discarded. And although at first the connection between a dislike of Homer and the destruction of the Bastille may not seem obvious, it is still logical.

Similarly, as Victor du Bled points out, the *Être Suprême*, who would have scandalized the Hôtel de Rambouillet, passed unchallenged at the Palais Mazarin; and here the chain of consequence is more apparent up to that culminating feast day of the Supreme Being under Robespierre. But if so, what then of another of Madame de Lambert's sayings: "Plebeians are those who think low and vulgar thoughts; the court is full of them"; and that remark about her unfortunate friends, the servants, which we have already noted? Yes, the wind as yet gave no more than a pleasant tang to discourse; Rousseau was still an infant; the young Monsieur Arouet at Madame de Villars's salon had not yet assumed the more sinister and famous surname of Voltaire; but the spirit of the new age had already crossed the threshold. It would grow bolder; and therewith also would deepen that sense of doom which attends the closing phases of a mature civilization. Much has been made of Chesterfield's political astuteness in foretelling the French Revolution, but in this, as in most things, he did no more than reflect the advanced thought of the times. Years earlier, his old friend Madame de Tencin had observed that "unless God intervened directly, it is humanly impossible to save the State. . . . Affairs have reached so terrible a pass, that it is best not to meddle with them. It will all end in some thunder-bolt." [5] The shiver of the oncoming storm would disturb increasingly the serenity of that generation.

It is almost unnecessary to point out how much in tune young Lord Stanhope was and would continue to be with this. He too hated Homer and abused Achilles; [6] he too rejoiced in modern writers, modern philosophy and ways as opposed to the old; he too professed a languid deism; he too was a parlor democrat.

The last clause needs elaboration, because the liberalism of Chesterfield, his lack of aristocratic prejudices, has been frequently emphasized, [7] and is, indeed, conspicuous in much of his formal writing. He would set up the busts of Adam de Stanhope and Eve de Stanhope in his library as a jibe at pedigree; he would make fun of royalty and royal pretensions; he would condescend to men of low estate. Nor was this insincere. It represented that cult of Common Sense to which he paid honest worship during the whole of his life. But there should be no mistake on two points: first, that such liberalism was the French philosophic vogue, in other words that it betokened no originality on the part of a man who belonged entirely to the French school — it was the enlightened, fashionable way of thinking; and, secondly, that such liberalism, such democracy, may be an evidence less of humility than of pride. Samuel Johnson's remark on this point is worth recalling. "Lord Chesterfield," he said to his friend Adams, "is the proudest man this day existing." [8] And making every allowance for the sage's hostility, there is a sense in which he spoke the truth. For the quintessence of pride is a condescension that passes as democratic, and the supreme gesture of aristocracy is the scorn of asserting itself. Throughout the letters, beneath their grace and graciousness, runs the undertone of an assumption so profound as to need no expression, the assumption of his own high place in the social hierarchy.*

After all, however, it was not the philosophy of the salons which would most influence him in France, but something still more subtle and pervasive. For want of better words, we may call it atmosphere, cachet, allure — nuances to be expressed more easily in music, painting, or aroma than in language. And here we approach that feature of Chesterfield which is nearest to greatness and nearest to passion, where for once he is more than a brilliant reflector of the spirit of the times and achieves individual rank. It is, on one hand, the extreme sensitiveness of his perceptions concerning matters of social conduct, and, on the other, his power of expressing them. It is decorum considered no longer as etiquette, but elevated to the plane of an art infinitely variable and delicate, whereof he was not

* Lord Burlington, he affirmed, had lessened his rank by too intimate a knowledge of the mechanical details of architecture (Letter to son, Oct. 17, 1749). "If ever the multitude deviate into right, it is always for the wrong reason" ("Character of Lord Bute," Chesterfield's *Works*, Mahon's ed., vol. ii, p. 494). Let his young friend Huntingdon beware of the "common herd of English who infest Paris." These are but three examples of a constant attitude. No proper estimate of Chesterfield can be formed if it be not steadily remembered that, for all his liberalism and common sense, he wrote as a great lord, brought up from his cradle in an aristocratic tradition of which it is difficult nowadays even to conceive the rigidity.

only a great master, but the unrivaled interpreter. "Do everything," he once wrote his godson, "in minuet-time; speak, think, and move always in that measure." [9] This was French, not English. It represented a civilization more artificial than that of Great Britain, although imitated there; a preoccupation with the exquisite trifles of behavior, as an art conducive to the most engrossing of human pastimes, the intercourse between perfectly well-bred persons. It sprang from a courtly tradition uninterrupted since the Renaissance, one that was absolutely mature and that, like the violin, required a lifetime of learning and practice.

Taine, quoting de Tilly, Necker, and others, observed that a great lady received ten persons with one curtsy, bestowing on each, through a movement of the head or by a glance, all that he was entitled to as regarded position, consideration and birth.

> She was never mistaken, and never hesitated in these subtle distinctions; with incomparable tact, dexterity, and flexibility of tone, she regulated the degrees of her welcome. She had one for women of condition, one for women of quality, one for women of the court, one for titled women, one for women of historic names, another for women of high birth personally, but married to men beneath them; another for women who by marriage have changed a common into a distinguished name; another still for women of reputable names in the law; and, finally, another for those whose distinction consists chiefly of expensive houses and good suppers. A stranger would be amazed on seeing with what certain and adroit steps she circulated among so many watchful vanities without ever giving or receiving a check. She knew how to express all through the style of her salutations; a varied style, extending through imperceptible gradations, from the accessory of a single shrug of the shoulder, almost an impertinence, to that noble and deferential reverence which so few women, even of the court, know how to do well; that slow bending forward, with lowered eyes and straightened figure, gradually recovering and modestly glancing at the person while gracefully raising the body up, altogether much more refined and more delicate than words, but very expressive as the means of manifesting respect. [10]

Youth was sacrificed to this training. The little girl in her whalebone stays, hoop skirt, and false curls, with a dash of rouge on her cheeks and maneuvering a fan; the little boy with his gilded cuffs and court sword, a chapeau under his arm, and with pomatumed hair, were launched into the beau monde almost before they left the nursery. George Sand, reviewing her own childhood, declared that she was rebuked for everything, that she could not make a movement that was not criticized.

Over such a world, the dancing master presided; and for forty years, Marcel of Paris occupied an unrivaled position among the virtuosos of the art. In 1717 the poet Gay referred to him as famous; he still held the stage in 1751.[11] Pupils flocked to him from afar — among them perhaps Lord Stanhope, but in any case long afterwards Stanhope's son, duly instructed by his anxious father that Marcel was of more consequence to him than all the bureaus of Europe, that he was the most useful and necessary of all the masters he had or could have. It was Marcel who exclaimed, "What a world in one minuet!" And to an English pupil, "Sir, people abroad only hop: it is in Paris alone that they dance." [12]

The snobs of England copied these graces at a wistful distance, but they never became native there. England, with its civil wars and religious quarrels, its masterful bourgeoisie, belligerent parliaments, harassed court and rustic aristocracy, could never compete with the manners of Versailles. But it was precisely to that alien, Latin culture that Chesterfield psychologically belonged. It has been frequently asserted that the awkwardness of his son called forth the torrent of lecturing on deportment which characterizes the famous *Letters*, that a different youth would have been differently addressed. This is true in a measure; but it is not altogether true. He lectured his godson in the same way, although the latter does not seem to have been unusually awkward. It was evidently a principle with him where education was concerned. The point, however, is that it was not a principle peculiar to him. In the eighteenth century everywhere, but deriving on the whole from Paris as the chief cultural center, deportment, the art of social living, had developed out of all proportion to its function as a means, and had become an end. It was Alexandrianism in conduct, the not too wholesome flowering of a civilization grown over-refined, old, and therefore pedantic. "A genuine sentiment," remarked Chamfort, "is so rare, that when I leave Versailles, I sometimes stand still in the street to see a dog gnaw a bone." [13] Behavior thus had become the obsession of a nation, the mightiest and most cultivated nation of that age. Chesterfield, born Alexandrian, delighted in it. "The English," he would observe long afterwards to his son, "are usually boobies; they lack the free and easy, yet polished manners of the French. Therefore consider the French and imitate them. . . ." [14]

At every other point, there was a similar agreement. The type of his wit, the flavor of his literary style, his choice of reading, the temper of his philosophy, his very cuisine were French.[15] It went farther, even to the matrimonial understanding with his wife. They agreed not to live together during the first years, but kept their separate houses and establishments. Many gentlemen in Paris did not live with their wives. The Duke of Lauzun, upon being asked what he would say if his wife, whom he had not seen for ten years, should inform him that she was *enceinte*, having reflected a moment, replied: "I would write and tell her that I was delighted that heaven had blessed our union; be careful of your health; I will call and pay my compliments this evening." [16] Such would be naturally the attitude of a gentleman and philosopher. Chesterfield might have expressed himself in the same terms.

But this affinity, to call it so, was mutual. If Stanhope admired the French, the French equally admired him. He was elected member of the Académie des Inscriptions; Montesquieu, Voltaire, Crébillon, Fontenelle, Mesdames de Tencin, du Boccage, de Monconseil, were among his correspondents; the salons of Paris, closed and cold to the usual English nobleman,* received him gladly. The following extract from a letter from Madame de Tencin to Chesterfield, recording the effect produced at her salon by the public reading of an epistle he had written her in French, is eloquent of more than flattery:

" 'Milord makes fun of us,' cried Monsieur de Fontenelle in concert with others, 'by writing our own language better and more correctly than we. Let him content himself with being the leading man of his nation, with having the parts and the depth of genius characteristic of him; but let him not also monopolize our airs and our graces.' The protests and murmurs of the company would be still continuing," added Madame de Tencin, "if, after having frankly admitted your faults, I had not taken care to recall the pleasure and charm of your conversation. 'Ah,' they exclaimed together, 'let

---

* Horace Walpole, as a youth, found this to be true. (See his letter to West, Feb. 27, 1740.)

him only come back to us, and we will forgive him for having more wit than ourselves!' " [17]

It would be interesting to know exactly what people he met in Paris during that late summer and early fall of 1715 — probably many who to the end remained acquaintances, correspondents, or perhaps friends.

There was, of course, the British minister, John Dalrymple, the Earl of Stair,* already a distinguished soldier and soon to be an even more distinguished diplomat. He was a Scotsman of charming manners and great gallantry, every inch a gentleman, who would later act with Chesterfield in opposition to Walpole. Now, as one of the Whig leaders and one of Marlborough's major generals, a man of real talent and address, no abler master for a débutant like Stanhope could have been found. As we have already pointed out, he was then absorbed in counteracting the schemes of the exiled Bolingbroke, though, in the character of an intimate friend, he welcomed him from time to time at his house.[18]

Thus, in addition to Stair, there was in Paris the brilliant leader of the Tory party himself; and the lifelong attachment of Stanhope for Bolingbroke probably dates from that period.[19] We have had a glimpse of the famous Viscount in St. James's Square; his importance in Chesterfield's life justifies a longer estimate.

The two men had a great deal in common, but with this difference, that both physically and intellectually everything in Lord Bolingbroke was heightened to a gallant and almost romantic pitch. His entire life, its stir and glitter, and sudden disgrace, its many accomplishments, has a dramatic quality wanting to Chesterfield's more prosaic career. Lord Bolingbroke was handsome of person; he was adored by women and admired by men; he shone as a statesman, orator, philosopher, and man of letters. The romance of glory and of misfortune attended him always.

He offers an extreme example of the brittleness of contemporary fame, for if that circle of wits and writers centering about Pope at Twickenham had been consulted, many of them would unquestionably have proclaimed him the most eminent stylist, the most profound thinker, of his age. Chesterfield admired him extravagantly, held him up as an almost universal model. He was the

* He was raised to the rank of ambassador in February 1719.

omnis homo, who showed how history should be read, who talked as elegantly as he wrote, who should be taken as a model for style; who deserved more than anyone else the character of all-accomplished; who equaled or surpassed even Cicero.[20] And Pope, similarly infatuated, declared that Lord Bolingbroke would be better known to posterity as a writer and philosopher than as a statesman; that he was superior to anything he (Pope) had seen in human nature; that he was much the best writer of the age;[21] that when a comet appeared, he was prone to fancy that it might be a coach to take Bolingbroke home! Today few even of the learned have read a single line of his many volumes. It seems to have been a case of those fireworks by which personality and fashion dazzle the eyes of contemporaries from seeing faults which are manifest when the display is over. "A showy actor," says Leslie Stephen, "declaiming popular platitudes without himself understanding them." [22] Even if we discount statements like this, there clings to Bolingbroke's memory something tinseled and rhetorical, a kind of Byronic grandiloquence.

Apart from such overtones, there was, as we have already stated, much in common between Bolingbroke and Chesterfield: passion for external grace whether of literary style or social manner, lack of tenderness,[23] scorn of idealism, worldliness. Above all they shared a common appreciation of France.

Like Chesterfield, Bolingbroke harmonized with a French setting. He too was perfectly at home amid the subtleties of exquisite conventions. If possible, he was even more debonair, more courtly. Perhaps it was the grace of his radiant, lovely second wife, whose very name is like a breath of spring, Marie Claire Deschamps de Marcilly, the Marquise de Villette, that lent him an added foreign charm. She, the adored of many, his mistress by the gallant code before she became his wife, devoted herself to him during an intimacy of thirty-five years. It was in her house in Nogent-sur-Seine that he found love and a refuge during his years of exile. And through her, as if by right, he stood related to the great world of the French noblesse: the Berwicks, the Torcys, the d'Uxelles, the Ragotskys, the Matignons, and a score of other clans with their intersecting orbits.

It was to this set also that Stanhope stood accredited. He might be King George's man, and Bolingbroke at the time might be acting as the Pretender's manager; but political differences could be shrugged aside in the neutral salons of Paris. Names, common to both, drift across their biographies: Matignon, Noailles, Coigny, Montesquieu, Tencin, Fontenelle. Of these the last two, whom he may easily have met at the time, should be glanced at briefly as representing phases of the intellectual Paris of Chesterfield's youth.

In the summer of 1715, Claudine-Alexandrine Guérin de Tencin had been only three years in Paris. She was an escaped nun with a turn for gallantry, who at length secured the papal annulment of her vows. At the house of an ecclesiastical brother, the Abbé de Tencin, she led a life distinguishable from that of a courtesan merely on the score of her birth and the distinction of her lovers. It is said that Lord Stair's predecessor, Matthew Prior, had been one of these. At any rate, their number was considerable; the Regent himself paid her a brief court; there followed Dubois, the Prime Minister, and, among others, the Chevalier Destouches. She bore the latter a son, whom she promptly abandoned on some church steps to the mercy of fortune, and who afterwards became the mathematician D'Alembert. In 1726, when she was forty-five, the last of her gallants, a banker, Charles de Fresnais, committed suicide in her apartment, and left a document accusing her of infidelity to him with her old lover, Fontenelle, and with her own nephew, accusing her also of cruelty, sharp practice, and the like. She even spent a short time in the Bastille because of this. But she was too beautiful, too witty, too popular for such severity. The Grand Conseil declared her innocent, confiscated the suicide's estate, had his will publicly burned, and posted the judgment on every street corner. From this eclipse she emerged more fashionable than ever to found the greatest salon of her time, frequented by old flames and admirers, a hotbed of advanced thought and political intrigue — pre-eminently a masculine salon. There appeared the wits, beaux, and roués of the 'thirties and 'forties: the veteran Fontenelle, La Motte, Montesquieu, Richelieu, Duclos, Marivaux, Marmontel, Helvétius, La Popelinière. . . . There in his middle age appeared the Earl of Chesterfield, no longer *le petit* Stanhope, but grown in fame if not in inches, an ambassador with ribbon and star. What did the past of Madame de Tencin matter — the cruelty, the faithlessness and lust, the sordid episodes? She was amusing and *spirituelle* and of inimitable tact. Like Circe of old, she could put her menagerie, as she termed her salon, through all its tricks: mother confessor to the inexperienced, purveyor of dubious jokes to the cynical. She excelled at everything; in intrigues, which gave the ecclesiastical brother a cardinal's hat; in literature, by producing one of the best French novels of the eighteenth century; as woman of the world by subjugating some of the most distinguished, some of the most profitable men. "Never rebuff anyone," she used to say, "for even if nine out of ten would not take a farthing's worth of trouble for you, the tenth might become a useful friend. Every tool has its purpose if one is clever enough to put it to work." [24]

Elle donnait le ton. The Abbé Trublet is quoted as stating that if it served her interests to poison anyone, her only concern would be in choosing the sweetest drug. It is certainly not impossible that she was one of the fine ladies Lord Stanhope met during that summer of 1715. Thirteen years older than he, and at the zenith of her beauty and her dissipation, what a *décrotteuse* for young gentlemen! What a devastating Lilith! *

One of her many lovers, an almost immemorial man about town, whom no aspirant of the *bel air* could have missed, was Bernard Le Bovier de Fontenelle, author of the *Pluralité des Mondes,* scientist, dramatist, poet, academician, nephew of the great Corneille, but above all, social lion. Immemorial, indeed, before the end! He was even at that time an elderly beau of fifty-eight, but stood only halfway in his career. He died forty-two years later, aged a hundred, and lion to the last. When his funeral cortege went by, Alexis Piron observed that that was the first time Monsieur de Fontenelle left his house without dining in town.

It is illustrative of the conventional in Chesterfield that there are numerous points of similarity between him and this monumental Frenchman. They were both of them too much children of their age for anything else to be true. Besides, Fontenelle was perhaps the finest example of the type that Chesterfield admired above all others. "He never laughed," said Madame Geoffrin, queen of the last salon he attended; "I asked him once, 'Monsieur de Fontenelle, have you never laughed?' 'No,' he answered, 'I have never gone:

---

* The probability of their meeting is all the greater because she seemed to belong to the English set — Prior, Bolingbroke. See C. B. Tinker, *The Salon and English Letters.* On the other hand, his letter to her, Aug. 20, 1742, while not excluding the possibility of a long acquaintance, does not somehow have the sound of one.

Ah! Ah! Ah!' — That was his notion of laughter: he merely smiled
at turns of wit; but he had no idea of any deep feeling." [25] The
same trait has been often recorded of Chesterfield. "Laughter," he
wrote, "is easily restrained by a little reflection. . . . I am sure that
since I have had the full use of my reason, nobody has ever heard
me laugh." [26] Similarly in regard to the expression of any emotion.
"He had never wept," continued Madame Geoffrin of Fontenelle,
"he had never become angry." To be sure, Madame Geoffrin ex-
aggerates. He did weep once in his hundred years of life, when
his friend Brunel died. He was actually seen to weep; and for that
one instant he merged with common humanity. As far as we know,
Philip Stanhope could not have been guilty of such weakness. It is
hard to imagine Chesterfield with tears in his eyes.

They were amateurs of the art of life — these two men. That is
why they submitted to such frigid discipline, for mastery in the art
of life needs a steady pulse. Like everything else, love itself was
reduced from passion to pastime. Women, as Louis Maigron put
it, loved Fontenelle in the same fashion as one loves a cat, expecting
no return.[27] For love, unless enjoyed as one enjoys bonbons, sets
too high a tax on life. For the same reason, anger as well should be
eschewed. It was the practice of Fontenelle never to answer an
attack, and in this connection one recalls the serenity of Chesterfield under the reproof of Johnson. Indifference to anything deeper
than the play of intelligence remained the cornerstone of their
egoism, and by long cultivation it became imperturbable. "He who
would be happy," said Fontenelle, "limits and contracts himself as
much as possible." Sainte-Beuve remarked that by a strange harmony even his illnesses showed a certain indolence and calm. Death
itself did not disturb him, but roused a faint curiosity. "It's the
first death I have watched," he said, and when asked by his doctor
whether he was suffering, answered, "I feel merely a difficulty in
being. . . ." [28] (*Je ne sens autre chose qu'une difficulté d'être.* . . .)
Chesterfield too would die with the same stoicism. Once Madame
de Tencin, touching Fontenelle's embroidered coat above his heart,
declared, "It's only another brain that you have there." [29] And perhaps nothing more on the subject needs to be said about either of
these life specialists. On the whole, Fontenelle surpassed even Stanhope as a philosopher of calm. No excess ever disturbed him except
his love for asparagus.

The likeness between Chesterfield and his French prototype extends to their literary work, the deftness, restraint, and elegance of their style; it includes also their tastes. Both were on the modern side in the Ancients versus Moderns controversy. Both were essentially stone-deaf in regard to poetry, but valued themselves on their poetic judgment. Both were absolute realists. Both had the same languid, polished wit. "Some day, we will be classics ourselves," observed Fontenelle, ridiculing the undue worship of ancient writers, "and we must hope that by virtue of the same superstition which we indulge, that it will be our turn to be admired excessively in future centuries. As compared with us, God knows with what scorn will be treated the wits of that far-off time, who might even be Americans." [30]

It was in company, in the parry and thrust of talk, in the scintillation of the epigram, that these two social geniuses inhaled the quintessence of life, like an exquisite aroma. How absorbing was the quest of the epigram! Like cameos finely wrought, such verbal trinkets passed among the salons — "As Monsieur de Fontenelle observes . . ." "As my Lord Chesterfield remarked . . ." — and spread the glory of their creators. Such men would manage to die with one last sally on their lips.

Fontenelle and Chesterfield esteemed each other unreservedly, and exchanged compliments on a note of despairing admiration. "It is a triumph for the French tongue," wrote the former, "that an English nobleman should have taken the trouble to learn it as perfectly as I see that you know it, my Lord; but permit me a word of advice in your ear: Please beware of drawing down upon yourself the jealousy of French writers. . . ." And in reply, Chesterfield, after lamenting that any letter of his should have been exposed to the criticism of such sovereign arbiters of taste and eloquence as the wits of Paris, adds with a flourish, "But however great the respect I owe these gentlemen, since I must be subject to your judgment, I am not concerned about theirs. I am sure they will pardon and, indeed, even approve, this sentiment." [31] And writing to his son in 1750, he referred to Fontenelle as "the foster-child and favorite of the Graces" (*le nourrisson et l'élève favori*).[32]

Although incapable of poetic emotion, Fontenelle was a clever versifier, and, among other trifles, composed the following adaptation of Hadrian's immortal poem. Like a breath of age-old laven-

der, it suggests all the delicacy, all the futility of that French world
— a nonchalant epitaph.

> *Ma petite âme, ma mignonne,*
> *Tu t'en vas donc, ma fille, et Dieu sache où tu vas:*
> *Tu pars seulette, nue, et tremblotante, hélas!*
> *Que deviendra ton humeur folichonne!*
> *Que deviendront tant de jolis ébats?*

It was therefore within the orbit of such men and women that
Stanhope continued his Parisian novitiate.* If one may judge from
subsequent associations at Paris (such as Madame de Monconseil,
Madame de Martel, whom we shall meet later on), his tendency was
toward the liberal rather than the conservative, toward the slightly
tarnished rather than the respectable, in brief toward the ultra and
the highly spiced. Picture him there among the scarlet-cheeked
beauties of the ruelles, with their short curly hair "powdered white
as snow," [33] among the youthful dandies and older noblemen, all
engaged in the endless chitchat of politics, letters or gallantry.

He was probably in Paris on September 1, when the news of an
event not less impressive because long expected swept across the
city — the death of Louis XIV. Not that many, except his personal
valets, regretted the King, nor that much stir was made. He had
lived too long; his wars had been too costly. In a simple coach,
without parade or any escort save for two chaplains, the royal
entrails were carried to Notre Dame. Cardinal Rohan left the King's
heart at the Grands-Jésuites, and the rest of Louis, with little pomp,
proceeded to Saint-Denis.[34] But sentimentally his death was still a
great event. He had created or at least had molded not only France,
but an entire age. All that Europe thought, read, or discussed, the
clothes worn, the houses built, the conventions followed, were
somehow emanations of the masterful, vain old king, now lying
so shriveled and tiny within his vast cocoon of Versailles. As in the
case of Victoria, his death heralded the end of the regime with
which he was identified. Chesterfield would write of him long after-

---

* It would appear from a reference in one of Lady Lansdowne's letters
to Mrs. Howard that he frequented even more exalted circles, such as that
of the Duke of Bourbon, successor to the Regent, and Prime Minister later
on. (*Suffolk Correspondence,* vol. i, pp. 80–81.) See also Chesterfield's letter
to the Duke of Richmond from The Hague in 1728, mentioning the Duchess of Portsmouth and other ladies in Paris, such as Mesdames de la Vril-
lière and St. Florentin.

ward that "he opened in a manner the human understanding in France, and brought it to its utmost perfection; his age equalled in all, and greatly exceeded in many things, the Augustan." [35]

From thenceforward, as time passed, would grow the conviction of a closing chapter.

PART TWO
1715 - 1732

CHAPTER VI
A Royal Family

As COMPARED with Bourbon Paris and the French urbanities, social London makes a rough, provincial impression in the year 1715. What might be styled the pudding-and-turnip decade had begun. St. James's Palace, to which society looked for its inspiration and *mot d'ordre*, was occupied by an unpopular, ill-tempered court, already on the point of those bitter internal quarrels that shortly afterward split it into opposing camps. There were assemblies enough of one kind or another, but no salons like that of the Palais Mazarin to welcome back the returning Lord Stanhope. The autumn air blew cold, smoky and damp then as now. From Parisian elegancies he re-entered the coarser practical life at home — the routine in parliament, his duties of attendance on the Prince of Wales, the ruder English pleasures.

But more important than anything else, the political situation would absorb him. For the next ten years he and the rest of the Whig party would be confronted by two major problems which would color the whole of his active life. They were: How, in the first place, to keep an unpopular but constitutional dynasty on the throne; and secondly, what side to take in the quarrels within that dynasty itself. It is important that his attitude toward these questions and toward the personalities they involved be understood.

The House of Hanover was unpopular because it was foreign and because it was so abysmally German. In the case of nations, as in that of individuals, distance lends enchantment. The irresponsibility, bigotry, and corruption of the Stuart kings, which while fresh in mind had procured for Dutch William the éclat of a liberator, had faded in vividness during the last thirty years. In the meantime, a Stuart queen had ruled not ingloriously. National sentimentality, an imponderable but considerable force, tended now to side with the exiled House. On the other hand, energetic, well-organized, and powerful, the Whig party, both by conviction and personal interest, stood committed to the Protestant succession and constitutional government. Here were ranged the practical sense and religious prejudices of the English people. With such support, a gracious king, whether foreign or not, trained in the manners, customs, and national foibles, with a smattering of the language, would have had small difficulty in recommending himself to popular approval. As it was, more than the usual degree of courtly complaisance was required to stomach the elderly, unpleasant *Deutscher* whom the chance of Protestant descent from James I provided. Even the Whigs were chilled; the Tories expressed their exultancy in lampoons.

George I was not only old and unpleasant; he was unpleasant in a middle-class manner, which implies always a total failure to understand the susceptibilities of other people. Greeting him with enthusiasm on his arrival, the English crowds expected at least a smile, a courteous wave; they encountered grumpish impassiveness. He knew no English, nor made the slightest effort to acquire it. He considered himself a sojourner in England, and took no pains to conceal his longing for Hanover, whither he joyfully departed for awkward periods amounting to an interregnum. He was a domestic tyrant who kept his wife, the lovely and unfortunate Sophia Dorothea of Zell, locked up until her death because of an apparently harmless flirtation with the Swedish Count Königsmark, and quarreled venomously with his son, the Prince of Wales. Without a queen, he held a tedious and dismal court frequented by German hangers-on and by a homely old mistress, German and rapacious. From the English standpoint, all that could be said for him was that, with a kind of rugged honesty, he kept his share of the bargain and allowed the Whig party to govern England. This one virtue was paramount. It speaks volumes for the strong stomachs, the constitutional Protestant fervor, and the necessities of the Whig leaders, that in their eyes it eclipsed everything else.

As for the Prince of Wales, subsequently George II, the prospect looked brighter. He spoke English, sought popularity, had an attractive wife, danced well, and possessed a not unmerited soldierly reputation. But to the end of his life he remained a conceited, pedantic, petty man, gross in the German fashion, who blustered and bullied, and was yet led egregiously by the nose — certainly not a gallant or a royal figure.

But the stars in their courses fought for Hanover. In the speculative regions of historical might-have-beens, there is no more fruitful chapter than the opportunities lost, the advice disregarded, the possibilities ignored by the Pretender, James Stuart. If he had had one ounce of leadership, one grain of common sense, if he had had even the luck of a fool, things might have gone hard with his successful rivals. As it was, in spite of his blunderings, the dynastic question remained open thirty years until Culloden.

Toward this most urgent political issue of his time, Chesterfield maintained an unswerving attitude. He was heart and soul a party man. He might ridicule and despise the King, Queen, and royal family, but he remained absolutely true to the monarchy as established by the Act of Settlement. Among many two-faced contemporaries, his own reputation stands untarnished as regards any dealings with the House of Stuart.* Thus, as early as April 24, 1716, his name appears on the majority list of the Commons [1] who voted to repeal the Triennial Act and to substitute for it the Septennial Act, whereby the Whig parliament, afraid to face a discontented country in the elections, prolonged itself for another four years. Throughout his life the security of the reigning house elicited his firm support. Though usually generous after the defeat of political adversaries, he showed himself intemperate toward any attempt to overthrow the existing dynasty. We have already recorded his philippic against the fallen Tory ministers, who were accused of negotiating with the Pretender; thirty years later, when Lord Lieutenant of Ireland, he demanded the sternest punishment of Prince Charlie's Highland rebels. [2]

It could not be otherwise with so shrewd and practical a mind. As opposed to romantic bravura, High Church enthusiasm, and Divine Rights, he preferred the realities of constitutional government and material progress. These were guaranteed by Hanover; they would have been jeopardized by the Stuarts.

---

* The only shadow of a doubt that can be cast on this statement was that in 1741 he visited Ormonde at Avignon. *Infra*, p. 190. But even if Horace Walpole's accusation is true, it was a political logrolling on the part of the Opposition, and did not involve treason.

But the established family, by its domestic feuds, incurred additional contempt and increased the difficulty of its position. These quarrels, originally personal, recruited adherents to one side or the other and created national parties which became of supreme political importance. The hellbroth of ambition, jealousy between father and son, the latter's anger in regard to his mother's treatment, the venom of court intrigue, which had been brewing before the accession of George I to the English throne, grew hotter until at length, on a trivial occasion, it overflowed. The story is familiar enough: how, Princess Caroline being brought to bed of a son, her husband, George Augustus, selected his uncle, the Duke of York, to act as godparent; and how his father, the King, for no clear reason except to show authority, imposed a sponsor of his own choosing, the Duke of Newcastle. And equally familiar is the scene of the christening: the Princess in bed, the court lined up on both sides of it, Prince George quivering with rage, the King, glum as ever, strolling out before the ceremony was over. And then the explosion, when George Augustus, rounding the foot of the bed, shook his fist in Newcastle's face, and cursed him for a rascal.

Tremendous doings! The Prince confined in his wife's apartment, while beefeaters guarded the door and with lowered halberds kept out even the Princess's bedchamber woman. Then the Prince set at liberty and ejected from St. James's Palace with no time for packing, but followed by the convalescent Caroline and accompanied by his court. That irrepressible Maid of Honor, Mary Bellenden, singing "over the hills and far away." A makeshift lodging at the house of the Prince's chamberlain, Lord Grantham, where his Royal Highness forthwith fell ill of the chicken pox, and the Princess continued her convalescence. The King, thirsting for vengeance, retained his son's children, among them even the newborn prince, who, cut off from his mother, languished away his three months of life. It was all of it a most lamentable exhibition. A Tory lampoon of the time expressed the general disgust.

> Now sire and son had played their part,
> What could befal beside?
> Why, the babe took this to heart,
> Kick'd up his heels and died.

God grant the land may profit reap
From all this silly pother,
And send these fools may ne'er agree
Till they are at Han-o-ver.[3]

There followed two years of war. The King proscribed his son
and his son's friends. The Prince set up a town and a country house
and held a separate court. Those who attended the levees and
drawing rooms at Leicester Fields or Richmond Lodge were excluded from St. James's. Foreign courts were notified of the Prince's
disgrace. Father and son did not meet, nor was the Prince permitted to have his children. Only on stated occasions could their
mother visit them. When the Princess Anne fell ill of the deadly
smallpox, we have the pathetic picture of her mother, Caroline,
begging leave to see her; and this being grudgingly accorded, the
wretched Princess of Wales, styled "that female devil" by her
father-in-law, waited every day at St. James's from eleven to three
and from six to eleven.[4]

This state of affairs continued from the end of 1717 until April
1720, when a surface reconciliation was imposed by the Whig
ministers, who, for the sake of the dynasty itself, could not permit
a perpetuation of the scandal.[5] But it amounted to no more than an
exchange of formalities. The Prince continued to reside at Leicester
Fields and Richmond Lodge; the King until his death kept possession of his grandchildren and excluded his son from any real share
in the government.

Under these circumstances — a pretext for ambition rather than
loyalty — the Whig leaders divided into two groups, the supporters
of the King, headed by General Stanhope and Lord Sunderland,
with the Hanoverian contingent, on one hand; and those of the
Prince, reinforced now and then by Sir Robert Walpole and Lord
Townshend, on the other. It was only natural that Philip Stanhope, as one of the Prince's gentlemen, should have been identified
with him. But in general his attitude was determined not by any
personal devotion to George Augustus and Caroline of Anspach,
whom he more or less openly despised, but by an antipathy between himself and an eminent statesman who from now on began
to dominate the political stage.

Scorn or admire, attack or defend him, the history of Sir Robert
Walpole becomes, until well-nigh the end of his career, the history

of England. For good or evil, there is something colossal about him. In spite of unscrupulousness, corrupt practices, vulgarity, and gross cynicism, he reveals a certain inspiring quality when viewed from our present distance. He recalls some headland, rough and forbidding on near approach, but, seen from afar, of stately and impressive proportions. In an age such as his, when the mind grows tired of admiring miniature virtues, it is refreshing to turn to that great human personality. He is the Hero as Politician, if such a hero can be said to exist. He boasted that he was no reformer. He dealt in compromise and in political expedient, but with a steady goal in view: the peace and prosperity of his country. These may not be the highest aims, but they are none the less massive desirables that all the heady talk of honor and national prestige can never quite discredit. Bluff, beefy, two-fisted, pragmatical, Robert Walpole represented many of the national characteristics. He recalled much in the past and stood prophetic of much in the future.

It is worth emphasizing him here, not only because he overshadowed Chesterfield's political life, as he did those of all his contemporaries, but because in contrast to him the Chesterfieldian qualities are more sharply defined. There is even something comical in the juxtaposition. What could there be in common between the big-bellied, hard-riding, hard-drinking Norfolk squire, storm center of political melees, and the French-minded aristocrat with his elegance and finesse? The oaken robustness of the one sets into relief the lacquer of the other. Between the two, a clash of personalities was inevitable. To the susceptibilities as well as to the ambitions of Chesterfield, the rough dominance of Walpole would be continually exasperating. This, far more than political principle, accounts for the former's long and often factious opposition. It was an opposition rendered still more bitter by its futility. It was an opposition of fencing foil to bludgeon, of clever intrigue against up-to-date demagogic method. Like a flock of woodpeckers, for years the so-called "patriots," headed by Carteret, Chesterfield, Bolingbroke, Pulteney, and others, would peck away vainly at Walpole's massiveness, and when at length he fell, it would not be their maneuvers, but an international tempest, that overthrew him.

There was at the outset another cause for this friction. The young Lord Stanhope owed much to his distinguished kinsman General James, afterwards Earl, Stanhope. Probably he owed him his position at court and his seat in the House of Commons. In any case, he appears to have regarded him with affectionate respect, if we can judge from a eulogy of him made in parliament shortly after his death in connection with the defense of another kinsman, Charles Stanhope, who stood accused before the House of South Sea peculations.[6] Similarly, on December 18, 1719, he voted in support of the Peerage Bill, which limited the prerogative of the Crown in creating peers, and was actually aimed against future creations by the Prince of Wales after his accession. It was a bill sponsored by the ministers then in power, Sunderland and Stanhope, and bitterly opposed by Walpole. It was an unwise and perhaps an unjust measure and was lost in the House. Although counter to the interest of the Prince of Wales, to whose suite he belonged, it is obvious that Philip voted here at his kinsman's direction.[7] And James Stanhope was the adversary of Robert Walpole.*

Thus in most issues, with the exception of a brief co-operation after the death of George I, during the next twenty-five years we find Chesterfield opposing Walpole. It explains, in negative terms, much of his political policy.

There remains to consider briefly the other two protagonists, not only of his life, but of the life of that entire generation: the Prince and Princess of Wales. George Augustus was past thirty when he became Prince, and had a not unpleasing figure; but he must have been an unspeakably heavy, selfish young man, fussy about little things, a slave to petty routine, of formal manners and low tastes. The glimpses afforded of him in the memoirs and letters of the time display invariably a Philistine and sometimes a boor, loving his wife in a bourgeois fashion, but with the silly vanity of being thought dangerous to women. Since it behooved every gallant prince to have a mistress, he appointed to that office the charming Henrietta Howard, Princess Caroline's bedchamber woman, whose apartment he visited at *precisely* nine o'clock every evening. But so regular

---

* Pope to Lady Mary Wortley Montagu, June 1717: "The political state is under great division, the parties of Walpole and Stanhope as violent as Whig and Tory." *Letters of Lady Mary Wortley Montagu (op. cit.,* vol. i, p. 429). It should be noted, however, that a year earlier, January 7, 1719, Philip Stanhope had voted against the Court party headed by his kinsman, and had voted with Walpole against the repeal of the unjust Occasional Conformity and Schism Acts, limiting the rights of Dissenters. But the repeal was carried in the House, 243 to 232. *Parl. Hist.,* vol. vii, pp. 585-588.

and calculated and cool were his attentions, that this lady enjoyed, if not an unblemished, at least a sedate and respectable reputation. Poor George Augustus! For all his effort, he could seldom appear other than absurd — even, for instance, at that supreme moment of his life when Walpole brought him the unexpected tidings of his father's death, and, roused from a nap, he stood without breeches, clutching that garment in the hand which Sir Robert reverently kissed.

Perhaps no better description of him has ever been written than that by Chesterfield himself a half century later. "Everything in his composition was little," observes this critic; "and he had all the weaknesses of a little mind, without any of the virtues, or even the vices, of a great one. He loved to act the King, but mistook the part; and the Royal dignity shrunk into the Electoral pride. He was educated upon that scale, and never enlarged its dimensions with his dominions. As Elector of Hanover he thought himself great; as King of Great Britain only rich. Avarice, the meanest of all passions, was his ruling one; and I never knew him deviate into any generous action. . . . He had no favourites, and indeed no friends, having none of that expansion of heart, none of those amiable connecting talents, which are necessary for both. This, together with the sterility of his conversation, made him prefer the company of women, with whom he rather sauntered away than enjoyed his leisure hours. — Upon the whole, he was rather a weak than a bad man or king. . . . For above thirty years I was always near his person, and had constant opportunities of observing him, both in his regal robes and in his undress . . . I have by turns been as well and as ill with him as any man in England." [8]

A similar analysis of the Princess Caroline survives in Chesterfield's pages; but the impartiality of it is less austere; a note of rancor emerges. It may be that her character has been magnified by subsequent historians, but we can be almost certain of detraction on the part of Chesterfield; he could not be expected to admit the eminence of any woman.

"I send you Gay's poem on the Princess," wrote Pope to Martha Blount in 1714. "She is very fat. God help her husband!" [9] And there clung to Caroline always, in spite of her greatness, something of the German *hausfrau* — in the docility to her husband, above all things, a meekness before his brutalities and appetites that not even her real power over him could excuse. He might snatch off her scarf to exhibit her bosom (proudly indeed) to his mistress; she did not resent it. She bore him children with monotonous regularity. She endured the tortures of the gout to take walks with him at his bidding. She abandoned her newborn babe and other children rather than that he should be driven from the palace without her. She put up abjectly with his insolence and his moods. To the end her every thought centered in him. Nor was her meekness a result of insensitiveness. "I can say, since the hour I was born," she told Lady Cowper once, "I have not lived an hour without suffering." [10] There is something heroic in this, but there is also something unpleasant, that makes one shrink from the hearing of it.

She displayed other traits of a Teutonic savor: a sly affability that deceived no one, a taste for gross words and gossip. Commenting on the destruction of Caroline's papers, Horace Walpole reported that Lady Suffolk (the Henrietta Howard already mentioned) had told him "that in truth many of the Queen's papers deserved to be burnt, particularly her correspondence with Madame the Regent's mother, to whom she sent all the scandals of the court." [11] Another attendant, the Lady Cowper, transcribing a conversation between the Princess and Mr. Secretary Craggs in 1720, quoted her as saying, " 'I was told that you condescended so low as to call me a bitch'; at which he began a volley of oaths and curses of the falseness of the assertions, for so long a time, and with so much vehemence, that she said to him; 'Fie! Mr. Craggs, you renounce God like a woman that's caught in the fact.' " [12]

But allowing for such flaws (and, indeed, in view of the customs of the time, much allowance must be made), she stands out as a sort of feminine counterpart to Walpole, whom she began by hating and ended by wholly depending on: [13] a robust woman, coarse-fibered but clearheaded and energetic, of strong will and purpose, utterly devoted to her family, with a taste, or perhaps rather a would-be taste, for intellectual and artistic matters. If Walpole's policies are to be approved, Caroline will be approved with them, for, as Queen, she became his most loyal coadjutor.

Speaker Onslow affirmed that "she was a very wise woman in what she knew, was an excellent wife and mother, had a high sense of religion,* and carried her state and dignity with ease and decency." [14] Horace Walpole in his *Reminiscences* recorded that "Queen Caroline . . . retained a most pleasing countenance. It was full of majesty or mildness as she pleased, and her penetrating eyes expressed whatever she had a mind they should. Her voice too was captivating. . . ." In her portraits, the impression given is one of force and stateliness. We need only read in Lord Hervey's *Memoirs* the ghastly story of her death to realize her indomitable character. When everything has been said, she remains one of the great personages of the eighteenth century; nor is this distinction dependent by any means entirely on her rank and position. It might be added she was of equal age with her husband and at the time of the Hanoverian accession was thirty-one years old.

* This may be questioned, at least from any orthodox standpoint, but Onslow was no doubt equating religion with ethics.

CHAPTER VII
The Young Court

THE COMING of the Hanoverians brought with it a release from the repressions which had been in force during the reign of the demure Queen Anne and the cold King William. One of those oscillations in manners and morals which make up the seesaw of ethical history took place. The swing of the pendulum on the liberal side did not reach perhaps the level attained at the Restoration; but that was owing rather to the progress in constitutional government and the rise of the middle classes than to any change of heart in the West End. There was less *élan*, less fire-eating and swagger in fashionable pleasures now than before; but otherwise Vanity Fair reopened all its booths. Looking back across the years, Chesterfield, an authority on the subject, recorded the change. It was no wonder, he wrote, "that pleasures pent up and in some measure incarcerated during two former reigns, should rush out with impetuosity in this; they did so *qua data porta*, and every door was willingly open to them. Drawing-rooms every morning at the Princess's, and twice a week at night; crowded assemblies every night at some house or other; balls, masquerades, and ridottos, not to mention plays and operas!" [1]

The King with his dowdy old mistress set an example; but it was especially the Prince and Princess of Wales who encouraged gaieties. Around them, still young and pleasure loving, gathered fashionable youth with whatever wit, beauty, and talent the times afforded. Here the elite of the next fifty years assembled for its first gala.

The court lists of the Prince and Princess of Wales, together with the names of those who at one time or another appeared at their court, form in large measure the dramatis personae of Chesterfield's life. Other and important names would be added later, but the cast, as a whole, is assembled and the stage set.[2] We should pause for a moment to consider both, transported by what imagination we can summon to one of Princess Caroline's evening drawing rooms in that unfamiliar London of two centuries ago, to follow through dark streets the jolting of stiff coaches with their cocked-hatted drivers up to the portals of St. James's Palace or to the unlighted precincts of Leicester Fields — then out of the darkness into a glimmering of many candles.

Most of the beau monde is here, the proud, calculating beau monde. It has been unintelligently romanticized in our day. A less romantic age would be hard to find. The glimmer of the candle-light on jewel and brocade has veiled its essential character. Charmed by its contrasts, charmed by its wit and grace, amused by its frivolities, poets and essayists, with few exceptions, have sinned against reality by failing to expose its inbred callousness. There is no use repeating the formula that human nature does not change. Types, indeed, remain; but the character of human society alters from century to century. Great men and women have lived since then, pioneers of the spirit, who have labored and suffered, and whose effort has not been without avail. Could it be seriously maintained that the Wesleys, Wilberforces, Burkes, Johnsons, Newmans, Nightingales, the poets, reformers and statesmen of the nineteenth century, have lived in vain? Since that day, incalculable sacrifices have been made to atone for it. There has been some loss, but there has been a greater gain. And if now in our fashionable assemblies we still find the cruel and the untrue, the vulgar and the base, these qualities are reproved by a new social spirit and by a sincere, if still vague, idealism.

Out of the dark, then, past powdered footmen, up the great stairway into the concourse of the great — phantoms of an unborn time, we and our criticisms do not trouble them. Seated at basset tables, they play for high stakes,* or they saunter here and there, or form groups to comment on the latest gossip. Rank and etiquette are the fibers of this society. The ladies of the bedchamber have precedence over bedchamber women, and lords of the bedchamber

---

* "In the evening I played at *basset* as low as I could, which they rallied me for." Lady Cowper's *Diary*, p. 14. At a Twelfth Night at St. James's Palace, no one could have a place at the royal table who would venture less than 200 guineas. *Ibid.*, p. 43.

over bedchamber gentlemen. Reputation and even birth may be equivocal, but the title makes amends. Those great ladies, for instance, the Duchesses of Shrewsbury, Buckingham, and Bolton, would have been regarded askance or, indeed, would have been excluded, except for their rank; as it is they dominate unchallenged. The Duchess of St. Albans, the peerless Diana de Vere, would, in humbler circles, have suppressed her husband's origin; but here such a name as Beauclerk, such parents as Nell Gwyn and Charles II, give added glamour to that husband's coronet. In some such drawing room old lady Dorchester, mistress of James II, upon meeting the old Duchess of Portsmouth, mistress of Charles II, and old Lady Orkney, mistress of William III, exclaimed jovially, "Who would have thought that we three whores should have met here!"

All were not of this stamp, and others again successfully eluded scandal. Lady Mary Cowper, for instance, she of the sparkling diary and skill on the harpsichord; or that belle of belles, the Maid of Honor, Mary Bellenden, racy of speech and flippantly chaste, who would fend off the Prince's attentions with folded arms; or gay Lady Bristol, stumping about on her swollen legs and writing to her husband, the dear angel, at Ickworth; or Maid of Honor, old Miss Meadows, whose prudishness was the butt of the court. There were others too whom life had not yet tainted: Molly Lepel, still Maid of Honor and not yet Lady Hervey; Sophia Howe, also Maid of Honor, still merely frivolous, and not yet seduced, abandoned, and dishonored; Henrietta Howard, not yet the languid, formal mistress of George Augustus. The gentlemen were still young and had not lost their teeth, nor fallen victim to the gout, stone, and other consequences of the great world. John Hervey had not become Pope's Sporus, nor had he dipped his pen into the bitterness of his terrible memoirs. Lord Lumley had not grown weary of living and had no thought of suicide. Philip Stanhope had not yet become the pedagogue of Vanity Fair. In short, youth, with whatever charms youth must always have, lingered in that drawing room. The lords and ladies of the Prince and Princess represented their class at its best, the good and evil together, but for the most part young, expectant, undefeated.

Yet, even at their best, there clings to them that miasma which forever attends sham, whether it be young and modish or not. The odor of rose water, pleasant and invigorating at first, grows op-

pressive when nothing else is breathed, until fresh air, unper-
fumed, becomes a necessity. These gatherings were not for the sake
of amusement. The ladies and gentlemen of the bedchamber were
tired with the dress parade and *qui vive* of attendance; [3] there were
aching backs and aching hearts among them. But they were there
in order to be seen, to cut a figure, in a word, as the phrase went, to
shine. It was all appearance, conventionally devised in every word
and movement to conceal reality. Henrietta Howard, writing to her
friend, the poet John Gay, with that accent of fatigue that would
grow stronger as the years passed, had something to say on this
point. "I (that am grown old in courts)," she sighed, "can assure
you, sincerity is so very unthriving, that I can never consent that
you should practise it." [4] And many others voiced the same opinion.
"That mask of constraint and hypocrisy essential to their stations," [5]
observed Hervey in reference to his courtly companions. "Caress the
favourites, avoid the unfortunate, and trust nobody," advised Lady
Mary Wortley Montagu, quoting a Turkish maxim, which, she
added, "includes all that is necessary in a court life." [6] "At court,"
remarked Chesterfield, "people embrace without acquaintance, serve
one another without friendship, and injure one another without
hatred. Interest not sentiment is the growth of that soil." [7] And
Sir Robert Walpole, broken at last and old, wrote from Houghton,
"My flatterers here are mutes; the oaks, the beeches, the chestnuts
seem to contend who shall please the Lord of the Manor; they cannot deceive, they will not lie." [8]

But for all that, because of youth, this court and these years
would be for many the gayest, the most gallant of their lives. The
ladies and gentlemen in waiting formed an inner coterie, an intimate group, which was the nearest most of them ever came to
real companionship. They were not always on dress parade. There
were gay suppers, for instance, in the apartment of Mrs. Howard,
to which afterwards her friends looked back with a sigh. They
grew familiar with each other's quirks and hobbies — Lord Herbert's fondness for his dog Fop, Mary Bellenden's unexpected sallies,
Miss Meadows's primness, Schultz the German equerry's puns,
Mademoiselle Schultz's tendency to cadge on all occasions, Mrs.
Howard's preoccupations with the building and design of her villa,
Marble Hill. They gave each other nicknames. Mrs. Lepel was "poor
Tom"; Mrs. Howard "the Swiss" and her apartment "the Swiss

Cantons"; Lord Hervey was "the Schatz"; Colonel John Campbell was "Jacky" Campbell. They developed slang of their own — "frizelation" for "flirtation," "dangleation" for "hanging on."

And then there were the daily squibs and happenings: Lady Cowper bit by a bedbug and forced to keep home a day to conceal her swollen eye; Prince George ill of a surfeit, but well enough to sit up while his lords and ladies played omber at his bedside; the latest story about old Madame Kielmansegge, the King's reputed mistress, to the effect that she carried about a statement from her husband, the General, certifying that she had always been a faithful wife; tremendous doings when George Mayo, drunk in the Prince's drawing room, pulled Sir James Baker's nose and had to be thrown out; tremendous doings when the Marquis Paleotti, the Duchess of Shrewsbury's ruffian brother, attempted to force his way into George Augustus's presence, and in his turn had to be thrown out; [9] still more tremendous doings when Mrs. Howard's irate husband, egged on by the King, threateningly demanded his wife from the Princess Caroline, and she was spirited away to Richmond Lodge under escort of the Duke of Argyll.

There was gossip of the rise and fall of favorites: the Duchess of Roxburghe coldly regarded by the Princess for recommending to court Mary Bellenden, too popular with the Prince, and the setting star of Lady Cowper. And there was talk of card games: Lord Scarborough's loss of £13,000 at Bath; [10] the luck of Princess Caroline and the Duchess of Montagu, who won £600 at a court Twelfth Night. There was the rat problem at Richmond Lodge, which must have set the ladies in a flutter, until that famous rat wizard, John Humphries of Dorsetshire, collected five hundred live rats in the place, which he exhibited "as a proof of his art." [11] There were jaunts to Tyburn to witness the hanging of such exceptional malefactors as James Shepherd, the eighteen-year-old boy who intended to shoot the King, an execution that Lord Stanhope himself was curious enough to attend.* There was the continual logrolling for government sinecures to supply greedy relatives or friends, a continual intrigue to oust one person at court in favor of another. There was the excitement of secret marriages and elopements, when Molly Lepel married John Hervey *sub rosa*, and when Mary Bellenden ran off with Jacky Campbell.

* This occurred on March 17, 1718. To his son, Sept. 13, 1748.

There were wars and rumors of wars to be discussed, as when Lord Peterborough, in love with the opera singer Anastasia Robinson, publicly caned Senesino, the leading tenor, for insolence to her, and was laughed at by Philip Stanhope as an old Quixote; whereupon Peterborough challenged him; Lord Delaware acted as second; the court was in a stir; but the duel was prevented — we suspect much to the future Chesterfield's satisfaction.[12]

Especially was the court drawn together in the great solicitude that attended a royal birth. Never alone, the Princess Caroline formed a center of a crowd on such occasions. What a to-do when she fell into labor on Sunday, November 4, 1716! She had a German midwife whom the English ladies, being "high dames," resented and threatened to hang if the Princess miscarried. But the Prince stood by the German, and swore he would fling from the window whoever pretended to meddle. The Duchesses of St. Albans and Bolton happened to come into the room and were saluted by these expressions. The poor Princess continued in a languishing condition till Friday night, when she was delivered of a dead prince.[13] At the birth of another prince the following year, there were present in the room the Prince of Wales, the Archbishop of Canterbury, the Duchesses of St. Albans, Montagu, and Shrewsbury, the Countess of Dorset, the Lady Cowper, the Duchess of Monmouth, the Countess of Grantham, the Countess of Picbourg, all the women of Her Royal Highness's bedchamber, Sir David Hamilton and Dr. Steigerdahl, her physicians.[14]

Moreover, there were factions at court — the German and the English faction — with all the talk and partisanship that this entailed. There were squabbles between the ladies, as at that dinner party described by Lady Cowper, where the fat Countess of Buckenburgh lamented that "English ladies did not carry themselves like women of quality or hold out their breasts enough." Whereupon Lady Deloraine replied, "We show our quality by our birth and titles, madam, and not by sticking out our bosoms."

Perhaps the greatest event of all, and long discussed, was the reconciliation at St. James's Palace between the Prince and King. It was only a gesture; but the Prince came home to Leicester Fields with a guard of honor which he had been thus far deprived of, and followed by hallooing crowds. The square in front of his palace filled with coaches, and his rooms with company — "everything gay and laughing," says Lady Cowper, "nothing but kissing and wishing of joy." Then, two days later, the young court paid its respects to the old court: a scene also described by Lady Cowper, who compared it to "two armies drawn up in battle array; for the King's court was all at the top of the room behind the King, and the Prince's court behind him. The Prince looked down and behaved prodigious well. The King cast an angry look that way every now and then; and one could not help thinking 'twas like a little dog and a cat — whenever the dog stirs a foot, the cat sets up her back and is ready to fly at him." Such was the atmosphere in the royal family.

The court of George and Caroline, however, was by no means composed merely of noble officials. Repelled by the dullness and indifference of the King, the men of letters of that time were to be found within the radius of Leicester Fields and Richmond Lodge. The Princess dabbled in philosophical and religious thought, corresponded with Leibnitz and patronized Whiston; but she would have gladly engaged, on reasonable terms, the homage of the wits. Pope, Gay, Congreve, Garth, Arbuthnot, Vanbrugh, Young,[15] and later (on a brief return from his Irish exile) Swift, together with the portrait painters Jervas and Kneller, appear some more, some less, upon the margin of her court. Addison, nearing the end of his life, was on the King's side relative to the Prince; and Steele, a supporter of Walpole's in parliament, tended in a like direction; Prior, tired and deaf, quitted London in 1719 for Down Hall, the final harbor of his storm-vexed life. But for a time in any case, these worthies also were upon the London horizon, and would be met here and there in the Saint James's end of town. With them should be grouped the literary and artistic dilettantes, half friends and half patrons of the others — such men as the Earl of Burlington (whom we met at The Hague), Lords Bathurst, Peterborough, Cobham, Warwick (who was Addison's stepson), Harcourt, Lansdowne, Scudamore, John Sheffield, Duke of Buckingham, Sir Paul Methuen, and many others — men who deserve at least a modest place in the history of art and letters, whether on the score of their own attainments, or because of the generous support they gave to greater talent. Lady Mary Wortley Montagu, still beautiful and still a friend of Pope's, belongs here, although she was perhaps even more popular at the old court, where King George made an exception in her favor to his dislike of English women.[16]

This association between the court of George Augustus and the intelligentsia of the times gave to the former its chief distinction. In retrospect, without the magic of those great names, the court would look rather tawdry; but the thought of them adds a brilliance and charm, an airy grace, which is imaginative rather than actual. The sylphs of "The Rape of the Lock," the picturesqueness of *Trivia*, the jauntiness of *The Beggar's Opera*, cast the reflection of their iridescence upon humdrum people and things; they lent the accompaniment of their minuet music to Hanoverian stodginess.

Then, too, the rural setting of London in those days, the traffic on the river, the imaginary savoriness of coffee house and country inn, the entire costuming of the period, throw a glamour over its workaday qualities. Even the highwaymen seem graceful. There has been such a deluge of operettas, adventure stories, *vers de société*, and anecdotes dealing with the eighteenth century that it is hard to recall its soberer aspect: the gin-soaked populace, the brutal laws, the universality of physical pain, beyond anything we can now have a notion of, the ignorance, superstition, and insensitiveness of the masses, the pervading sensuality. There was now and then a row of decaying human heads on Temple Bar; there was the weekly macabre show at Tyburn; people were still pelted to death in the pillory with refuse and ordure. A Papist chairman who insulted and spat at the Princess Caroline was whipped from Somerset House to the end of Haymarket. Picture the scene if possible: the cart, the half-naked victim, and the crowds yelling "Whip him!" The executioner, "who followed his work pretty close" and was applauded by the people, made the fellow cry "God bless King George" before he had done with him.[17] Jervas and Kneller need to be balanced off by Hogarth.

But one of the darkest features of that time, and one that receives too slight a historical emphasis, was the prevalence of suicide, which impressed all foreign visitors to Hanoverian London. Montesquieu refers to it frequently in his various writings;[18] Voltaire describes it;[19] César de Saussure devotes the greater part of a letter to manifestations of this strange mania.[20] They all agree in ascribing it to physical causes: the climate, the smoke, the east wind, etc. But none of these factors had been eliminated in the nineteenth century, and some at least had become aggravated, such as crowded city conditions and the like; whereas, on the other hand, the suicide rate in England had by that time fallen to half of the French rate. In view of this, it would seem justified to seek for other contributing causes for suicide in Hanoverian England, and of these not the least would appear to be the religious and moral bankruptcy of that period. Indeed, if we consider the phenomenon of suicide in the world at present correlated with a similar spiritual retrogression, it is difficult to escape the conviction that one is, at least in a measure, the reflection of the other, and that belief in nothing tends to result in an abhorrence of life itself. At any rate, the prevalence of suicide and insanity during three quarters of the eighteenth century casts a shadow not easily lightened by wit, costume, and picturesqueness.

It is in the country even more than in London that one likes to think of the young court. Before the quarrel with the King, they spent their summers amid the magnificence of Hampton Court, and afterwards at Richmond Lodge, purchased by George Augustus from the Duke of Ormonde's confiscated estates. It was at the former palace that Pope visited his friends the Maids of Honor and Mrs. Howard in September 1717. He met them returning with the Prince on horseback after a day of hunting, had dinner with them, and ended with a moonlight stroll accompanied by Molly Lepel. They encountered, he says, "no creature of any quality but the King, who gave audience to the vice-chamberlain all alone, under the garden wall." [21] This letter to Teresa and Martha Blount is so familiar that it needs no repetition here, but it reflects charm and gaiety of a rural kind. From now on, Twickenham, too, begins its historic role. And in general the country interrupts with serene passages the intense urbanism of the time. Here, if anywhere, the romance of the eighteenth century is to be found. There was a good deal of hunting, of interest in horses and dogs, a good deal of visiting at country houses and delight in the laying out of gardens. There were adventures on the thief-infested roads, as when Bridget Carteret, a Maid of Honor, was robbed of her jewels on the way to Richmond Lodge in June 1719, and was reimbursed by the Princess with a diamond necklace and a watch. There were many journeys to and from Bath. The country life even of the beau monde is a relief to read about after the formalities of London.

Among the members of this court, there were three who especially concern us as intimates of Chesterfield, and of these one was his greatest and perhaps his only friend.

The character of Richard Lumley, Earl of Scarborough, belongs to the few of that age who seem to be lost and alien there. Inevitably his name rises in answer to Thackeray's famous question, "Whereabouts in this court is the honest man?" Pope extolled him; even the venomous Hervey admired him. In a world of busybodies, gossips, and libelers, not one breath of scandal attached itself to him. Whenever we encounter him, it is always in a gracious, kindly, dignified connection. Courteous, charming, grave, but ever a little distrait, a forceful speaker, a great gentleman, he gives the impression of having strayed by mistake into the chilly, glittering maze of that century and to have felt somehow puzzled and aloof until, distaste turning to despair, he put a bullet through his brain.

If contemporaries such as Lord Hervey wondered at the friendship between Scarborough and Chesterfield,[22] we, at this distance, are still more astonished. Superficially considered, they would seem to have had no common ground. But the fact of their intimacy remains. Perhaps each found in the other what he himself lacked; or perhaps the speculative, Hamlet mind of Scarborough, piercing beneath externals, discerned in Chesterfield what only at rare intervals and then indirectly comes to light, a kind of weariness with the baubles by which ostensibly he set so great a store, a stifled hunger beneath his sophistication — such as appears, for instance, in his love of little children — an inarticulate idealism. To this one man, he may have disclosed what no one else was ever permitted to see, and in regard to which we can only theorize. In the "Character" he drew of him long after his death, there appears for once a different quality in Chesterfield's writing, a solemn tenderness, a passionate respect. "To his friendship, as well as to the public notoriety of it," he confesses, "I owe more than my pride will let my gratitude own. . . . The most secret movements of his soul were, without disguise, communicated to me only. . . . I owed this small tribute of justice, such as it is, to the memory of the best man I ever knew, and of the dearest friend I ever had." *

At a considerable remove in the scale of intimacy, but still a life-long and cordial acquaintance, stands Molly Lepel, the Maid of Honor already mentioned, who secretly married in 1720 another member of the young court, the handsome Lord Hervey. She was second in beauty only to Mary Bellenden. She became *par excellence* Chesterfield's ideal woman of the world. It was to her that he especially recommended his son during a winter she spent in Paris thirty years later. "She has been bred all her life at Courts," he wrote, "of which she has acquired all the easy good-breeding, and politeness, without the frivolousness. . . . No woman ever had more than she has, *'le ton de la parfaitement bonne compagnie, les manières engageantes, et le je ne sais quoi qui plaît.'* " [23] Even in the early years, they seem to have been on peculiarly warm terms. She mentions him repeatedly in her letters to Mrs. Howard; it was for her that his rather lame Muse burst into doggerel, of which the following verses may serve as an example:

> Bright Venus yet never saw bedded
> So perfect a beau and a belle,
> As when Hervey the handsome was wedded
> To the beautiful Molly Lepel.

> Old Orpheus, that husband so civil,
> He followed his wife down to hell,
> And who would not go to the devil
> For the sake of dear Molly Lepel?

She was also a great friend of Pope's, who carefully excluded her from his terrible attack on her husband. Indeed, she visited him and his mother for a while in March 1720, not long after her marriage.[24]

Stanhope's third intimate friend at court was Henrietta Howard, George Augustus's official mistress, Caroline's bedchamber woman,

* Mahon, *op. cit.*, vol. ii, pp. 477-481. The "Character" was written in 1759. Since there was no portrait of Scarborough existing, Chesterfield had a pencil drawing made from memory by Worlidge, showing him and his friend seated at table together. As a likeness of Scarborough, it is probably vague, but gives additional evidence of Chesterfield's affection. It is reproduced in Carnarvon's edition of *Letters of . . . Chesterfield to his Godson,* facing p. li. *Cf.* also Dobrée's edition of the *Letters,* Introduction, p. 89.

and later, as Countess of Suffolk, her mistress of the robes. She was Chesterfield's friend and the friend of countless others, one of the best beloved women of her time. "I really do believe," wrote Mrs. Campbell, the former Mary Bellenden, to her, "you have as many people that love and value you as ever came to one woman's share." [25] Her life was a running commentary in a placid, demure hand on the tedium and futilities of the courtier's career. Married early to an impecunious and brutal younger son, she and her husband sought their fortunes at Hanover in the Electress Sophia's time; and, as English gentlefolk were popular there in view of the coming accession, they were attached to that court even before the death of Queen Anne. It is said that on one occasion she sacrificed her splendid head of hair to the wigmaker, in order to defray the cost of one of her husband's strategic dinners to the German lords.[26] In England, as we have seen, she became ultimately the mistress of George Augustus, both as Prince and King. Her mercenary husband, after the proper amount of fury, was bought off to the tune of £1200 a year payable quarterly in advance. When he had inherited the earldom of Suffolk and had conveniently died, she remained at court as Countess for a year longer, and at length, middle-aged and deaf, weary and out of favor, she retired in 1734 to the peace of Marble Hill and a convenient marriage with Chesterfield's college friend, George Berkeley. Thirty years later, a very old woman, but still elegant and serene, we have a glimpse of her chatting on autumn evenings with Horace Walpole, and supplying his insatiable hunger for anecdotes with stories and gossip of the distant past.

At the heyday of her career, upon the accession of the Prince as George II, a number of her friends, notably Pope, Gay, Swift, and perhaps Chesterfield, deceived themselves with the idea that she, like other official mistresses, would exercise considerable patronage and influence, and upon discovering their mistake, visited her with unmerited coolness. It was then that the "heartless Chloe" appeared in the *Moral Essays* and that Swift, who had once presented her with the crown of Lilliput, treated her to an overimpartial analysis of her character. But she had made no promises and could not be blamed for her friends' disappointment. On the whole, in favor and disfavor she retained her popularity, her gentle heart, and grave ways. "I have been a slave twenty years," she wrote pathetically to Swift in 1727, "without ever receiving a reason for any one thing I ever was obliged to do." [27]

It is pleasant to revive her memory, adorned as it is by at least two great lyrics — Pope's "On a certain Lady at Court," and Peterborough's "I said to my heart." This inflammable nobleman, dying at the age of seventy-eight, addressed her in a kind of prose swan song, asserting that he had learned "how a soldier, how a philosopher, how a friend of Lady Suffolk's ought to die." [28] Even her lap dogs retain a modest place in literature; Swift wrote an epistle to her dog Fop, and Pope composed his epitaph.[29] One of Chesterfield's earliest letters is addressed to another of her lap dogs, Marquise.

It is a moot point as to how much Chesterfield expected from her influence at court, and whether or no he was disappointed in her lack of it. Horace Walpole declares that by paying his addresses to her he incurred the enmity of Queen Caroline; but Walpole's testimony is often more amusing than exact. If one may judge from Chesterfield's "Character" of her, he had not been one of "the speculative politicians of the antechambers, who know everything, but know everything wrong," and had therefore entertained no illusions. Certainly the tone of his letters to her, after he had been dismissed from the court in 1733, shows no change from earlier letters. They are charged throughout with gaiety and apparent affection. As late as 1766, he wrote her an account of himself in the person of his footman — an example of the comic spirit rare in his correspondence. There is no reason, then, to refuse him the benefit of the doubt or to believe that his liking for her was materially alloyed with self-interest. She remained an old, pleasant acquaintance.

CHAPTER VIII

The Earl of Chesterfield

IT IS AN INTERESTING, if elusive, problem to determine exactly what was Philip Stanhope's position at the young court we have just described — that is, what the degree of his importance there was — and it is especially interesting in view of the orthodox assumption that he must have played a brilliant role. This may indeed have been the case, but from contemporary mention, there are no indications of it. On the whole, his name is conspicuous by its infrequency, as compared with those of several others.

A note even of disparagement emerges in such a remark as that of Lady Cowper, when she records that "the Prince has been so rough with little Lord Stanhope about voting in the South Sea affair, that he has talked of resigning for a good while." [1] Evidently in this lady's eyes, little Lord Stanhope was no very arresting figure. Pope mentions him with a group of others in a letter of November 8, 1717, as having received Gay's letters, and in the summer of 1723 he appears to have been on the footing of an informal caller at Twickenham. [2] But Gay omits him from the list of Pope's friends who in 1720 were eagerly awaiting the completion of the *Iliad* — and this in spite of the fact that on the list of subscribers he is put down for two sets of volumes — a reason *ex silentio* for assuming that he did not at that time rank among the poet's intimates and therefore probably did not rank as a wit.

Estranged from his father, and on a scanty allowance, his impatience for the paternal estate seems to have been commonly known by his friends, if we may judge from a reference in one of Lady Hervey's letters to Mrs. Howard, where, after commenting on the marriage of the Earl of Pembroke with Mary Howe and the probably fatal result to a nobleman of that age, she adds, "You had best advise Lord Stanhope to procure Lord Chesterfield a bride, and himself the estate." [3] These notices together with the part taken by him in the defense of his kinsman after the South Sea Bubble and in the Septennial, Peerage, and Schism debates, as well as in the affair with Peterborough, nearly complete the list of contemporary evidence until his accession to the title in 1725. Other records of that period are drawn from later sources.*

To conclude, therefore, from the references which have been preserved, his position at the young court was not a peculiarly brilliant one. His short stature, large head, and unprepossessing figure, together with his lack of funds and a turn for raillery, occasioned, no doubt, the "uphill game" to which he referred long afterwards in a letter already mentioned. His parliamentary attitude would serve to reflect a growing unpopularity with the Prince and Princess.

This view is worth presenting because it involves a process frequent in the biography of distinguished men, which is that of viewing a person's youth in the light of subsequent achievement and reflecting back upon it the brilliance of later fame. It is especially to be guarded against in the case of Chesterfield, because his reputation for wit and elegance, the fruit of many years, easily tempted such later contemporaries as Horace Walpole and Dr. Maty to assume that he had always possessed it. Indeed, his whole life is an example of this illusion. There can be little doubt that except for the posthumous publication of the famous *Letters* and of the *Miscellaneous Works*, Chesterfield, like many of his greater contemporaries, would be but vaguely remembered. What does the general reader now recall of Carteret, Pulteney, Pelham, Newcastle, Hardwicke, and a dozen others? Yet each of them occupied a more important place in the public eye than did Chesterfield. The epigrams and social address which gave him his great reputation during life [4] would have proved ephemeral. It was his writings and the classical expression of a certain philosophy that permanently established him, so that almost at once after death he became more

---

* Maty affirms, for instance, that such store was set by Lord Stanhope on the part of the King's faction, that a dukedom was offered his father, if Stanhope would desert the Prince. This he honorably refused to do (vol. i, p. 27). I can find no reference to this elsewhere, although there had been some discussion of a dukedom for the second Earl of Chesterfield. (*Cf.* the *Verney Letters of the Eighteenth Century*, vol. i, p. 108.)

famous than ever; and even on the part of his earliest biographers and commentators, it is this literary fame which has lent adventitious importance to his courtly, political, and diplomatic career.*

A case in point may have been the much quoted anecdote recorded by Spence, that in the days of the young court Stanhope belonged to a literary club known as the World which was held at the King's Head in Pall Mall, where on one occasion, as the gentlemen were inscribing verses on their wineglasses, Dr. Edward Young borrowed Philip's diamond and cut the following epigram:

> Accept a miracle instead of wit,
> See two dull lines with Stanhope's pencil writ.[5]

There is no reason to doubt the existence of the club, although I can find no other reference to it. Indeed, the name may have been perpetuated later in the famous magazine, *The World*, to which Chesterfield was one of the chief contributors. But the epigram itself would have had little point at that time, when, as far as we have reason to believe, Stanhope had written nothing but some wretchedly mediocre verse. At least the suspicion lies near at hand that the anecdotist is here projecting back an epigram more appropriate to a later period, when Chesterfield's skill as an essayist had been recognized.

To return then to his position in London at that time, it is likely that he was gradually acquiring that reputation for epigram and table talk to which his subsequent rank and wealth gave an added luster. It is likely, too, that with the inner fire of an ambition which he knew so well how to conceal, he was becoming a finished, perhaps a too patently finished, public speaker. It is probable that, while disliking the rough-and-tumble of the House of Commons, he took his parliamentary duties seriously.[6] "I was early convinced of the importance and powers of eloquence," he declared, "and from that moment I applied myself to it."[7] And in 1720, on a visit to Paris, he wrote back concerning the possibility of coming into "business [political affairs] and leaving an idle life he had grown weary of." By well-timed support of a royal measure for augmenting

* Horace Walpole reproves Dr. Maty for comparing Chesterfield with Sir Robert Walpole, as if they were political equals. Chesterfield, he says, was never at the head of the court party or of the Opposition. *Marginal Notes on Maty.*

the army, and through the patronage of his friend Lord Townshend, who succeeded Earl Stanhope as Secretary of State, he was
rewarded in 1723 with the Captaincy of the Yeomen of the Guard,
his first considerable office.[8]

This in a sense inaugurated his larger career. It shows that the
"uphill game" had at last been won. With the gold-tipped ebony
baton and uniform of his rank, but above all with the salary of a
thousand pounds a year,[9] he was now independent of his father and
had become a personage in the court world. It is related by Maty
that Lord Townshend, who preceded him in this post, "advised
him to make it more profitable, than he himself had done, by dis-
posing of the places." "I rather for this time," answered Lord
Stanhope, "wish to follow your lordship's example than your advice!" — an instance both of his courtliness and of his incorruptibility
as far as money was concerned. He lost this position in 1725 by
ridiculing Sir Robert Walpole's re-established Order of the Bath,
which would not be the last time he incurred that statesman's resentment; but he was then close upon his title, and besides the holding of one office sets a precedent for other offices.

Such was the graver aspect of these years; but on the other hand
they were those of a young man about town, a young man superficially idle and secretly alert, intent upon learning the ways and
means, the expedients and strategies of the world. He gambled both
in London and Bath. He indulged certain other tastes with cour-
tesans, like Constantia Phillips, who in a letter addressed to him
long afterwards refers to "the gay, pleasure-loving, wild, unthink-
ing Lord Stanhope, amidst . . . companions of the same age." * He

* Relying presumably on an unsupported statement in the *Dictionary of
National Biography* (*vide* Phillips, T. C.), Mr. Dobrée in the Introduction
(pp. 175–177) to his recent edition of Chesterfield's *Letters,* asserts that
young Lord Stanhope, under the alias of "Thomas Grimes," seduced Constantia Phillips when she was about fourteen years old, and that in 1748
she demanded from him an annuity of £500, in default of which she
threatened to publish an account of their relations. According to Mr.
Dobrée, Chesterfield refused to be mulcted in this fashion, and therefore
An Apology for the Conduct of Mrs. Teresia Constantia Phillips was published 1748/49. There appears not to be the slightest justification for this
story in such documents as are available in the British Museum, to wit:
the *Apology* itself. *A Letter Humbly addressed to the Right Honourable
the Earl of Chesterfield by Mrs. Teresia Constantia Muilman,* April 5, 1750;
A Defense of the character of a Noble Lord, 1748; *A Counter Apology,* 1749.
In none of these does any connection appear between "Thomas Grimes"

wrote to George Bubb that "balls, assemblies and masquerades have taken place of dull formal visiting days." [10] He dabbled in poetry, wrote letters to lap dogs, and advice to fine ladies, such, for instance, as the following:

> Asses' milk, half a pint, take at seven or before;
> Then sleep for an hour or two, and no more.
> At nine stretch your arms, and oh! think when alone
> There's no pleasure in bed.—Mary, bring me my gown! [11]

But we must remember his discipline of early rising, the ceaseless effort at finish and eloquence, the stolen hours spent in the study of ancient and modern thought. For to become even a great man of the world, one cannot be merely a fribble, but must practice the iron hand under the velvet glove.

Meanwhile, the skein of events in England and on the Continent was being spun out into history. The strands of the skein are for the most part colorless, but here and there at intervals they are diversified by brilliant details that catch the eye and serve as points of reference. These were the days of the naval war with Spain, of the Triple and Quadruple Alliance between England, Holland, France, and ultimately the Empire, of Admiral George Byng's victory over the Spanish fleet off Cape Passaro in 1718. They were the days of the South Sea and other bubbles in 1720, that ruined multitudes of the English people, but established Walpole and raised him to his long premiership. They were the days of Marlborough's decline and death, with the memories they recalled of Blenheim, Ramillies, Oudenarde, and Malplaquet. But they were also the days of obscure, though not less important, beginnings. The population was increasing, new methods and products of agriculture were being introduced, Liverpool had become a port, the colonies were being developed: in fine, the wealth of England, and with it her modern power, had dawned. William Pitt was at Eton and John Wesley at Oxford.

*   *   *

---

and Lord Chesterfield. Moreover, the *Letter Humbly addressed* is couched in the most respectful and flattering terms, and is clearly a device for capturing a respected name to give prestige to her *Apology*. Finally, none of her references to "Grimes" fit either the character or the circumstances of Chesterfield. Unless Mr. Dobrée has had access to documents of which we are ignorant, it would appear that this episode never took place.

On October 9, 1725 Miss Dorothy Dyves, an attendant on one of the young princesses, wrote to Mrs. Clayton, Caroline's bedchamber woman, "We hear that Lord Chesterfield is either dead or dying, and that Lord Stanhope was sent for from the Bath." [12] Philip and his two brothers had spent a part of that summer with the sour Earl at a health resort, probably Buxton,* in the Peak country of Derbyshire, and Philip, at least, had felt unutterably bored by the experience. "Had I been a Papist," he wrote Mrs. Howard, "(as thank God I am not), I should have thought myself in purgatory; but, being a good Protestant, I was obliged most orthodoxly to conclude myself to be in Hell." Now, summoned to Bretby, the ancestral hall, he prepared to go through the gestures of filial piety.

But he had long to wait. October, November, December, and most of January dragged by, while the stubborn old Earl clung to life, and detained his son from London. It was a final act of spite. "Ever since my father had his fits," he lamented to Mrs. Howard, "(which were such and so many as I believe no other body ever survived) he has continued entirely senseless: in which condition it is impossible for me, upon many accounts besides filial piety, to leave him. How long he will continue so, I cannot tell; but this I am sure of, that if it be much longer I shall be the maddest of the two: this place being the seat of horror and despair, where no creatures but ravens, screech-owls, and birds of ill-omen, seem willingly to dwell; for as for the very few human faces that I behold, they look, like myself, rather condemned than inclined to stay here."

This was humorous exaggeration of course. Bretby Hall, to judge from the engraving by Kip, was a very splendid manor, indeed, a kind of miniature Versailles, upon which the second Earl of Chesterfield had lavished time and money. He had made it one of the celebrated estates of the county.[13] It had a noble *corps de logis*, with a mansard roof, and two long wings, the whole enclosing a spacious courtyard. It had formal gardens on either side, and formal plantations beyond them. It had a miniature lake, long vistas, and apparently all other accessories of a French park. Hamilton de-

---

* In 1707 the second Earl had taken the waters of Buxton, and had been attended there by his son, who now in 1725 was being in his turn so attended. *Hist. MSS. Comm.*, MSS. of the Earl Cowper, vol. iii, p. 168.

scribed it as "a very beautiful house, situated on the margin of a stream, in the midst of the most agreeable and laughing country-side that one could ever see." [14]

But it was winter now. The trees were leafless and the gardens desolate. And it was tedious waiting for an unloved old man to die. Not even the fashionable *Mémoires de Gramont*,* which had described at length the misadventure of George Hamilton at Bretby, when he followed there on a false rendezvous the lovely Countess of Chesterfield in 1664, not even this could render the place fashionable in the eyes of Lord Stanhope. He disliked the country, and he had not the faintest interest in out-of-date love affairs. His heart was in London. Of Bretby, as of the Peak, he wrote, "Were I inclined to a religious melancholy, I should fancy myself in Hell: but not having the happiness of being yet quite out of my senses, I fancy — what is worse than either — that I am just where I am, in the mansion-seat of the family, and that, too, not my own." Being reassured in regard to hell by Mrs. Howard, he replied, "I am afraid you are too much in the right when you tell me I am in purgatory; for souls always stay there till they go to Heaven, which I doubt will be my case; whereas I should be very glad of baiting a considerable time at London in my way to it."

The sour Earl continued to hang on. Stanhope felt that the sacrifice demanded of him was excessive. He made no pretenses; once the dying man asked him to lower his head so that his faint voice could reach him, "But," said Philip afterwards, "I would not come so near, for I thought he wanted to bite my ear off." [15]

This lingering death at Bretby is a curiously sinister and revealing episode. An arctic cold of the heart surrounds it. But it would be a mistake to cast up our eyes at Lord Stanhope's callousness. Certainly none of the outer proprieties were transgressed; the old man was not neglected. No, it is rather the general than the personal implication which is revealing, an example of the *quid pro quo* in human relationships, untouched on either side by a spark of love. The old Earl had been accused of a like insensibility in turn by his father; [16] he had given nothing all his life, and he received nothing now. It was simply the way of the world.

At last his irksome life flickered out, and his successor could draw

---

* They had been published in 1713, and became, according to Chamfort, *"le bréviaire de la noblesse."*

a deep breath of relief.* At the age of thirty-two, Lord Stanhope was at length Earl of Chesterfield and Baron of Shelford. His title stood twenty-first on the list of earls, that is, well toward the top. It was a respected title backed by broad estates. † A seat in the House of Lords, vastly increased prestige, an unhampered career, lay before him. With such assets, the "uphill game," already won, could be now forgotten.

We may be sure that he lost no time in returning to London. Two months later, in company with Dr. Arbuthnot and Pulteney, we find him escorting Swift on a course through town. He even condescended to call first on the famous Dean.[17] Bolingbroke also had returned from exile, and entertained Swift at Dawley near Uxbridge, so that the Parisian acquaintanceship with Chesterfield must have been renewed.

There can be no doubt that his new title heightened Stanhope's position in the literary world: he had now become a potential patron. Voltaire, who began his long visit to England that spring,‡ was indebted to him for the favor of the Princess Caroline.[18] Whether or not they had met previously in Paris may remain uncertain; but as one of the literary circle which included Bolingbroke and Pope, Chesterfield saw much of the distinguished Frenchman during this period. They were alike in many ways: in the point of view reflected by their admiration for the philosophy of Locke, in a common passion for literary form, in a common cynicism. It is related of Voltaire that he found the tipping system imposed by the servants of his noble English hosts too exorbitant for a poor poet, and nowhere so oppressive as at Chesterfield's house in St. James's Square. Being asked by Stanhope to return, he declined, because, as he said, his lordship's table was too dear. But such a contretemps, if it actually occurred, had no effect upon their lifelong friendship. In the future, upon every publication of a new, epoch-making volume from Voltaire's pen, we find a fresh outburst

---

* The third Earl of Chesterfield died Jan. 27, 1726. Mahon's edition of Chesterfield's *Works*, vol. iii., p. 22 *n*.

† Chesterfield inherited from his father the whole of the latter's personal estate, "together with the two real estates in Derbyshire and Nottinghamshire, and the reversion of that in Buckinghamshire." Maty, *op. cit.*, vol. i, p. 207.

‡ He landed on Whitmonday, May 30, 1726, according to Collins, *Voltaire . . . in England*, and remained until March 1729.

of enthusiasm on the part of Chesterfield; and the latter has received perhaps no finer encomium than one addressed to him at the end of his life by the Sage of Ferney.

Meanwhile, it can be assumed that he plunged with new gusto into the social world, after his temporary eclipse in Derbyshire. We find him dining with his old friends Lady Bristol and Lord and Lady Hervey at Richmond in July of that year.[19] In 1727 he set up an establishment befitting his rank in the new house, No. 18 St. James's Square, which had been erected on the site of the now demolished Halifax House.[20]

About this time also occurred another and certainly a regretted death in that of his grandmother, Lady Halifax, who died of an apoplexy in 1727. She was buried in Westminster Abbey.[21]

As regards Chesterfield's political attitude in the House of Lords immediately following his succession to the earldom, he seems to have spoken on two occasions in opposition to the King [22] and therefore to Walpole, a policy looking perhaps to the future; for Walpole's power could not be expected to survive the King, and as the latter was old his reign could not last much longer. Actually it ended abruptly on June 12, 1727, at Osnabrück in Germany, whither he had departed on a visit to his beloved Hanover. The Prince, now George II, was free at last to hang up the portrait of his mother, the late Sophia Dorothea, in the Queen's dressing room.[23] As in the case of Chesterfield there were no pretenses of grief at the demise of his father. He promptly pocketed the latter's will, and that document disappeared forever.

It is unnecessary to repeat here the somewhat humorous story of how George Augustus attempted to free himself from Walpole, and how he discovered that he could not do without him, and how the Queen had her way. Great was the chagrin of Sir Robert's enemies, and, among them undoubtedly, of the Earl of Chesterfield. The King received £130,000 per annum more from the public revenues, and the Queen £50,000. Such was the cost to England of Walpole's continued office.

Meanwhile, the court prepared itself for the supreme ceremony of the coronation, which "was performed on October 11 with great magnificence, the Queen being ablaze from head to foot with jewels, most of them hired." [24] The value of the stones on her petticoat amounted to £100,000, rented from Shirar, the jeweler, for £600. It was so "immensely stiff and heavy," wrote Horace Walpole informed by Lady Suffolk, "that as she could not have knelt to receive the sacrament, it was contrived to draw up with pullies like a little curtain, and had leads to weight it down again." He adds, and there is something peculiarly significant in the remark, that after the state dinner, the Sword of Justice was discovered to be missing. "The Herald that held it was slipped into a brandy shop." [25]

CHAPTER IX
Ambassador

O N JUNE 27, 1727, following the King's address to the House of Lords, the Earl of Chesterfield moved an answering address of condolence, congratulation, and thanks, which was unanimously voted.[1] At the same time, he was daily expecting his appointment as ambassador to France.[2] Thus, at the outset of the reign, he made his debut as one of the King's principal henchmen and a leader of the court party.

Baron Lovel, coming up to London hungry for preferment, sounded him by observing that he did not know how to vote.

"Why," said Chesterfield, "with the Court, of course."

"If I vote with the Court," answered Lovel, "I expect to be paid for it."

Chesterfield asked how, and was informed that the title of earl or viscount, at least, was not more than he, Lovel, ought to receive.

"But that," replied the other, "is more than the King can do."

"Is not his Majesty," retorted Lovel, "the fountain of honor? If he has made me a baron, cannot he make me an earl?"

"No," returned Chesterfield, "for it is a maxim of our law that the King can do no wrong." [3]

But if George Augustus could do no wrong, it was not equally clear, as the months passed, that he would do right — at least by Philip Stanhope. There were Walpole and the Queen to be reckoned with, and in relation to them Chesterfield stood on the opposite side. With all his address, he seldom contrived to wager on the right horse. He was a protégé of Lord Townshend, whom the King despised, and whose power had lapsed at the death of George I. His former opposition to the once again omnipotent Sir Robert, an opposition aggravated by mockery, still rankled with that statesman. He had vented his wit on the Princess of Wales, who now, as Queen, had no reason to trust him. Indeed, Hervey records that in the old Leicester Fields days she had warned him more than once that although "he had more wit than her yet she would assure him she had a most bitter tongue, and would certainly pay him any debts of that kind with most exorbitant interest." [4] Finally, to cap his offenses, he was too much the friend of Henrietta Howard, whom Caroline would tolerate, for fear of worse, as the royal mistress, but took care that she should never be anything more.

The appointment to Paris did not come. In vain Dr. Arbuthnot communicated with his brother the banker there, to the effect that his lordship desired his assistance in settling with a large retinue; nothing happened. Walpole apparently opposed the nomination, and Cardinal Fleury seems also to have opposed it, on the grounds that a person of Chesterfield's "youth, wit, and vivacity was not the properest minister to treat with one of his Eminence's age, meekness, and sedateness." [5]

Instead of this, he received nothing at all — not even an appointment to the Privy Council, until six months later. His position as lord of the bedchamber, which he had occupied at the young court after succeeding to his title, was the only official place allowed him during the better part of a year following the accession of George II. Then, by the personal influence of the King, who insisted that something be done for him, he was appointed ambassador to Holland. He had become a man of sufficient importance to merit recognition, and Walpole would rather have him abroad than intriguing at home. There is probably a good deal of truth in Lord Hervey's observations on this point, as well as to the effect that Chesterfield could serve more comfortably at a distance than in daily contact with a minister whom he had bitterly opposed. [6] The inferior appointment was perhaps sweetened, as Maty declares, [7] by the hint of a removal to Paris after the termination of his embassy at The Hague. Meanwhile, Sir Robert's brother, Horatio Walpole, retained the post in France, and when he relinquished it two years later it was in favor of Lord Waldegrave.

Paris, indeed, must be considered the premier British diplomatic post at that time, as at almost every other period; but second to it, The Hague and Vienna divided the honors. It was upon the United Provinces, as an ally, that England had for some time counted most to assist her in maintaining the balance of power. To keep them in step with British interests, as these were affected by the veering interrelationships of France, Spain, and the Empire, often required dexterous diplomacy and a shrewd diplomat. Chesterfield, as it turned out, proved of far greater use to England at the Dutch capital than he could have been at Versailles, for he was largely responsible for concluding the Second Treaty of Vienna.

With this appointment to an active career, the historical Chesterfield emerges. His correspondence became extrinsically of greater importance and was preserved, so that it becomes possible to follow step by step the course of his development. For the next twenty years, whether in or out of power, he remained continually in the public eye. During this period he achieved the reputation of an able diplomat, a pleasing orator, an enlightened administrator, and a disinterested patriot. Hervey and other political opponents might sneer at him; panegyrists, on the other hand, might exalt him in too glowing colors; but when in 1748 he retired finally into private life, it was with a name for political integrity that many of his contemporaries might envy. He lived twenty-five years longer, respected for his sagacity and wit, a patron of the arts and *grand seigneur;* and he died at length, if not in the odor of sanctity, at least in that of eminence and universal esteem. Warburton, annotating the Epilogue to Pope's *Satires,* referred to him as one "commonly given by writers of all parties for an example to the age he lives in, of superior talents, and public virtue." Lord Sackville, in 1764, was glad that one of his friends, Sir Laurence Dundas, was known to Chesterfield. "Approbation of such men as his lordship must be most acceptable, as it cannot be purchased even by his great fortune." [8] In 1766 the Earl of Dartmouth turned to Chesterfield for advice in reference to American affairs.[9]

It was, however, not as a statesman, but as a writer, that his lasting fame was destined to be established. The publication of the *Letters* forced a reappraisal of his character upon an astonished and somewhat shocked public. His political career became thereafter subsidiary to a philosophical and literary interest; and if, in the following chapters, we review rapidly the various stages of his public life, it will be in relation not to the political importance of his actions, but to the other more permanent aspect. In other words, what he did becomes the background and the sanction of what he wrote. It establishes fully the value of his witness in regard to human nature and the ways of the world. The reflections on this subject of a relatively inexperienced man would carry little weight. It is the fact of his experience, the fact that, within certain limits, he had made a long and practical study of life under conditions most favorable for such a study, that lends importance to his conclusions.

In the spring of 1728, he prepared for Holland by appointing the staff of his embassy. The diplomatic service, as such, did not yet exist. In general the King was represented by residents in the various important capitals, who combined the diplomatic and consular functions. Envoys and ministers were also sent upon special missions. The office of ambassador plenipotentiary, which implied a compliment to the state to which he was accredited, fell usually to some great lord who would lend dignity to his charge. It was not a permanent means of representation at The Hague or Paris or Vienna, but arose in connection with an important or ceremonious occasion. In the case of Chesterfield, his embassy was in response to a formal deputation from the United Provinces congratulating the King upon his accession. The ambassador was the special legate of the monarch — in theory his other self; as such he had the right of public entry into the capital of his destination and had precedence over other envoys. It was his duty, indeed, to insist on such precedence, lest the dignity of the monarch in question suffer an affront. The staff that supported him was the personal retinue of a viceroy.

The Honorable John Stanhope, Chesterfield's favorite brother, became his official secretary. Mr. (afterwards Colonel) Rutter occupied the post of equerry. James Hammond, a poet who later celebrated his patron in not unpleasing pastoral verse, accompanied him now as a kind of attaché. There was a Prussian by the name of Holingbore, who probably acted as clerk or amanuensis.[10] For the domestic chaplaincy, there seem to have been several candidates. One was the Reverend Cornelius Ford, whom the younger Richardson qualifies as "an infamous fellow of much off-hand conversation and wit," and he gives the terms in which Chesterfield rejected him.

"I would certainly take you," said the ambassador, "if you had one vice more."

"I thought," said the Reverend Cornelius, "I should never be reproached for my deficiency that way."

"But if," rejoined the other, "you had one more, almost worse than all the rest put together, it would hinder these from giving scandal." [11]

In the end, he appointed Richard Chenevix, who had been recommended to him by Scarborough.

The new chaplain was a son of Major Chenevix of the Guards, who had been killed at Blenheim, and grandson of a Huguenot pastor, refugee in England after the revocation of the Edict of Nantes. He had served as domestic chaplain of the Earl of Scarborough and latterly of Lord Whitworth at the Congress of Cambray, was a graduate of Cambridge, and spoke French as well as English. He and Chesterfield became lifelong friends. It was a relationship of generous patronage on one hand and of equal gratitude on the other. Chenevix followed the Earl's fortunes, accompanied him as his principal domestic chaplain when he went to Ireland as Lord Lieutenant in 1745, was raised by his influence to the Irish bishopric of Killaloe and subsequently of Waterford. He seems to have been a man of real piety and benevolence, an eighteenth-century churchman of the best sort, perhaps not too spiritual, but upright and thoroughly correct. If there is truth in the adage that a man can be judged by his choice of friends, it is worth repeating that of the few who may be called friends of Chesterfield in the more intimate sense, there were two like Scarborough and Chenevix. It reveals a strain in him deeper than the social glitter, deeper than the worldly philosophy of the *Letters*, an instinctive discernment of worth and, however starved, a desire for human affection.

So accompanied, he proceeded to The Hague, and announced his arrival there in a letter to Townshend dated May 7 (New Style), 1728.[12] *The Craftsman*, which was being published by his friend Lord Bolingbroke, under the pseudonym of Caleb Danvers, although an opposition paper, burst out into a hymn for the occasion. One suspects that even then Lord Bolingbroke may have regarded the young Earl as a potential ally. At any rate, in effusiveness the verses left nothing to be desired. They compared him to Marlborough; they extolled his skill in upright measures, his generous heart, his scorn of low cunning. The following are samples:

Ambassador

O Chesterfield, with early laurels crown'd
For poignant wit and nervous Sense renown'd,
Whom all the Powers of Eloquence adorn,
For publick Scenes and great Employments born;
A while indulgent to my Verse attend,
Of every Art the Judge, to every Muse a Friend.

. . . .

By no mean Arts, or servile Courtship rise,
But Virtue mark't you out to Brunswick's eyes;
In knowledge, Sense, and Honour you confide,
And your high Lineage is your meanest Pride.
Already, conscious of thy spreading Fame,
The Belgian Powers thy timely Presence claim.

. . . .

For, if the sanguine Muse aright presage
From thy known Talents, which forerun thy age,
By prudent Counsels and deliberate Schemes
(Proving all Ways, and shunning all Extremes),
The Broils of Europe thou shalt still compose.

. . . .

That Work performed, a Work of so much Art,
That only Stanhope can sustain the Part!
Thy native loud-applauding Shores regain,
And in the British Senate shine again,
Again thy Sovereign's Smiles and Counsels share,
By all the Nation bless'd, recover'd from Despair.[13]

A magnificent send-off!

It is beside our purpose to record the minutiae of diplomatic business that absorbed him during the next four years — the affairs of the ill-fated Altona Company, sponsored by Denmark as a rival to the Dutch and English East India trade; the North German interests of the King of England as Elector of Hanover in regard to East Friesland, the Duchy of Mecklenburg, and the tiny estates of Jülich and Berg, or his relations with Prussia; the question of Dunkirk, which, pursuant to the Treaty of Utrecht, should have been, and was not yet, dismantled by the French; Jacobite plots at Rotterdam; the Congress that went on deliberating at Soissons without reaching any conclusions; the Treaty of Seville on November 9, 1728, between England, Spain, and France, into which the Dutch had to be brought. The very mention of all this is well-nigh extraneous, except for one point — that they reveal the energetic application of the new ambassador to his work. His letters to the

Secretary of State, of which there is still preserved an average of one for every third day, show an unremitting alertness and industry, the will here as elsewhere to succeed, to excel.[14]

In this, he exemplified the English aristocratic tradition at its best, the right to rule purchased by the ability to serve. In the exercise of official duties, now or later, he spared neither himself nor his fortune. Sufficient the reward of power and reputation without any other incentive; and to secure it, he underwent the discipline, however concealed, of infinite pains. From entering a drawing room to negotiating a treaty, it was a maxim with him that anything worth doing at all was worth doing well. Secondary post as it was, by seizing every opportunity he turned his embassy at The Hague into a lasting personal triumph. And the official letters we have mentioned, tedious as they are in point of intricate and now unimportant detail, express one of his essential qualities.

In the thicket of affairs already mentioned, there were two major issues that chiefly concerned him, and of which the happy conclusion owed much to his skill. The first of these was the projected marriage between Anne, Princess Royal of England, and the Prince of Orange: a scheme that involved far more than the susceptibilities of the bridal couple or of their respective families, and tangled itself into the skein of Dutch political faction. This, in turn, affected the alliance with England, and might, therefore, affect the balance of power in Europe. The United Provinces formed, at that time, a republic, and though a strong monarchical party continued to agitate, an effective majority supported republican principles. They wanted no stadholder, and they feared, not without reason, that the young Prince of Orange, backed by the prestige of a British royal marriage, would follow the example of his ancestors in forcing himself as stadholder upon the country. It required, therefore, infinite tact and caution to guide the project through such a political danger zone.

On the other hand, the personal problems involved were exceedingly delicate; for the young Prince was misshapen, if not actually deformed,[15] and from the standpoint of the King of England had no position to offer commensurate with the dignity of the Princess Royal; indeed, George II referred to him flatly as a baboon. Altogether the match appeared more sordid than was usual even among dynastic marriages: the Prince of Orange and the fat little Princess were each paying a price: he to become stadholder, which was finally achieved in 1747, and she to become a wife, for it was this princeling or no one.

Undeterred by the difficulties of the problem, Chesterfield began adroitly to prepare the ground: paid his court to the Prince, at that time a youth of eighteen, was charmed "with his precocious parts and knowledge"; reported favorably on his manners and person, which though deformed, was not as deformed as had been rumored; sounded out this person here and another there; advised that when the time came for raising the Prince of Orange to the stadholderate, "a general insurrection of the people might with very little difficulty and expense be procured, and a stadholder imposed upon the province"; arranged a meeting between the Prince and King George upon the latter's return to England from a visit to Hanover.[16] The marriage did not take place until 1734, two years after Chesterfield's recall, but he deserves the credit for having set on foot all the necessary preliminaries.

Of wider importance, and representing his greatest diplomatic success, was the second of the two issues we have mentioned, involving as it did the reversal of British policy during the last fifteen years. In this case his efforts bore definite fruit in a treaty which profoundly influenced the politics of Europe, and with which his name is forever associated.

Since the death of Louis XIV, there had been a transformation in England's age-old attitude toward France. The immemorial rivals had co-operated, now against Spain, now against Austria, and again against the two combined. It was a regrouping of European power in a new system. The Treaty of Seville between England, France, and Spain, but excluding Austria, may be regarded as the culmination of this policy.

But the situation was too unnatural to last. France, by political and religious tradition, by a vastly superior population, by its competing interests both in America and the Indies, and by its menacing vicinity, remained potentially too dangerous for British peace of mind. It was imprudent to confide overmuch in this powerful ally and neglect other combinations, such as Austria, the convenient and traditional counterweight on the French frontier. The triumphs of Marlborough and Prince Eugene were still vivid in memory and had a sentimental appeal. Last of all, there was the exasperating

Ostend Company that operated from the Austrian Netherlands, a thorn in the flesh of similar Dutch and English enterprises, which might be abolished through a proper understanding with the Emperor. Such an English, Dutch, and Austrian alliance constituted the Old System, to which it was now resolved to return. During the last eighteen months of his office at The Hague, that is, from the latter part of 1730 till February 1732, it was this problem with which Chesterfield was primarily occupied.

It is hardly necessary to recall that the Emperor Charles VI, intent upon the succession of his daughter, Maria Theresa, to his undivided dominions, was prepared to concede almost anything in return for the guarantee of the European powers to the Pragmatic Sanction. In this instance, he sacrificed the Ostend Company, and acceded to the Treaty of Seville,* while England on her side pledged support to the succession of Maria Theresa. The articles of the new treaty, to be known as the Second Treaty of Vienna, having been agreed on at The Hague between the Grand Pensionary of Holland, the British ambassador, and the Austrian envoy, Count Sinzendorf, it was definitely concluded, as far as England and Austria were concerned, on March 16, 1731. But Chesterfield and the Grand Pensionary, van Slingeland, had the further and arduous duty of securing the agreement of the Dutch provinces, a process that took a year longer and required the utmost patience as well as skill.

Chesterfield's correspondence during this period shows the working of his mind at its smoothest and most effective. It reveals also in full play his qualities of adaptability and self-control. The red tape and delays of the Viennese court, the pedantry of the Dutch and Hanoverian demands, the straining at gnats on the part of everyone — all this is reflected in the current of the ambassador's diligence and perseverance. He was sometimes at the point of despair, but never quite despaired. He was often at the end of patience, but still kept his temper. "I don't know," he wrote to Robinson at Vienna, "whose situation is the most disagreeable, yours or mine; you have to do with obstinate and able people, I with obstinate and ignorant ones. Yours won't hear reason, mine can't understand it if they hear it." [17] Or again, "I am sensible what a silly figure I make in the meantime, labouring in vain for about six

---

* By permitting Spanish troops to garrison Parma in behalf of Don Carlos's succession.

months, to get the Republic into measures, which for their own
interest they ought to have come into in six days. But I have not to
do here with ministers, and people of sense, but with a tumultuous,
ignorant, and obstinate multitude." [18] In the end he succeeded; the
treaty was signed. It established his reputation throughout Europe
as an able negotiator.

No better school of diplomacy than was The Hague at that particular time has ever existed. It was a school in self-restraint, dissimulation, the knowledge of human nature, intrigue, cajolery, suav-
ity, and persistence. Without unification in a central authority, the
seven provinces, each a sovereign state, sent deputies to the States-
General, but so circumscribed their authority that independent
action of an executive kind by this parliament had become impossible. Constant reference of every minute point by the deputies to
their constituents introduced delays to concerted action, which
made diplomatic business an ordeal of patience, tact, and manipula-
tion. Only the predominance and power of the province of Holland
among the other provinces permitted international dealings at all.
It was with the chief civil officers of that state, the so-called Grand
Pensionary and Greffier, or Secretary of State, that diplomatic
representatives to the United Provinces had to do; and these officers
in turn bullied or cajoled measures of policy through the States-
General. A shopkeeping pedantry of small minds and interests, the
corruption of the rich, and discontent of the populace added
further complications to the parliamentary difficulties. Finally, the
very smallness of The Hague, the fact that it existed only as a diplomatic and governmental center, made it a hotbed of scandal, espionage, gossip, and rumor, from which the diplomatic novice either
learned, or did not learn, sagacity. The clinical opportunities here
for studying the intricacies of the human mind were unlimited.

To deal with such a government and such a situation was to deal
with a vast number of individuals. Although this must always be
true of the negotiator, it was apt to be truer then than now because
of the greater influence wielded by the individual at that time.
Beginning with the king or chief magistrate and with the latter's
wife, mistresses, favorites, ministers, extending through the wives,
mistresses, favorites, servants of the above in an ever-widening nexus
of relationships, it was the individual, the interaction of personalities, which in a large measure determined events. The foreign

minister of that age did not, as a rule, think in terms of groups, but of persons, the idiosyncrasies, habits, ambitions, foibles of A or B, and how best to exploit them. Chesterfield's letters to his son were colored by and dealt with this problem. "There is, at all courts," he writes, "a chain which connects the prince or the minister with the page of the back-stairs, or the chambermaid. The king's wife, or mistress, has an influence over him; a lover has an influence over her; the chambermaid, or the *valet de chambre*, has an influence over both; and so *ad infinitum*. You must, therefore, not break a link of that chain. . . ."[19] If such a condition (which might be termed the supremacy of the individual) prevailed in general through eighteenth-century Europe, it was accentuated at The Hague by the republican anarchy of the Dutch government. The number of individuals that had to be dealt with must have been unusually great.

But it was precisely in dealing with individuals that Chesterfield showed his greatest skill. Although he became, by application and practice, a finished speaker, and although his poise, his sense of justice and public spirit, made him an excellent administrator, he was pre-eminently and naturally a diplomat. At The Hague he found both the finishing school and the arena for his native talents. Never at his most effective in the alternating tides of parliamentary debate, nor in the rough-and-tumble of party leadership, he felt at ease in the subtleties of diplomatic negotiation, in the secret maneuverings of policy behind a screen of affable pretensions, in the strategy or intrigue of private interviews. These talents were more successful and more appreciated on the Continent than they could be in England. They belong to that side of his nature most nearly related, in its passion for finish and finesse, to the French genius. There can be no doubt that this career was the one he most loved and the one to which he looked back with the fondest memories. It should be noted that it was primarily for the foreign service that, with a sort of vicarious gusto, he prepared his son.

If there could be any doubts as to Chesterfield's charm, the winsomeness of his manners, and his proficiency in the art of pleasing, his personal success at The Hague must certainly dispel them. Simon van Slingeland, the Grand Pensionary himself, became an ally and intimate. Years later, the Earl wrote of him that he was the "ablest Minister and the honestest man" he ever knew. "I may justly call him my friend, my Master, and my Guide," he went on; "for I was then quite new in business: he instructed me, he loved, he trusted me." [20] It is unnecessary to point out of what value to an ambassador and to the nation he represents such a connection must be. Chesterfield and van Slingeland conversed of Dutch affairs with a frankness which, on the part of the latter, would appear, at this distance, almost indiscreet.* Toward the end of the Earl's residence at The Hague they formed a kind of secret partnership for the purpose of steering the Second Treaty of Vienna through the delays and objections of the States-General. Being on such terms with the chief civil officer of Holland, he enjoyed, by that very fact, a privileged position and secured the Pensionary's active cooperation in most of his projects. Even the marriage of William of Orange and the Princess Royal, which van Slingeland by his very position was forced to oppose, became no stumbling block to their friendship. His opposition remained passive; it was at no time a source of inconvenience to the British negotiator.

The Grand Pensionary was merely the most prominent of a host of friends. Chesterfield captivated equally the Secretary of State, Fagel, for whom he had also deep respect on account of his business experience and sound judgment.[21] Then there was Baron Torck, an important nobleman of the Province of Gueldres, with whom the Earl carried on a sprightly and intimate correspondence for some time after leaving The Hague; there was van Linden, an active adherent of the Prince of Orange; there were the Kreunigens; there was Count William Bentinck; there were the Count and Countess van Wassenaer, "people of the first rank and consideration"; there was the Austrian ambassador, Count Sinzendorf — these and many others.

* See the report of a conversation with the Pensionary in Chesterfield's "Account of the Government of the Seven United Provinces" (Mahon's edition, vol. ii, p. 401 f.). It is debatable whether or no the trust of the Pensionary in his English friend was justified. The latter made no scruple of reporting their confidential interviews to the English Secretaries of State. Nor did he scruple to lie to van Slingeland when occasion demanded it, as, for instance, in regard to this very marriage of the Princess Royal, which had been explicitly entrusted to him. When asked by the other whether he knew anything about it, he replied that he had not been informed one way or the other. But, of course, this was diplomatically necessary. (Letter to Townshend, Mar. 5, 1729.)

Unwearied in attentions, the soul of affability, stooping to conquer with the greatest adroitness, forever alert to the value of trifles, Chesterfield went on his way, attracting, flattering, impressing. He gives a glimpse of himself as he was at that time in a letter to his son written twenty-five years later. "Comte de Wassenaer and his wife," he wrote, " . . . had a little boy of about three years old, of whom they were exceedingly fond; in order to make my court to them, I was so too, and used to take the child often upon my lap and play with him. One day his nose was very snotty, upon which I took out my handkerchief and wiped it for him; this raised a loud laugh, and they called me a very handy nurse; but the father and mother were so pleased with it, that to this day it is an anecdote in the family. . . . Where one would gain people, remember that nothing is little." [22] In brief, he became all things to all men so that he might gain some, and left behind him a lasting popularity. Van Wassenaer himself bore witness to it seventeen years later, when congratulating him on his promotion as Secretary of State. He calls him that "man of all the world, whom I respect, admire, esteem, and, in short, if you will permit me, whom I love the most." And again, "You cannot be ignorant, my lord, to what a degree you are loved and honoured here." [23]

Chesterfield, like most able and energetic men of affairs, disliked the parade of business. If he must pose, it would be rather the affectation of a languid serenity. No fussiness, hurry, and fever, no continual harping on office matters. He might employ a gentleman recommended to him by Professor Vitriarius of Leyden to live at his house and instruct him in civil law and the Imperial code; [24] he might devote himself to grasping the tangle of the Dutch government and politics; he might watch catlike every point of interest to the Home Office; but all this went on behind an external leisure. Ten days after arriving, he wrote Mrs. Howard: "My morning is entirely taken up doing the King's business very ill, and my own still worse; this lasts till I sit down to dinner with fourteen or fifteen people, where the conversation is cheerful enough, being animated by the patronazza, and other loyal healths. The evening, which begins at five o'clock, is wholly sacred to pleasures; as, for instance, the Forault [Voorhout, the Mall] till six; then either a very bad French play, or a reprise at quadrille with three ladies, the youngest upwards of fifty, at which, with a very ill run, one may lose, besides one's time, three florins; this lasts till ten o'clock, at which time I come home, reflecting with satisfaction on the innocent amusements of a well-spent day that leave no sting behind them, and go to bed at eleven, with the testimony of a good conscience. In this serenity of mind, I pity you who are forced to endure the tumultuous pleasures of London." [25]

Of course the picture here has been tinted, for comic effect, with the rose water of a mock innocence; but it reflects the persiflage of the man of pleasure that concealed the man of affairs. It was all part of the screen behind which policy or ambition could work undisturbed. Indeed, he was very much a man of pleasure at that time. The respectable age of the card-playing ladies mentioned above may almost certainly be doubted; for the new ambassador cultivated Venus more than his health in those days, and suffered in consequence.[26] He upheld his position at The Hague on a splendid scale, entertained lavishly, and, according to Horace Walpole, pleased the Dutch by losing to them enormous sums at play.[27] We find him writing to Paris for a cook to replace one he had already hired from thence, who was "not of the first rate"; and he appealed to no less an expert than the Duke of Richmond, who was visiting in Paris his mother, the Duchess of Portsmouth, to help him in the matter. He wanted a *"maître cuisinier d'un génie supérieur,* who should be able not only to execute but to invent *des morceaux friands et parfaits"*: in short, such a one as might be worthy to entertain the Duke's distinguishing palate, if he came to The Hague. He wanted only a master, one whom the whole of Paris allowed to be at the top of his profession. Probably as gifts for his ladies, he imported other articles from Paris: *lunettes d'opéra,* for example, that showed one object while they were directed toward another, or such toys as were *"fort à la mode et tout à fait charmants."* [28] It would be interesting to know more about that cook and about those opera glasses and the occasions they served. Since the house he had taken proved too small for his taste in entertainment, he added at his own expense a ball-and-supper room fifty feet long and thirty-four wide, to be "handselled" as he put it, on the King's birthday.[29] Such an item alone is indicative of the establishment he maintained. It embarrassed him financially, and left him with a diminished fortune;[30] but that too is a perquisite of the aristocratic tradition.*

Man of pleasure, gamester, gallant, the charming host, the amiable friend, the witty table companion, we can only guess of what he must have been from brief allusions and from the reputation he achieved. Flickerings of this, sometimes gay, sometimes odd, lighten here and there the monotony of the more sober correspondence. We hear the laughter of women, the flutter of violins, the ring of coin, appetizing gossip, courtly protestations of love. Who was "la Caroline," and who "Miladi" of the letters to Torck?[31] What a pity that only the mention remains of those "dinners, suppers, and balls" that attended the visit at The Hague of the Duke of Lorraine, who liked him so much and condescended so far as to be made a Mason by Lord Chesterfield![32] What entertainments the Prince of Orange must have received to give even the prudent English ambassador a headache![33] What, too, of Chesterfield playing blindman's buff till past three in the morning? Was it as innocent as all that? "We had music in the wood," he adds; "parties out of town . . . quadrille and scandal. . . . We have even attempted two or three balls."[34] And more than before, perhaps, when he had at length received his diamond star and ribbon, ladies were apt to sigh and languish at him. There were trysts and triumphs.

It was during this period, no doubt, that on one occasion he attended a great dinner given by the Spanish ambassador. At the conclusion of it, when the moment for the drinking of healths had arrived, the host begged leave to propose his master, the King of Spain, whom he compared to the sun. Then followed the French ambassador with a health to the King of France, whom he likened to the moon. It was now Chesterfield's turn. "Your excellencies have taken from me," he said, "all the greatest luminaries of heaven, and the stars are too small for me to make comparison of my royal master; I therefore beg leave to give your excellencies — Joshua!"[35]

* "I assure you," he wrote modestly to Mrs. Howard, "you need not be alarmed at what Lord Albermarle and Mrs. Macartney are pleased to call my magnificence; for it is nothing like it, and only what is barely necessary; and as for the expense, I should be very sorry to be a gainer by this or any other employment that the King may ever think fit to give me. Whatever my actions may be, interest shall never be thought to influence them; and if I can procure any credit to my master or myself, at the expense, not only of what he allows me, but even of my own, I shall think it very well bestowed." July 26, 1729.

Through the correspondence of those years, one turns the coin of his character over and over: on one side, the gay, the punctilious, the insinuating, and, on the other, the intent, the efficient, the unyielding representative of England. To gain van Wassenaer, he might condescend to wipe a child's nose; but let the envoy of Prussia overlook his diplomatic precedence when paying official calls, and there could be no forgiveness short of complete apology.[36] He might associate with von Sinzendorf on a footing of intimacy; but let the Austrian envoy attempt to outmaneuver in the smallest trifle the British ambassador, and Chesterfield would admit of no compromise.[37]

So much for the diplomat. Firmness and suppleness are the outstanding characteristics of Chesterfield as a man of affairs. It would be always so with him — reflected in the maxims he loved to repeat: *suaviter in modo, fortiter in re; volto sciolto, pensieri stretti;* reflected in the ingenuity of his mind, which could devise, one after the other, twenty different drafts of a treaty clause in search of the satisfactory wording;[38] reflected in the grace and hardness of his thought, that revealed exactly what he wished to reveal, but nothing more; reflected in his very style with its clarity and balance, thrust and parry of antitheses. At The Hague, all these qualities in him reached their maturity.

CHAPTER X
"These Trophies, Stanhope..."

AﾒﾒBASSADORS who are young, ambitious, and men of the world, do not labor merely for the sake of laboring. The pride of work well done is not wholly enough for them; they expect at least a tangible recognition, if not a reward. Their gaze is frequently turned from the capital of their residence and the problems of their office back to the source of good things in their native land; and sometimes they go home on leave, partly to keep in touch, and partly to push their interests. Chesterfield's life during his years of foreign service falls naturally into two divisions, the diplomat on the one hand, the aspiring English nobleman on the other. His time was divided also between The Hague and a year's leave in England. Intent on efficiency at his post, he still kept a shrewd eye on the court in London and on future prospects; when the proper moment arrived, he returned home to lend those prospects the benefit of his personal supervision.

There can be no doubt that he plied the trade of courtier at this time in all the usual implications of that term. Though allowances should be made for the ceremonious phrases of the day, no devoted servant ever expressed himself more humbly, more obsequiously than he did in his references to the King. He is sensible of his own inabilities; he must beg that His Majesty's indulgence will, in favor of his known zeal for his service, excuse, etc.; he cannot express the sense he has of His Majesty's goodness; if anything could add to that zeal with which he shall always endeavor to obey His Majesty's commands, it would be that indulgence he is pleased to show to his want of abilities to execute them; he will throw himself at His Majesty's feet; he will always receive and obey His Majesty's orders with the utmost submission. Nor is it easy to escape

the doubt that his letters to Mrs. Howard, though dictated by friendship, were spiced with policy. She could be counted on to report
his compliments and protestations to the King or Queen. Indeed,
he once asks her "to let drop in a proper place" the reasons of his
failure to entertain on the anniversary of His Majesty's coronation
day.[1] In like manner, he depended on his old patron Townshend
for similar offices.

Even the Queen, whom he described later under the pseudonym
of Agrippina as having been "born with an understanding and
dispositions, which could, at best, have qualified her for the sordid
help-mate of a pawn-broker or usurer,"[2] and who had always been
distasteful to him, came in for the proper amount of suave attentions. His quondam comrade of the bedchamber, Lord Hervey,
remarks in a celebrated passage that "nobody who had not tam-
pered with our chief priestess ever received a favourable answer
from our god,"[3] a sentiment that seems to have inspired Chesterfield
in those days. He wrote to Mrs. Howard that, knowing the Queen's
love of china, he had purchased "some of a very particular sort . . .
a service for tea and chocolate, with a basin and ewer"; that it would
not become him to take the liberty of offering them to Her Majesty,
and would Mrs. Howard manage it so that he would not seem
impertinent? Were they not baubles, he would not presume to offer
them to Her Majesty at all; and as they are such, he is ashamed
of doing it. However, if, notwithstanding these difficulties, Mrs.
Howard commanded him to send them . . . The Queen very
rightly considered it a bribe and very bluntly hinted as much, but
accepted the china. Whereupon, his lordship was extremely sensible
of the great honor the Queen had done him, and added unblush-
ingly, "Her Majesty need not apprehend being bribed by me; she
is only to be bribed by merit, a bribe which it is not in my power
to offer."[4] But what a grimace of the mind as he penned this
flourish!

He was not content, however, in sowing the problematic seed
of gallantries and gifts. Some might bear a hundredfold, but he
realized perfectly that the major part would come to nothing unless
backed up with more direct attention. The realist does not cast
his bread upon the water in pious hope, but makes certain that
it returns to him in the near future. Chesterfield believed in insisting on it.

What he wanted at this moment was the Order of the Garter, the premier decoration at the King's disposal, the most illustrious decoration in Christendom.

Aside from everything else, it was a gorgeous ornament of dress, in a day when Knights of the Garter and the Bath put on their ribbons and stars as a part of daily apparel. The broad blue ribbon expanded even a narrow chest; the blazing diamonds of the huge star over the heart dazzled beholders with awe and veneration. Ambassador Chesterfield entering a salon without this splendor was relatively a little naked man compared with Ambassador Chesterfield clothed in such insignia. As he put it eventually to Sir Robert Walpole, "I am a man of pleasure, and the blue ribbon would add two inches to my size." [5] But primarily, of course, it was the symbolic character of these trappings that gave them their essential value. To be one of twenty-five selected from the entire nobility of England, to be one of an inner circle already four hundred years old * — the merit lay in this rigid exclusiveness.

He had hardly been four months in Holland when he applied to Lord Townshend for one of the two Garters then vacant, on the score of its advantage to him in his diplomatic work; [6] but he received only a vague though encouraging answer. He applied again the following March [7] in a somewhat crisper fashion. It was generally believed and hoped at The Hague that he would receive one of the vacant Garters; it would not be very advantageous for him if he failed to receive it. But once more the reply was evasive: the King had not yet filled up the vacancies. It was a clear case of keeping him zealous by postponing the reward, and he had no other choice than to go on pursuing the elusive ribbon down the pathway of service, however much this dangling must have infuriated him.

In addition to the Garter, he kept a jealous watch on diplomatic promotions and sent in a request to be made ambassador to Berlin, if there should be question of an embassy thither in relation to a possible marriage between the Crown Prince Frederick and one of the English princesses. But this did not succeed either. Another request of about the same time was for preferment in behalf of Dr. Michael Stanhope, his kinsman, grandfather of his successor and heir-to-be, the fifth Earl of Chesterfield.

* The Order of the Garter seems to have been founded about 1346.

Meanwhile, in the spring of 1729 he entertained Lord Town-shend *en route* with King George to Hanover,[8] and on the royal return, waited upon His Majesty at Hellevoetsluis. Meanwhile also, he maneuvered the Dutch into agreement with the Treaty of Seville. But when a year and a half had gone by since his appointment to The Hague, he began to yearn for England. Ill-health and private affairs were the ostensible reasons of his demand for leave, and undoubtedly both were in a depleted state; indeed, the symptoms of that partial invalidism which exercised so marked an influence on his life began at this time. But there can be no question that the desire to return to headquarters was the dominant motive. Townshend perhaps had hinted something in regard to the possibility of his becoming one of the Secretaries of State. Certainly Maty believed that he had.[9] But in any case, the man in the field is always at a disadvantage in comparison with those at home. Plums have the habit of falling perpendicularly, and exploits abroad are not worth the quarter of a few tête-à-têtes near the fount of power. Accordingly he obtained leave, summoned his yacht toward the latter part of October, and finally reached England on a Thursday morning, October 25 (New Style), 1729.[10]

His reception at court the following day left much to be desired. His old enemy, Sir Robert, encountering him at St. James's, eyed him coolly and remarked, "I find you are come to be Secretary of State." "Not I," disclaimed the Earl, "I have as yet no pretensions, and wish for a place of more ease. But I claim the Garter, not as a reward for my late services, but in virtue of his Majesty's promise while Prince of Wales."

Likely enough the old political chief took the statement about the cabinet position with a pinch of salt; but he laid the blame on Townshend: it must have been his intrigue, and, of course, it could lead to nothing; Chesterfield could not be Secretary of State. As for the Garter, concluded Sir Robert, he should be beholden for it to nobody but himself: a very vague, and, considering their past relations, a dubious promise.[11]

Indeed, the prospect of anything at all grew less and less. At the beginning of the year, the brothers-in-law Townshend and Walpole reached the end of their long political partnership, quarreled for the last time, separated, and Townshend was forced out of the cabinet. This left Chesterfield without a patron and in imminent danger of having to pay the reckoning for his previous errors of judgment in regard to the power of Walpole and the Queen.

His ill-health, induced by fever at The Hague, was perhaps not improved by the bleakness of the general outlook. He fell into a dropsical condition that resisted the poultices of doctors Mead, Broxholme, and Arbuthnot over a period of six months. In despair, he confided his case to Palmer of St. Thomas's Hospital, who reversed the process, and made him soak his legs every morning in hot brine which had had meat salted in it, by which enlightened process he recovered in three weeks.[12]

We can picture him soaking in this matutinal brine and pondering his future. But the winter of his discontent turned to summer at last. Walpole kept his promises; the philosophy of "in sight, in mind" justified itself. Obstacles to the award of the Garter disappeared; Chesterfield not only obtained it, but was appointed Lord Steward of the King's household. Was it the Earl's courtcraft or insistence, was it Sir Robert's magnanimity or calculation, that retrieved the loss? Perhaps a mixture of all this. Certainly Walpole hoped that the little Earl might be won by generosity, and indeed, if Lord Hervey is to be credited, Chesterfield abounded in "the warmest professions to Sir Robert Walpole that it was possible to utter, acknowledging that his attachment this winter to Lord Townshend gave him no right to expect this favour, and he concluded with saying, 'I had lost the game, but you have taken my cards into your hand and recovered it.' "[13]

To be sure, on the one hand, Sir Robert had already offered the Lord Stewardship to Lord Carteret, who had refused it, so that the appointment was the less flattering; and, on the other, all the protestations of gratitude on earth would not prevent Chesterfield from aiming at Sir Robert's overthrow when the proper moment arrived. Meanwhile, they remained for a time on apparently good terms.[14] The Earl was installed Knight of the Garter at Windsor on June 18, 1730, together with his old friend Lord Burlington, and the King's second son, the Duke of Cumberland. His Majesty was present at the ceremony, and did him the added honor of paying the expense of the installation. On June 19 he received the white staff of Lord Steward. Whereupon a young poet, Soame Jenyns, tuned his lyre and presented the new dignitary with a graceful compliment:

These trophies, Stanhope, of a lovely dame
Once the bright object of a monarch's flame,
Who with such just propriety can wear,
As thou, the darling of the gay and fair?
See ev'ry friend to wit, politeness, love,
With one consent thy Sovereign's choice approve!
And liv'd Plantagenet her voice to join,
Herself and Garter both were surely thine.[15]

It was a straw showing how the wind blew. "Darling of the gay and fair" might be a little strong, but it reflected his vogue. Moreover, it should be observed that the reputation for wit and politeness was already popularly established.

The Lord Stewardship was the first office at court. It fell always to a peer and Privy Councilor, and at that time carried cabinet rank. Theoretically the Lord Steward is overseer of the King's household; he presides at the Board of Green Cloth, a committee formed by him and his subordinates, such as, at that time, the officers of the almonry, the treasurer, comptroller, master, coroner, and paymaster of the household, who examine and pass on the household accounts. Under him also were the cofferer of the household, the treasurer of the chamber, the paymaster of pensions, and the six clerks of the Board of Green Cloth. He, together with the treasurer, comptroller, and master of the household, were known as "the lords with white staves." He received a salary of £1460 a year.[16] The place, however, was a sinecure and a flattering unction. Its actual duties were performed by the master of the household, who resided permanently at the palace. This will explain how Chesterfield, as Lord Steward, could also continue his embassy at The Hague during the next two years.

It has seemed not altogether irrelevant to describe the office of Lord Steward, as this will give some idea of the multiplicity of court positions, and will account for the swarm of job-hunters who immediately beset each new official. There can be no question that certain incumbents of the chief posts made a business of the sale of places; but whatever charges may be leveled against Chesterfield's moral character, that of jobbery at least cannot be one of them. He turned no one out of his place at court, and appointed others to vacancies from a waiting list drawn up, it would seem, according to the priority of application. When Dean Swift, for instance, appealed to him in behalf of a relative's hus-

band, one Launcelot, "an honest man," he replied frankly as to what
his obligations were, and what were the ultimate chances of according the petition. The Dean, who is not at his best when sneering at
courts and whining over his own obscurity, replied with venom. But
for all that, Launcelot, in due time and contrary to expectation,
received a place.[17]

Attendance in the House of Lords, illness, the Garter, and the
pursuit of other plums, did not, of course, occupy the whole of
his leave, which, as we have noted, began to draw out to a goodly
length. The winter had its social phase — the beginning of new, the
continuing of old acquaintances. It was particularly distinguished
by an addition to the number of his friends in the person of a very
great Frenchman. This was Charles Louis de Secondat, Baron de la
Brède et de Montesquieu, who on his travels through Europe had
been making notes of laws and customs, and who had turned up at
The Hague two weeks before Chesterfield sailed. He brought with
him not only a letter of introduction from Lord Waldegrave in
Vienna, but all the aroma of beloved Paris. He was the friend of
many in the Earl's French coterie, and was already noted as the
author of the *Lettres Persanes*. They became immediately intimate
on the score of an absolute congeniality.

There was nothing of the indigent literary man about Montesquieu; he was first an aristocrat, and only in second place an
author.* He was that fine flower of eighteenth-century culture, the
philosophical nobleman. Lucid, detached, skeptical, with a strain
of sensualism, it is unnecessary to point out in how many ways he
resembled Chesterfield. "His virtues did honour to human nature;
his writings to justice," declared the latter years afterward.[18] Now,
he took him to his heart and offered him a berth on his yacht. It
was at Chesterfield's house in St. James's Square that Montesquieu
spent a part of that winter. His host introduced him at court, and
contributed to his election to the Royal Society. Thenceforward
they remained mutual admirers and in frequent correspondence.[19]

Among his English public, it was Chesterfield's approbation of

---

* John Churton Collins, *op. cit.* Collins points out that while in England,
Montesquieu did not meet the literary men, but spent his time with great
noblemen.

his supreme work, the *Esprit des Lois,* that Montesquieu most coveted, and with which he was most delighted.[20]

Montesquieu himself described one episode of their intimacy which is both amusing and instructive. It was on the occasion of his presentation at court by the Earl, and the scene was Kensington. It presents Chesterfield, the French philosopher, and Queen Caroline earnestly engaged in discussing Shakespeare; and a more unlikely trio of critics in regard to the great dramatist never assembled.

"How is it," asked the Queen, "that Shakespeare, who lived in the time of Queen Elizabeth, has made his women talk so badly and such fools as well?"

The shades of Rosalind and Portia, of Juliet and Viola, did not disturb the two gentlemen, who sincerely agreed with Her Majesty. Chesterfield answered that it was because women in Shakespeare's time did not go to the theater and only the poorer actors took female parts, so that Shakespeare did not trouble to make them speak well.

"But I," says Montesquieu, "suggested another reason." It was that book knowledge alone was sufficient to supply the diction for masculine characters, but that in order to invent the proper dialogue for women, "a poet must have a knowledge of the world and of good manners," the implication being that Shakespeare had neither.[21]

It would be hard to find a more perfect instance of the blindness that literary conventions of one age induce toward the masterpieces of another. Here were three exceptionally intelligent people, two of whom would take permanent rank in literary history, and yet they discussed the greatest of modern dramatists with as little understanding as would have been shown by city apprentices.

It would be delightful if more such glimpses of that winter had been preserved: a conversation with Bolingbroke, now in the heat of his philippics in *The Craftsman,* some treasonable sparks of sympathy passing between the two; or a visit from Arbuthnot, famous physician in spite of the unlucky poultices,[22] but still more famous as a good companion, whom the Earl loved and of whom he wrote after his death that "to great and various erudition, he joined an infinite fund of wit and humour," that his imagination was almost inexhaustible, and whatever subject he treated or was consulted upon, he immediately overflowed with all that it could possibly produce. As spring advanced and the famous grotto at Twickenham yielded a pleasant shade, we can picture the two of them there with Pope, indolent after the labors of the *Dunciad*.* Bathurst and Queensberry would be there perhaps, and John Gay, affluent from the subscriptions for *Polly* and at length snug in the harbor of the Queensberrys' patronage. Burlington would be there, and Cobham, Pulteney, Lyttelton, Marchmont, and others: [23] a half-political, half-literary group.

We know the Earl's opinion of some of these men, of Lyttelton's awkwardness, of Burlington's too plebeian interest in the details of building, of Pope's inconsistency, of Pulteney's avarice. His liking or admiration for them was always tempered by a just perception of their faults. What, exactly, was their opinion of him? It is doubtful if affection played much more of a part in it. They would admire his wit and grace, but probably enough they would have echoed the sentiments reflected in a witty letter addressed to him at The Hague by Mrs. Howard not long before. Referring to a recent illness he had had, she affirmed that the London surgeon, Cheselden, had reported his death together with the results of the autopsy: "that his head was perfectly right, but that there was no sort of communication between that and his heart; and that the part of his heart most susceptible of impressions in others, had a hard substance over it, which resisted everything but steel; and that his death was owing to climate; but that infallibly if they had removed him into France, he might have been alive at that time." [24]

The Earl himself enjoyed his own reputation for cool nonchalance. Swift, writing to Mrs. Howard in 1731, spoke of Chesterfield's "hardened soul" (*âme endurcie*), and added significantly that, "having once charged him with it, his lordship did not dislike it." [25] Their interchange on the subject of Launcelot, which we have already mentioned, illustrates perfectly the point at issue. As in the Johnson episode years afterwards, no impartial critic of the data concerned but will admit that Chesterfield was right and that his celebrated critics — Swift first and Johnson later — were not only wrong but surly and ungenerous. In the case of both of them,

* There had been a third and enlarged edition the preceding autumn.

Chesterfield did more than he promised and more than could have been expected of him; but, for all that, Johnson denounced him in his famous letter, and Swift remained unappeased by Launcelot's appointment. The point is, that although wrong and ungenerous in the special case that provoked their anger, both Swift and Johnson reacted to a certain quality in Chesterfield that exasperated them. It was precisely what the phrase of Swift implies: want of heart, or perhaps better still, a lack of emotional warmth. He could be liberal and friendly, he could even be affectionate, but it was a friendship and affection cooled with reason and controlled by common sense. Whim or impulse had no part in their composition. On the other hand Swift and Johnson were men of quick feeling, who valued emotions or were at least sometimes governed by them. They were far removed from the Earl's intellectual detachment. Instinctively they abhorred it. And thus their criticism, wrong in the special instance, was still fundamentally right: that is, if heartiness and glow are attractive, and if flawless self-control, however estimable, is sometimes unlovely. In any case, they pointed to a characteristic of Chesterfield's apparent to people of discernment long before the publication of the letters to his son had emphasized it, and of which there will always be apologists and critics according to the diversity of human opinions.

Refreshed by his leave in England, adorned with a ribbon and a star, rewarded with a new and shining position, Lord Chesterfield returned to The Hague in the summer of 1730 prepared for the long negotiations that culminated in the Second Treaty of Vienna. The trophies which life had thus far brought him, of earl, ambassador, Knight of the Garter, and Lord Steward, were weighty and imposing. But we have yet to mention one more of a different kind, which, from the standpoint of English letters and from that of his own permanent fame, was of greater importance still; for if he had not seduced Elizabeth du Bouchet, a governess or companion in the house of one of the van Wassenaer family,[26] his ill-starred son would not have been born, nor would Chesterfield's commentaries upon life have been written, at least in their present version.

That so little is known about Mademoiselle du Bouchet is itself significant of this affair. She was not an important conquest;

possibly she was not a conquest at all in the sense that much art or persuasion had been required in the winning of her. Lord Chesterfield, beribboned and diamond-starred, ambassador of England, with his fine house and splendid entertainments, his retinue of gentlemen, his flunkeys and coaches, the principal foreign official at The Hague, an intimate of princes and of their High Mightinesses of the States-General — such a patrician would not need more than a conventional flourish of compliments to win an obscure dependent like Elizabeth du Bouchet. He had nothing to boast about in regard to her. She belonged to the category of purchasable gratifications and had exactly the brief importance of such.

She was of good French Huguenot ancestry.[27] In his letters to Torck, her lover refers to her simply as "la Bouchet" without any other qualification or trace of affection, as, in short, one would refer to a negligible mistress. It has been noted by various biographers that in the letters to his son he speaks of her always with respect, and so he does (when he speaks of her at all), if such phrases as "compliments to your mamma" may be so designated. But there are also indications that he does not take her very seriously and is at no pains to conceal the fact from his son. Thus, writing from Dublin in 1746, he instructs young Philip as follows: "Pray tell your mamma, that I really have not had time to answer her letter; but that I will see what I can do about it when I return to England. . . . Send me, in your next, that Ode of Horace that begins with *mater saeva Cupidinum*." This is respectful enough, but casual. We would hardly suppose that he would gratuitously insult her. Nor in all probability was that clause of his testament bequeathing her "five hundred pounds as some compensation of the injury" he had done her, intended as an insult. It was simply the largesse of a nobleman to an inferior, whom he had paid off and on whom he was now bestowing a bonus. Too much has been made of this episode. Elizabeth du Bouchet, in all likelihood, was an uninteresting woman, who had once been plump and pretty and had pleasant manners,* of whom he had tired within a year or two. She had sold herself partly from vanity, partly for an easier life than that of upper

---

* To his son, no date (Strachey-Calthrop edition of Chesterfield's *Letters*, vol. i, p. 129): "As nobody can instruct you in good breeding better than your mamma, be sure you mind all she says to you upon that subject."

servant in a Dutch household; and she achieved her object in the form of an annuity sufficient for a decent maintenance. It had been a common-sense, lackluster bargain, palliated by the conventions of the time. Under the circumstances, Chesterfield acted according to the code of his world until he reached the above-mentioned clause of his testament. That was a mistake, a cracking of the veneer, and was so regarded by contemporaries. In spite of apologists, it was a tactless and rather gross gesture, the appropriate finale to an unromantic amour.

Meanwhile, as we have seen, by cajolery, finesse, and patience supplemented by more cajolery, finesse, and patience, the last of the United Provinces had been brought into line with the Second Treaty of Vienna, and the ambassador could regard his work as finished. The promotion to Paris had fallen through, and to remain longer at The Hague was a waste of time. "When the treaty is once signed," he wrote Harrington, "I shall be entirely useless, and a very unnecessary expense to his Majesty here, so that I could wish his Majesty would permit me to return to the employment he has honoured me with, near his person [the Lord Stewardship], which as yet I have neither deserved nor executed." [28] And a month later, when young Hammond had been dispatched to England with the Act of Concurrence, "Thus is this affair at last finished after a very tedious and probably a very unskilful negotiation on my part. Its own weight and his Majesty's great credit and influence here have alone carried it through and overcome the many difficulties that wrong judgements, private interests, personal piques, and the poor remains of an expiring French party had raised to obstruct it till now. I am happy in having been the instrument the King has employed to put the last hand to the settlement of the present tranquillity and future security that he has procured for Europe. But I am still happier in the assurances your Lordship has given me of his Majesty's gracious approbation of my conduct, when all I could hope for was only his forgiveness of my faults." [29] It was a letter calculated for the royal eyes.

Chesterfield's correspondence at this period breathes the impatience of a courtier too long from court. He obtained his recall, once more summoned his yacht, turned over official routine to the King's Resident, James Dayrolles, bade farewell to the States-

General in a letter full of diplomatic compliments,[30] and set sail at the end of February.[31] It is uncertain whether or not Mademoiselle du Bouchet accompanied him. In any case, she appeared with him not long afterward.[32] His son was born on May 2, 1732.*

* To his son, letter in Latin, dated Kalend Maii, 1741, and referring to his birthday as "tomorrow." I see no reason to suppose, as have Coxon and Dobrée, that he was not born in England. Chesterfield, in his first letter to Philip, when the latter was five years old and was on his way to Holland, speaks of the boy's beginning his travels by way of Holland, and does not refer to it as the place of his birth. His reference in his nondated letter to Torck (Dobrée, *op. cit.*, vol. ii, p. 258) speaks of "*la belle que je lui* [her employer] *ai enlevée*" and "*il n'y avait pas moyen de l'éviter*," which would indicate the approaching birth. Chesterfield would hardly have left her in Holland under the circumstances. Besides, in a letter to Torck dated London, June 23 (Old Style), 1732, he refers to "la Bouchet" and the child as near him.

PART THREE
1732 - 1745

CHAPTER XI
The Patriot

CHESTERFIELD returned to London, to the Lord Stewardship and the comforts of St. James's Square, with a still sanguine ambition. He left behind him on the Continent a record of real ability and of real achievement. Before leaving The Hague, he had assured his friend and chaplain, Chenevix, that he intended to shine as an orator in the House of Lords;[1] and there lay before him also the reasonable prospect of higher administrative positions in the government. He stood well with the King, and, superficially at least, even with Walpole — a definite supporter of the administration under an unclouded sky.

But it was one thing to be an ambassador, the most important foreign representative in the small world of The Hague, courted, consulted, and admired, absorbed in matters of high policy and negotiating treaties, and it was quite another to become at a stroke merely one, and by no means the most prominent, of the London court circle. Reichenbach, the Prussian envoy, wrote to Minister Grumbkow at Berlin that "Lord Chesterfield passes here for a fair enough kind of man and is a favourite with the King, but nobody thinks him such a prodigy as you all do in Germany."[2] Once more distance had lent its false enchantment. The reality of home seemed drab and without glamour. Here there were ministers, politicians, and great lords who bulked larger than himself and must be deferred to; there was that vulgarian, Walpole; there was the fat Queen and the pompous King. He disliked the English manners and missed his friends and the amenities of The Hague. What were the latest social events there? Was faro still being played? Count Bentinck was a wretch not to have written to him. His mind continued to run in the recent grooves, more concerned with diplomacy than British politics — the schemes of France, Spain, and Austria, the minutiae of Berg, Jülich, and Ravenstein.[3]

In brief, four years on the Continent had made him sensitive to British angularities. Moreover, he found his health and his fortune both impaired; and, as the raw March weather harassed London, there crept over him and into his correspondence the shadow of a depression hitherto undiscernible there — for him the herald not of oncoming spring but of approaching autumn, the intimation of life's receding tide. He was thirty-eight years old. For a man of pleasure, as he liked to call himself, this meant the beginning of middle life. He was one of those who had spent a slender capital of health too lavishly. More and more often now would come a sense of vertigo and of collapse. Still a few years of women and white nights (even in his prudent use of them fewer than he thought), before the inevitable fireside chair and cushions and the long tedium of retirement. As this was so, he was forced to accept the unavoidable, to think of settling down, and, as the principal feature of that sad process, to consider even marriage. Having emptied three quarters of his cup, he had still a fraction left above the dregs to bestow upon a wife.

Probably no one has ever approached marriage in a mood of more dispassionate, not to say dreary, appraisal. He had never been one to delude himself about anything or to dress up fact in romantic spangles. Granted the materialism of his life, his sincere expression of it is absolutely admirable. It is this that gives him permanent value and makes him a clear-cut type. He did not pretend to himself or to others that he felt more, that he believed more than he did. And let this honesty, even in a desolate cause, be his memorial. From such a man, thirty-eight years old, the veteran of courts, ruelles, tea tables, and gaming rooms, who regarded women as objects of aesthetic, sexual, or financial gratification, no lyricism on the subject of marriage could be expected. He looked over the field with cynical eyes.

He makes the fine gesture to Baron Torck of thinking of la Bouchet — "but she knows me too well to want me. And besides it is better for us both that I find someone else, upon whom I can saddle my past pleasures, and who will furnish a bit to the support of la Bouchet and her child." [4] And later, he doubts whether he will be able to make a find like his friend, who was marrying a Made-

moiselle van Wassenaer, "For I want merit and I want money —
two qualities rarely united. Feminine merit without money would
not be enough; money without merit would furnish a bad alloy." [5]
And later still, after admitting that the routine of his life suggests
marriage and that he would be inclined to marry: "But here's the
difficulty: I need a woman who in every way would be content to
give much and to receive little, who in a word would put up with
an outworn body, and would patch up an outworn fortune. I fear
that such an one would be like the wife of La Fontaine, who never
existed and will never exist." [6]

If these smooth passages are analyzed, their frankness must evoke
real admiration. He wants a wife who will support his mistress and
her child, one who will give everything and expect nothing. Under the circumstances, it was small wonder that the marriage market
offered little to choose from. Of course there was always Melusina
de Schulemberg, Countess of Walsingham, bastard of the old King
by the skinny Duchess of Kendal.[7] He had courted her once in his
indigent youth, but had been turned down by the King on the
score of his gambling.[8] She spoke English with a broad German
accent,[9] and gossip, probably mendacious, affirmed that, as a girl
in Germany, she had been married to her uncle, the Count von
Schulemberg.[10] But she was a great fortune, whose mother had made
money in George I's days by an occasional bribe for backstairs
influence: £11,000, indeed, from the Marquise de Villette, Bolingbroke's wife, to permit that nobleman's return to England.[11] In
point of rank and money, she was therefore eligible, and yet it is
hard to avoid the conjecture that, for the time being, Chesterfield
regarded her as a final resort. She would be available, perhaps, if
nothing else turned up. Presumably, then, he considered that season's
bevy of unmarried women with increased attentiveness; and during
the summer at Scarborough, whither he went to bathe and to drink
the waters, the heiresses at that agreeable seaside place were weighed
and valued.

Meanwhile, the birth of his son in May had kindled a small taper
that was destined to become an absorbing flame. The exquisite
gentleman with his star and ribbon, with his schooled face and
practiced eyes, looked down at the becapped infant that stared
back at him from the cradle and grasped his extended forefinger
with a moist, tiny hand. He felt a new throb, a curious warmth

under his figured waistcoat. Love was born. There can be no doubt of Chesterfield's love for his son. If the giving of one's innermost self, of one's time and thought, implies love, if the expenditure of that which is hardest for a selfish man to spend implies it, then no paternal devotion has been more abundantly proved. Money is nothing; money is often no more than the compounding with conscience for indifference. But to curtail leisure and sleep for the sake of a child, to yearn and brood over him, to dream and scheme for him, are the marks of true paternity. A thousand letters, with all that lay behind them of anxious thought, bear witness.*

And yet Chesterfield at the cradle of his son is as pathetic and, in one sense, tragic a picture as can be imagined. The practiced eyes of the Earl had become nearsighted with their own shrewdness. His love, real as it was, hardened too soon within the mold of his own ambition and rationalism. He could not be other than himself; he could not give what he did not possess. In the grip of that imperious love the child would be stretched out on the framework of a system; the screws would twist and tighten year by year. Crammed and lectured from babyhood, vamped up, laced in, and spurred on, he would grow into a mediocre manikin, without home or country, drifting in a dull Odyssey from capital to capital at his father's bidding, hounded by the Graces, deluged with advice, his awkward body and commonplace mind sweating toward a goal they could never reach. Under the inquisition of that great love he would be early taught the boundless selfishness of humanity, the ambition or avarice of men, the frailty of women, and he would be shown the tricks of managing both to his advantage. There would be room within the system for every rational virtue and for every polite sin; but there would be none for enthusiasm of mind or heart or soul.† Possibly, indeed, it was only another example of the sow's ear. Under any circumstances young Philip Stanhope, perhaps, would have remained a mediocrity, but he would have been spared at least the life-crushing burden of that pedantic love.

Biographers have pitied Chesterfield, and there is reason, indeed, to pity him for the dust and ashes of so much effort and hope; but

---

* There are four hundred and twenty letters extant. Everything indicates that more than that number have been either lost or suppressed.

† With regard to Chesterfield's insensibility to great poetry and to music, see *infra*, p. 209 *n.*, and p. 293.

there is an even greater pity due his son, the harassed apprentice to the beau monde, who remained inadequate. A cold breath of emptiness and decay rises from the memory of these vain oblations.

Six weeks after Philip's birth, the triumphant father wrote to Baron Torck that his son was becoming a regular fellow (*un gaillard*) and gave every sign of some day having great merit. The germ of the thousand letters is already there.

We know little about Chesterfield during the rest of the year 1732. After the season at Scarborough he went south to his estates, breaking the monotony of his journey by visits at the country houses of friends. In September he stopped at Bretby,[12] the disliked, in order to give an eye to land and tenants before returning to London. In December he appears briefly at Westminster Abbey, as pallbearer at the funeral of John Gay.

That false friend of the simple poet, as Lady Suffolk called his heart, "the foolish tender thing"[13] which had kept him poor and made him beloved, was still at last. Pope was a fellow pallbearer and our old acquaintance George Berkeley, and General Dormer, Lord Cornbury, and Mr. Gore.[14] The Duke and Duchess of Queensberry were there, whose devotion to Gay would be sullied by styling them his patrons, and who had been exiled from court on account of raising subscriptions within St. James's for the indiscreet *Polly*. Doubtless Bolingbroke was there and most of the wits: a grand cortege for a humble man of letters.

It may be questioned how much Sir Robert Walpole, who knew everything that went on, liked the report of this ceremony; for it represented not only his declared opponents, but the growing opposition within his own ranks, the elusive intellectual opposition, lords of anonymous pens and pamphlets, lords of tea-table epigrams that roused dangerous laughter behind the chief minister's back. Chesterfield, Berkeley, that Jacobite Cornbury, Lucifer St. John, venomous Pope, the entire coterie of Lady Suffolk, a seditious clique. There were hints of storm on the political horizon. It was a storm which would largely determine the balance of Chesterfield's active life.

For the better part of a year now, and growing in volume with every month, a wave of opinion throughout the nation had been rising against Sir Robert Walpole's fiscal policy, insofar as it contemplated the imposition of excise duties on tobacco and foreign wines. It was a policy aimed to correct certain flagrant customs abuses, to discourage smuggling, and by a more efficient method of tax collection to effect economies which would permit the reduction of the land tax by one shilling in the pound. It entailed no rise in the cost of tobacco or wine; its advantages to all but customs cheats and smugglers were apparent to any unprejudiced mind. There were already twenty-four other commodities subject to excise duties, so that the extension of the list to include two more did not constitute a fiscal innovation. In brief (for a discussion of this measure is beyond the scope of our study), it was a sound little revenue act dictated by wise statesmanship and one that has since been unanimously acclaimed by practical economists.[15] In this, as in many another policy and expedient, Robert Walpole stood in advance of his age.

But the word "excise" bore a sinister reputation in England. It recalled the tyranny of the Stuarts, the exactions of the Long Parliament, the burdensome imposts of grievous wars. Its connotations in the popular mind were all detestable. An extension of the excise, however, would not in itself have provoked the tempest of fear, rage, riot, and general disaffection which now burst upon the stalwart chief minister. The parliamentary opposition, directed by Bolingbroke and profiting from an unguarded phrase or two of Walpole's, spread the report throughout England that the tax measure in question was to serve merely as prelude to a general excise upon all commodities whatsoever; that the cost of living would be multiplied; but, worse still and intolerable, that the constitutional liberties of Englishmen would be invaded by an army of excise officers who, no longer content as at present with the inspection of shops and of warehouses, would extend their intrusions to the search even of private houses. Reason had no longer any part in the national reaction. Panic, rhetoric, and patriotic slogans took control. It would be difficult to find a more cogent illustration of popular dementia than that which now beset the English people on the subject of a businesslike revenue bill coupled with the term excise.

Meanwhile Chesterfield marked time. He was of cabinet rank by virtue of the Lord Stewardship and held that office as one of the court party. On March 6, 1733,[16] he spoke with grace and effect in

support of the Government against a minority measure to reduce
the land forces from eighteen to twelve thousand men, insisting
that "the present number was barely sufficient for the security of
the nation." [17] It was a speech entirely to the taste of the King, and
should be noted as one of those opinions that Chesterfield saw fit to
reverse later on when he had gone over to the Opposition.

But, though officially still on the side of the ministry, there can
be no doubt that personally he disliked Walpole and rejoiced at his
present dilemma. He owed him, indeed, both the Garter and his
employment at court; but such favors were not enough to overcome the fundamental antipathy. Between the bluff commoner and
the suave aristocrat there was simply no meeting ground; and we
have, therefore, every reason to believe that at this juncture the
Earl privately undermined Sir Robert Walpole whenever possible.
We can only conjecture what his actual opinions in regard to the
merits or demerits of the excise plan may have been. Without the
slightest disloyalty he may well have shared his friend Scarborough's
conviction that, whatever the excellence of the bill, it could not be
imposed upon an antagonistic country.* But there can be no doubt
that it was not the minister's fiscal policy, right or wrong, that
chiefly concerned him, but the effect that the inevitable failure of the
Excise Bill would have on the minister himself.

For twelve years Walpole's domination had been complete. His
ungainly, solid figure had blocked the avenues of ambition for a
dozen proud noblemen who considered themselves his superiors
in ability as well as rank. But the plums remained in his basket and
were handed out by him in return for obedient service. A tribune
of the middle classes, he stood for the supremacy of the House of
Commons. He stood for the humdrum virtues of peace, trade, and
sound finance. Bolingbroke, Pulteney, Wyndham, and latterly Carteret, the Tories and malcontent Whigs, had declaimed, obstructed,
protested, and intrigued in vain; Walpole's massiveness had not been

---

* From the rather vague phrasing of his letter to the King (April 16, 1733),
it might be inferred that Chesterfield doubted the practicality of enforcing it.
However, we can lay hold of nothing definite in his statements. On the other
hand, *vide* the "Character" of Lord Bute (Mahon, *op. cit.,* vol. ii. p. 498),
where he discusses the excise laid by Bute upon cider: "Though the thing was
right, the name was odious; and Lord Bute, if he had had more experience, and
known the temper of the people, would have known, that even right things
cannot be done at all times."

even so much as shaken. But now that the voice of the nation roared against him, the long-desired, the ever-deferred hour of the Opposition had struck. They were at last sure of their quarry, and it was now or never the occasion for all those who, like Chesterfield, rebelled against the dictator to take thought for their share of his spoils. So the astute Earl spoke and voted for the ministry, while biding his time to throw the weight of his influence against it at the crucial moment.

The story of the Excise debate has been repeated often enough to require only the briefest mention here: how from March 4 [18] till April 10 the battle raged; how Walpole's majority melted away; how oratory silenced reason; how the London mob, incited by agents of the Opposition, clamored and demonstrated at the doors of parliament; how the minister, reduced to a bare seventeen votes in his favor, sat, on that April evening, in the emptying House of Commons, with his hat pulled over his eyes, and admitted at last that "this dance must no further go." Next day, hemmed in by his enemies, he adjourned indefinitely the second reading of the bill.

London burst into an orgy of delight and triumph. The ministry had yielded. Throughout the night joy bells pealed. On many a bonfire effigies of the fat minister and fat Queen Caroline were burned. Surrounded by a handful of his friends, Walpole, refusing to leave Westminster by a back entrance, faced the mob, was attacked, shouldered and shoved his way through to his coach, although four of his friends were hurt in the melee.[19] Could any chief of government be more discredited or in a more hopeless situation!

Although the Excise Bill had never reached the House of Lords, Chesterfield had expressed his disapproval of it in the strongest terms. Moreover, his three brothers, Sir William, Charles, and John Stanhope, had voted against it in the House of Commons.[20] Thus he had shown his colors definitely against Sir Robert Walpole at the moment of the latter's greatest need over a measure which was the apple of the chief minister's eye. It was also a measure warmly supported by the King and Queen. He had, however, been playing a safe game on the winning side.

But against every appearance, against almost every certainty, the full triumph of the Opposition languished. Walpole, though at bay, was not yet beaten. The veteran politician showed himself more than a match for the elegant wits that assailed him. They attended his parliamentary execution in the finest fettle and with watering mouths, only to discover, after a pass or two, that the victim had become the aggressor, that he was escaping them and had fallen upon their flank. It appeared suddenly that yesterday's patriots of the Opposition had stirred up a homicidal mob not only with the intent to injure Walpole (a minor matter), but to overawe and coerce parliament itself, and that the very foundation of British liberties was thereby threatened. The House, jealous of its dignity, took fire. The Opposition, thrown in its turn upon the defensive and eager to clear itself of such charges, joined the now rallying majority in resolutions condemning all "actors, abettors, promoters, or encouragers of these violent tumultuous transactions." Yesterday's favorites, the city members, were ordered to carry these resolutions to the Lord Mayor with the command to publish them. Walpole's regular supporters, now that the opprobrium of the excise had been removed, flocked back to him. And once more the malcontents of parliament perceived the colossus re-enthroned, and realized that they had dreamed a dream.

On April 13, two days after the withdrawal of the bill, when Chesterfield, returning to court from the House of Lords, ascended the great stairs of St. James's Palace, he was stopped by a servant of the Lord Chamberlain, the Duke of Grafton, with a message that the Duke wished to see him at his house on important business. Aware that this could mean but one thing, he returned home immediately, and received the Duke, who, as instructed by the King, demanded his surrender of the white staff of the Lord Stewardship.

Of course, there was noble posturing and the tone of martyrdom. He "begged of his Grace to assure his Majesty, that he was ready to sacrifice everything for his service except his honour and conscience"[21] — which meant nothing, but read well. The King, unimpressed, administered an icy snub at the Earl's next appearance at court, so that he did not venture into St. James's again until the following year, and then only as spokesman of a committee of three delegated by the House of Lords to present its congratulations to the Queen on the marriage of the Princess Anne and the Prince of Orange. This may have been an attempt to ingratiate himself again, or as the Queen believed, it may have been intended as an insult; though certainly, as the first negotiator of the marriage in question, his appearance on this occasion was appropriate enough. In any case the Queen, highly incensed at what she considered his impudence, decided "to receive him as an Earl sent by the House of Lords whom she had never seen before in her life." Hervey relates the episode vividly. The Queen received the three members of the committee — Chesterfield, Scarborough, and Hardwicke — in her bedchamber, with no one present except her children, the servants, and Hervey himself. "Lord Chesterfield's speech," he reports, "was well written and well got by heart, and yet delivered with a faltering voice, a face as white as a sheet, and every limb trembling with concern. — The Queen's answer was great and natural, and delivered with the same ease that she would have spoken to the most indifferent person in her circle." [22] After this unequivocal rebuff, he did not return to court again for many years.

Thus Chesterfield, for the second time, had been dismissed from office at Walpole's nod. Once more, as in the days of George I, or at the beginning of the present reign when siding with Mrs. Howard or Lord Townshend, he had ventured to oppose Walpole and had been promptly stranded. The sure instinct, the infallible astuteness on which he prided himself never seemed to work as far as this incalculable minister was concerned. In spite of what had seemed to be a certain triumph, all that he and his influence and the Lord Stewardship had achieved was to serve as a caveat to the world that anyone, however prominent, who defied Sir Robert did so at his peril. Chesterfield was the only member of the administration distinguished by wit and fashion, he was a brilliant figure, and his dismissal, following immediately upon the failure of the bill, gave notice to the country that Walpole was sure of himself and stood dependent on no man. It gave notice also that hereafter he demanded absolute loyalty from his colleagues, and would tolerate no mutiny. In the past Chesterfield, whether on account of youth or the favor of the King, had retrieved his position with Walpole; but an atonement now, even if he had cared to make one, was out of the question. On one hand the King and Queen made common cause with Sir Robert; and on the other, the Earl's disgrace had been too conspicuous. The issue was joined. Henceforward, there was no other course open to him save warfare in the ranks of the Opposition.

It would be unjust to censure Chesterfield's political conduct during this episode. However mistaken his judgment of the Excise Bill may have been, we have no proof that he acted against his honest opinion in opposing it. But admitting this, it is still true that his views accorded with what he believed to be his interest. Briefly, he acted as most other politicians would have acted, neither altruistically nor yet dishonestly. It was the way of politics; only, for the time being at least, it had not been successful.

But disgrace at court brought advantage elsewhere. He entered the Opposition as something of a hero, much lauded by the Opposition press,[23] and with high hopes for the future. Other lords, included by Walpole in the same proscription and dismissed from their employments, came to swell the ranks. They were Clinton, Marchmont, Stair, Burlington, Westmorland, Cobham, the Duke of Montrose, and the Duke of Bolton. Moreover, parliament had only one year longer to run, and there could be no doubt in regard to the next elections. The country, indignant at the Excise plan, would have no more of Walpole under any circumstances. The triumph of the Opposition was merely delayed.

Chesterfield's letters at that time reflect this confidence. Summering again at Scarborough in company with other leaders of the malcontents, such as Stair, Marchmont, Anglesey, Pulteney, and Carteret, he no doubt shared in conferences and plans for the overthrow of the common enemy. He wrote to Lady Suffolk, the former Mrs. Howard, in high good humor, declaring that since the King of England was allowed to be the master of the seas, and that "as bathing in the sea was becoming the general practice of both sexes," a design had been made to impose an excise on the water, so that every person bathing should be measured, and "pay so much per foot square as their cubical bulk amounted to." [24] And he added that this would be a better tax than the late lamented bill. Similarly, in October he assured Baron Torck in an exceedingly buoyant letter "that there was no prospect at all of the ministry lasting six months; but that it was absolutely impossible for it to stand after the election of the new parliament, of which a great majority will most certainly be against it, so much has the temper of the entire nation been roused." [25]

But once more the Opposition had counted its chickens before they were hatched, and once more the astuteness of the Earl was at fault. They underrated the efficiency of Walpole's machine. The liberties of the kingdom might be at stake; Britain, preserved from excise by the efforts of patriots, might now be standing at the cross-roads between freedom and slavery; but the British electorate, re-covered from its panic of a year ago, yielded to the humdrum diligence of the Duke of Newcastle, Walpole's manager for Eng-land; and the Scottish electorate, still more mercenary, gave heed to the "practical" arguments of Lord Islay, manager for Scotland. Money changed hands, but the result justified the means. For when all was over and the dust had cleared, the amazed Opposition beheld Sir Robert Walpole still in the saddle, and with a majority sufficient to keep him there many years. From now on, a note of disillusionment and bitterness clings to Chesterfield's political letters. Once again he had backed the wrong number. His role henceforth, until close upon the end, would be that of a patriot indignant at his country's wrongs, protesting against corruption and the supineness of the Government.

Oppositions the world over are alike. Their function at every turn is to criticize, harass, and discredit the Majority, but above all to acquire popularity by championing now one and now the other popular cause. They must pose as defenders of the oppressed and as superlative lovers of their country. Without responsible commitments, they can indulge the luxury of fine feeling and of noble oratory. Thus in Chesterfield's time the Opposition came to be known as "the Patriots" in contradistinction to the "Court" party. Generally speaking, however, it was a matter of words rather than of principles — the old conflict of the outs and ins — for when at length, by the force of events rather than of his enemies, Walpole fell and the Opposition rose to power, its conduct differed little from that of the former dictator save on the point of efficiency. The history of the subsequent ten inglorious years, as one writer expressed it, wrote the eulogy of Walpole's administration.

In the meantime it is not surprising that Chesterfield, excluded from office, came increasingly to enjoy among the laymen of his party a reputation for distinguished eloquence and patriotic fervor. To this his abilities, his freedom from governmental responsibility, and his audience alike contributed. He took exquisite pains in the preparation of his speeches, was careful to be exactly informed of the subject discussed, and won his hearers by the grace of his style or stung them with the mordancy of his wit. He shone in exposition rather than in debate. His age was unanimous in declaring him an eminent, if not the most eminent, orator.* Moreover his political sentiments, unhampered by any immediate prospect of effective execution, appealed to the rank and file of sympathetic idealists. A friend of poets, he had all the gifted pens of the day on his side, and they have transmitted a highly colored portrait. We approach him from a new angle in the following lines from Thomson's revision of *The Seasons*.† The only excuse for quoting them at length is that they reveal Chesterfield, so to speak, in full dress and as viewed by the public during those Opposition years.

> O, thou, whose wisdom, solid yet refin'd,
> Whose patriot virtues, and consummate skill
> To touch the finer springs that move the world,
> Join'd to whate'er the Graces can bestow,
> And all Apollo's animating fire,

* The Earl of Orrery was particularly eulogistic. On Feb. 2, 1743/4, he writes Lady Orrery: "He [the Duke of Newcastle] was followed by the Earl of Chesterfield in all the weight of Eloquence, the superiority of Argument, the dignity of Genius, and the sweetness of Persuasion. No Syren had ever half his Power. . . ." *Orrery Papers*, vol. ii, pp. 179–180. But there was general unanimity in regard to Chesterfield's eloquence. Speaker Onslow of the House of Commons (certainly no partial critic) reports that he was "a very graceful speaker in public, had some knowledge of affairs, having been ambassador in Holland, and when he was engaged in debates always took pains to be well informed of the subject, so that no man's speaking was ever more admired or drew more audience to it than his did, but chiefly from those who either relished his wit or were pleased with seeing the Ministry exposed by his talent of ridicule and the bitterness of jest he was so much master of and never spared, and this made him so very terrible to the Ministers who were of the House of Lords that they dreaded his wit upon them there, and his writings too, for he sometimes, as it was thought, furnished the weekly paper of the Opposition with the most poignant pieces it had." *Hist. MSS. Comm.*, 4th Report, Appendix, Part IX, p. 472. *Cf.* also Sir Thomas Robinson to Lord Carlisle, June 2 and 7, 1733, and March 1, 1736, commending Chesterfield's speeches on those occasions (*Hist. MSS. Comm.*, MSS. of the Earl of Carlisle, p. 119). Also Horace Walpole to Horace Mann, Dec. 10, 1741: "Lord Chesterfield made a very fine speech against the Address, all levelled at the house of Hanover." And again, Dec. 15, 1743: "I was there [in the House of Lords], and heard Lord Chesterfield make the finest oration I ever did hear." Other encomiums on his oratory are to be found in the *Gentleman's Magazine* for 1740, pp. 101–102, where he is described under the name of Castroflat; Smollett's *History of England*, vol. ii, p. 215 (the Playhouse Bill, 1737); Lady Hervey's *Letters* (Feb. 6, 1744); *Parl. History*, vol. xiii, p. 274; Yorke's *Earl of Hardwicke*, vol. i, p. 614.

† Between 1738 and 1740.

Give thee, with pleasing dignity, to shine
At once the guardian, ornament, and joy,
Of polish'd life, permit the Rural Muse,
O Chesterfield, to grace with thee her song!
Ere to the shades again she humbly flies,
Indulge her fond ambition, in thy train
(For every Muse has in thy train a place),
To mark thy various full-accomplish'd mind:
To mark that spirit, which with British scorn,
Rejects th' allurements of corrupted power;
That elegant politeness, which excels,
Ev'n in the judgement of presumptuous France,
The boasted manners of her shining court,
That wit, the vivid energy of sense,
The truth of Nature, which with Attic point,
And kind well-tempered satire, smoothly keen,
Steals through the soul, and without pain corrects.
Or rising thence with yet a brighter flame,
O, let me hail thee on some glorious day,
When to the listening senate, ardent, crowd
Britannia's sons to hear her pleaded cause.
Then drest by thee, more amiably fair,
Truth the soft robe of mild persuasion wears:
Thou to assenting reason giv'st again
Her own enlighten'd thoughts; call'd from the heart,
Th' obedient passions on thy voice attend;
And ev'n reluctant party feels a while
Thy gracious power: as through the varied maze
Of eloquence, now smooth, now quick, now strong,
Profound and clear, you roll the copious flood.[26]

Nothing could be better than this. The Earl's former attaché at
The Hague, James Hammond, hymns more sweetly:

Stanhope, in wisdom as in wit divine,
May rise, and plead Britannia's glorious cause,
With steady rein his eager wit confine
While manly sense the deep attention draws.[27]

It is unnecessary to repeat the "Attic wit" allusion of Pope's [28]
or the much-quoted verses of Sir Charles Hanbury Williams.[29]

Such vivid colors fade when exposed to the light of reality. There
is no question of depreciating the qualities of Lord Chesterfield
as an orator or a wit; but in forming a final estimate of his worth
as a man, and hence of the philosophy identified with him, we must

beware of that tendency to whitewash by which several of his biographers have been led astray. That he had a sincere if not an unmingled love for England, that he was not less patriotic than the other, and perhaps than the more disinterested, Opposition leaders, we may admit at once without reservation. But that he exhibited a peculiar consistency of patriotic devotion, that he occupied a unique position in regard to this among the statesmen of his time, seems to be unsupported by fact.

The "Patriotic virtues" lauded by Thomson suffer an abatement if we recall that at the outbreak of the war of the Polish Succession, when increased solidarity with Holland became a national need, he wrote to Baron Torck approving the Dutch aloofness, urging its continuance, and advising that a deaf ear be turned to the solicitations of Horatio Walpole, Sir Robert's brother, who was proceeding on an embassy to The Hague.[30] Why? There could be no doubt that the concerted action of England and Holland in the affairs of Europe was to the advantage of British policy. Chesterfield himself had spent four years at The Hague endeavoring to deepen and cement this alliance. He would repeat the effort some years later when he was again in power. There was nothing new in the present emergency. And yet privately he used his influence in Holland to defeat a negotiation of obvious national value. Of course the reason is both apparent and contemptible. He desired merely to embarrass the administration by a diplomatic failure, against the interests of his country. This was hardly patriotic. To give it a blunt qualification, it was dirty politics.

Similarly in regard to the British scorn that rejected "the allurement of corrupted power," we find no trace of it when he gratefully accepted the Garter and the Lord Stewardship from Walpole's hands. And considering the diatribes, the sneers and insinuations he launched against that minister for his use of political bribery, it is interesting to read his suggestion to Marchmont, after the elections of 1734, that Scottish peers might be bribed to appear at the bar of the House of Lords and admit that they had received money to vote for the court list.[31]

Furthermore, if we look for consistency in his parliamentary record, we are not impressed by any conspicuous example of it there. He voted with the Majority for the Septennial Bill in 1716, and he voted with the Minority to repeal it in 1734. He voted against the reduction of the land forces in 1733, but voted against the army in 1736. He supported the motion in 1737 for an appropriation from the Civil List of £100,000 per annum for the Prince of Wales;[32] but in 1739 he opposed the settlement of £39,000 yearly as a provision for all the other royal children.[33]

Times change and opinions must reflect them; we hold no brief for consistency; but it is hard to avoid the conclusion that Chesterfield, like other "Patriots" of this period, was guided as much by faction as by patriotism.* And it is difficult not to agree with Dr. Maty, who observes that Walpole's "most unpardonable fault was to have kept his rivals out of his place so long."[34]

Except on the score of factiousness, how can Chesterfield's veering attitude in regard to Walpole's military policy be explained? When the minister insisted on preparedness in view of the Polish war and the Continental turmoil, the Earl opposed it not only in parliament but by letters to Holland.[35] When Walpole, whose chief object was to keep England at peace, sought to avoid hostilities with Spain in 1739, the Earl, applauded by a gallery of militant noblewomen[36] who had forced their way into the House of Lords, championed the war and precipitated England into a costly and sterile conflict. His speech was a fine one;[37] but to an impartial mind Sir Robert's remark on the subject of the Polish war outweighs such eloquence. "There are fifty thousand men slain in Europe this year," he said, "and not one Englishman."

Except as factiousness, it is impossible to explain the Opposition policy, shared by Chesterfield, of supporting and inflaming the Prince of Wales against the court, with all the division, disaffection, and even national danger that such a course entailed.[38]

"I have opposed measures not men," he wrote Chenevix in 1742,[39] but the assertion must be qualified: That Chesterfield's resentments were acid rather than passionate is likely enough, from the cool temper of his mind; but they were quite personal and human. With him, it was a question of persistent dislike rather than of hatred, with one exception — he hated the Queen. His "Character" of Caroline, written long after her death, still bears the impress of

---

* It is interesting to note that the historian J. R. Green (*History of the English People*, ed. 1879, p. 704) calls this Opposition "more factious and unprincipled than had ever disgraced English politics."

rancor. "Neither strength of parts nor judgment," "cunning and perfidy," "a dangerous ambition," "neither esteemed, beloved, nor trusted," are some of the phrases he uses to describe her. He acknowledges the Queen's intrepid death under torments which, as reported in the pages of Hervey, recall the horrors of a torture chamber; but no touch of pity, no respect for the tomb, prevented him from attacking her memory in a satirical epitaph immediately after her death:

> Here lies unpity'd both by Church and State
> The subject of their flattery and hate,
>
> · · · · · ·
>
> In Tindal's and in Hoadley's paths she trod,
> A hypocrite in all but disbelief in God,
> Promoted luxury, encouraged vice,
> Herself a slave to sordid avarice.
> True friendship's tender love ne'er touched her heart,
> Falsehood appeared, in vain disguised by art,
> Fawning and haughty, when familiar rude,
> And never gracious seemed but to delude,
> Inquisitive in trifling, mean affairs,
> Heedless of public good and orphans' tears;
> To her own offspring mercy she denied,
> And unforgiving, unforgiven died.[40]

This ugly caricature of Queen Caroline redounds only to the shame of its author, and throws a more searching light upon his character than upon hers. In this connection it is illuminating to recall his elaborate flattery of her while ambassador at The Hague.[41] Amid the general mourning at her death, it caused a flurry of comment that he refused ostentatiously to wear any himself or to change the livery of his servants. Nor did he send condolences to the palace.[42]

Toward the King and Walpole, on the other hand, his resentment was at least temperate enough to cool off in later years, and restrained enough to give vivacity and humor to his satire. But he left no shaft untried which would contribute to their discomfort. Thomson to the contrary, it was not a kindly satire. He ridiculed their appearance, their morals, and their policies. He assailed them with light and heavy artillery, lampoon and jibe, essay and oration. A squib on the court painter, William Kent, who had finished a portrait of the King, may serve as an illustration of the former:

As to Apelles, Ammon's son
   Would only deign to sit;
So to thy pencil, Kent! alone
   Will Brunswick's form submit.

Equal your envied wonders! save
   This difference we see,
One would no other painter have —
   No other would have thee.[43]

His political essays modeled on Swift reach a level not much inferior to that of their prototype. "The Waxwork Army," [44] for instance, which attacked Walpole's military policy in 1736, ranks among classical examples of its kind. "On Ear-Ticklers," [45] "On the Political Dangers of Glasses," [46] "On the Advantage of weighing Kings and Statesmen Annually," [47] "The Rat in the Statue," [48] wherein Walpole plays the part of the rat, may be mentioned among others. Chesterfield's literary work, taken as a whole, will be considered later. Suffice it for the moment that, as penman for the Opposition, he composed articles that almost transcend the level of fugitive pieces. Here, as in everything he wrote, the form at least is distinguished. At the moment they gave body and backing to his social reputation as a wit.

But not content with attacking Walpole while the latter was in power,* his opposition became revenge after the minister's fall in 1742. He wished him joy, to be sure,[49] of the new title of Orford that raised the old dictator to the House of Lords, and marked the close of his parliamentary effectiveness; but there was an ugly menace of irony behind the congratulation, for he set about actively to secure his impeachment on the ground of corrupt practices. Evidence against Walpole was to be encouraged by indemnifying witnesses, a base and puerile bill that was promptly defeated. In like manner, the investigation committee appointed to discover Walpole's peculations arrived at nothing. Chesterfield's malevolence was once more, and this time finally, baffled by his undaunted enemy.

No wonder the King hated him! He had insulted and traduced

---

* Some indication of his animus against Sir Robert may be gathered from the fact that in the debate on the motion against the minister of Feb. 13, 1741, "Lord Chesterfield, tho' forbid by his physicians, came and gave his vote and proxies, with blisters upon him. . . ." (Philip Yorke to the "Club" at Cambridge, Yorke, *Earl of Hardwicke,* vol. i, p. 252.)

the only woman whom George II had ever loved; he had attacked, ridiculed, and sought to disgrace the only minister he had ever trusted; and worst of all, he had made light of royalty itself.* "Bolingbroke," said the King, "is a scoundrel, but he is a scoundrel of a higher class than Chesterfield. Chesterfield is a little tea-table scoundrel, that tells little womanish lies to make quarrels in families, and tries to make women lose their reputations, and make their husbands beat them, without any object but to give himself airs, as if anybody could believe a woman could like a dwarf-baboon." "A little chattering cur" was another favorite qualification.[50] King George reminds one of a fat, stupid bull goaded by an expert picador.

It would be unprofitable here to trace skirmish by skirmish the struggle between the Opposition and Majority parties during the years from 1733 to 1745. I have mentioned a few of these, and, for the rest, must refer the reader to more politically minded histories and biographies. In general, whatever the Government supported, Chesterfield opposed; and, unfortunately for his subsequent political fame, the Government at that time rested in the hands of a capable and farsighted statesman, whose policy later events have vindicated. As time passed, and disease, together with the changing world, portended Walpole's fall, rifts and rivalries began to appear in the Minority ranks. Lord Carteret, an abler politician than the Earl, overshadowed him. Pulteney, the chief leader of the Patriots, antagonized him. And when at length the longed-for opportunity occurred and the King in tears accepted Sir Robert's resignation, Chesterfield, excluded from the new ministry, remained in even bitterer opposition. From his letter to Chenevix already quoted [51] one gains the impression that he would not co-operate in a government of whose measures he disapproved. Horace Walpole, on the other hand, declares that "there was no unwillingness on his side," but that Pulteney and Carteret, together with Lord Hardwicke and the Duke of Newcastle, had formed a closed corporation without place for him.[52] At all events, by February 1743 he was asserting that his old colleagues, the new ministry, had acquired "more infamy in ten months, than their predecessors, with all the pains they took,

---

* Cf. the two lampoons, too coarse to reprint here, that Chesterfield composed on George II's relations with Queen Caroline. Hervey's *Memoirs*, vol. iii, p. 652.

could acquire in twenty years." He accused them of "treachery and connivance," of "sneaking and abandoning their principles," and called them "the reproach or scum of their party." [53]

Oppositions are not always factious, nor are they always wrong. In the debate on the Licensing Act in 1737, we find Chesterfield (through the stately periods of Samuel Johnson, who rewrote his speech for the magazines) [54] defending one of the cardinal principles of liberty, the freedom of books from governmental censorship. [55] To be sure, the bill in question contemplated merely the regulation of the stage, and has had in practice few of the disadvantages he prophesied; but the thesis was a sound one and appears to have been ably presented. Similarly in regard to the Gin Act of 1743, which was designed to raise taxes by the public intemperance, [56] and throughout the whole of his anti-Hanoverian agitation, [57] he undoubtedly strove for the best interests of England. Moreover, as a warning to an otherwise arrogant power, the service of an Opposition is obvious. But the question may fairly be raised as to the effect of their role, if too long continued, upon the opposers themselves. Generally speaking, it is a negative role, a practice of plots and cabals, petty obstructions and mean expedients. It is a deterrent, not a constructive, force, and is therefore intrinsically sterile. What, we may ask, was the fruit of so much eloquence, so much writing, scheming, and maneuvering? A few speeches and essays no longer read, a few samples of wit preserved in contemporary letters and memoirs. And what was the effect upon Chesterfield himself of this long opposition? A growing bitterness, apathy, and chagrin.

It could not be otherwise. For more than ten years he had spent himself in a guerilla warfare that effected nothing at last but the replacement of one ministry by another less capable. He had achieved none of the satisfaction or experience that comes of responsible and constructive service, but had given the best of his life to a negative cause and to evanescent issues. It is not surprising, therefore, that a sense of futility, a deepening cynicism, oppressed him at the threshold of old age. Each year contributed to the pervasive disillusionment. In 1739 he wrote of his companions in the Opposition: "They consider money as their only interest, and would not venture the suspension of a quarter's salary, to save the whole nation. This . . . is our wretched situation, from whence, I think little good can arise. Union among ourselves cannot be expected, where our views are so widely different . . . I despair of either doing good or seeing any done; yet while I live, I assure you, I will endeavour it." [58] And to Lyttelton in 1742, announcing the death of Hammond: "Such is the folly, knavery and futility of the world, and such was his truth, fidelity and attachment to me, that in my opinion, I have lost more by his death than he has." [59] And again to Marchmont in the same year he referred to "the ill fortune that commonly attended him in everything." [60] A habitual pessimism in regard to the future of England settled upon him as the years passed.[61] The nation was always upon the brink of calamity, and yet the glorious era of William Pitt stood close at hand. Such defeatism, psychologically speaking, is merely the projection of personal defeat.*

Perhaps all this may not have been the fault of Chesterfield, but it was certainly his misfortune. When at length by a shifting of parliamentary coalitions, Lord Carteret fell in the autumn of 1744, and Chesterfield as head of the Opposition became allied with the Pelhams in the Broad-bottomed Ministry, it was too late. The sands of his active life were running low. Time had been, and time was past.

* See also letters to Marchmont, April 24, 1741. In justice to Chesterfield, it should be added that many of the finer spirits among his contemporaries shared his pessimism during those years which marked the close of Walpole's ministry and the rise to power of Pulteney and Carteret. It is reflected in the Marchmont, Orrery, and Pope correspondence. In this connection, the latter's diatribe which concluded the First Dialogue of the *Epilogue to the Satires* (1738) will be recalled:

> See all our nobles begging to be slaves!
> See all our fools aspiring to be knaves!
> The wit of cheats, the courage of a whore,
> Are what ten thousand envy and adore;
> All, all look up with reverential awe,
> At crimes that 'scape, or triumph o'er the law:
> While truth, worth, wisdom, daily they decry —
> "Nothing is sacred now but villany."

But Chesterfield's pessimism began with the period of his opposition and continued during the rest of his life. Maty observes, vol. i, p. 179: "Lord Chesterfield . . . it must be owned, was rather inclined to despondency on many occasions."

CHAPTER XII
Melusina

A MAN'S OFFICIAL CAREER is seldom the most important factor in his life. It gives him a rating and index number among his contemporaries; if successful, it brings with it position and other emoluments; if thwarted, it colors his attitude toward the world. But after all, the ex officio hours, which are by far the most numerous, his social contacts and personal problems, the state of his health or of his purse, his avocations, habits, and philosophy, are the determining and revealing elements of his biography. They constitute the essential man whose career is more often than not merely a reflection of these other influences.

In the *Gentleman's Magazine* for September 1733 there appears, as the most important marriage announcement for that month, the following notice: "The Earl of Chesterfield, married to Melusina de Schulumbergh, Countess of Walsingham in Norfolk, and Baroness of Aldborough (both Royal Titles) conferr'd on her by Letters Patent, dated April 10, 1722. Her portion is said to be 50,000 *l.* down, and 3,000 *l.* per ann. payable out of the Civil List Revenue in Ireland, during her life. Soon after they were married the Prince of Wales sent his compliment to them thereupon."[1]

So, after all, Melusina had been the best he could do.* The marriage notice is eloquent of much that can be read between the lines. A woman who, in spite of wealth, titles, and a royal connection, had remained unmarried until the ripe age of thirty-eight was presumably not distinguished for her attractiveness. Nor

---

* With regard to Chesterfield's suit for the hand of Lady Diana Spencer, the Duchess of Marlborough's granddaughter, and his rejection in 1731, while he was ambassador at The Hague, see Connely, *op. cit.*, pp. 116 f.

are there indications that she was anything but matronly. An age fertile in compliments restricted itself, when it praised her at all, to encomiums on the "amiableness of her character, the accomplishments of her mind," and her qualities of "prudent management." Dr. Maty ventures a bit further in asserting that "her taste for the fine arts, and in particular for music rendered her a fit companion for Lord Chesterfield." [2] But as the Earl disliked music and became increasingly deaf, it might be doubted whether this statement was as accurate as it was well intended. In her youth, while her father, the old King, lived, she had been paid a certain amount of social homage, if we can judge from a letter of Lady Hervey's to Mrs. Howard in 1725, where the former refers to a number of balls at Bath in honor of Lady Walsingham; [3] but her heyday was brief, and only at rare intervals does she emerge from the background. Indeed, references to her are extremely few and casual. She seems to have been a kindhearted and perhaps sentimental, but withal a thrifty, German woman, speaking English with a broad accent, though tongue-tied and probably a little awkward socially. Jewels delighted her; and she had a large supply of them, worn maybe too conspicuously at times. A comfortable, mediocre, dull person — such is the impression conveyed by chance remarks in the correspondence of that age, bracketed, as it were, between Horace Walpole's estimate of her as "an exemplary wife" at one end, and Lord Hervey's as "an avaricious fury" at the other. [4]

But the size of her dowry and of her pension should be noted. They would be large even in our day; they were triply so then. Chesterfield, naturally extravagant and a gambler to boot, found here the mainstay of his dilapidated fortune. When the Duchess of Marlborough bequeathed him twenty thousand pounds in 1745, it was rumored that he had at that time an income of only eight hundred pounds from his own estate, and he deplored the bequest as having roused up his creditors. "My doors were quiet," he said, "I went in and out unmolested, but now they assemble in my hall, they stop me as I pass, and they require not only twenty, but forty thousand pounds." [5] In such predicaments his wife's fortune remained a refuge. The magnificence of Chesterfield House in Mayfair was no doubt in large part due to her money. The expensive education of young Philip Stanhope on the Continent was made possible by her. And Melusina's thrift, in spite of her husband's prodigality and gaming losses, kept him a wealthy man.*

It will be recalled that the Earl was in search of a wife who would give much and demand little, and he had found one. A mature bride of thirty-eight had no right to demand much. He gave her an old title, the nimbus of his social prestige, a rescue from spinsterhood. There can be no doubt that he treated her always with his perfect grace and affability. Perhaps even he paid her some conjugal attention.[6] But if she expected more than this, she was disappointed. Love had no place in the bargain, and even companionship was excluded. It was an exemplary marriage of convenience. To be sure, he took the trouble of moving from St. James's to Grosvenor Square, so that he and his wife (who continued to live with her mother, the Duchess of Kendal) could be next-door neighbors. Dr. Maty, urbanely concerned to sprinkle rose water over the arrangement, observed that "he divided his time between his business in his own house, and his attentions and duties at the other. Minerva presided in the first; and in the last, Apollo with the muses." [7] It is one of those occasions when the reader blushes for Dr. Maty. The Earl seems to have harbored the traditional attitude of a son-in-law toward the Duchess of Kendal, whom he describes as a "considerable sample of George I's bad taste and good stomach." [8] She does not accord very well with Apollo and the Muses.

Now and then husband and wife appeared together, sometimes at Isleworth, a suburb where the Duchess of Kendal had a summer villa,[9] and again, more often, at Bath, but it was many years before they lived under the same roof. As one follows the life of Chesterfield, it requires something of an effort to remember that he had a wife at all, so dim and effaced is the relationship. Nor should this be put down, as is the way with apologists, to the customs of a century dominated by the French code. His conjugal indifference impressed even so tolerant a French woman as Lady Bolingbroke, who observed to a friend, the Countess of Denbigh, that Lord Chesterfield spent six days of the week on his own affairs in the city, to the chagrin of both his wife and mother-in-law.[10]

---

* Apparently Chesterfield threatened the King with suit to recover a bequest to Lady Walsingham by George I in the will which George II destroyed. This was said to have been settled out of court for the amount of £20,000. Walpole, *Marginal Notes on Maty*, vol. i, p. 71, and Chesterfield to Newcastle, March 20, 1746, also the *Gentleman's Magazine*, June, 1774, p. 265 ff.

He seems to have regarded his marriage as a kind of humiliation, a bourgeois compromise and, with his customary frankness in such matters, waved aside the congratulations of his friends. To a letter from Marchmont in October, he replied that he would not take up his time in returning compliments to him for his good wishes: "It is inconsistent with that real zeal and truth with which you know I belong to you." [11] To the Earl of Essex in November he was more explicit, but no more sentimental. It should be remembered that he had now been married two months. "To a man," said he, "who marries for the first time with fear and trembling, the congratulations of a friend, who has tried that state twice with success, are exceedingly comfortable as well as obliging, and give one reason to hope it may not be so bad as is generally represented. For my own part, I found both my constitution and my fortune so much the worse for wearing that they would neither of them pay at sight; from whence I concluded it was high time to lay aside the fine gentleman, and to think of repairing them." [12]

There are no illusions apparent in this extract, and he remained forever disillusioned. "It is possible, though not very probable, that there may be joy in marriage," he wrote long afterwards.[13] And again, as an old man, to his relative Arthur Stanhope: "I must freely tell you, that in matters of religion and matrimony I never give advice; because I will not have anybody's torments in this world or the next laid to my charge. . . . I may possibly be in the wrong, but I tell you very sincerely, with all due regard to the sex, that I never thought a woman good company for a man *tête-à-tête*, unless for one purpose. . . . Upon the whole, you will marry or not marry, as you think best: but to take a wife, merely as an agreeable and rational companion, will commonly be found to be a great mistake. Shakespeare seems to be a good deal of my opinion, when he allows them only this department,

> To suckle fools, and chronicle small beer." [14]

At the extreme end of his life, he had no doubt his own experience in mind when he wrote the following to be delivered to his godson and heir after his death: "There are but two objects in marriage, love or money. If you marry for love, you will certainly have some very happy days and probably many very uneasy ones; if for money, you will have no happy days and probably no uneasy ones; in this latter case let the woman at least be such a one that you can live decently and amicably with, otherwise it is a robbery." [15]

This was his last word on the subject — to live decently and amicably with a wife, as the best of a bad business.

It is useless to moralize the point. Chesterfield's attitude on this question, like most of his opinions, reflected the mode of thought current among the emancipated wits of the age, such, for example, as Pope. It was one of the many similarities between the Earl and his friend the poet. They echo each other reciprocally, and both echo the prevailing cynicism.

> Most women have no characters at all [rhymed Pope].
> Matter too soft a lasting mark to bear,
> And best distinguished by black, brown, or fair.

> Woman and Fool [he remarks further] are two hard things to hit
> For true No-meaning puzzles more than wit.[16]

And the current satires, in poetry or prose, abound in like sentiments. This was the somber lining to the high-flown gallantry of the day, and perhaps sincerity lay somewhere in between.

One thinks of poor Melusina, the financial milch cow, with a kind of pity. To be sure, she was homely and middle-aged and spoke bad English; to be sure, also, she had the honor of belonging to a famous man; but somewhere in her vague, docilely corseted heart, there must have been an ache until time and resignation smoothed it away. Married to Lord Chesterfield, the ever gracious and inscrutable, his compact little person as hard and scintillating as his diamond buckles, the master of cutting epigram and of studied eloquence, the social paragon, and she only a convenience of which he was slightly ashamed. Did she deceive herself about him at first? Did she preen before the mirror and put on her jewels and rouge and patches, and then wait long hours, to be greeted at last by his finished smile and unrevealing eyes? Married to Lord Chesterfield! Let any feminine reader imagine herself in that predicament.

Melusina had soon more to complain of than simple neglect. The hours of dereliction at Grosvenor Square might not have been quite so forlorn if it had been merely the House of Lords or even White's that claimed the Earl's devotion. Madame du Bouchet was no secret and could be accepted with a pinch of snuff as part and parcel of the past. A former bourgeois mistress, now grown stale and quasi-respectable as a mother, need not give a moment's concern to Lady Chesterfield. With her natural kindness of heart, Melusina received la Bouchet in her drawing room,[17] accepted la Bouchet's son and apparently befriended him. But a fashionable liaison, one with a reigning beauty of rank, was a different matter. The slighting implications of that could not be shrugged off. The lines of a poem ascribed to Lord Chesterfield became a popular song, and the affair identified with it was common property to the polite of Bath and London. It ran as follows:

> When Fanny, blooming fair,
>   First caught my ravished sight,
> Struck with her shape and air,
>   I felt a strange delight
> Whilst eagerly I gaz'd
>   Admiring every part,
> And every feature prais'd
>   She stole into my heart.
>
> In her bewitching eyes
>   Ten thousand loves appear;
> There Cupid basking lies,
>   His shafts are hoarded there;
> Her blooming cheeks are dyed
>   With colour all their own,
> Excelling far the pride
>   Of roses newly blown.
>
> Her well-turn'd limbs confess
>   The lucky hand of Jove;
> Her features all express
>   The beauteous queen of love:
> What flames my nerves invade,
>   When I behold the breast
> Of that too-charming Maid
>   Rise, suing to be pressed.
>
> Venus round Fanny's waist,
>   Has her own cestus bound,
> With guardian cupids graced,
>   Who dance the circle round.
> How happy must he be
>   Who shall her zone unloose!
> That bliss to all but me,
>   May heaven and she refuse.[18]

If Chesterfield actually wrote this gay lyric, we might forgive him a good deal; for why, after all, need his wife's bleakness as she read it, concern us? But unfortunately it must be admitted that one of the Earl's well-known foibles was not to disclaim literary productions of merit that were attributed to him; and although the actual author of "Fanny, blooming fair" appears to have been an obscure dramatist by the name of Thomas Philips, his lordship permitted it to be included with other of his verses in Dodsley's collection.[19] On internal evidence, besides, the poem appears a bit too good for Chesterfield's humdrum poetic vein, unless we may assume that for once the alchemy of love transmuted it. But the authorship of "Fanny" is a minor matter. It suffices that the poem became identified with Chesterfield and with the charming belle, the Lady Frances Shirley.*

She was a younger daughter of the Earl of Ferrers, lived at Twickenham, and belonged to Pope's coterie.[20] She was twelve years younger than Chesterfield. No precautions were taken to conceal, nor were any gestures of secrecy made in regard to their mutual philandering, which was as open as the noonday sun. Melusina, as usual, might just as well not have existed. Lord Lovel, he of "the King can do no wrong" epigram, like Chesterfield middle-aged, and a somewhat humorous rival, informed the Earl of Essex that

*Four months before his marriage, an apparently authentic poem by Chesterfield appeared in the *Gentleman's Magazine*, May, 1733. It was probably also intended for Lady Fanny. It reads as follows, and is the happiest product of his poetic vein:

> Mistaken fair, lay Sherlock by,
> His doctrine is deceiving;
> For whilst he teaches us to die
> He cheats us of our living.
>
> To die's a lesson we shall know
> Too soon, without a master,
> Then let us only study now
> How we may live the faster.
>
> To live's to love: to bless, be blessed
> With mutual inclination:
> Share then my ardour in your breast,
> And kindly meet my passion.
>
> But if thus bless'd, I may not live,
> And pity you deny,
> To me at least your Sherlock give,
> 'Tis I must learn to die.

Lady Fanny was quite lost to him. "That foul fiend Chesterfield has bewitch'd her and, under pretence of serving me, has intirely defeated me and is in full possession of the Lady's soul; as for her body, that is so glorifyed that I presume none of our grosser mortal substance can ever think of that. . . . I find great ease in . . . tiring all my acquaintance with my grief. My Rival triumphs so publickly that I hear of nothing from London but his success, all Summer, parties by water, rides in Bushy park, etc.; and Old Bitches begin to be censorious, which the nice Lady however stands, and, since she herself knows there is no harm, dos not mind what others say." [21] And a little later: "That beauty you think so cold shows herself warmer than any Lady in England, but not with me; all I can flatter myself with at most is to have been her dunkerer; I attack't (tho' not boldly) in front; dazzled by her beauty I could scarce approach, while that sly Chesterfield, like the toad in Milton, came privily behind and fastened on her ear and that way found access to her heart, the descent from which to her — is pretty easy, but how that fort still resists I know not, but when the town is taken, the castle seldom holds out long. In short they live together, ride together, walk, go by water, etc. etc., in the face of the whole world, and this cold, shy beauty as you call'd her bears up, I do assure you, more than ever I yet saw either married or unmarried Lady. The great trouble they have is that when they ride out his Lordship is forced to stand on his stirrups while she makes her back ake with stooping to hear him." [22] These extracts reflect the gossip of polite and elegant London.

There were surmises at the time, and there have been many since, as to the nature of the intercourse between Chesterfield and Lady Fanny. It began not later than 1735 [23] and continued for many years. In his poem "Isabella or the Morning," which appeared considerably later,[24] Sir Charles Hanbury Williams, referring to Chesterfield and Fanny, could still make the lovelorn Lovel complain of

> That eternal whisper which begun
> Ten years ago, and never will be done,
> For though you know he sees her every day,
> Still he has something ever new to say.[25]

And when Chesterfield resigned his office of Secretary of State in 1748 and retired from politics, he procured Lady Frances a pension from the government of £800 a year.[26]

So much is fact, the rest is speculation. Horace Walpole spoke roundly of a long amour. Lord Lovel's surmises were definite enough. Moreover, the Earl himself has left no doubt regarding his attitude toward women. On the other hand, Lady Bolingbroke considered it a platonic friendship,[27] and there remains a shrewd suspicion that in affairs of sex the Earl liked rather the reputation than the fact. Indeed, his advancing age and chronic ill-health favored a platonic friendship. Writing to Robert Nugent in 1739, he asserts that far from thinking now of giving existence to others, he had much ado to preserve his own.[28] And, on the whole, increasing familiarity with the eighteenth century leads to the opinion that much of its scandal was a matter rather of conventional loose talk, social gossip, and pretense than of actuality. Chesterfield's affair with Frances Shirley may have had its more passionate phase, but for the most part it was certainly a case of prolonged philandering — or call it friendship, if the implication of middle-age *douceurs* be consistent with that term.

The question is of importance because of the light it throws on Chesterfield's conduct. To understand the art of life which he elaborated so completely for his son, it is necessary to know how he himself lived. But from the standpoint of Lady Chesterfield, the discussion might well be considered academic. As Lady Bolingbroke shrewdly pointed out, "Madame de Chesterfield should be more wounded by a Platonic love-affair than by any other. One has no right to be jealous save of preferences in sentiment." All the conjugal fidelity on earth and all the graces will not compensate for the more fundamental desertion. And this was to be her lot. She would endure it, would accept what he gave for lack of better, would prove uncomplaining, faithful, and submissive. But, on one hand, the long habit of years, and on the other, serenity, decorum and impeccable politeness have their worth. When, for the last time, to the indignation of her friends, he had neglected her in his will, she could still write to Dayrolles of that "very dear and very worthy man, my late Lord Chesterfield," and could refer to "his merit and his rare talents." [29] Such is the temper of old age. Of what importance, at the vesper hour, are the heartaches of noon: Frances Shirley and the others (for there were others), Madame de Monconseil, Madame de Berkenrode,[30] the handsome Miss Pulteney who,

Horace Walpole says, broke her heart for him,[31] and the other flirts or bluestockings of the past? * Wind-strewn ashes.

As for Lady Fanny, the face of her old admirer must have been a study when he heard of her conversion to Methodism in 1749. A thin smile, raised eyebrows, a pinch of snuff. What delightful hours they had spent in their "eternal whisper," what nuances of sentiment, what palpitating delicacies! And now sanctification, egad! After that she fades from his biography.

The railers had their sport of her. "Saint Frances" begins to figure in Walpole's letters. She "has chosen this way of bestowing the dregs of her beauty upon Jesus Christ," he wrote to Mann. . . . "The Methodists love your big sinners as proper subjects to work upon." [32] Or in the *Twickenham Register*, he puts her to rhyme:

> Here Fanny "ever blooming fair,"
> Ejaculates the graceful prayer:
> And 'scaped from sense, with nonsense smit,
> For Whitfield's cant, leaves Stanhope's wit.

The same scoffer gives her a casual death notice in 1778. "Fanny, blooming fair, died here yesterday of a stroke of palsy. She had lost her memory for some years, and remembered nothing but her beauty and not her Methodism. Being confined with only servants, she was continually lamenting, 'I to be abandoned that all the world used to adore!' She was seventy-two." [33]

Let this lament be her epitaph: "I to be abandoned that all the world used to adore!"

---

* Chesterfield's admiration for Lady Hervey, the former Molly Lepel, was well known. Possibly Melusina was jealous of her, if that construction can be put on the following remark to his son, July 8, 1751: "*A propos* of her [Lady Hervey]; remember, when you are with me, not to mention her but when you and I are quite alone, for reasons which I will tell you when we meet; but this is only between you and me; and I desire that you will not so much as hint it to her, or to anybody else."

CHAPTER XIII
Drinking the Waters

PERHAPS Chesterfield would have defined gallantry as the nosegay and marriage as the underwriting of life. But though decorative or useful, they were not for him at any time absorbingly essential. Women, those "agreeable trifles," exerted no compulsion upon his will. He was never a Casanova. The society of men in pleasure or business; a mixed society of well-bred people assembling for the supreme sport of intelligent conversation; books on one hand, cards on the other, and, in between, the pageantry of the world: these things made up the truly important objects of living. In this chapter we will glance at the environment and at certain aspects of his social career, to establish, if possible, the effects these may have had upon his philosophy.

In the first place it should be noted that, the reverse of effeminate, he was par excellence a man's man, a clubman, with headquarters at White's and his sanctum at the gaming tables. Other clubs were associated with him — the Rumpsteak, for instance, a political organization of the titled Patriots, which met at the King's Arms, Pall Mall, during the parliamentary sessions of 1734 and 1735 [1] — but White's remained the favorite resort. He called it the "established church." [2] There, for hazard or faro, assembled the curiously mixed sporting membership of that distinguished club's infancy. It had not quite lost its first tradition as White's Chocolate House, where even a well-groomed gunman, expert in cards and highways, might attend for the mere payment of the charges. [3] It had grown, to be sure, more exclusive than this, but was still not inclined to probe too deeply into the antecedents of occasional visitors who were superficially genteel and at the same time addicts of chance. For, as chocolate house or club, White's

represented the inner shrine of gambling and high play, London's
most famous altar to this special vice. How many ancestral manors
and farms have been dealt away in sessions at White's! How many
panic-cold hearts concealed by the prescribed smile has that place
contained! The misery of families, the obscure sacrifices imposed
on women and children, has paid the scot of many an evening's
glorious fever there. And how often has the door at White's, opening upon the dawn in St. James's Street, closed finally upon a
member of the club returning to his apartment for his final venture, suicide! You could bet on anything for any sum at White's
— on a man's death or marriage or prowess in this or that, on which
of two women would bear children first, on which of two men
would survive the other — and old betting books still record the
fantastic wagers. Lord Mountford and Sir John Bland made bets
on whether Beau Nash would outlive Colley Cibber, but both Sir
John and his lordship had blown out their brains before Nash
and Cibber died. Play was terribly deep. Lord Carlisle lost £10,000
at the club one night, a great figure for the day; Charles Fox lost
thousands there; Chesterfield, though restored to affluence by
Melusina's dowry, crippled his personal fortune there.[4]

It is worth noting that rationalism is apt to explode at one point
or another. Chesterfield had no god but his reason, and that failed
him in this particular. Self-controlled in eating, drinking, and
women, unruffled by passion, undisturbed by any enthusiasm, he
made an utter fool of himself over cards. At that one point reason
with all her precepts was ignored, and he capitulated openly to
folly. For he was not even an adroit gambler. His friends made
merry on the subject. Pope in "A Poem" in 1740 refers to

> Chesterfield, who speaks so well and writes,
> Whom (saving Walter) every sharper bites.

Horace Walpole relates that a German baron, a noted cheat, in
prison for debt at Bath, used to be released by his creditors when
the Earl reached town, as that was the best chance they had of
recovering their money. Although quite aware of the baron's
crookedness, Chesterfield could not resist playing with him.[5] And
Maty's much-quoted anecdote will be recalled of how, on one
occasion at Bath, the Earl warned a young gentleman against
cardsharpers with whom he himself at once proceeded to play.[6]

It was "no less disgraceful to his understanding than detrimental to his reputation," scolded Maty elsewhere,[7] and in still another place he called Chesterfield's passion for gaming "the least excusable of all, especially when not fostered by want, or accompanied by skill," and one that in every period of his life "was equally detrimental to his character and his fortune. It engaged him every night," continued the Doctor, "in the company of people, with whom he would have been ashamed to have been seen at any other time. He knew, and despised, yet could not shun, them."[8] It was apparently this vice that prejudiced George I against him and delayed the marriage with Melusina.[9] "He gamed away his credit" with Melusina's mother, the immensely wealthy Duchess of Kendal, who for that reason overlooked him in her will.[10] Moreover, he frequently admitted the weakness in letters to his son, but, so to speak, with a sigh of resignation, as of a foible about which nothing could be done.[11]

Such supineness on the part of a man like Chesterfield, zealot of the will and apostle of common sense, is little short of amazing. It would seem to indicate that will and common sense are subject to limitations. He could lecture his son and godson upon the evils of gambling, but the homily rang false, because of the unregenerated homilist. If forbidden the exercise of any nobler passion, irresponsible nature protests against the strait jacket of prudence by venting itself on the grosser plane.

Of course, apart from the excitement of deep play, gambling is at least the foster child of vanity. On his own admission, he contracted the habit when a mere youth at The Hague, because it was the polite thing to do.[12] The bravura of the gaming table, the swagger of the clubroom, nourished it. A sporting attitude and flourish, the gallant reputation cheaply acquired at cards, were strong temptations to a man who relished social applause. No more fitting stage for the fine gesture or polished epigram could be found than the card table with the flashing of lace cuffs and jeweled hands above the pyramids of gold. "Crowds," said Maty, "flocked round the gaming table," and "while his pocket was picked, the applause, which the repeated flashes of his wit drew from all around, seemed to make him abundant amends for his losses."[13]

This is understandable enough, but as the years creep upon him a clubman, however witty, runs the risk of becoming a fixture or

perhaps even a little stale. After retiring from politics, Chesterfield, who during his brief tenure of office had refrained from cards,
returned to White's and, as Walpole puts it, lived there "gaming and
pronouncing witticisms amongst the boys of quality." [14] In time
the witticisms began to creak a little, savoring of premeditation.
It began to be expected that his lordship, upon rising from play
and passing through the supper room, would utter the daily joke
for fashionable London. One of the boys of quality, George Selwyn,
lampooned the regularity of the Earl's effusions with customary
bluntness, and the jibe reached Chesterfield's ears. It must have
been a bitter moment for him, a straw that showed clearly how the
wind was blowing: the end even of his supremacy at White's, the
bursting of his most cherished bubble. Walpole declares that he
never returned to the club again. [15]

Thus, by no means the least important element in his life, but
rather characteristic of it, was that atmosphere of club and gaming
room where, as veteran cardplayer, he watched the succession of
fashionable games go by: brag and crimp, basset and hazard, commerce, quadrille and whist. [16] Dissector of human nature as he was,
he found here, among other things, an excellent observation point
for certain aspects of it. Meanwhile, increasing invalidism, by sending him on the circuit of health resorts and gaming rooms through
England and even to the Continent, forcibly widened his horizon
still further.

It was "forcibly," because, though in the end resigned to his
yearly sojourns at Bath and Tunbridge, or Cheltenham or Spa,
he would not of his own choice have left the vicinity of London,
except for Paris. As we have seen elsewhere, he was fanatically
urban in his tastes and habits, a characteristic that he shared with
most of his eminent contemporaries. London, he declared, was the
only possible abode for a gentleman. An intense absorption in
humanity with all its infinite facets, social, artistic, ethical, and
scientific, typified the age; and national capitals, the seats of courts
and academies, clubs, parliaments and exchanges, provided the
richest means of satisfaction. The only difference between Samuel
Johnson and Chesterfield in this particular was that the former
would have been unhappy outside of London and that the latter,
a thorough cosmopolitan, would have been equally happy in Paris. [17]

What Chesterfield's malady was, that drove him twice a year

into exile from the city, is difficult at this distance precisely to
determine. Likely enough, there was rather a complication of ailments: the general collapse of a constitution never robust and
prematurely overtaxed. He had been ill of fever, possibly malaria,
at The Hague, and this had been followed in London by a dropsical
condition of the legs. The effects of this illness in turn lingered on;
for subsequent to the Dutch embassy he was never a wholly well
man. Some form of gout or rheumatism he had, of course, as had
most of his generation; but, as an illness peculiar with him, he became increasingly subject to attacks of dizziness followed by extreme weakness, which, as time passed, seem to have run parallel
with a deafness that at last grew almost complete. It will be recalled
that his father had become deaf at an even earlier age, so that this
and the accompanying symptoms were perhaps hereditary. At all
events, after the age of thirty-eight he began a search for lost
health that lasted for the rest of his life and, as time went on,
deepened into confirmed invalidism. Naturally, in the circumstances, there remained for a man of means and leisure no other
resource than "to drink the waters." We may find specified reme-
dies sprinkled through his correspondence, such as vomits, asses'
milk, alkalized mercury and Burgundy; [18] but the main treatment
for his ailments, as for all other ailments at that time, was "to
drink the waters."

In general, the beau monde of Hanoverian England required a
great deal of patching and purging. Ignorance of hygiene, lack of
exercise, excessive indulgence in meat and drink, the amazing ineptitude of medical treatment, supplied sickness enough; but, if real
ills were lacking, there were plenty of imaginary ones. It was a
valetudinarian age, a period much afflicted by nervous disorders
and shadowed by insanity. We have already recalled the prevalence
of suicide at that time, and the words "spleen" and "vapors" are
among the most typical of the eighteenth-century vocabulary. For
all this mass of real or fanciful ill-health, for the apoplectic and
alcoholic, for the gouty and graveled, and even for the depressed
or bored, there remained one universal nostrum equally appropriate for all — "to drink the waters."

In this prescription merciful Providence no doubt protected the
beau monde from its physicians, who would else have bolused and
bled it into extinction. But by virtue of the waters, invalidism be-

came almost a pleasure and ill-health a pastime. The waters could do no harm at least, and they certainly did much good. Moreover, they provided an excuse for superbly fashionable gathering places.

It would be absurd to pity Chesterfield's exile at the Bath or other health resorts too much. It is true that at times he lamented with David: "Woe is me that I am constrained to dwell with Meshec, and to have my habitation among the tents of Kedar"; [19] but the spas provided a diversity of amusements and social contacts, a correct and elegant milieu, second only to London. He would find himself inevitably among friends and acquaintances, and perhaps with this advantage over London itself, that there was ample leisure there and greater opportunity for gossip.[20] Even at this remove, the buzz of it reaches us in the lines of such a letter as the following to his old friend Lady Suffolk. It represents perfectly the come-and-go, the graceful triviality of health-resort life, which, after all, has changed little but its costume in the last two hundred years.

MADAM [he wrote],

A general history of the Bath since you left it, together with the particular memoirs of Amoretto's * life and conversation, are matters of too great importance to want any introduction. Therefore, without further preamble, I send you the very minutes, just as I have them down to help my own memory; the variety of events, and the time necessary to observe them, not having yet allowed me the leisure to put them in that style and order in which I propose they shall hereafter appear in public.

Oct. 27. — Little company appeared at the pump; those that were there drank the waters of affliction for the departure of Lady Suffolk and Mrs. Blount.† What was said of them both I need not tell you; for it was so obvious to those that said it, that it cannot be less so to those that deserve it. Amoretto went upon Lansdowne to evaporate his grief for the loss of his Parthenissa, ‡ in memory of whom (and the wind being very cold into the bargain) he tied his handkerchief over his hat and looked very sadly.

In the evening the usual tea-table met at Lyndsey's, the two

---

* The Honorable Robert Sawyer Herbert, brother of the ninth Earl of Pembroke, a middle-aged beau and mutual friend, jovially chaffed but apparently much liked by Chesterfield and Lady Suffolk.
† Martha Blount, Pope's friend.
‡ Mrs. Blount.

principal persons excepted; * who, it was hoped, were then got safe to Newbury. Amoretto's main action was at our table; but, episodically, he took pieces of bread and butter, and cups of tea, at about ten others. He laughed his way through the girls, out of the long room into the little one,† where he *tallied* till he swore, and swore till he went home, and probably some time afterwards. The Countess of Burlington, ‡ in the absence of her Royal Highness, held a circle at Hayes's, where she lost a favourite snuff-box, but unfortunately kept her temper.

Oct. 28. — Breakfast was at Lady Anne's, where Amoretto was with difficulty prevailed upon to eat and drink as much as he had a mind to. At night he was observed to be pleasant with the girls, and with less restraint than usual, which made some people surmise that he comforted himself for the Lady Suffolk and Parthenissa, by the liberty and impunity their absence gave him.

Oct. 29. — Amoretto breakfasted incognito, but appeared at the ball in the evening, when he distinguished himself with his *bons mots*. He was particularly pleased to compare the two Miss Towardins, who are very short and were dancing, to a couple of totums set a-spinning. The justness and liveliness of this image struck Mr. Marriott to such a degree, that he begged leave of the author to put it off for his own, which was granted him. He declared afterwards to several people, that Mr. Herbert beat the whole world at similes.

Oct. 30. — Being his Majesty's birthday, little company appeared in the morning, all being resolved to look well at night. Mr. Herbert dined at Mrs. Walter's with young Mr. Barnard, whom he rallied to death. Nash § gave a ball at Lyndsey's, where Mrs. Tate appeared for the first time, and was noticed by Mr. Herbert. He wore gold laced clothes on the occasion, and looked so fine, that, standing by chance in the middle of the dancers, he was taken by many at a distance for a gilt garland. He concluded his evening, as usual, with basset and blasphemy.

Oct. 31. — Amoretto breakfasted at Lady Anne's, where, being now more easy and familiar, he called for a half-peck loaf and a pound of butter — let off a great many ideas; and had he had the same inclination to have let anything else, would doubtless have done it.

* Lady Suffolk and Mrs. Blount.
† The card room.
‡ Chesterfield's half-aunt, Lady Dorothy Savile, daughter of the Marquis of Halifax by his first wife (Dobrée's note).
§ Beau Nash.

The Countess of Burlington bespoke the play,* as you may see by the enclosed original piece; the audience consisted of seventeen souls, of whom I made one.

Nov. 1. — Amoretto took a vomit in the morning, and then with a clear and excellent stomach dined with me, and went to the ball at night, where Mrs. Hamilton chiefly engrossed him.

Mrs. Jones gave Sir Humphrey Monoux pain with Mr. Browne, which gave Sir Humphrey the toothache, but Mr. Jones has since made up matters between them.

Nov. 2. — . . . Mrs. Hamilton bespoke the play at night, which we all interested ourselves so much to fill, that there were as many people turned back as let in: it was so hot that the Countess of Burlington could not stay it out.

You now see, by this week's journal, how much you have lost by leaving the Bath so soon; at least I can assure you we feel what we lost by your leaving it before us. . . . This day fortnight I hope to have the pleasure of finding you at St. James's, much the better for the Bath; where, over a hot roll with Mrs. Blount, I propose giving you next week's journal by word of mouth.

After having troubled you so long already, it is only in compliance to the form of letters that I add so unnecessary and so known a truth, as the assurance of the respect and attachment with which I am, Madam, yours, etc.†

There is something eternal in all this, the classic expression of watering-place temper, with its private jokes, short but vivid intimacies, and magnified minutiae. But it will be allowed that Chesterfield's regimen did not weigh heavily on his mind.

He became forever identified with the gay little capital of Somerset. The house he occupied in tranquil Pierrepont Street still retains its graceful outlines. He was one of the first governors of the Hospital.[21] His name is associated with that of Beau Nash, whom he lampooned, with Gainsborough, who painted his portrait here, with the Duchess of Marlborough, Allen of Priors Park, William Pitt, another famous invalid; with all the belles and gentlemen,

---

* I.e., engaged the entire playhouse — a dingy, small building — for the evening. *Cf.* Sitwell, *Bath,* p. 238.

† To Lady Suffolk, Nov. 2, 1734. He never again, however, called at Lady Suffolk's apartment in St. James's Palace. She returned from Bath to such obvious marks of her royal lover's indifference that on November 12 she resigned her employment as Mistress of the Robes to the Queen, and retired from court, "which makes a great noise." *Marchmont Papers,* vol. ii, pp. 55–56.

statesmen and adventurers, who passed through the Pump Room during forty years. It is at Bath that we find him together with Pope at the end of the poet's life entertaining him *en malade* and for the sake of his company putting up even with the garlic prescribed by Pope's physician.[22] It was here in the autumn of 1738 that he received Their Royal Highnesses the Prince and Princess of Wales, now in open rebellion to the King and visiting Bath at the Earl's suggestion in order to hold a conference with the leaders of the Opposition. Dr. Maty puts on his gaudiest prose for the occasion. Beau Nash built an obelisk in its honor. "Bath," says Dr. Maty, "was the spot fixed upon for that purpose [the conference]. This elegant town much resembles the Bajae of the luxurious Romans. Like that, it is distinguished by its water, its magnificence, and its pleasures. It is there that, twice a year, health, diversions, politics, and play, attract what is called the best company. . . . The royal and much-beloved pair received the homage of the numerous concourse of people of every rank, who flocked thither to make use of a liberty they were restrained from in the capital. Sumptuous entertainments were given by the corporation, under the direction of the famous Nash. Lord Chesterfield did the honours of the place, and his servants were employed to attend."[23] Only the shrewd Lady Mary Wortley Montagu, who was present, casts a shadow upon the éclat of the ceremonies. She found that Chesterfield was playing "an under-part in a second-rate theatre," and adds with a sneer, "to me that have always been an humble spectator, it appears odd, to see so few desirous to quit the stage, though time and infirmities have disabled them from making a tolerable figure there."[24] One suspects that the hatred for Pope included his friends.

The quaint, gray city of today — so lovely and unchanging an heirloom of Hanoverian England — still reflects Lord Chesterfield's personality. Here the frivolity and coarseness of that age, washed off, as it were, by time, have left its imperishable essence in decorous house fronts and serene squares, leisurely streets and sunset vistas. His life in a real, but elusive, sense has contributed to this impression: a neat, smiling, sensible impression without a trace of grandeur but of pleasing harmony. The Circus and Royal Crescent rather than the modern pump room recall him. They are not so much architectural groupings as a composite spiritual portrait of an age and of the men and women in it. As these are, so were they, so was the eighteenth century. The thought lies near that such earth-bound spirits as frequented Bath in its great period still find a refuge there from the uncongenial vastness of eternity, still haunt this tiny remnant of the world they knew, fearful of the time when at length it also will have been swept away. And surely if any place, enthu-siastically lived in, is ever revisited by departed spirits, it must be this pleasant town so representative of the life and pleasures, thought and death of an epoch. Perhaps in this tenuous realm of lingering shadows, Lord Chesterfield still pronounces the inevitable epi-gram. . . .

Bath had two seasons, the autumn and spring, and as far as can be judged from the headings of his letter, Chesterfield regularly sojourned there during both. In summer it was the turn of Tun-bridge Wells,[25] which Beau Nash similarly ruled as Master of Cere-monies. But the Earl's attendance here was less inevitable than at Bath. Cheltenham might be taken as a substitute. And twice he deserted England entirely for Belgium.

It was on one such occasion in the spring of 1741 that he passed through Calais, Dunkirk, Lille, and Ghent, and broke the journey at Brussels, where he spent several days with his old acquaintance Voltaire, who read aloud to him some passages from the newly written *Mahomet*.[26] We can picture the two of them, so curiously alike in mental temper, tasting, in some high-ceilinged drawing room, the rich delight of polished style and brilliant satire. The English lord, more conservative if not less skeptical than the French-man, deplored the latter's attacks on religion as undermining the foundations of morality. Such satire, he thought, made for disorder and was hence pragmatically bad. They disagreed doubtless, with mutual compliments, however, and Chesterfield went on by coach to Aix-la-Chapelle, to drink the waters there.

These, he informed his son, were very warm and very disgusting and smelled like rotten eggs. He found the company Germanic and heavy,[27] and after several weeks moved on to Spa for a month and a half.[28] According to Maty, it was at this more cosmopolitan water-ing place that he met a Prussian diplomat, who, by reporting to Berlin his encomiums of the young king Frederick, already promi-nent, but not yet the Great, evoked a corresponding esteem for the Earl on the part of that monarch — an esteem productive of some

handsome compliments and of some useful civilities to Chesterfield's son when the latter appeared at Potsdam.[29]

By the end of August he was sniffing blissfully the air of Paris,
and exclaiming over it. "A most magnificent town," he wrote,
"not near so big as London, but much finer; the houses being
much larger, and all built of stone . . . a prodigious number of expensive buildings, and useful and charitable foundations, such as
libraries, hospitals, schools, etc. And the people here are well-
bred . . . they are not awkwardly bashful and ashamed, like the
English; but easily civil, without ceremony. Though they are very
gay and lively, they have attention to everything, and always mind
what they are about." [30]

But for the moment this was no more than a glimpse. He was
already posting south to spend three days with Bolingbroke, who
had returned to his French exile at Argeville.[31] Then on through
Dijon, Lyons, Vienne, and down the Rhone by boat to Avignon.[32]
His health, he asserted, needed baking "by the sun of Provence
and Languedoc" [33] — which may have been true, though Sir Robert
Walpole's secret service discovered another and less avowable
reason for visiting the City of the Popes. Indeed, his proceedings
there required a rather elaborate camouflage, and by a legalist
might technically have been construed as treason; for it seems fairly
evident that his primary object at Avignon was to secure the Pretender's mandate to the Jacobites of the House of Commons to act
solidly with the Opposition for the overthrow of Walpole. Negotiations for this were carried on with the Pretender's chief agent,
the Duke of Ormonde, a distant relative, at whose house Chesterfield was entertained.[34]

They had not met since the latter's boyhood, when the Duke had
been one of the nonpareils of London, at the height of his splendor.
Now, as aged and middle-aged men, they met in this arid Provençal
town, the shabby refuge of exiles. It is a curious episode in the Earl's
decorous career — these days in the Jacobite camp at Avignon, over
fruit and wine of an evening with the ruined, homeless Ormonde.
It may be, he felt uncomfortable and strained. Some dramatist
might find it amusing to recreate their conversation.

After a view of the Riviera, Toulon, and Marseilles, he returned
to Paris, put up at the Hôtel de Luxembourg, Rue des Petits Augustins,[35] and spent a refreshing month in the salons of Madame de

Tencin and Madame de Monconseil, with his friends Fontenelle, Crébillon, and Montesquieu. He was no longer the little Stanhope of twenty-five years before, but an internationally celebrated name, a figure in parliament, a great lord, something of a littérateur, above all acceptable in France as a noted wit and master of the graces. True, he had no longer the health of youth, and his gallantries must be largely verbal, and he stooped somewhat, and his teeth were discolored.* But then what manners! What address! What an air accompanied the sparkling of his diamond star! He had a good time in Paris. Most of his French correspondence dates from this visit.

So, half for pleasure and half for health, but with an eye still on politics, he frequented the watering places of England and the Continent. One likes to think of him especially in the little village of Spa, installed at the Court of London or the Golden Sun, treated with the deference due his rank, but mingling affably with the genteel throng of Bobelins depicted by Baron von Pöllnitz in his diverting book.[36] One pictures him at the Pouhon spring in one of the open squares of the little town, handing, with inimitable grace, glasses to fair invalids, abounding in perfect French and well-turned phrases, the cynosure of observers who would delight in the elegance of his manner and treasure his pleasantries. There would be dangling from the lapel of his coat one of the ivory dials that registered the number of glasses absorbed. He would distinguish some lady or ladies (Miss Ann Pitt and the Countess of Cardigan were at Spa during his visit in 1741[37]) with superlative attentions, escort them shopping for lacquered ware, a specialty of the village, inspect the display of tables pictured with scenes from Ovid's *Metamorphoses*, the quadrille boxes, watch cases, dessert baskets, snuffboxes, and would present the ladies with some trinket they fancied. Lacquered canes, inscribed with gallant and perhaps naughty devices, were especially in evidence and a prolific source of repartee.

There were other springs than that of Pouhon, however, which lay outside the town and formed a goal of interesting excursions

---

* We have already noted Chesterfield's association with Montesquieu. He was in correspondence with Crébillon. He imported that author's *Sopha* and had it put on sale at White's in 1742 (*cf.* Walpole's *Letters*). On this visit to Paris he seems to have heard Fontenelle read two of his comedies aloud (to Madame de Boccage, Jan. 14, 1751).

over roads rough enough and through country wild enough to give the ladies a flutter of adventure: the springs of the Geronstère, the Souvinère, Tonnelet, and Barissart, each with its own properties and virtues endlessly discussed. Then, too, in Spa itself there were places of fashionable promenade: the Four O'Clock Meadow, the Seven O'Clock Meadow, the garden of the Capuchin monastery. One reads a good deal of orchestras playing here and there, of the Ladies' Assembly, of frequent dances. Drinking the waters at Spa in those days was a fairly strenuous and regimented process: up at daybreak, assembly *en déshabillé* at the Pouhon spring at four A.M.; at five the departure of excursionists for other springs; at nine a recessional in order to dress; at ten, mass for the devout; at half-past eleven the coffee house, if it rained, otherwise a promenade in the streets; dinner at half-past twelve; formal calls or the Ladies' Assembly at two; at four o'clock the play or a stroll in the Capuchins' garden or Four O'Clock Meadow; supper at six; the Seven O'Clock Meadow at seven; and then wigs off, stays unlaced, and nightcaps on; not a sound in the streets, save on gala occasions after a ball.*

The moral of this for our purpose may be summed up in the words of one of the ladies in Pöllnitz's book: "Methinks," says she, "here's Europe in her undress; I see it, as it were, on a great stage, and am prodigiously delighted with the comedy. . . . Nothing can better express the miscellany of good and bad qualities which are here exposed to view, and open a vast field of reflection to philosophical tempers. . . . I regard the season of the waters as a most useful book to those who have a mind to study the world by reading the world itself; because these places of assembly are an epitome of the most considerable parts of the known world." [38]

Lord Chesterfield would have agreed with this observation. At least, Spa or the Bath represented a cross section of the only world worth knowing from his standpoint. And if so, he had leisure to study it from every angle during his long years of invalidism.

It was not only here or in Parisian salons, in clubrooms or parliament, that he watched the ever-similar and yet ever-changing

* This applies strictly to his first, and, it would seem, his most pleasant visit. When he returned in 1754, deafness and invalidism had made life a burden, and he found the place and the company "detestable." Letters to Dayrolles, June 4, 12, 1754, and Chenevix, June 15, 1754. But even in 1741 his first impression of Spa was that it was a "damned disagreeable place." To Nugent, June 20, 1741.

kaleidoscope of mankind. Essentially an extrovert, concerned in
the panorama about him, any place of social concourse attracted
him. Even the slightly promiscuous pleasure gardens had their
charm.

Ranelagh, which was formally opened on May 24, 1742, is too
much a puppet booth of Chesterfield's world, too much a microcosm of its personalities and interests, to be disregarded in any study
of his life. As Beresford Chancellor points out, the shape of its
famous Rotunda "somehow bulks in the background of all the
social annals of the day, and forms, as it were, the characteristic
hallmark of the fashionable life of over half a century." Around it
lay the gardens, a Canaletto with Chinese House and Venetian
Temple, lined with an avenue of trees — gardens where one could
saunter on a summer's night under colored lanterns to the accompaniment of an orchestra playing Handel or Arne. But the Rotunda
was the heart and focus of Ranelagh: an amazing structure, a
hundred and fifty feet wide, five hundred and fifty-five feet around,
faced on the outside with an arcade and gallery, lined on the inside
with two tiers of boxes each capable of seating eight people and
with a total capacity of eight hundred and thirty-two. Refreshments were served in the boxes, which were decorated with lamps
and pictures. In the center of the floor, around and between the
pillars supporting the ceiling, lay a further seating space with chairs
and tables, and between them and the lowest tier of boxes, which
were level with the floor, extended an ample, circular promenade,
where people could stroll around beneath the scrutiny and the
lorgnettes of the seated spectators. On one side was reserved a
stand for the orchestra with an organ behind it. "The whole of
the interior of the Rotunda was elaborately painted and gilded,"
writes Chancellor, "and from the ceiling, which was tinted in olive-
green and across which a rainbow flashed its varied colours, hung
a number of chandeliers suspended by long ropes from the roof.
Entrance to the place was by four Doric doorways, and sixty windows above afforded ample light." [39]

Picture this Rotunda on one of the concert evenings,* or better
still during one of the frequent masquerades or ridottos, such, for
instance, as that occasion recorded by Horace Walpole where a

* These were Mondays, Wednesdays, and Fridays. The concert began at
seven and continued till eleven or twelve.

traffic jam of coaches on the way to Ranelagh lasted thirty-six minutes.[40] The King is there "incognito" in a red damask box, and the Duke of Cumberland and all the nobility and all the fashionables and all the would-be fashionables and cits in their best clothes, who paid the entrance charge for a glimpse of so much grandeur. With the glittering of chandeliers, glow of lamps, and flashing of rainbow colors, the place must have resembled internally an illuminated beehive, in front of whose brilliant cells the eternal promenade went on.

If it is a night of costume, there are Shepherds and Shepherdesses, Pierrots and Columbines, Punches and Harlequins. In the cool air outside, as one writer describes it, "festoons of coloured lamps hang down from the branches of trees that shade every walk; and beneath their canopy, bright eyes make answer to the tale which is seldom told with more effect than in the intervals of music and dancing. . . . Meanwhile," he continues, "the bosom of the Thames is covered with barges and wherries, all of them laden with the most distinguished fashionables of the day; and all steering their course from Westminster stairs . . . to a landing place below the Rotunda."

Meanwhile, too, the unbroken line of coaches is rolling up. Coroneted panels swing open and steps rattle down before the belles and beaux of the season. Here are the two lovely sisters, Ladies Emily and Georgiana Lennox; there are the Ladies Lucy Manners, Caroline Darcy, Lucy Clinton, Harriet and Anne Wentworth, Charlotte and Sophia Fermor, Camilla Bennet, Elizabeth Le Neve. There are the young bloods Horace Walpole, Lord John Sackville, Lords Ancram, Holdernesse, Ashburnham, Howard, Hartington, and Castlehaven; Messrs. Colebrook and Poulett, General Churchill, young Bob Carteret, Colonel Maguire, and Sir William Boothby.[41] Save for one or two of them, all but their names have now vanished with myriad beaux and belles of other years and other pleasure gardens. And from his box, the middle-aged Lord Chesterfield, thinly smiling, looks down with approbation on so much impeccable gentility. He is delighted with the place, "goes there every night and declares that he designs to live there soon altogether," [42] "is so fond of it," according to Horace Walpole, "that he says he has ordered all his letters to be directed thither."

Walpole continues significantly to inform Seymour Conway: "If you had never seen it, I would make you a most pompous description of it, and tell you how the floor is all of beaten princes — that you can't set your foot without treading on a Prince of Wales or Duke of Cumberland. The company is universal: there is from his grace of Grafton down to children out of the Foundling Hospital — from my Lady Townshend to the kitten — from my Lord Sandys to your humble cousin and sincere friend." [43]

Finally, let the glories of Ranelagh be rehearsed by Tobias Smollett's Lydia Melford: "It looks," she exclaimed, "like the enchanted palace of a genie, adorned with the most exquisite performances of painting, carving, and gilding, enlightened with a thousand golden lamps that emulate the noonday sun; crowded with the great, the rich, the gay, the happy and the fair; glittering with cloth of gold and silver lace, embroidery, and precious stones. While these exulting sons and daughters of felicity tread this round of pleasure, or regale in different parties, and separate lodges, with fine imperial tea and other delicious refreshments, their ears are entertained with the most ravishing delights of music, both instrumental and vocal." [44]

In addition to orchestral music there was singing; there were fireworks; there was a barge paddled about on the Canaletto; there were other amusements. But these were adjuncts and side shows. The heart of Ranelagh, its *raison d'être*, its unfailing charm, consisted in that circular strip of floor between the hub and rim of the Rotunda, between the center tables and the loges around which sauntered, night after night, the stream of promenaders. It was to see and be seen that people went to Ranelagh. It was humanity absorbed in itself. And here from his box, as in the Pump Room at Bath, or the Four O'clock Meadow in Spa, as in Madame de Tencin's "Menagerie," or at the hazard table at White's, or from his chair in the House of Lords, Chesterfield studied the world and analyzed it, and drew his conclusions.

Enough has been said to demonstrate his right of judgment, the rich and long experience of men and women upon which it is based, and therefore the validity of that critique of life upon which his fame rests. As far as his field of observation extended, and it extended far, he speaks as a master and with authority. No worldly wisdom, using "worldly" in its special sense, has ever stood upon a broader foundation. No realistic philosophy of behavior and social intercourse — Montaigne's or La Rochefoucauld's or La Bruyère's — has been more amply documented. It is precisely this breadth of foundation which has given Chesterfield's pronouncements on the way of the world a value beyond their own age, a sort of perennial value in each succeeding century. Human nature perpetuates certain types. It was Chesterfield's genius that his mind instinctively selected the typical from the multitudinous phenomena with which it dealt. As was the man or woman of the world then, so essentially is he or she now. As were the threads of desire or self-love by which amoral nature manipulated the human puppets then, so are they now.

But if the reader reflects a moment not only on the kind of world it was whose ways Chesterfield so ably interpreted, but on the special angles under which he viewed it, limits to the universal truth of his conclusions will appear. We have already noted that his opinions were formed from the study of one class only: the privileged upper class, with its dependents and parasites. He was never personally acquainted with the rudimentary problems of life, the struggle for such necessities as food, clothing, and shelter, material sacrifices for the well-being of a family, the weight of financial worry and insecurity. He knew only those to whom work was a career, not a treadmill. And on the other hand, he did not know at all the virtues that thrift, self-sacrifice, and fellowship in the enterprise of ordinary life, bring into family relations. Particularly, he knew women as ornaments or playthings, not as wives, mothers, and focal centers of households. Hence, his opinions on that side are especially defective.

It is not this concentration upon one social class to the exclusion of others, however, that constitutes the most serious limitation to the justice of his worldly analysis. The truth of Kipling's remark as to the sisterhood of the Colonel's Lady and Judy O'Grady needs for its acceptance only to be stated. If allowances are made for the duke's coat, income, and habit of environment, the rest of him, anatomical and psychological, is fundamentally similar to a stevedore; and the essential motives, foibles, vices, and illusions of Chesterfield's elite are reproduced in a cheaper edition among the populace. It is rather the light under which he studied the men and women of his class and the setting in which he encountered them that render his verdicts upon human nature suspect. Courts and parliaments, health resorts and pleasure gardens, salons, gaming rooms, embassies, and ruelles are surely the places where mankind appears at its most frivolous, greedy, selfish, and insincere. In such surroundings, even men and women of worth are viewed under trying colors. The exceptions to self-seeking and self-advertisement merely emphasize their predominance.

What must be the attitude toward life and humanity evolved exclusively upon such a stage? To make this question vivid, we should transpose the terms and ask ourselves what we would think of our fellow men after fifty-odd years not at Bath or Spa, but at Newport or Miami, Brighton, Torquay, or Cannes — with their endless parade of idlers. What deductions about human nature would we make from a contemplation four decades long of Parliament or Congress with the accompanying obbligato of London or Washington society — the receptions, teas, dinners of those forty years? What would we learn of men from a life of clubs and casinos? Of women, from the monotony of debutantes and society hostesses or the equally monotonous demimonde? These questions answer themselves. No other than a cynical verdict is possible upon such a show.

Many acquaintances, but no comrades; a code of behavior, but no religion; parents, but no love; a wife, but no household; a marriage, but no children — such are a few of the lacunae that invalidate Chesterfield's conclusions upon the art of life. The pity of it is that in spite of these, in spite of everything, so many of his comments remain accurate.

CHAPTER XIV
Vexilla Regis

MEANWHILE the personnel of his world was changing around him. Lady Suffolk, the dear "Swiss," the rallying point of so many memories, no longer received her countless friends in the apartment at St. James's. For some time now, King George had fidgeted to the Queen about her, complaining of "the old deaf woman of whom he was weary." At length Caroline, though fearful of younger and less docile successors, allowed him to cashier the official mistress, and the court world rocked with excitement. The Opposition took him to task for using a woman of Lady Suffolk's "merit, prudence, and understanding" so ungratefully; and Lord Hervey remarked that, to hear them, one would have imagined "that the King, instead of dropping a mistress, to give himself up to a wife, had repudiated a virtuous wife in order to take a mistress." But her withdrawal from court would represent to Chesterfield, Herbert, Burlington, Scarborough, and others a page turned over upon their youth.[1]

This was in 1734. The following year another link with the past was broken by the death of the beloved Dr. Arbuthnot. "Pope and I were with him the evening before he died," wrote Chesterfield.[2] ". . . He took leave of us with tenderness, without weakness, and told us that he died, not only with the comfort, but even the devout assurance, of a Christian." What a strange, eighteenth-century deathbed scene as one thinks of it! — Pope, Chesterfield, and Arbuthnot, a touch of formality to the very end, a bleak but virile courage.

And there were other deaths: that of his friend and enemy, the gallant Lord Peterborough, in 1735,[3] of his brother Charles in 1736, of his old patron Lord Townshend in 1738, of his protégé James Hammond in 1742, of his mother-in-law the Duchess of Kendal in

1743,[4] of his benefactress the Duchess of Marlborough in 1744 —
some for whom he cared, others to whom he was indifferent.

On May 30, 1744, died Alexander Pope, and with him the so-
called Augustan Age. He and Chesterfield had been friends since
the days of the Young Court. Thirty years before, the Earl had
spent a week at a time in the house of the poet at Twickenham and
had, as he put it, seen his mind in its undress. They belonged to
the same circle, and they shared the same enmities. More important
still, they both reflected similar tastes in books, art, manners, people,
and philosophy. They each appreciated the distinction of the
other. De Pesters, writing to Lady Denbigh, speaks of them as
together at Lord Cobham's with "much wit and a good dose of
satire." They were together at Bath and visited the Duchess of
Marlborough at the same time. William Warburton, Pope's protégé
and editor, was patronized by Chesterfield, who promoted his
writings and offered him a chaplaincy in his household while Lord
Lieutenant of Ireland. Warburton dedicated the new edition of his
Alliance between Church and State to this Maecenas. But in spite
of all that, one feels that Chesterfield never ranked among the poet's
closest friends, though he remained an admirer of his genius. "The
Character of Mr. Pope," written after the poet's death, reveals no
trace of affection, is more than usual icily objective. After balancing
praise and blame of Pope's character, he reserved his enthusiasm
for the poetical works, which he considered superior to those of
Horace. Nor, on the other hand, did Pope leave him, among the
many other bequests to friends, any token in his will. Was it the
wretched scandals and controversies that stained the satirist's memory which induced this coolness? The fact of it is strange, because
in that generation it would be difficult to find two minds more
naturally harmonious.[5]

Insensibly the drawing rooms and assemblies were filling up with
new faces. A generation that but dimly remembered George I and
had not known Queen Anne nor the worthies of her reign, let alone
those of King William or King James, was now thrusting itself
forward. Lord Chesterfield's world was growing old.

At the assembly room in Bath or in one of the great houses on
St. James's Square, now gray and weather-stained, but which he
could remember spick and span in the new London of forty years
ago — in the ballroom of such a house and surveying the rouged

and wrinkled faces of once lovely women, the toasts of his youth, surveying too the wear and tear and dregs of time about him, it is not unlikely that some of Pope's great verses crossed his mind. They are more desolate than Villon's "snows of yesteryear"; their thin, hard music expresses perfectly the sense of winter deepening across that age. Fat and lean, bejewelled, titled and unsavory, the poet, sneering at old women, his contemporaries, consigned them and the world they represented to the rubbish heap of his lost illusions:

> As hags hold Sabbaths, less for joy than spite,
> So these their merry, miserable night;
> Still round and round the Ghosts of Beauty glide,
> And haunt the places where their Honour died.
> See how the World its Veterans rewards!
> A Youth of Frolics, an old age of Cards;
> Fair to no purpose, artful to no end,
> Young without Lovers, old without a Friend;
> A Fop their Passion, but their Prize a Sot;
> Alive, ridiculous, and dead, forgot.[6]

At eight o'clock on the evening of January 29, 1740, Chesterfield was called suddenly from the House of Commons (where he had been attending the debate on the Place Bill) by the news that Lord Scarborough was dead or at the point of death from a stroke of apoplexy. He had had one or two previous attacks, so that the news could not have been altogether a surprise. But when Chesterfield reached his house, he found that the cause of death had not been apoplexy but suicide. Scarborough had ordered his chair for six o'clock in the evening to carry him to Lady Hervey's. When he failed to appear, a valet entering the Earl's room discovered that he had put a bullet into his head.[7] He had spent that morning with Chesterfield, discussing, among other matters, Sir William Temple's negotiations. The latter's memoirs stood open at a page that had been mentioned, as if, says Maty, Scarborough "in his last moments had been attentive to his friend, and desirous that he should know he was so."[8] Maty adds that to the end of her life Lady Chesterfield could not speak without emotion "of the manner in which his lordship, on her return home at night, acquainted her with his loss of that amiable nobleman; and he ever after lamented that he did not detain him at his house, saying he might perhaps have been saved, if he had not been left to himself that day."

But Scarborough's life and death are significant of a conflict which has a general application, and for this reason a certain emphasis has been laid upon them. It was an obvious case of maladjustment between temperament and environment, but an unusual case because of Scarborough's virile and magnanimous character. He was no weakling nor recluse nor failure, but universally popular, a brave soldier, an effective speaker, a finished courtier. The age, ruthless in slander, extolled him with an awe-struck respect, his sense of honor, his benevolence, tenderness of heart, sincerity of purpose. Ethically, he held a unique position among his contemporaries, and because of this his social and political influence was considerable. Yet such a man, the *preux chevalier* of his time, perhaps its noblest and best-beloved figure, killed himself. Illness and a hereditary taint may be made to cover the event; but there is something about Scarborough's death that conveys the impression of an inarticulate criticism and protest.

What escape was possible for those tired of the arrogance of fashion in thought and conduct, tired of the prudent, reasonable and genteel, tired of common sense, tired of the Alexandrine rhythm? [9] There was no escape except pious fortitude or impious satire, worldly distraction or bewildered hopelessness. Chesterfield, perfectly adapted to the age though he was, felt the tedium and ache of living, but took refuge in an amiable stoicism; Scarborough could not fit the mold, and so shot himself. If only he had been detained a little longer that day at Grosvenor Square, might he have been saved? No, there was required to save such men as he and such a century a message more profound than that of Grosvenor Square. "I know not what posterity may think of us," wrote the Earl of Marchmont to the Duke of Montrose, "but I am of opinion they can scarcely think worse of us generally than what we deserve." [10]

And yet, even while he was writing, strange events were on the march. Not only was the population of the West End changing; England herself was changing, or stood rather upon the threshold of an amazing transformation.

The Great Revival, which may be said to have begun with John Wesley's conversion on May 24, 1738, is one of the most dramatic movements in history; and by the contrast it provides with the ostensibly important personages, events, and tendencies of the century, a searching light is turned upon the reality of their importance and upon the entire scale of usually accepted values. It is dramatic, because of the odds it had to encounter, because of the gallantry and devotion of its leaders. It is socially and ethically instructive, because, together with the industrial development of the time, it far overshadows, as a formative national influence, the wars, politics, ministries, and schools of wit or conduct which at a given moment bulked much larger in the public consciousness. What comparison could be drawn between the unimportance of George Whitefield addressing crowds of smutty miners on some commons and the pre-eminence of Sir Robert Walpole managing parliament? What an immeasurable distance in the public estimation between shabby John Wesley ambling into Bath on his cob, and Philip, Earl of Chesterfield, rolling into it in his coach! But by one of time's ironies, there are few intelligent people nowadays who would maintain that, however constructively Walpole administered the national finances, there is anything therein comparable to the spiritual, and therefore civic and moral, awakening of the lower classes inspired by Whitefield; nor that any contributions made by Philip Stanhope to English letters or philosophy are even remotely comparable to the influence of Wesley upon the history both of England and America.

It is because of the clearer insight obtainable into Chesterfield's character and the world he represented by a contrast with the purposes and personages of a movement towards which he showed himself either indifferent or opposed, that the Great Revival is worth considering. The ultimate value of his attitude toward life is more definitely appraised by comparing it, not with similar standards of his class and age (as better here or worse there), but with motives and ideals diametrically different — different in sanction, different in effectiveness. Chiaroscuro must always remain one of the most vivid methods not only of painting, but of exposition.

The spiritual miasma of the eighteenth century hardly requires mention. If Matthew Arnold more than a hundred years later lamented the ebbing of the sea of faith, he might have taken heart by considering what the extent of that ebb had been in the days of his great-grandfather. Even our own complacent generation, parading its skepticism as modern and up-to-date, is too self-conscious about it for comparison with the apathy of that more sophisticated era.

It was not that religion seemed dead two hundred years ago, but it was embalmed, and kept, so to speak, as a state exhibit. It sanctioned law, morality, and common sense, provided topics for theological argument, and, for the rest, displayed the value of a venerable antique. Montesquieu observed calmly that there was no religion in England. "In the Houses of Parliament prayers are never attended by more than four or five members, except on great occasions. If one speaks of religion, every one laughs." [11] Lord Hervey records that "the fable of Christianity, as Leo X called it, was now so exploded in England that any man of fashion or condition would have been almost as much ashamed in company to own himself a Christian as formerly he would have been afraid to profess himself none. Even the women who prided themselves at all on their understanding took care to let people know that Christian prejudices were what they despised being bound by. Many of the best writers of the age had indeed written so forcibly and so openly against this system of religion that it was not surprising they gained so many converts, especially when those whose trade and interest it was to write against them defended Christianity so ill. . . ." [12] And Bishop Butler in the preface to his *Analogy of Religion* gives episcopal sanction to this statement. "It has somehow come to be taken for granted," he writes, "that Christianity is not so much a subject of inquiry, but it is now at length discovered to be fictitious. . . . Men treat it as if in the present age this were an agreed point amongst all people of discernment, and nothing remained but to set it up as a principal subject to mirth and ridicule."

Against this sort of disdainful and massive languor, against the bleakness of fashionable deism, against smug and decent morality, against a social order among the poor that was incredibly brutal, ignorant, and debased, John Wesley flung himself more recklessly than did ever Quixote at the famous windmills. Up to the moment of his conversion, he had been rather a failure than a success. Thereafter his life becomes a miracle, an ardent flame, burning up and down through England during fifty years. He gathered followers, groups of reformed sinners, from the lower classes for the most part, some illiterate, a handful of the nobility, and with such scattered troops we find him carrying on the ceaseless campaign

along his battle line of half a century. The victorious results of this
we know. Perhaps the Methodist Church, with its thousands of
parishes throughout the world, is the least of them. His greater
glory was the spiritual quickening of an entire race, whether
the new vitality showed itself in poetry and art, in milder laws,
in more enlightened education, or in social reform and nobler
customs.

But this day was not yet. The world of Chesterfield, respectable
and self-contained, would face him many a long decade still, and
would imagine that it had outfaced him to the end. Let the reader
think back for a moment to the picture we have drawn of it, and
then let him imagine John Wesley, as he stood that August day [13]
in the Oxford pulpit and threw down his challenge to the assembled pundits. Let him also bear in mind the most perfect
example we have of this world, Lord Chesterfield, with his cool
intellect and amused smile. "Generation of triflers," said Wesley,
"triflers with God, with one another and with your own souls. . . .
It is time for Thee, Lord, to lay to Thine hand! . . . Lord, save, or
we perish! Take us out of the mire, that we sink not! . . ." [14]

Of course, the polite world, goaded by such impertinences, struck
back. Methodism, in the person of Whitefield, found itself in
the *Dunciad*.[15] The author of the *Analogy*, Bishop Butler himself,
forbade Whitefield and the Wesleys to preach in his diocese "though
all around his cathedral city lay the most degraded and hopeless
class in England — the coal-miners of Kingswood." [16] Such an ir-
regularity as sermons preached not in a church, but out-of-doors,
filled him with indignation. Scandalized magnates here and there
stirred up the mob, and the Methodists' lives were often in danger.
The wits, such as Horry Walpole, took flings at them, of which the
following may serve as an instance. It is an instance too of an epigram becoming unintentionally a very handsome compliment:

When Whitefield preaches, and when Whiston writes [jingled Horace],
All cry, that madness dictates either's flights.
When Sherlock writes, or canting Secker preaches,
All think good sense inspires what either teaches.
Why, when all four for the same gospel fight,
Should two be crazy, two be in the right?
Plain is the reason — every son of Eve
Thinks the two madmen, what they teach, believe.[17]

But in spite of ridicule, interdicts, and violence the campaign went on and in its progress, swept away much that opposed it.

A feature of the Great Revival was its ubiquity, due to the tirelessness of its few leaders. No gentleman, however fond of his ease, could ever feel entirely safe from harrying and challenging. His wife might suddenly adjure him as to the state of his soul; his mistress might turn Methodist and undertake his conversion; his friends might pester him to attend meetings. Even Bath, gouty Mammon's favorite refuge, was not safe, although Beau Nash did what he could to exclude the disturbers of sleeping consciences. The entries in Wesley's *Journal* that are concerned with Bath are peculiarly illuminating. If we consider them, scattered through the years from May 1739 to March 1790, they represent the progress of the Revival under the least favorable circumstances.

There was great expectation at Bath [he records in June 1739] of what a noted man [Beau Nash] was to do with me there: and I was much entreated not to preach, because no one knew what might happen. By this report I also gained a much larger audience, among whom were many of the rich and great. I told them plainly "the Scripture had included them all under sin, high and low, rich and poor, one with another." Many of them seemed to be not a little surprised, and were sinking apace into seriousness, when the champion appeared, and coming close to me asked, "By what authority I did these things?"

I replied, "By the authority of Jesus Christ, conveyed to me by the (now) Archbishop of Canterbury, when he laid his hands upon me, and said: 'Take thou authority to preach the Gospel.'"

He said, "This is contrary to Act of Parliament. This is a Conventicle."

I answered, "Sir, the Conventicles mentioned in the Act (as the Preamble shows) are seditious meetings. But this is not such. Here is no shadow of sedition. Therefore it is not contrary to the Act."

He replied, "I say it is. But besides, your preaching frightens people out of their wits."

"Sir, did you ever hear me preach?"

"No."

"How then can you judge of what you have never heard?"

"Sir, by common report."

"Common report is not enough. Give me leave, Sir, to ask, is not your name Nash?"

"My name is Nash."

"Sir, I dare not judge of you by common report. I believe it is not enough to judge by."

Here he paused a while, and having recovered himself, asked: "I desire to know what these people come here for?"

On which one replied, "Sir, leave him to me. Let an old woman answer him. You, Mr. Nash, take care of your body. We take care of our souls, and for the food of our souls we come here." [18]

Methodism had therewith struck root in Bath, and though Nash carried on a warfare of petty annoyances, such as drowning out open-air meetings with patriotic band music, the Revival continued slowly to advance even within the precincts of the Pump Room. One cannot but feel for some of the moths fluttering about the flame of the great evangelist. Under Monday, January 24, 1743, we read:

> I preached at Bath. Some of the rich and great were present; to whom, as to the rest, I declared with all plainness of speech, 1. That, by nature, they were all children of wrath; 2. That all their natural tempers were corrupt and abominable; and 3. All their words and works — which could never be any better but by faith; and that 4. A natural man has no more faith than a Devil, if as much. — One of them, my Lord ——, stayed very patiently till I came to the middle of the fourth head; then starting up, he said, " 'Tis hot. 'Tis very hot," and got downstairs as fast as he could. [19]

One can imagine Lord Blank's disapproval and agitation as he clattered downstairs.

Next year Wesley records that "many of the audience appeared to be deeply convinced; and one, though a gentlewoman, could not conceal the emotion of her mind, but broke out into strong cries and tears. Perhaps even here, the bread we have 'cast upon the waters' shall be found after many days." [20]

So the entries continue until twenty years later. On March 8, 1767, we read: "I know not when I have seen a more serious, or more deeply attentive congregation. Is it possible? Can the Gospel have place where Satan's throne is?"

Beau Nash and Beau Nash's world were gone. Almost all had vanished except old Horace Walpole, who lived to titter over every person and thing in his century, but John Wesley still rode his circuit. A long-contested redoubt had fallen. On March 25, 1790, he wrote at Bath: "Indeed, the word of God seems to flourish here, deepening as well as widening." The bread "cast upon the waters" had been found after many days.

So much for the Revival itself. It was, we repeat, one of the two most important national movements of the period. And if we are right in considering Chesterfield as representative of worldly rationalism, it should be interesting to consider his attitude toward, his relationships with, this transforming current that led out into modern times. A new measure of the man and of what he stands for may be derived from such an inquiry.

To begin with, we should be very much in error if we imagined that Chesterfield was opposed to Methodism. While in Walpole's letters the subject is never mentioned without scorn and is sometimes treated with evident hostility, there is not a single passage of the sort in Chesterfield's writings. Nay more, it is likely that if *some stranger* had asked him his serious opinion of the movement, he would have replied that it undoubtedly made for a heightening of the moral tone and therefore served a useful purpose in government.[21] He observed on one occasion with apparent approval that Lady Huntingdon, the matriarch of the Calvinist Methodists and an intimate of Whitefield, bore a very popular character, which her religious enthusiasm had raised with some people and had lowered with none.[22] He went to hear Whitefield preach and gave his friend Bolingbroke "an extreme good account of the sermon."[23] Officially then his opinion would be favorable, and in this respect, as compared with Walpole, he showed himself more mature, more sagacious — one might almost say more sophisticated. For your true man of the world is wise enough to welcome the conservative, stabilizing influences of religion, even if it be of the vulgar evangelical kind.

On the other hand, if *an intimate* had asked him his serious opinion of Methodism, he would most probably have felt a certain surprise. How could anyone who knew him imagine that he would have a serious opinion of it at all? Neither scorn nor hostility appears in his references to the Revival; but somehow the impression is given that he has some difficulty in keeping his face straight. A suppressed smile struggles beneath the surface.

On the whole, as Moses to La Fontaine, so was Wesley to

Chesterfield, "*Ce Wesley là, n'était pas son homme.*" If he frequented clergymen, he preferred them decorous and worldly, like Chenevix or Warburton. Of this gentle mirth, his description of the popular Methodist divine, Dr. Madan, is a case in point. Though he took his ear trumpet with him, he could not understand a word that was said; but, as an expert in such things, he appreciated the doctor's manner, which he compared to that of a parlor magician. "He is a very fine figure," wrote the Earl, "has very graceful actions, white hands and white handkerchief, both which he displays properly to his audience, and shows them that all is fair" — that recalled the eternal theme of good breeding; and he went on to point out that "these little external advantages will have more weight with the wisest man in the world, than he himself is aware of or could believe." [24] Lady Huntingdon, who saw only the poised ear trumpet, hoped that her right noble friend was in the throes of rebirth. In point of fact he was simply being polite, for in the same letter he declared that by his attendance he was now "extremely well with Lady Huntingdon and all those who are of the Household of Faith."

The pursuit of Lord Chesterfield by evangelical ladies of rank forms one of the humorous chapters of his biography. As we have seen, the high priestess of the movement, Lady Huntingdon herself, was an intimate friend. Her sister and convert, the Lady Fanny Shirley, had been his reputed mistress; another acquaintance, Fanny's sister-in-law, the Lady Margaret Hastings, married Benjamin Ingham, a disciple of John Wesley; [25] Chesterfield's sister, Lady Gertrude Hotham, and his sister-in-law, the Countess d'Elitz, became Methodists; finally, Lady Chesterfield herself seems to have been converted. [26] Thus, ringed about by a feminine phalanx zealous for his salvation, the Earl without question heard enough of the Great Revival. With angelic complaisance he now and then went to a meeting and heard more. "That saint, Chesterfield!" chuckled Bolingbroke when he learned of it. [27] Moreover, he even dipped into his pocket and offered Lady Huntingdon twenty guineas toward the building of the new tabernacle. [28] There can be no doubt that this band of great ladies plotted and prayed for him. Such a recruit, they well might argue, would vastly benefit the reputation of the movement. But his smiling politeness kept eluding them. With no greater incongruity, Goethe might have displayed him Mephistopheles similarly pursued. Horace Walpole relates how, when Chesterfield was close upon death, his sister, Lady Gertrude, and Lady Huntingdon visited him in a last attempt, as Walpole puts it, "to get at his soul through a cranny in his health. If they could only lure him to one of their Methodist seminaries in Wales, the feat might be managed. So they extolled the prospects — and then there were such charming mountains! 'Hold, ladies,' said the Earl; 'I don't love mountains, — when your Ladyships' faith has removed the mountains, I will go thither with all my heart!' " [29]

Thus he merely smiled as the Great Revival swept on. It was another human illusion, comical enough, though socially useful; but not to be taken seriously by a philosopher. Deaf to great poetry and to music, the still more ethereal world of spiritual experience was equally closed to him.*

"The soul?" asked one of the animals in Madame de Tencin's menagerie. "What is the soul?" Marivaux answered modestly that he had no idea. "Very well, then, we'll ask Monsieur de Fontenelle." "Ah," said Marivaux, "he has too much sense, to know more about it than I." [30]

The smile of a Marivaux or a Chesterfield may be one of life's greatest tragedies.

* *Cf.* his opinon of Homer, Virgil, Dante, Petrarch, Shakespeare, and Milton, *infra* p. 293. His insensibility to music is also noteworthy. Writing his godson, Feb. 19, 1773, he observes: "I do not know by what strange luck music has got the name of one of the liberal arts. I don't see what can entitle it to that distinction. I declare that I would rather be reckoned the best barber than the best fiddler in England." Sidney L. Gulick, Jr., *Some unpublished letters of Lord Chesterfield*, University of California Press, 1937. *Cf.* also Chesterfield's essay on *The Italian Opera*, published in *The World*, Nov. 14, 1754. Mahon, *op. cit.*, vol. 5, p. 308. Other slighting references could be added. This was the age of Bach, Handel, Arne, Gluck, etc.; but music seems to have meant nothing to him except as an occasion for ridicule.

PART FOUR
1745 - 1748

CHAPTER XV
Lord Lieutenant

AT THE OUTBREAK of the Spanish war in 1739, about which there had been such a hullabaloo of patriotism, Sir Robert Walpole remarked, "They may ring their bells now, but they will soon be wringing their hands," a prophecy amply verified by nearly a decade of expensive and useless strife. For the naval war with Spain — a commercial quarrel — was caught up in a sudden maelstrom of conflicting ambitions and policies that embraced most of Europe, and has since been known as the War of the Austrian Succession. During the course of it, ministries rose and fell with the flood and ebb of fortune; new men came into prominence, others dropped away; treaties were made and broken and remade; the diplomatic kaleidoscope exhausted its patterns; political parties fused and separated and swung into new alignments.

There can be no question here of describing that complicated tangle. As we have already observed, it was still the day of individuals rather than of masses, I had almost said, rather than of nations; at least the whims and foibles of personality were then, far more than now, conspicuous in affecting the course of events. George II's hatred of Frederick the Great, Maria Theresa's ambitions, the astuteness of Charles Emmanuel of Sardinia, the maternal solicitude of Elizabeth Farnese of Spain, the languor of Augustus of Saxony — all these human traits combining with the temperaments and intrigues of princes, ministers, and generals, confuse the main currents of European policy at that time with a bewilderment of intersecting ripples. They are fascinating to the historian, but would be here both repetitious and unrelated to our main intention, which is that of portraiture rather than of narrative. Only such details as are indispensable to a survey of this closing and crowning phase of Chesterfield's political life will be retained; and insofar as they do not affect the more personal appraisal of him, will receive merely a passing mention.[1]

He rose to power on one of those sudden gusts of public petulance which had overthrown Walpole in 1741, and which now in 1744 ousted the latter's successor, Lord Granville. The one had prosecuted the war too languidly for the national taste; the other's grandiose schemes against the Bourbon powers had crumbled suddenly upon Frederick the Great's re-entry into the war on the side of France, and had strengthened in England the growing desire for peace. Though, together with other "Patriots" in 1739, he had hounded and denounced Walpole's reluctance to defend the honor of England against Spain, Chesterfield turned rapidly pacific when the war became multinational and demanded military rather than naval effort. With characteristic distrust of English and admiration for French power, he could see nothing but bankruptcy, defeat, and ruin ahead for Britain and her continental allies as a result of any protracted struggle, and believed that as early and as good a peace as possible should be negotiated. It was, therefore, as leader of a pro-peace Opposition that he, together with such adherents as the Dukes of Bedford and Devonshire, Lord Cobham, Lord Gower, etc., entered a coalition with members of the Walpole and Granville cabinets (Henry Pelham, his brother, the Duke of Newcastle, Lord Hardwicke, and Lord Harrington) to form what would now be called a national cabinet, but was then known as the "Broad-bottomed" ministry because of the diverse elements it bracketed.

Politically speaking, this was indeed a varied assortment, ranging from Tories like Gower and Sir John Hynde Cotton to Whigs like Hardwicke. The bitter opponents of ten years' standing became colleagues under the undoubted predominance of Walpole's old election managers and henchmen, the Pelhams, Lord Hardwicke, and Lord Harrington; except that the great chief minister himself had fallen, his cabinet remained intact. It meant that for personal, political, and national reasons the Chesterfield "Patriots" must be reconciled with Walpole's disciples — as long as it suited the convenience of both. And the formula of reconciliation uniting Whigs and Tories, pro-war and pro-peace men, was a device which has remained modern ever since, namely, war to end war. In other words, the peace party and militarists could agree on one final campaign, which should be so vigorously ensued as to obtain an advantageous peace.

When we speak of Chesterfield's rise to power, it is in a distinctly restricted sense, which means simply that from being chief of the Opposition, he became an important member of the administration. Whatever his ambitions may have been, he never directed its policies, but remained to the end at first a willing and at last a disappointed subordinate. Indeed, upon the formation of the ministry, his place, if dignified, was one of the least influential; for he sought and obtained the nomination of Lord Lieutenant of Ireland. Hervey in his memoirs refers scornfully to this position as the "honourable Irish exile," [2] and Chesterfield himself felt constrained repeatedly to furnish his friends with his reasons for desiring it.[3] They were not altogether adequate. He pleads indolence and that the place was an easy one; that he wished to reward some "little people who were attached to him and had suffered for him"; that after all it was a cabinet place and gave him access to the King when he chose, etc. The fundamental truth was, in the first place, that the King at this time detested him to such a degree that he could not bear the sight of him.[4] If his leadership in parliament made a cabinet post necessary, let it in any case be one that would keep him as far as possible from a meeting with the outraged monarch. For years he had endeavored to thwart the latter in every cherished plan, had stirred up his own son against him, had ridiculed the persons and things he cared for, had even satirized the dead queen. And now if the "little tea-table scoundrel" and "dwarf-baboon" had become so important that he must be conciliated with a post, let him be kept out of sight. George II hated the whole ministry and clung to Carteret, Lord Granville, whose policies he endorsed and whom these puppies, because of their parliamentary power, replaced; but bad as most of them were, they shone by comparison with Chesterfield.

There is evidence, however, that apart from royal disfavor, the Earl would still have sought the Irish appointment;[5] and his reason for this reveals one of the salient traits of his character. Though one of the most sociable of men and though repeatedly used to negotiate peace between conflicting factions or persons, he was never at his best as a collaborator, but rather as a free agent. If

he could not act on his own responsibility, unhampered by colleagues of the council board, he was apt to discharge punctiliously
the duties before him and then at length, scornfully indifferent, give
up the game. There was in his attitude on this point something of
the hauteur expressed by Landor's celebrated line — "I strove with
none, for none was worth my strife." But, on the other hand, permit him to carry out a mission unaided, or to fill an independent
office, and his performance would be of distinguished brilliancy
and adroitness. It was so throughout his career. He excelled as a
lone wolf, but did not thrive in harness. Consciousness of this must
in some way have colored his choice of the Lord-Lieutenancy.

It is no use speculating upon the presumable state of his mind at
this wished-for culmination of ten years' political striving. As sparks
fly upward, so it is the end of politicians to hold office. He desired
power and had had little of it in his life. Now, though late in the
day, the opportunity of office, of accomplishment, and of national
recognition, had come as the appropriate crown of his public career.
Moreover, in regard to personal ambition, the future was unusually
bright. Walpole was gone; the brilliant Carteret and Pulteney,
Chesterfield's former allies and recent opponents, had had their day.
Of the coalition cabinet, he might reasonably consider himself the
ablest member, with the exception of Lord Hardwicke; and Hardwicke was a great lawyer rather than a statesman. The others were
prominent mediocrities obviously inferior to the Earl on many
counts. At the very outset of the coalition, it was he who was
welcomed by the old ministers on an even footing with themselves
and most possessed their confidence.[6] It was, therefore, by no means
too much to hope that the Lord-Lieutenancy, supreme in Ireland,
might lead eventually to a position equally supreme in England. The
only barrier to such a consummation was a personality who, alone
of the ministers in question, requires more than a passing reference,
for it was the obscure conflict with him that determined the outcome of Chesterfield's cabinet experience. This was his distant relative, the Duke of Newcastle, at that time, with another relative,
Lord Harrington, one of the two Secretaries of State.

He is, perhaps, the most absurd chief minister who ever ruled a
great nation for a considerable time. One somehow thinks of him
as an enormous bluebottle, forever busy and forever buzzing.
"Hubble-bubble," Shelburne's nickname for him, expresses the idea.

His passion was to be continually in the public eye and to have
the reputation of controlling everything. He loved crowded levees,
and had the politician's effusiveness. For the rest, he was timid,
jealous, vain, a poor speaker, an irresolute statesman, a confused
thinker. At first glance it would seem that Chesterfield, the disciplined, logical and lucid, must inevitably surpass and govern such
a rival. What the outcome of that rivalry was, we shall soon learn.
It went on behind a smoke screen of mutual compliments and apparent confidence. But in the meantime it should be remembered
that Newcastle, however inferior, at least desired office with every
faculty he had, and was prepared to sacrifice everything to obtain
it. Single-minded persistency is one of the most powerful forces in
nature — as the fable of the hare and the tortoise or the experience
of Chesterfield with Newcastle shows.

The campaign which was to procure a peace favorable to England and her allies, Austria, Sardinia, and Holland, was by necessity,
as so often in the past, to be fought out in the Netherlands; and
Holland, for various reasons, must be induced to do most of the
fighting. Austria was preoccupied with defending or recovering
Bohemia and Silesia from Frederick of Prussia, and was far more
interested in them than in holdings in the Netherlands. England,
fearful of invasion by the French and the Jacobites, dared not strip
herself of troops for Continental service. It was Holland, therefore,
menaced by the projected French campaign against the Austrian
Netherlands, which, together with the barrier fortresses, served as
her buffer, who was most directly concerned in their preservation
and from whom the most strenuous efforts might be expected.

But the Dutch States were no longer the hardy and dauntless
people of William the Silent. Long commercial prosperity had had
its usual effect in relaxing moral fiber and in carnalizing moral
issues. Freedom itself had lost some of its potency as a word to con-
jure with. There was a strong peace party with French leanings,
who were wholly antagonistic to the war, and feared that to pro-
long it would result (as it actually did result) in the destruction of
the republican form of government and the erection of a stadholderate. As between foreign domination and domestic tyranny,
they preferred the former. Another party — that of the merchants
and financiers — desired to preserve a nominal neutrality and to
profit on both sides. Therefore, the problem of English diplomacy

was to bring an unwilling country aggressively into the war; and to this end the British government must find an appropriate negotiator and be prepared to pay an appropriate price.

That the new Lord Lieutenant of Ireland should be appointed ambassador to Holland at this crisis was practically inevitable. His name was current in that connection even before the formation of the coalition government.[7] The achievements of his first embassy fifteen years ago were still enthusiastically remembered. Besides that, he had always been *persona grata* with the Dutch; had a profound knowledge of their character and of the intricacies of their government; and had retained many influential friends among them. So, for the second time, we find him ambassador plenipotentiary and extraordinary. He reached The Hague on February 2, 1745, having been a member of the Broad-bottomed ministry hardly more than a month.

The appointment, though inevitable, had been conferred ungraciously by the King. It was the custom for an ambassador to take courtly leave of the monarch before setting out, and to receive the King's instructions. George II refused this audience to his well-hated envoy; Chesterfield, powerful enough at the moment to dictate, insisted on his right; the King gave way, but had the best of it by seizing the opportunity of his compliance to administer as harsh a snub as he could contrive. The interview lasted about ten seconds. The Earl in triumph entered the closet, asked for his instructions. The venom of ten years burned in the curtness of the reply: "You have received your instructions, my Lord." A blow in the face could not have been more explicit. Henceforward, during the next year or so, Chesterfield "dodged" the King upon all occasions.

This second Dutch embassy need not detain us. On paper, at least, every objective was obtained. The Dutch agreed to support 60,000 men in the field, to come roundly into the war, and to accept the young Duke of Cumberland as nominal commander-in-chief of the allied army, with the Austrian Marshal Königsegg as advisory commander. But England paid heavily for these concessions, which, as it turned out, were but half-heartedly performed.[8] Moreover, Chesterfield had hardly concluded negotiations when the French victory at Fontenoy on May 11, 1745, showed the weakness of a patchwork army opposed to a unified command under such leaders as Marshal Saxe.

The Earl, however, was not to blame for military defeats. From the diplomatic standpoint, he did well to bring Holland into the war on any terms; and that these last were expensive could not be helped; the Dutch were in a position to name and to exact their own price.

We catch glimpses of him during these months, strenuously busy as always when on a mission, absorbed as always in making a good job of it, too absorbed, indeed, to think even of his health. On one occasion, and it was doubtless not the only one, we find that he has been working fourteen hours without a break.[9] His letters, as usual, are frequent, forceful, and alert. But one cannot demand of the eighteenth century a modern fever of business. Between negotiations and interviews, he still found time to cultivate the charming, giddy, pretty Madame de Berkenrode, to philander in her salon, or, as he expressed it tenderly some years later, "to wear her chains."[10] One would like to know more about Madame de Berkenrode, a woman out of the "Toccata of Galuppi," an iridescent, frivolous memory upon the crowded stage of his life. Luynes speaks of her as "young, pretty and fond of dancing."[11] Perhaps it is all one needs to know. Her husband became the Dutch ambassador in Paris ("She will pass her time well there," wrote Chesterfield, "and she deserves it"); she was caught tripping in some amour; they were separated. But she was still Madame l'Ambassadrice when Chesterfield's son reached Paris six years later, and became at his father's command one of her train. The Earl's young protégé, Lord Huntingdon, was similarly referred to her. "She was infinitely agreeable," sighed Chesterfield. "I hope your servitude has been better rewarded than mine was."[12]

Meanwhile, however preoccupied at The Hague, he kept a watchful eye on home politics and especially on his own status in the cabinet. The whole ministry stood on treacherous ground — indeed even wondered at times whether they were ministers at all. The King made no secret of his dislike for them and of his preference for the recent chief minister, Lord Granville, who retained his confidence and acted as a secret adviser. It was, of course, the old problem, then approaching the final stage of its solution, as to whether a ministry should consider itself responsible to parliament or to the King. Chesterfield, who had no royal favor to lose, was all for the high hand: Lord Granville must be crushed; the King must be coerced by a simultaneous resignation of all ministers; no *respectful-ness* to him, no "little notions of frivolous decency or compliment" must enervate the ministerial position. "Your strength is in Parliament," he wrote the timorous Newcastle, "and you must use it while you have it." [13] Here, as so often throughout history, a decision of the utmost importance was being worked out in terms of petty personalities. Though always a constitutionalist, there can be no doubt that Chesterfield's attitude at this time had not been sweetened by repeated rebuffs from the King. It was perhaps fortunate for the future of parliamentary government that the second and third Georges had very little notion of tact. The Crown might have retained its authority for a considerably longer period if, at this critical stage, it had more often stooped to conquer.

There was, for instance, the affair of Chesterfield's protégé and chaplain, the respectable Dr. Chenevix. As Lord Lieutenant of Ireland, the Earl had, subject to the King's approval, a right of nomination to bishoprics that fell vacant within his jurisdiction. Accordingly, two months after his own appointment, he nominated Chenevix to the small bishopric of Clonfort. And at once the King refused his assent — another obvious slap in the face. Whereupon his lordship made it a test case, set his political life upon the hazard of that die and declared that either Chenevix would be Bishop of Clonfort or he would not be Lord Lieutenant. It had been a silly, peevish gesture on the part of the King, as ill-considered as it was insulting, for it challenged not only Chesterfield but the other ministers as well, notably Henry Pelham and the Duke of Newcastle, who had invited his co-operation. "If my recommendation to the dirtiest Bishoprick in Ireland," he wrote Newcastle, ". . . is not to prevail, it can only be because it is mine. An indignity by which I am distinguish'd from all my predecessors, and to which I will upon no account submit; and I think it but fair to give your Grace and our friends notice that, upon this foot, I will not be Lord-Lieutenant of Ireland one hour after my arrival in London." [14] The King, unable to resist the corporate will of his ministry, had to yield; and Chenevix obtained the slightly better bishopric of Killa-loe, whence in due time he passed to the see of Waterford and a revenue of £1400. [15] In this affair, Chesterfield had scored a notable triumph, and could return from The Hague to London with heightened prestige. He did not dare jeopardize it, however, by meeting the King, and arranged his departure so as to avoid waiting upon the sovereign and his suite at Hellevoetsluis, when George and Lord Harrington set out for Hanover in May.[16]

On the whole, Chesterfield's second embassy to The Hague was a success on various counts. He had obtained more favorable promises from the Dutch than had been anticipated, and in general had strengthened his position in the cabinet. Henceforward during the next years, at any crisis between England and Holland, his name was sure to be prominent.[17] Moreover, on his return to England in May 1745,[18] he entered the inner circle of the ministry and practically discharged the duties of Secretary of State that summer during Lord Harrington's absence.

He had been now for six months Lord Lieutenant of Ireland and was in no hurry to begin duties there, when a sudden event took place that recalled the absent King to England and dispatched Chesterfield himself to his post. It was one of those events that give to the eighteenth century its picturesque, dramatic, and unexpected character. It was the landing of the Pretender's son, Bonnie Prince Charlie, upon the shores of Scotland.

Time has concealed the grave of that episode beneath the myrtle and ivy of romance. Historical fiction, which thrives on gallantries and lost causes and stirring incident, has surrounded it with the haunting charm of "far-off things and battles long ago." But to Chesterfield hastening to Dublin as fast as Captain Mercer's frigate of ten guns could get him thither from Holyhead,[19] the affair was simply an outrageous annoyance. Unlike Newcastle, the Earl refused to believe that the undisciplined swarm of Highlanders who backed the Prince's venture could prevail against the numbers and organization opposing them. It was only a question of how much damage this crowd of Scottish ruffians would effect before they were driven back again to their mountains. There was no more romance about it from the Lord Lieutenant's standpoint than would attach itself nowadays to a sizable raid of bandits from across an exposed frontier. And though at Prestonpans and later at Falkirk the Highlanders did better than he expected, the course of the revolt proved him right. England, tutored by Walpole, had given up political sentimentalism. The Jacobites of the Lowlands and of the northern counties, upon whom the Stuart cause had chiefly re-

lied, did not raise a finger in support of the fetish of "auld lang syne."
The Prince marched by, and the people watched him pass. From
Derby to Culloden the inevitable ebbing went on. There remained
at length only to hang or otherwise punish the scoundrels who had
disturbed the King's peace, and to take preventive measures against
the recurrence of such a revolt in the future.

So much for England. But however skeptical of Jacobite success
the Lord Lieutenant might be, Ireland, as usual, needed careful
watching. In the first place, like the exiled House of Stuart, it was
Roman Catholic, and for the great majority of its inhabitants Protestantism had long been synonymous with oppression. Therefore
it was likely enough that Prince Charles would be presented to
them in the guise of a liberator. But secondly, and more important
still, was the danger throughout that year, both in England and
Ireland, of French invasion, and the Irish southwest coast was peculiarly vulnerable. Accordingly, the moment demanded quick de-
cisions and unremitting vigilance on the part of the government
at Dublin.

It is against this background of potential danger and absorption
in preventing the spread of sedition from Scotland that we should
study Chesterfield during his residence in Ireland. If the limitations of the man have become apparent in other connections, his
fine qualities are nowhere more obvious than during this period.
The world and its ways have, indeed, a certain worth, are conducive to a certain discipline, and bear a definite fruitage by no
means to be despised. Out of the training of the past, out of the
effort and study and rich experience, had been evolved a character
and a philosophy, coupled with an insight into human nature, that
stood Chesterfield and England in good stead at this point. His
government of Ireland and the letters to his son are the two most
excellent products of his active and reflective life. Neither is, nor
could be, supremely great; but each, as far as it goes, exhibits a
finish and perfection of its own.

Chesterfield reached Dublin on August 31, 1745, two days after
the marshaling of the clans around Charles Edward's standard in
Glenfinnan. He left Ireland on April 23 of the following spring,
just a week after Culloden, so that his absence from England was
almost exactly coextensive with the Stuart revolt. He was therefore par excellence a wartime governor of Ireland, and a consider-

able number of his measures had a military purpose. Fortifications were to be repaired; troops were to be shipped to England; new levies were to be raised, equipped, trained, and held in readiness; possible sources of supply to the rebels in Scotland were to be cut off; fears were to be calmed on one hand, and the constant surveillance of danger points was to be exercised on the other. All this and similar routine finds expression in his correspondence; but it turned out to be only precautionary. Indeed, it was the backstage management of as peaceful a scene as Ireland has ever enjoyed.

From the very moment of landing to the tune of drums, trumpets, and salvos of artillery, his due as viceroy of the King, he seems to have been popular. The Irish liked his good manners and talent for repartee. They reveled in the impression he was able to diffuse of an almost paternal interest in the people and the national welfare. Repressive measures in view of the situation might have been and doubtless were expected, but none occurred. "Sir," he informed a Papist gentleman of means, who was suspected of being an agent of the Pretender's and whom he summoned to the Castle, "I do not wish to inquire whether you have any particular employment in this kingdom, but I know that you have a great interest amongst those of your persuasion. I have sent for you to exhort them to be peaceable and quiet. If they behave like faithful subjects, they shall be treated as such; but, if they act in a different manner, I shall be worse to them than Cromwell." [20]

A blundering governor, in those days of political religion, would have closed the Roman Catholic chapels as a matter of course — in point of fact this had been the procedure in London — but Chesterfield not only left them open, but encouraged their use by protecting the worshipers from mob violence. He was a philosopher who, as we have seen, accepted religion of any but the most tenuous kind as one of life's foibles; and religious persecution was temperamentally odious to him, as long as civil peace and the constitution remained unjeopardized by any given cult. He even proposed replacing the oaths of supremacy and abjuration, which only sycophants and perjurers among the Roman Catholics could take, by a straightforward oath of allegiance. [21] All this — especially his attitude towards Catholic churches — was not merely humane, but adroit. It left him the means of keeping watch on the possible

Stuart sympathizers; for his secret agents attended mass as well as the faithful, and noted who came and went.

There can be no doubt that his benevolent attitude was due to a sincere desire to rule well, or, in other words, to make a success of his administration. Whether in trifles or in serious affairs, in the composition of a casual letter or a literary essay, in building a house, or in the conduct of a public office, he had, as a never-failing characteristic, the passion for a task well done. "Anything worth doing at all," he wrote once, "is worth doing well." It was perhaps his greatest quality. It colored everything about him — is reflected in the clarity of his thought, in the precision of his style. Moreover, under his rationalism, conventionality, and veneer, there was a vein of real benevolence that in some cases verged even toward tenderness and was often prone to compassion. He might be formally hard or pedantic, but there was not a trace of deliberate cruelty in him. He sincerely pitied the Irish and unquestionably desired to serve them.[22]

So much should be granted; but it is no detraction from this — indeed, it is perhaps rather an addition that gave edge and effectiveness to his purpose — that he had the politician's flair for the charming word and the noble gesture. He knew the importance of manner, and no small share of the art of government consists in this knowledge.

Did the panicky vice-treasurer, Mr. Gardner, report in a fright that the people of Connaught were rising, Chesterfield looked at his watch with composure and replied, "It's nine o'clock, and certainly time for them to rise; I therefore believe your news to be true." [23] Such flippancy spreading among the Dublin mob would be worth an added regiment to the King.

Was a poor tradesman of County Kerry horsewhipped by the servants of a rich debtor for dunning him with an old bill too often, the Lord Lieutenant heard the man's complaints in person and sent a special commission to try the case, with the result that the debtor in question "was fined in a very heavy penalty." [24]

Did the privates of his guard despair of an increase in pay because "they had no influential friends," Chesterfield remarked, "What do you think of me? . . . I will be your friend," and raised their pay accordingly.[25]

Was his coachman accused to him of being a Roman Catholic

and attending mass — a heinous crime, indeed, to the Protestants of that day — the Earl merely replied, "Does he indeed? Well, I will take care he shall never carry me there." [26]

Was it a question of promoting the Irish manufactures, there would be a ball at the Castle where Lady Chesterfield set the example of wearing only Irish poplins.[27]

The Lord Lieutenant condescended even to flatter the Dublin belles in rhymes that passed current from lip to lip, and lost nothing to Irish ears because of a tinge of ribaldry. There was Miss Eleanor Ambrose, for instance, a very celebrated beauty whom he addressed in the following jingle:

> In Flavia's eyes is every grace,
> She's handsome as she could be
> With Jacob's beauty in her face,
> And Esau's where it should be.[28]

The delighted newspapers took up the tune and replied:

> Flavia's a name a deal too free,
> With holy writ to blend her;
> Henceforth, let Nell Susanna be,
> And Chesterfield the Elder.[29]

As an example of how far the world has wagged since then, this trivial episode will serve as well as one more important. An English viceroy at a critical period endearing himself to the hearts of his subjects by rakish limericks, and a lovely debutante highly complimented by them, gives a picture of manners and customs which are entirely of the eighteenth century. But it illustrates also Chesterfield's insight into the character of the people he was dealing with. The Latin quality of his mind has been pointed out more than once, and there is a certain affinity between the Latin and the Celtic, which is entirely absent between the Celtic and the Anglo-Saxon. All the phrases and flourishes we have quoted were no doubt sincere, but they were also the result of a technique which had become natural. It is such little things as these that charm a people as they charm a drawing room. A stiff, dour governor may be ever so able, but other things being equal, he will certainly be surpassed by one with the gift of blarney. "I would be much rather distinguished and remembered," wrote Chesterfield, "by the name of the Irish Lord-Lieutenant than by that of the Lord-Lieutenant of Ireland." [30] There in a nutshell lies the reason for his success.

And it was a great success. Even the grandiloquent Maty did not exaggerate the facts. "A phenomenon took place," he observes, "not often beheld in times of tranquillity. Protestants and Roman Catholics, natives and strangers, well-wishers and enemies to the Pretender, all alike influenced by the example of their benevolent governor, indulged, respected, and would have loved one another, if he had continued a longer time among them." [31] Poets deluged him with dedications and with complimentary verses. Instead of the bullets that might have been singing at that moment, melodious praises fluttered up.

> Stanhope each purpose of his breast [breathed one]
> 　To gen'rous views consign'd:
> And chose his method to be blest,
> 　By blessing all mankind.
>
> Stanhope, though high thy transports glow,
> 　To one false step descend;
> Or you'll incur the dangerous woe
> 　Of him whom all commend. [32]

Furthermore, one must recognize the solid underpinning to the façade of his Lord-Lieutenancy: the conscientiousness, for example, that slighted no work and eliminated middlemen. Being compelled to have a secretary, he appointed a "genteel pretty young fellow" named Lyddel, whose value was purely decorative, and informed him frankly, "Sir, you will receive the emoluments of your place, but I will do the business myself, being determined to have no first minister." [33]

More impressive still, because more costly and because it exhibits an ideal of responsibility rare for the time, was the self-restraint he practiced in regard to his passion for gambling. During the months in Ireland and during his subsequent term as Secretary of State, he refrained rigidly from his favorite vice. It would have occasioned remark only among the strait-laced and the unfashionable if gaming for high stakes had gone on at the Castle, as it went on at St. James's Palace, but he forbade faro there and every other kind of high play during his tenure. [34] Maty ascribes it to a sense of respect for the dignity of his office, and this is doubtless right. He believed that a governor ought morally, as well as in other respects, to stand as a model to the governed, that this was one of the duties of his office, and he was prepared to discipline himself to that end. It represented the peak of the moral code, the Ciceronian ideal, he followed.[35] At this point, there begins to emerge another side of Chesterfield which we shall have increasing occasion to observe and study: the Chesterfield of later life, the philosopher, still worldly, still obstinately disillusioned, but mature in the Greek or Roman fashion.

With gaming eliminated, the Castle enjoyed a period of good behavior such as it had never experienced. The new Lord Lieutenant had always been temperate in meat and drink; the vice of drunkenness was his special abomination. Curiously enough, indeed, he can be regarded as one of the first temperance agitators, though with him the goal was extreme moderation rather than total abstention. It was against the Irish abuse of alcohol, with its inevitable lessening of economic efficiency, that he contended, not only during but after his stay in Ireland.[36] "It will be now too late," wrote Baron Bowes to George Dodington a month after his departure, "it will be too late to tell you of our gaiety and our sobriety whilst Lord Chesterfield was here, and unnecessary to tell you we are returning to old habits now he is gone. This I must say, his example has convinced that people may be cheerful, though sober." [37]

If we recall, then, the underpinning of industry, honesty, and self-discipline beneath his administration, we are not surprised to discover that beyond the details of wartime government, beyond the spacious word or act, he was deeply interested in the fundamental development of the Irish people. "Think of your manufactures," he wrote Prior, "at least as much as your militia, and be as much upon your guard against Poverty as against Popery; take my word for it, you are in more danger of the former than of the latter." [38] We find him encouraging such industries as those of paper, linen, and glass,[39] a patron of the philanthropic Dublin Society,[40] suggesting the introduction of French Huguenots into Ireland as a valuable laboring element,[41] encouraging the Charter Schools, advocating new methods of starch manufacture,[42] and the like.

"I am sensible," he wrote, "that I shall be reckoned a very shallow politician, for my attention to such trifling objects as the improvement of your lands, the extension of your manufactures, and the increase of your trade, which only tend to the advantage of the public; whereas an able Lord-Lieutenant ought to employ his thoughts in greater matters. He should think of jobs for favourites, sops for enemies, managing parties, and engaging Parliaments to vote away their own and their fellow-subjects' liberties and properties. But those great arts of Government, I confess, are above me, and people should not go out of their depth. I will modestly be content with wishing Ireland all the good that is possible, and with doing it all the good I can." [43]

Finally, we should repeat that Chesterfield's government of Ireland was strictly a one-man affair. From beginning to end, he made it evident that he would not tolerate any interference. Even Newcastle, who sought to pay a political debt with an Irish bishopric, was sent roundly about his business. [44] According to Maty, he declared openly, "that if, during his stay in Ireland, any person should make a successful application to the King, for any place in his Majesty's gift, through any other channel than his own, he would immediately throw up the Lord-Lieutenancy." [45] And this purpose was never challenged. Similarly, from subordinates in the government, he brooked no disobedience. The Master of the Rolls, having raised a flurry of opposition in the Irish House of Commons, was brought up sharply by the Earl, who told him, "Master, you must do the King's business, or be turned out of your employment, and if you are . . . you shall never come in again as long as I have any power." [46] Thus, if his government was efficient, it was also autocratic. In such an atmosphere of independence and unshared responsibility, his highest self and his worthiest talents could show themselves unhampered.

Meanwhile, a gradual change occurred in his relations with the King. Whatever the defects of George II may have been, faintheartedness was not among them, and while Newcastle trembled before the advance southward of the Highlanders, the King was demanding drastic, soldierly methods. With this policy Chesterfield, who, like most Englishmen of his time, bitterly detested the Scotch and Scotland, agreed. One of his letters to Newcastle, which fell under the eyes of the sovereign, did much to atone for the past. [47] He wished that the King's second son, the Duke of Cumberland, might return from the Netherlands and take command of the royal army; he advised the utmost severity against such men and officers as had shown the white feather at Prestonpans; he urged that no quarter should be given to the rebels in the future, even though the innocent might suffer with them. As regards the defense of Ireland, he outlined the immediate and effective measures he had taken. All this, as Newcastle wrote back, was music in the King's ears. "The spirit, the solidity, and the *bravery* of your letter," wrote the Duke, "had a wonderful effect. *Chesterfield is in the right; it is the wisest letter that ever was wrote,* and in short everything was liked." [48] Other letters in the same vein no doubt improved the good impression. The most ardent fire-eater in England could not have expressed himself in more vigorous terms. "Starve the whole country indiscriminately by your ships," he wrote Newcastle in the spring of 1746, "put a price upon the heads of the chiefs, and let the Duke put all to fire and sword." [49] His opposition to volunteer or, as he called them, "mob" regiments, raised by members of the nobility, was also pleasing to the King, who had a sound German belief in regular troops.[50]

A good many of the wartime utterances of Chesterfield must be taken with a grain of salt. They were colored partly by the excitement of the moment, and were intended for home consumption. As for the fire-and-sword element in them, he simply did not mean what he said. Two years later, at dinner with Lord Marchmont, Lord Huntingdon, and General Huske, he was advocating schools and villages to civilize the Highlands.[51]

Along with prejudices like these should be classed such remnants of earlier intolerance as even the most enlightened governor at that time could not be wholly free from. Thus, he approved of the Gavel Act, which automatically made any Protestant relation of a deceased Papist his sole heir, and hence set a premium on apostasy.[52] But such flaws were contrary to the whole trend of his mind and character. They were the unheeded cobwebs of the past.

On the whole, such was the quality of Chesterfield's performance as Lord Lieutenant, that one would be inclined to rub one's eyes and admire his perfection were it not that the other side of him, overshadowed by the achievements in Ireland, appears now and then in his correspondence, and the tip of the fox's ear peeps up through the lion's skin.

This hocus-pocus of letters, for example, the device of "private" and "very private": letters which could be shown to others to pro-

duce a certain effect, and letters which must be kept under lock and
key; "my lord," as a form of address designating one kind, and
"my dear lord" designating another; or two letters written at once
to the same person, one of them to be passed on and the other
withheld — what of them? It will be urged, of course, and with
obvious truth, that such expedients are unavoidable in business or
politics. And in any given case Chesterfield might have pleaded the
virtue of necessity. But throughout his correspondence there is
enough of this kind of thing to suggest that he rather enjoyed the
deftness of it, the wheels within wheels and clever management.
We find it afterward in his letters to Dayrolles, where detachable
postscripts instruct the latter how most adroitly to use the main
body of the text, how to waken curiosity on the part of a certain
person to see it, how to be persuaded reluctantly to show it, and so
on.[53] We find it even in relation to his son and the system of benevolent espionage with which he surrounded him.[54] We would not
make a mountain out of a molehill in regard to this, but would
merely suggest that it reflects an attitude of mind, and that the constructive statesman interested in the question of Irish manufactures,
schools, morality, and trade, kept equally in hand the arts of the
courtier and diplomat.

Or take that passage in a letter to Newcastle about the King's
now reigning mistress imported from Germany. "Would it be
amiss," he hints, "for you to cultivate Lady Yarmouth more than
you have hitherto done? She certainly can give good or bad impressions [to the King] in the many hours' conversations she has;
for even the wisest man, like the cameleon, takes without knowing it more or less of the hue of what he is often *upon*. Now Die-
maar's pension of a thousand pounds a year upon this establishment expires next month, and why should not your Brother * hint
to her a grant of that pension for a term of years? I dare say she
would understand so much English as that perfectly well!" Newcastle, in reply, thanks him for his "very kind and very wise" suggestion.[55] O subtle eighteenth century! But the Lord Lieutenant
has not greatly changed from the former Lord Steward.

Nor has his fundamental point of view altered. The Jacobite
revolt may be crushed; the menace of foreign invasion may vanish;
he may himself achieve solid results in his government of Ireland;

* I.e., Henry Pelham.

but he remains a pessimist in regard to the general situation. Everything internationally was going from bad to worse; the English Ministry was in a position where nothing good could be done; [56] the war on the Continent was drifting toward certain defeat for England and her allies. The negative attitude acquired during his years of opposition lingered on. He would never get rid of it. At most, in the serene philosophy of later life, he would become a resigned and affable defeatist.

Parallel with this trait continued inevitably another. There is no one who enjoys prophecy so much as a pessimist, and no prophet is more frequently wrong. We have touched on this characteristic of Chesterfield's before, and need not enlarge on it here. He had a supreme confidence in his acumen for foretelling the dismal future, and an absolute passion for doing so. That he was seldom right never discouraged him, nor roused any suspicion in his own mind as regards his competency. An occasional lucky hit atoned for a hundred errors. This foible is worth emphasizing as an example of how the shrewdest people are fooled about themselves, and of how convinced realists are usually eluded by reality. Lord Chesterfield's letters from Ireland are full of gloomy forebodings that for the most part came to nothing.

As the months passed in Dublin a further characteristic, still more individual with him, made itself apparent. Although, as we have pointed out, a firm believer in doing thoroughly whatever came to hand, he was an expert in the short task rather than the long one, and grew easily impatient of routine. This had been true of his first embassy to Holland; it was true of his leadership in the Opposition; it was to be further exemplified in his rivalry with Newcastle. And now in Dublin, the same trait became operative. In brief, he grew tired of his job.

There is a certain neutral quality in Chesterfield that gives a singular unity to his character. The spring bent now upon the positive, now upon the negative side, though tending toward the latter, maintained in general a middle position. It was this that prevented any long-continued creative work. It made him a letter-writer and essayist, though both by training and talent he might have written great history or valuable memoirs. It gave him brief periods of political brilliance, but forbade a sustained career. If

Newcastle had been forced out, and if the premiership had devolved upon him, it is still inconceivable that he would have remained long in power. The blight of indifference, apathy, weariness — call it what you will — would have set him sighing after lost leisure. His capacity was quick, varied, and rich, but lacked the depth that gives continuance.

From the outset he had chafed. "Pity me a little," he had written the Duke two weeks after arriving, "me, who am as much plagued with little business as you can be with great. . . . Every connection, nay almost every family, expects to govern, or means to distress, if they can't govern, the Lord-Lieutenant." [57] And when, after eight months of exile, circumstances permitted his return to London, he embraced the occasion joyfully. "Though I am obliged to you for wishing me in England," he wrote Newcastle in February, "I assure you, you need not invite me there. I have had royalty enough, God knows, and am very impatient to return to the state of an English subject." [58] In March he was counting the days with impatience; [59] in April he could not tell the Duke how impatient he was to assure him in London that no man there was more faithfully and inviolably his.[60]

So, at length, he rushed the necessary bills through the Irish parliament, prorogued it, and could make arrangements for departure. Ostensibly it was on leave of absence, but neither he nor anyone else was deceived on that point.[61] He had finished with the Lord-Lieutenancy.

The regret was universal. A bust of him "placed in the castle," says Maty, "does him the greater honour, as it was fixed with public acclamations, and out of part of the savings of the public money." Maty continues: "To be," he says, "as much regretted when he quitted his employment as he had been extolled when he entered upon it, is a glory singularly attached to the Earl of Chesterfield, whose name still continues dear to that grateful and respectable people. . . . Persons of all ranks, denominations, and religions, followed him with his lady to the water-side, to which he walked, and from which he *publicly* embarked. The Bishop of Waterford, who was present at this pleasing but melancholy procession, expresses in the most feeling manner the universal acclamations of the people who praised him, blessed him, and intreated him to return." [62]

It is an old-fashioned, pretty scene, the departure of Chesterfield, his lady on his arm, down the cobblestone street, through the ranks of people, his wig immaculate, his laced hat gracefully doffed. And at the water front, with the big-bellied frigate, the plying of small boats, the fluttering of flags, the smell of tar and cordage — a final bow from the deck, a debonair wave of the hand, a final curtsy of Lady Chesterfield — then salvos of cannon and rolling of drums.

As in the case of the embassies in Holland, his reputation lingered and was cherished in Ireland. "Lord Chesterfield's influence," wrote the Earl of Orrery, "like the departing sun, has left a warm and serene sky behind it." [63] As late as 1754 there was talk of reappointing him Lord Lieutenant "to quiet the minds of the people," [64] for his successors had neither his tact nor his moderation. He had set a standard in government which would remain authoritative long afterwards. [65] Moreover, as after the diplomatic missions, he returned home with enhanced prestige and an embellished record. His success in Ireland had become public talk. [66] There was considerable gossip as to what the plans for him were: an embassy to Spain, to Paris, or The Hague. [67] But as a matter of fact an even higher post was imminent. After an illness that sent him to vegetate for a while at Bath, he was able, at the end of October, 1746, to address his letters from Whitehall, as one of His Majesty's two Secretaries of State. [68]

CHAPTER XVI
Coarse Pulleys and Dirty Ropes

THE FIGURE cut by Chesterfield as Secretary of State is so diminished in comparison with that of the Lord Lieutenant that biographers ever since have felt compelled to apologize and extenuate. If he had retired from public life on his return from Ireland, he would have left a clean-cut, brilliant record. As it was, his career faded out in a kind of pathetic insignificance. From being an active, autocratic and constructive governor, he declined (in spite of his cabinet rank) into the position of a mere clerk, a rubber stamp for Newcastle. And, what is more, he accepted this indignity for over a year. The reasons for such a decline are worth establishing. They are speculative in part, but, however we theorize or condone, they are never entirely to Chesterfield's credit.

It will be recalled that he entered the Broad-bottomed ministry as leader of a pacific Opposition urging peace with France as early and as favorable as possible; but that the formula binding together the peace and war elements of the cabinet had been the plan of a vigorous campaign in order to secure advantageous terms. Since then the fortunes of war had, on one side, given Cape Breton, the key of Canada, into the hands of the English and, on the other, had left France in control of the Netherlands. Meanwhile also, the French Foreign Minister d'Argenson had come forward with peace terms which Chesterfield, Harrington, and Henry Pelham considered sufficiently favorable to serve as a basis for discussion. They included the return of Cape Breton to France, the neutrality of the Netherlands, and a concession to Spain at the expense of Austria's holdings in Italy. But to these terms the war half of the cabinet, to wit, the Duke of Newcastle and Lord Hardwicke, supported by the pugnacious King, were for various reasons bitterly opposed; and the turn of events gave additional weight to their opposition. The hope could plausibly be entertained that Spain (at the death of Philip V) would be detached from her alliance with France; that the latter by an invasion of Provence would be forced to evacuate the Netherlands; that Cape Breton need not be surrendered.

Such, in general, was the situation at the end of the summer of 1746. Newcastle was in the ascendancy; an envoy of pro-war leanings and directly responsible to him, the Earl of Sandwich, had been sent to the peace conference at Breda with instructions to delay any conclusion. All the indications were that the war would go on.

Up to this point Chesterfield had consistently, though without rancor, opposed the Duke, as far as the latter's diplomatic program was concerned. On his return to England he had declined Newcastle's proposal that he succeed Lord Harrington as a Secretary of State in the event of the latter's resignation, and he had similarly declined being sent as an envoy to Breda. His answer had been that "he would keep Ireland as long as he was in place." [1] He was opposed to the war and would not collaborate in prolonging it. [2]

Then an amazing *volte-face* occurred. Chesterfield returned from Bath and called on Newcastle in the morning of October 28. The Duke, having outlined the political situation, suggested once more that Chesterfield should succeed Harrington as Secretary of State, and regretted that it was chiefly a difference of opinion in regard to the continuance of the war that prevented this. Whereupon, to Newcastle's complete surprise, [3] the Earl (and here we quote Newcastle himself) answered that "of all things he did not desire to be Secretary of State; that, as to the difference of opinion in foreign affairs, he had been, and still was, of opinion that peace should have been made pretty much upon the foot of d'Argenson's project, but that now the die of war was cast, and that he thought it should be carried on in the strongest manner, and particularly that we should give £900,000 for 30,000 Russians if we could have them, and upon this foot would accept the Secretary's office." "He allowed me," continued Newcastle in his letter to Hardwicke, "to acquaint my brother with this and even the King. This I thought determined him the successor, in case the King liked it." [4] Almost simultaneously with this, Lord Harrington, cold-shouldered out of his place, resigned. The King, mollified by Chesterfield's Irish record, accepted the latter as his successor — at least conditionally.

"You shall help get rid of him," he told Newcastle, "if I don't like him."

"That is already done," replied the Duke. "The moment the King dislikes him, he told me he would make his bow."

And at once Chesterfield, having called on the King and having been cordially received, accepted.[5]

The change of front in regard to the war is sufficiently puzzling, but attendant circumstances make it more puzzling still. These are connected with Newcastle's personality, and with the status in relation to the Duke which the office of Secretary of State implied. It was not as if Chesterfield had known little or nothing of Newcastle's peculiarities. He knew them intimately. "We were," he wrote long afterwards, "contemporaries, near relations, and familiar acquaintances."[6] He was perfectly familiar with the Duke's thirst for prominence and with the jealousy and pettiness that accompanied it. Nor was there the slightest secret as to the ultimate cause or the immediate occasion of Lord Harrington's resignation. The complicated system that permitted two Secretaries of State, one for the northern and one for the southern international fields, rendered co-operation between them exceedingly difficult if one of them, like Newcastle, endeavored at all costs to monopolize power, and if the other, standing on his dignity, refused to be shelved. This had happened in the case of Harrington, who learned that Newcastle, to cap his interferences, was carrying on a secret correspondence with Sandwich, the British ambassador to Holland and therefore belonging to Harrington's province. It indicated not only that the Duke was running his department for him, but that subordinates in that department recognized the Duke's authority. When it appeared that the King not only knew but approved of this practice, Harrington gave up the Seals.

Now, Chesterfield not only accepted the vacant post, but he accepted it with full knowledge that the correspondence between Newcastle and Sandwich would continue. Nay, he even approved of this correspondence, though doubtless he considered himself man enough to outbulk Newcastle eventually in Sandwich's eyes. "Pray continue," he instructed the latter on February 20, 1747, "to write separate letters to the Duke of Newcastle, if you would continue to be well with him; for he is a jealous lover of paper." In brief, then, he who had entered the coalition government as leader of the peace party, and who, as Lord Lieutenant of Ireland, had not permitted the slightest interference in his province, had now performed a complete change of front in every particular: he agreed to the prosecution of the war, and he accepted not only interference in his departmental affairs, but cheerfully played second fiddle to the Duke. Why?

Biographical problems, as a rule, would be much simpler if biographers, enamored of their heroes, did not muddy the waters by too ingenious apologies. In the first place, it is important to remember that Chesterfield was a politician by career and that politicians (even aristocrats of the eighteenth century) have, as their chief aim, the holding of office. It is absurd to contend that he was coaxed, jockeyed, or deceived into accepting one of the most important posts in the cabinet. To assert this is to make a fool or weakling of him. During the months that had passed since his return from Ireland in June, his political ambition, momentarily satisfied by the Irish viceroyalty and certainly dampened by a serious illness, had no doubt reawakened. Newcastle's offer of the Seals in October was a different, more immediate prospect than earlier offers had been. What additional considerations may have contributed we have no means of knowing — the future of his son, advantages to friends and relatives — but it is unnecessary to seek a more unusual motive than the love of place and power with all that that means of eminence. His interview with Newcastle shows this. He protested, indeed, that "of all things he did not desire to be Secretary of State," and then proceeded to fall in completely with Newcastle's policies or actually to improve on them in the direction of war, concluding that on such a foot he would accept the Secretary's office. This does not look like reluctance, but like eagerness. To be sure, also, he wrote the following lines to one of his French friends, Madame de Monconseil, a month later: "Here I am then withdrawn from an honourable and lucrative place, of which the duties did not encroach too much upon the time that I like to spend upon the amenities of society or even of indolence. I enjoyed therein both leisure and dignity; whereas at present I find myself, as it were, raised to a public pedestal, an eminence which my person, by no means a colossus as you know, will never be able to sustain; and I am burdened, moreover, by work that exceeds the strength of my body and mind. Ought I to be congratulated, or ought I not rather to be pitied?" [7]

Whatever *ought* to be the case, he knew that Madame de Monconseil *would* congratulate him, would admire the "public pedestal," and among her friends in Paris would not fail to refer with a negligent pride to her correspondent, the English Minister of State. A screen of courtly modestly conceals no small elation. As to his regrets for the Lord-Lieutenancy, we have already seen that he was tired of the post. It was simply a habit with him to deprecate the present, to augur ill of the future, and to sigh over the past. No importance can be attached to such utterances.

But if love of power was the chief incentive to his action at this point, it is by no means probable that he took the Seals with the idea of subservience to Newcastle, or that he desired merely to enjoy an empty title. Mr. Dobrée, in the Introduction to his edition of the *Letters*, sets forth, I believe, the only tenable theory in this regard. With all due modesty, Lord Chesterfield could not but feel his intellectual superiority to most of his colleagues in the ministry, and especially to Newcastle. Admitting that the Duke had had a longer training in government, and that he had perhaps derived from Walpole something of the latter's parliamentary astuteness, there could be no comparison between him and Chesterfield on the score of address, versatility, self-discipline, and mental power; nor can Chesterfield be blamed for regarding him with obvious contempt. "He was always in a hurry," wrote the Earl in his later "Character" of Newcastle, "never walked, but always ran; insomuch that I have sometimes told him, that by his fleetness one should rather take him for the courier than the author of the letters. — He was as jealous of his power as an impotent lover of his mistress, without activity of mind enough to enjoy or exert it, but could not bear a share even in the appearances of it. . . . Upon the whole, he was a compound of most human weaknesses. . . ." [8] Therefore with whatever seeming compliance Chesterfield entered the cabinet (and there can be no question but that the Duke regarded him as entirely under his direction), it is inconceivable that he did not expect eventually by his own weight to exercise greater influence than his shallower colleague. This confidence is clearly apparent in a letter to the Earl of Sandwich written several weeks after taking the Seals. "Though upon my coming into this post, the Duke of

Newcastle desired you to drop your separate correspondence with him [it had been this correspondence which had caused Harrington's resignation], yet I find he expected you should sometimes write to him as friend. He dropped something of this kind the other day, and I thought it right to inform you of it. Therefore pray send him a friendly letter once a fortnight or so. There are certain weaknesses that it were weak not to conform to. I have many of my own, but jealousy and suspicion are not of the number." [9] And similarly a month afterwards: "The Duke of Newcastle was pleased with your letter; pray refresh him now and then with one, and mix some business in it. I assure you *I shall not be jealous*." [10]

It is clear that Chesterfield considered himself above the need of jealousy; he belonged to a higher sphere than Newcastle,[11] and took it for granted that Sandwich realized it. But even after it became apparent that Sandwich was bearing complete allegiance to the Duke rather than to the chief of the Northern Department, even after negotiations involving Holland's policy toward the war had been entered upon over his head and without his participation, Chesterfield, as Mr. Dobrée points out, continued to believe that he would eventually outdistance Newcastle. He "would hold out longer than people thought. Besides, things might mend"; [12] he "was growing daily stronger with the King"; [13] he "was quietly permitting Newcastle to display his incompetency." [14] It was a dignified, inactive role that depended too much on his own merit unadvertised and unsupported by effort. Not until eight months had passed did he realize that his passive campaign against Newcastle had been lost, and that in politics as in affairs generally it is not so much merit as stir and noise that count.

Odd that so shrewd a man had not foreseen this. Others had foreseen and warned him. An anonymous pamphlet with the title *An Expostulatory Letter to a Certain Right Honourable Person upon his late Promotion,* which appeared not long after Chesterfield's transfer into the new position, undoubtedly represented a point of view shared by others than its author. In any case, it foretold with amazing precision what actually happened. After emphasizing the success of Chesterfield's administration in Ireland, the respect and affection for him of the Irish people, the independence enjoyed by him in that post, the certain prospects of future achievement, it went on to demand, "Why then, my Lord, did you slight the Affection of a People that was growing to the highest Pitch of Fondness, and among whom you had no Controuler or Associate, to accept a Charge which at best is burthensome and envied? [15] . . . Take care, my Lord; for I am afraid that you who so long held out against the *master* [Walpole], have at last been shamefully taken in by the *scholars*. . . . I doubt if it will turn out either to your *honour* or your *satisfaction*. If you go into all the measures of these men, you will manifestly be led by them, and contradict in actions what you have so often advanced in words. . . . If you oppose them too strongly in their darling scheme of administration, is it not probable that we shall see one of the effects of your promotion; either that you are overruled and make a cypher in all debates, or are obliged in disgust to quit your seat and office? Neither of which, I presume, will be very satisfactory to a man of your Lordship's elevated spirit." [16]

But Chesterfield, as we have seen — for instance, in regard to his fondness for political prophesying — did not set a low estimate on his astuteness. It was one of his weaknesses, deepening as the years passed, to believe that he knew much more about human nature than he actually did know. Indeed, this is one of the defects to which that type of mind is almost inevitably subject, for to no one more than the realist and the rationalist are the words appropriate, "Let him that thinketh he stands take heed lest he fall." Like a chess player who imagines that he sees a move ahead of his opponent, Chesterfield proudly overlooked the board, and when the openings were over, discovered that he had been checkmated. It is distressing to trace step by step the course of his gradual humiliation. The impression is given of a weakening grip, a growing bewilderment, a clinging to appearances, and then the recognition that his day was done. It is the politician's vesper hour. People were beginning not to take him seriously.

For one thing he had become a courtier again, and he who but a few months ago was advocating high-handed measures in regard to the King was now bending a supple back at St. James's and by propitiating the King and the royal mistress was attempting to outrival Newcastle. We find him, for instance, in one of the anterooms expending his graces on a small boy whom he supposed to be Master Louis, the King's son by Lady Yarmouth. He is prodigal of his deep regard for the lad's mamma. "The shrewd boy," says Horace Walpole, "received all his lordship's vows with indulgence, and without betraying himself — at last he said, 'I suppose your Lordship takes me for Master Louis, but I am only Sir William Russel, one of the pages' ": [17] a story that would go the rounds of fashionable London accompanied by a devastating titter. Or again, we find him making the King laugh at a joke like the one recorded by Maty where the King refused the appointment of a certain person to a great position on the ground that he "would rather have the devil. 'With all my heart,' replied the Earl, 'I only beg leave to put your Majesty in mind, that the commission is indited to *our right trusty and right well-beloved cousin.*' " [18] He made headway in the royal closet and won the friendship of Lady Yarmouth; [19] but this very success redoubled Newcastle's jealousy of him, [20] and the day was past, as Lord Carteret had discovered to his sorrow, when a King's or a mistress's pleasure outweighed more solid considerations.

Meanwhile, week by week, his influence ebbed. The initial self-reliance became less serene and rather dogged. Lord Sandwich, who, as a younger man, had been one of his political protégés, sensed the decline and veered over to Newcastle. By June 1747, the new Secretary of State for the Northern Department had barely authority sufficient to secure the appointment of his young friend, Solomon Dayrolles, as Resident at The Hague: an appointment bitterly resented by Sandwich, who believed, not without reason perhaps, that Dayrolles would serve as Chesterfield's personal spy on his actions. In the same month it became apparent through advices from Dayrolles that Newcastle was encroaching still further upon the Earl's department by negotiating directly with Count Bentinck, the leader of the Dutch war party. [21] In view of this, Lord Chesterfield was little better than an upper clerk to whom routine business was entrusted. He hung on during the summer with some remnant of hope, but with increasing heartache. On August 25 he wrote Dayrolles: "I don't at all wonder at Lord Sandwich's proceeding with you, as it is conformable to his conduct with regard to me. His Lordship has for some time made his option between the Duke of Newcastle and myself, and I suppose thinks he has chose the best, in which however he may some time or other find himself mistaken. Bentinck follows his example, and never comes near me nor speaks to me about business, though in my province, but confers wholly with his Grace." [22]

A month later that trait which we have already noted — the tendency to grow tired of any situation or problem if too long unchanged — had become operative, and amid gloomy forebodings he gave up the contest. "He [the Duke of Newcastle] is the only person here weak enough and ignorant enough to support those wild schemes which I fear will end in the ruin of the Republic [Holland], and, in consequence, of England. I am concerned for the public, which I take to be in a very dangerous situation; as to myself in particular, I am extremely easy. I will continue in public life, while I can do it with honour; and, when I cannot, I shall enjoy private life with pleasure, and I hope some reputation." [23]

But in point of fact, he had already in a sense outstayed his honor and he lingered another four months at his derogatory post. Hardwicke, the Lord Chancellor, gives a striking picture of him during this phase, a self-pitying impression. "Lord Chesterfield," he records, "never avowed an opinion in the closet contrary to the King's . . . would never propose a plan of peace, tho' for one on any terms . . . [was] never explicit in his opinion . . . would only write just as he was bid; told a foreign minister that he had *beaucoup à faire, rien à dire;* again that he was the 3rd commis [or clerk] in England." [24] A silly and peevish and baffled state of mind, for nothing prevented his resignation. He stayed on apparently to save appearances and to avoid confessing defeat. Besides, there may have been a vague hope from day to day that some change would occur.

It was about this time that an elephantine, middle-aged hack writer named Johnson, who was known chiefly for a poem called *London* and a life of the poet Savage, addressed the Plan of an English dictionary to Lord Chesterfield. He had long been contemplating this project, and had contracted for it with the publisher Robert Dodsley, in conjunction with several of the other London publishers; but, being of a dilatory turn, had put off even writing a prospectus. The address to Chesterfield was Dodsley's idea; the Earl was by now a leading Maecenas, famed for his friendship with Pope, Montesquieu, and Voltaire, one of the Twickenham elite, a patron of the lesser fry, English and Irish. On the pretext that dedications to such a nobleman took time, Johnson gave himself the benefit of further delay. In the end, the Plan was finished and presented. Chesterfield, who had already heard of it, was interested, received the author in a gracious interview, enchanted him with his manners, and discussed the prospectus with him in detail.[25] As a return for the dedication of the Plan, he made Johnson a gift of ten pounds, which, by the way, had been precisely the amount derived from the sale of the poem *London*.

Here matters rested. Any sensible person would suppose that Chesterfield had acted properly and even generously. But Secretaries of State are busy men; he did not cultivate Johnson's further acquaintance. The gracious interview had perhaps given rise to false hopes; it is possible, indeed, that the lexicographer may have waited once or twice on the Earl without seeing him. After all, what credentials did he have except an unprepossessing exterior and the plan of a dictionary not yet, and possibly never to be, written? He was not yet the great Dr. Johnson; but he was the same man, and he had the pride of Lucifer.

Years passed; no dictionary appeared; Chesterfield forgot all about Johnson. As far as one can see, there was no compelling reason why he should have remembered him. And here we will leave the episode in order that the reader may gain a proper perspective for judging the end of it seven years later. Unjustly and curiously enough, it is one of the most famous passages in Chesterfield's life. Such is the distorting power of a great literary name and a mischievous pen.

Perhaps instinctively to compensate himself for a dwindling importance in the world of affairs and to salve the pain of unacknowledged failure, it was during these same months of discontent that Lord Chesterfield laid the foundations of a residence so splendid as to stir the admiration of an age accustomed to noble domestic architecture and to magnificent decoration. Let petty and vulgar men triumph, here at least would rise a monument to his taste and urbanity, his learning and his lordliness. It should perfectly represent him, as the outer casket of his personality, the intricate symbol of a versatile and patrician mind. It should reflect his superiority, his scornful indifference to the poor business of courts and council rooms. He would withdraw hither proudly from that sordid arena which failed to appreciate him, and in the serenity of his palace would say to his soul, "Thou hast much goods laid up for many years."

Subconsciously thoughts like these, however unexpressed, attended the building of Chesterfield House. They are implicit in the pride with which he proclaimed the superiority of certain rooms to any in London, the superiority of his gardens, the superiority of his paintings. They are implicit in the loving attention to details of ornament or furnishing over a period of two and a half years. Chesterfield House should interpret him triumphantly to the world.

Of course it was in the French style, "with plentiful sculptures and gildings" [26] (*avec force sculptures et dorures*). Any other type of decoration would have been inappropriate in his case. And he had a great reception court and spacious gardens — "rarities in London though usual in Paris." [27] The French soul of the Earl demanded a habitation reminiscent of the Faubourg St. Germain. His boudoir was "so gay and so smiling" that one would never be able to *bouder* there. "Its ceiling and woodwork are of a lovely blue," he wrote, "with many mouldings and gildings; the tapestries and upholstery are of a flowered design in *petit-point,* a splendid pattern on a white background; over the mantel-piece of Giallo di Sienna marble, there is much mirror and moulding and gilding which surrounds the portrait of a very handsome woman painted by Rosalba." [28] It was as French as possible. The Marquise de Monconseil in Paris supplied it with porcelain sconces which were warmly appreciated. "I am proud of them, Madame, as of a fair mistress, but I am also jealous of them. If I do not show them, my vanity will suffer, and if I do, who knows? They are fragile; others will touch them, will break them perhaps. . . . Decide what I ought to do. They fit the two sides of my boudoir mantel-piece, as if they were made to order. . . ." [29]

From the summer of 1747 over a period of three years he was building and tinkering and adorning. Politics and his retirement were forgotten in this new interest. He employed his protégé, Dayrolles, to secure him paintings. "I have already, as you know," he wrote, "a most beautiful landscape by Reubens, and a pretty little piece of Teniers; but if you could meet with a large capital history, or allegorical piece of Reubens, with the figures as big as the life, I would go pretty deep to have it, as also for a large and capital picture of Teniers. . . . What I want to complete my col-

lection, is only two or three of the most eminent Masters. . . ."
And what elation when a capital painting by Rubens, secured
through the dutiful Dayrolles, arrived! — the most graceful and
beautiful figure of a Virgin he ever saw, and "not so Flemish-built
as most of Reubens's are." "All the Reubenses in England," he declared subsequently, "must strike to mine." He negotiated with the
Chapter at Rheims for a Holy Family by Titian, and was bitterly
disappointed when judges acting for him at Paris affirmed it to be a
"damned" copy. He visited print shops, and studied auction cata-
logues for objects of virtu, "bustoes and vases" — a Hermes, a
Bacchus, a Priapus.[30]

Next to his boudoir, the library at Chesterfield House absorbed
him. He called it the best in England.[31] We will deal with the
contents of it later, a map, as it were, of his intellectual range and
interests; but, for the moment, think of a quiet, spacious, and very
stately room, lined, halfway up the walls, with books, and above
them, close together, the portraits of eminent French and English
authors. Upon the mantelpieces and cabinets stood busts of old
orators, "interspersed with voluptuous vases and bronzes, antique or
Italian, and airy statuettes of Opera nymphs." * The whole room was
surmounted by a frieze inscribed with verses from Horace:

> *Nunc veterum libris, nunc somno, et inertibus horis*
> *Ducere sollicitae jucunda oblivia vitae.*[32]
> (Now with old books and sleep and languid hours,
> To taste the longed-for bliss of private life.)

But Chesterfield House was symbolic not only of its owner, but
of the period which he so peculiarly represented: in the bleak discomfort of the bedrooms, for instance, as compared with the downstairs spaciousness and splendor, an arrangement reflecting the
all-importance of the social, as opposed to domestic, life. Its classical
taste appeared in the far-flung colonnade connecting the two wings
of the house with the central mass, and in the lawns and formal

---

* *Cf.* Lord Brougham's article, *Quarterly Review*, vol. 76, 1845, p. 484. The
library and boudoir were unaltered when he wrote. Horace Walpole relates
that there were also busts of Adam de Stanhope and Eve de Stanhope in ridicule of genealogical pretensions; but this is probably only another version of
the anecdote recorded some years earlier by Miss Talbot, writing to Mrs.
Carter, May 23, 1743, to the effect that the Earl had inscribed an ancient family
portrait group, Adam and Eve, Cain and Abel Stanhope. Mrs. Carter's *Letters*,
1809, vol. i, p. 33.

gardens extending behind, and presenting, as the Earl expressed it,
"a scene of verdure and flowers not common in London." [33]

In short, the magnificence of the Italian Renaissance as expressed by Palladio, adapted by Inigo Jones, and readapted by
Chesterfield's friend, Lord Burlington and the Earl of Pembroke,[34]
this magnificence had not yet given way to the Victorian ideal of
the quaint, the somber, and the quiet. The patrician epoch, now
in its sunset glory, stood revealed in the formality, the generous
façade, the serene aloofness of Chesterfield House.

It stood in Mayfair facing the Park, a suburban neighborhood
at that time and one of sinister reputation, so much so that the
Earl spoke of living "among a parcel of thieves and murderers,"
and returned home from the club at nights under an escort of his
footmen armed with blunderbusses.[35] As the name of the district
indicates, it was the site of the noisy and disorderly May Fair that
was held annually (with occasional suppressions) until after 1766,
when the Earl of Coventry, aided perhaps by Chesterfield, secured
its final abolition.[36] That the latter chose to build in such a neighborhood is one more evidence of his progressiveness, which fore-
saw the development of London in that direction, and of his love
of space and of gardens.

More impressive, more significant, however, than anything else
in regard to Chesterfield House is the time consumed and the
personal care expended in building it. Native as we are to an age of
rapid construction, where an imposing mansion is run up and
finished within six or nine months from the signing of the contract,
the three years [37] required for the erection of this particular house
remind us of the efficiency and progress achieved in building since
then. But if there has been an enormous gain in speed, there has
been also something lost in less measurable values: the intangible
charm that work done by hand gives to anything, the minute
irregularities that lend personality and mellowness to surfaces or
decoration. The pride of craftsmanship leaves a subtle beauty as
its memorial that no amount of machined exactness can achieve.
Indeed, time itself would seem to lend an irreplaceable increment
of grace that defies imitation. For this reason nothing of permanent
value, none of those elements which are the flower and fruit of
civilization, can be quickly produced, no matter with what energy
or scientific method they are attempted. But add to this the second

factor mentioned above — namely, personal superintendence by the owner himself — and it becomes apparent how great and individual houses evolve, and why the comfortable prairies of modern architecture so seldom are relieved by any distinguished landmark. Isaac Ware was the architect of Chesterfield House, but Lord Chesterfield sat at his elbow. Nor were interior decorators required for the furnishing of halls or galleries or apartments. It was the Earl himself, his own personality and no one else's, that the house was expressing.

As a consequence, Chesterfield House, so lovingly and carefully built, remained to the end * (though deprived of its former spaciousness by the denseness of the city) a peculiarly revealing monument to its first owner. Here, as in other enterprises of his life that offered a definite, limited task, he achieved a singular perfection. Nor is it a small thing for anyone to bequeath such an interpretation of himself to posterity.

Absorption in building, decoration and art-collecting, which reveal the sophisticated mandarin quality both of the Earl and of his period, were not the only recreations of these last months of his political career. Sufficient traces of his correspondence remain to prove the increasing gusto that he took in letter writing. The famous epistles to his son are accumulating; the no less delightful letters to Dayrolles are acquiring an added sparkle. We shall discuss Chesterfield as a letter writer in another place; but at this point the addresses of several to whom he was writing should be recalled as significant. It will be remembered that a long and arduous war was in progress and that Chesterfield was one of the King's Secretaries for Foreign Affairs. A modern mind will be therefore impressed by the nationality of some of his most valued correspondents. They were French noblemen and ladies. His Majesty's Secretary of State was corresponding with the enemy.

That he did so without the least embarrassment or prick of conscience is creditable both to him and to his age. Our day of inflamed nationalism had yet to dawn; manufactured hatred had not yet become patriotism, nor did declarations of war destroy international friendships. To enlightened people, war remained a political matter requiring loyalty, but not imposing rancor. It was, at that time, perhaps too much of a game and too coolly perpetrated; but

* It was demolished in 1934.

the attitude of personal detachment regarding it had at least certain advantages over our present acrimony. Thus, no amount of bloodshed by sea or by land produced the slightest ripple in the relations between Chesterfield and his intellectual flirt, the Marquise de Monconseil. He remained firmly English, and she, no doubt with equal firmness, upheld her own country, but the subject, as far as their mutual sentiments were concerned, was academic and remote.

"I assure you," he declared, "that I wish for peace every bit as much as you; and I believe that, if it depended only on the two of us to bring it about, it would soon be made. But, as it unfortunately does not depend entirely on us — what's to be done? You desire it on your terms, which would in no way suit us. We desire a just peace, and you want an advantageous one, so that I fear it is farther off than ever. We seek only liberty and the safety of Europe; you are interested only in your despotism. How then can we get together? Only leave to our queen [i.e., Maria Theresa] what belongs to her and what you have guaranteed her, and do not demand for your queen [i.e., Elizabeth Farnese of Spain] what in no sense belongs to her, and then we could come to terms." [38] Whereupon, in the next paragraph, he discusses the education of his son, whom he plans to send to Paris as soon as the war is over, so that he can acquire that "easy polish, those manners, that attractiveness, which surely is found only in France." And on this far more interesting topic, he asks the Marquise's advice.

An international tennis match today would heat the pulse of moderately interested people to about the same degree as the War of the Austrian Succession stirred emotionally the beau monde of that decade. This interchange of letters continued during Chesterfield's entire term of office. It accompanied also an occasional interchange of gifts such as dress material,[39] or porcelain, and the like.

The Marquise de Monconseil was not the only French person on the Earl's list of correspondents. There were the Duke de Nivernais (to whom Philip Stanhope, the younger, owed a pleasant reception at Rome) and the Chevalier de Mirabeau. There was the Duke de Nevers, for whom Chesterfield spent two years in search of a proper English stallion; and when the animal had been found, he dispatched it to the Duke with a gelding from his own stables as a token of esteem. There was the Abbé de Ville, his opponent during

the second embassy to Holland, a beloved enemy, who kept him
supplied with the latest French books. There was the Maréchal de
Coigny, with whom he condoled upon the death of a son killed in
a duel.[40] No doubt there were others. He was always partial to
France and to the French; [41] his retirement from office was keenly
regretted in Paris.[42]

Thus, at a point, sophistication with its cosmopolitan attitude,
its cool tolerance, produces an effect resembling Christian charity.
Absence of emotion may counterfeit love. For Chesterfield and
other *grands seigneurs*, there extended above the frontiers of country
or religion a common atmosphere — not of human nature, not of
mutual affection, but of a class ideal dominating vulgar emotions
and fanaticisms. It was the ideal of good form.

Towards the end of the year 1747 he had given up the political
game. The bubble of that ambition had burst; his eyes smarted a
little, but, after all, so much remained: the society of his friends,
the cultivation of leisure, the career of his son. There may have
been a hint of the sour-grapes philosophy in his attitude at the
time, but there was, far more than that, a sincere desire for private
life. What bitterness was left could be almost completely dis-
sembled. He had grown tired of affairs altogether, as in the past he
had tired one by one of his separate employments. And now, as
progressively in the years to follow, there was a taste in his mouth
of dust and ashes. The fruit of the long effort had not seemed
worth striving for. According to Pope, the triumph of wisdom was
"well-tim'd retreat." He would retire to the elegances of Chesterfield House and sip the cup of social pleasures.

On the day before Christmas, 1747, he presented his friend the
Earl of Marchmont with a veritable litany of dissatisfaction. He had
resolved to give up his office. His advice in regard to the war had
been ignored. He had been discredited with the King by the Duke
of Newcastle, who undermined him in that quarter and opposed
him in every way possible. Why, even such a trivial matter as the
promotion of his relative Lieutenant Colonel George Stanhope to
the command of a regiment had been passed over five times in spite
of his recommendation, to show that he had no credit. Everyone
must be thinking that he continued to hold office for the sake of the
£5000 a year! To this he added a list of other grievances:

... that he was everyday setting his hand to what he disapproved, and carrying on measures he condemned, and acting as the Duke of Newcastle's clerk; that he was identified with a bad war which would end in a bad peace; and of this he would be held responsible, as having always been for peace; that the nearer it came to this last period, the more difficult his situation grew. He would tell 'em that his health would not permit him to go through the fatigues of an office wherein he could do no service beyond another. He would tell the King the same thing, and that he had not enough credit with him to serve him to his satisfaction, that his advice had no weight in the conduct of his affairs, which he thought in a very desperate state, that he would continue to support his government and measures without any employment and with better effect out than in. He would tell everybody that he was employed in the care of his health and finishing his new house. He would go to Bath for a month and leave his proxy with Lord Gower to show he had no quarrel with the government.[43]

But his resignation hung fire. On January 26, 1748, he wrote Dayrolles in the same vein as his conversation with Marchmont, but more temperately and with great objectiveness. Indeed, this letter reflects so perfectly his entire state of mind at the moment of quitting office that the relevant parts of it should be inserted here. His obvious sincerity makes any further comment superfluous.

Neither the state of foreign nor domestic affairs will permit me to continue much longer in my present situation [he asserted]. I cannot go on writing orders, of which I see and foretell the fatal tendency. I can no longer take my share of either the public indignation or contempt on account of measures in which I have no share. I can no longer continue in a post in which it is well known that I am but a *Commis;* and in which I have not been able to do any one service to any one man though ever so meritorious, lest I should be supposed to have any power and my colleague not the whole. And lastly, I tell you very truly, I long for rest and quiet, equally necessary to my present state both of body and mind. Could I do any good, I would sacrifice some more quiet to it; but, convinced as I am that I can do none, I will indulge my ease, and preserve my character.

I have gone through pleasures while my constitution and my spirits would allow me. Business succeeded them; and I have now gone through every part of it, without liking it at all the better for

being acquainted with it. Like many other things, it is most admired by those who know it the least. And this one consideration
would alone disgust one of it, even if one had the sole power;
which is, that in this country one must, for political reasons, frequently prefer the most unworthy to the most worthy, and prostitute to importunity and undeserving greediness the rewards of
merit. Thus weary of business, you will easily imagine, that in
retiring from my present business, I shall not engage in any other;
but far from embarking upon any account in cabals and opposition,
whenever I do take any part in the House of Lords, it shall be
in support of the Government. Do not think neither that I mean
a sullen retirement from the world; on the contrary, my retreat
from business will give me both more time and better spirits for
the enjoyment of social life, from which I will never withdraw
myself.[44]

Finally, on the pretext of Colonel Stanhope's delayed promotion,
he resigned the Seals on February 6, 1748. The King was most
gracious, regretted his resignation, declared that "he had served
him with fidelity, exactness, and ability," [45] offered him the choice
of a pension or a dukedom. They were both getting old, and both
realized that this was the end of their mutual chapter. It had begun
long ago in the days of the Young Court, and each represented to
the other the span of active life, the halcyon days as well as the
storms of it, vanished ambitions and faces, griefs and pleasures.
They had been friends and enemies; each in a sense formed part
of the other, and at the moment of farewell each bade adieu not so
much to a person as to the drama in which they had both been engaged.

The pension and the dukedom were declined; but Lady Fanny
Shirley received a pension, Colonel Stanhope a regiment, and the
Earl's brother, John Stanhope, was given a place at the Board of
Admiralty.[46] The Duke of Newcastle seems to have been equally
pleasant.[47] In brief, Chesterfield's political career ended beneath a
cloudless sky. On the night of his resignation, the gentlemen at
White's welcomed him back to the gaming tables after an absence
of three years.[48]

There can be no doubt that the Earl expected his retirement to
produce a furore and that the event must have disappointed
him. Having taken refuge in Bath, he repeatedly informed his cor-

respondents that he had done so not on account of the waters but to be absent from London "while he was the only subject of conversation there." [49] Actually his resignation does not seem to have caused more than a ripple. On February 9, Lady Westmorland, writing to Lady Denbigh, observed that it was of little importance, "for as his going in produced no good effects, his going out can produce no bad ones." [50]

All men of public life flatter themselves upon their consequence to the nation, and all, if they live, discover in turn the dismal fact that they are of small consequence indeed. From one day to the next, the places that knew them know them no more. Lord Chesterfield cannot be blamed for clinging a trifle pathetically to his relinquished greatness. He inspired a pamphlet called *An Apology for a Late Resignation*,[51] where an attempt is made to defend or perhaps to glorify what no one was any longer interested in. The book fell as flat as the resignation it defended.[52] Similarly we find him asserting that the King had now come around to his opinion regarding the situation in Holland and had declared in council that Chesterfield had told him six months before that such and such was so.[53] After the Peace of Aix-la-Chapelle, he maintained that it was his resignation which brought it about. "I may add," he wrote, "that my resignation made this peace, as it opened people's eyes with relation to the imminent dangers of the war, and made the continuation of it too strong a measure for our Minister to stand. As a proof of this, I resigned on the 6th of February last, and on the 9th Lord Sandwich had orders sent him to make the best peace that he could, but to make any rather than none. The Republic is saved by it from utter ruin; and England from bankruptcy." [54] So Lord Chesterfield had saved Europe after all! This and similar extracts from the letters of these months, which explain how he had foreseen and foretold what would happen, are to be both excused and expected. They are the lingering glances of a retired politician who looks back a little pompously and perhaps a little wistfully over the field of his former efforts.

But after all, he was content. The feeling of futility and emptiness, the shiver of *vanitas vanitatum* which had weighed upon him during the last year of office reconciled him now to the joys of retirement. Surely these would not elude him nor prove of tinsel.

"All the busy tumultuous passions," he wrote Dayrolles, "have subsided in me; and that not so much from philosophy, as from a little reflection upon a great deal of experience. I have been behind the scenes, both of pleasure and business. I have seen all the coarse pulleys and dirty ropes, which exhibit and move all the gaudy machines; and I have seen and smelt the tallow candles which illuminate the whole decoration, to the astonishment and admiration of the ignorant audience." [55]

PART FIVE
1748 - 1773

CHAPTER XVII
Indian Summer

THERE COMES A PERIOD in most lives when the upward climb resolves itself into the level of the summit, when, for a space, the crest is followed before beginning the descent. It was this season of upland life, warm and golden with an autumnal richness, a life of placid retrospect as yet untroubled by imminent forebodings and physically still enjoyable, that Lord Chesterfield now entered. Indeed, for the time being, his retirement improved his health and gave him a sense of exhilaration such as he had long been denied. He exulted in it. "I am now returned from Bath," he wrote Dayrolles, "in a state of health, which I have not known of some years, and which is owing to quiet of mind and exercise of body. I am now master of my own time, and of my own motions. I do whatever I please, whenever I please, and am mightily pleased with it." [1]

If the Lord-Lieutenancy, as we have seen, represented the zenith of his political career, it was in this period that his literary and social talents reached their utmost development, that his essential qualities bore such perfect fruit in their kind as henceforth to be considered illustrative of a type, and to deserve their own rubric. There has been some discussion whether or no Chesterfield's character underwent a change in later life — a question which, like many others, may be convincingly argued on either side. Actually the answer depends on what meaning is ascribed to the word "change." A serenity, kindliness, and tolerance, a depth and flavor, absent in his earlier manhood are progressively apparent in middle and old age. But these are autumnal colorings, the effect of time acting on elements present throughout. It is the aging of wine, the mellowing of pigment. In this sense there was indeed change. But on the other hand, if transmutation be meant, a conversion to something wholly new, there is nothing in the later phases of Chesterfield's life to support such a conclusion. Among the characteristics of his old age, none are entirely new; none of his more youthful tendencies have been entirely suppressed.

This, however, must be said, that, as the years passed, he developed in the direction of his better, and away from his baser, qualities. Like others of his type, old rationalists of the world, he might have degenerated into a trivial, materialistic old age, the decayed clubman, the pestiferous invalid. Instead, all that was wise and just and refined in him progressively triumphed. He became increasingly the suave philosopher resigned to the ills of life, an Epicurean, in the best sense, rather than a Stoic, extracting from the diminished years what he could of urbane pleasure, and shrugging his shoulders, sometimes a trifle wearily, about the rest. Therefore, he presents rationalism at its human best, not without even a touch of the heroic in his quiet acceptance of destiny. All that the will and reason, in conflict with the vicissitudes of life, can accomplish was achieved in him. If his philosophy fails, as an answer to human need, it was that philosophy at its highest and embodied in one of its ablest interpreters.

The building of houses and laying out of gardens belongs to the Indian Summer of life. As if Chesterfield House had whetted his appetite for such things, he took over his brother John Stanhope's villa at Blackheath after the latter's death in 1748 and proceeded to enlarge and beautify it. "*Il ne faut jamais faire les sottises à demi,*" he explained to his old friend Chenevix.[2] The Marquise de Monconseil had named her country house in the Bois de Boulogne "Bagatelle"; Chesterfield paid her the compliment of imitation and called his place on the Thames "Babiole."

It stood a hundred paces back from the river; and he added a gallery with three bow windows which gave him "three different and," as he boasted, "the finest prospects in the world."[3] He would sit there and watch great merchantmen and frigates of war glide past. The walks too were fine, and the air excellent.[4] That such a confirmed devotee of cities should at last be praising the country walks and air is significant of change, but more impressive still that he should begin pottering with melons, pineapples, and gardening. He took especial pride in his cantaloupes and more than once commissioned Dayrolles to send him seeds from Holland. "As for my melons," he announced to the Marquise, "they are *arch-melons*. By dint of skill and care, I defy our climate, and produce such delicious melons, that if there were means of serving you as the emperor of the moon is served, with crossbow flights, I would shoot you some melons from time to time all the way to Bagatelle, and they would put your better climate to the blush." [5]

When a man about town takes to gardening, his autumn has begun.

Meanwhile the whirlwind of politics drifted further and further away. Whig or Tory no longer meant a great deal to him. He began to feel that England would have been as well served by one party as the other; that it was not the difference in political principles, but the misconduct of individuals contrary to the principles they professed which caused governmental failure or inefficiency. [6] He could advise Dayrolles, without apparent resentment, to flatter "the silly vanity" and quiet "the silly jealousy" of the Duke of Newcastle. [7] "I thank God I am out of the galley," he wrote six months after his retirement; "but, however, I wish it fair weather and a good voyage." [8] Of course, he retained an emeritus interest in his old profession and now and then took the trouble to review events and to make political forecasts. The Duke of Newcastle and others frequently called on him for advice, or made use of his good offices as a political mediator. Although he rejected it, his reappointment to the Lord-Lieutenancy of Ireland was even mooted.* But the former earnestness had passed. Indeed, he had little choice in the matter. His compromise with Newcastle had lost him his former authority in parliament. William Pitt now headed the Opposition. By necessity as well as by preference he was irrevocably out.

And yet oddly enough, it was at this point that he managed to drive through parliament a reform of great importance and of lasting value, which remains honorably associated with his name. Hitherto his triumph as a leader in the House of Lords had been

---

* He declined the Presidency of the Council in 1750 (Walpole to Mann, Dec. 19, 22, 1750); an opportunity to re-enter politics was offered him in 1757, but was again declined (Lord Waldegrave's *Memoirs*, p. 110). On the question of the second Lord-Lieutenancy, *cf*. letter to his son, Feb. 26, 1754.

forensic merely. What, as politically powerless, he now achieved was both solid and durable.

For generations England, as ever conservative and glorifying this quality even when it became a vice, had clung to the old and admittedly faulty Julian calendar, whereas the more considerable nations of the Continent had long since gone over to the Gregorian reckoning. A result of this was an ever-widening gap between the date of the month in England and in most of the civilized world. It entailed numerous inconveniences to any international dealing public or private; it confused history and cumbered correspondence. An analogy to it nowadays may be found in the Anglo-Saxon standards of measurement as opposed to the metric system.

Such a problem, definite, limited, and useful, appealed naturally to Chesterfield's mind. It was a clear-cut objective that could be perfectly attained in a short time. Moreover, it represented the cosmopolitanism of France as opposed to British insularity. He documented himself through his foreign correspondents, particularly the French chancellor Daguessau, and having secured the support of the learned Earl of Macclesfield, President of the Royal Society, proposed a bill for the reform of the calendar on February 25 (Old Style), 1751.[9] As usual, the timid Duke of Newcastle trembled for the consequences, called it newfangled, begged him not to stir matters that had long been quiet.[10] The populace, misinterpreting what they could not understand, regarded the measure as a conspiracy to rob them somehow of eleven days — the difference between the Julian and Gregorian systems.[11] But Chesterfield's wit, eloquence, and charm, surpassing themselves on this occasion and allied with Macclesfield's expert knowledge, prevailed. The bill was readily approved by both houses.[12] Altogether it was a highly characteristic episode reflecting the Earl's adroitness, his intelligence and public spirit.

Parliamentary reappearances, however, even in support of nonpartisan measures, became increasingly rare. The pleasures of retirement absorbed him more and more. Not infrequent glimpses of him on horseback in the Park drift across the glass of his correspondence. He rode regularly and for the sake of exercise, but he liked quiet horses.[13] Or again, as in the past, we find him at Vauxhall and Ranelagh, though little by little the charm of them is wearing off.[14] Or he appears at the King's birthday dressed in "a brown suit with a very rich gold button." [15] Or he delights in entertaining with his exquisite French cuisine Parisian bluestockings, like Madame du Boccage, the authoress, or great personages like the French ambassador and his wife, the Marquis and Madame de Mirepoix. Or he regales himself with the latest French books, such, for example, as de Graffigny's *Lettres Péruviennes,* that his friends on the Continent, Baron Kreunigen, the Abbé de Ville, and others, kept him supplied with.[16] Serious and frivolous reading went on side by side, for his tastes were catholic and he kept himself abreast of the times.

It was thus an absorbing, delicious, and many-sided life that he led during these October years. It was the life of the exquisitely cultivated and disciplined aristocrat, than which, perhaps, human society has never evolved a more attractive or more brilliant type. Wealth and rank are its essentials; good breeding, self-control, leisure, and taste must support it, it is nurtured by the arts rather than the sciences. Inevitably it is the fruit of an old civilization, nor can it be produced in shorter space than many centuries. The trouble is that, from the standpoint of society, such a quintessence is absurdly expensive to evolve, and connotes sacrifices which achieve in the end nothing of obvious utility. The eternal problem recurs, as to whether one ephemeral perfection is worth the cost necessary to produce it. For a further disadvantage of the mode of life in question is its brevity, that perforce it must resemble a goblet of imperial wine soon emptied. Its supreme sparkle and grace depends on too many casual elements in the control of fortune. Health or wealth vanishes; time impairs; the flowers wither. They may leave steel fibers about which they clung; but there is no comfort in cold steel. In brief, there is an inner vacancy behind the Epicurean façade that tends to grow cold in winter.

But winter was not yet; only the purple, crimson, and golden colors of maturity. The leaves had not yet begun to fall.

To this season belongs peculiarly the gentle art of letter writing, and it is during this period that Chesterfield attained an eminent rank among the letter writers of the world. The most famous letters of all, those to his son, deserve separate treatment; but some characteristic examples of his familiar correspondence may be reviewed here. The latter has been unjustly overshadowed by the more celebrated collection, and should be more widely known.

Indeed Chesterfield the man, as distinct from the pedagogue, is rarely encountered in the parental letters; if he is ever to be met, it is in the correspondence with friends. I say, if he is ever to be met, because his tendency is to wear a different costume, perhaps even a different mask with each one of his correspondents. In his letters to the Marquise de Monconseil he is not the same person as when writing to Dayrolles; there is a shift again in the letters to Chenevix, to Madame du Boccage, or to Lord Huntingdon. This, to be sure, is in part unavoidable, on account of different interests and different relationships; but there is a further, deeper cause than these, a fundamental reserve, coldness, insincerity — call it what you will — a reluctance or inability to express his inner self.

For the sake of convenience, the letters of these years may be roughly divided into five parts: those to Irish acquaintances in Dublin; to Chenevix, Bishop of Waterford, similarly in Ireland; to French women of rank and talent, Madame de Monconseil and Madame du Boccage; to Lord Huntingdon; and to his young protégé, Solomon Dayrolles, British Resident at The Hague.* There are, of course, various letters to other people, which have been accidentally preserved, but the above classes represent long-continued and cordial attachments.

We may leave aside the correspondence with Dublin as of importance only in showing the ex-Lord Lieutenant's continued interest in Ireland. A certain complacency at the success of his administration may be forgiven him; and with this his benevolence gladly allied itself. Work devoted to a place or a country constitutes an investment to which the heart remains always attached. Chesterfield's letters to his good friends the Dublin burghers, though few in number, reflect a trait which must never be forgotten in any estimate of him: a real kindliness and a desire for the public good.[17]

It is, however, in the long-continued and intimate correspondence that we discover the more personal and perhaps more dominant characteristics. Let us first consider the letters to Madame de Monconseil.

*   *   *

---

* The letters to Baron Torck and Lady Suffolk are finished; the letters to his godson have, of course, not yet begun at this period. It should be repeated that we are dealing here with the *familiar* letters and not the *political* or *business* correspondence.

Cécile-Thérèse de Monconseil was tall and thin but with good eyes and a good complexion. Her father had been the Marquis de Curzay and at eighteen she had married the Marquis de Monconseil, a former page of Louis XIV and subsequently lieutenant general. One thinks of her as typical of the period: alert, intelligent, witty, steeped in political intrigue, mercenary, and somewhat hard, but with all the polish that an incessant life at court or in the best Parisian society could give. From 1726, the year following her marriage, until more than forty years afterwards, she was involved in plot, counterplot, and faction — a complete woman of the world. Chesterfield, scanning the circle of his friends at Paris, could think of no one more competent to initiate his son in all the finesses of social intercourse. Madame de Monconseil's cross seems to have been her mother, the old Marquise de Curzay (born plain Mademoiselle Blondot), who had been a great beauty and wanton in the Regent's time, had ruined in turn her two lovers, Auguerre and Bossoré, and in the early forties, after her husband's death, had ended by keeping a gaming house. Later on she lived with her daughter, Cécile-Thérèse; but her reputation frightened off even the sophisticated ladies of Paris, so that, as Chesterfield pointed out to Lord Huntingdon, although the best masculine society frequented the Hôtel Monconseil, the feminine element was conspicuously lacking.[18] The Marquise, however, seems to have endured her mother with filial patience. Perhaps also it was the masculine callers who most interested her. We should add that at the time of Chesterfield's retirement in 1748, she was forty-one years old, that is, thirteen years younger than the Earl.[19] He had presumably met her on his visit to Paris seven years before, and had paid her the kind of court which finds its satisfaction in flourishes and gallantries. Their correspondence continued indefinitely along the same line.

O, the delicate game of a gallant correspondence! A fine perfume of wit, tenderness and sentiment, an exquisite titillation of the heart — we have nothing like it nowadays. It is a completely lost luxury. What was the point of it? A sincere exchange of ideas? No, for one of its conventions was a graceful and transparent insincerity. Moreover, Chesterfield scorned the mentality of women too much to admit the value of such an exchange. Was it the expression of an old passion cooled to a lingering fondness?

No, for their acquaintance never seems to have included anything more intimate than the compliments of the drawing room. Did it reflect at least a long companionship? No, for in all probability they had met each other during no longer period than a month. And yet on the basis of so slight an intercourse, they corresponded for the rest of their lives! One is reminded of Horace Walpole and Madame du Deffand. In each case the incentive to so much writing was the same: not friendship, not love, not the commerce of thought — at least not primarily these — but the passion for correspondence itself, for the polished phrase, the gallant sentiment, the nuance of wit, the humorous conceit, the elegant gesture. It was the delight in superficial, but ingenious and exquisite self-expression. As compared with profounder and serious interests, it occupies about the same place as the pinch of snuff, the aroma of the scent bottle, a glass of Madeira, or the tinting of a fan in relation to more robust sensations. It is the most delicate, most elusive flowering of immemorial culture.

We have no time for it nowadays, nor for what it symbolizes. The art and the motives have alike vanished. But we can still admire its deftness and technique and infinite sparkle. Consider the dexterity of the conclusion alone with its arabesques and flourishing of courtly plumes.

> Five hundred years ago [wrote Chesterfield] it would have cost some fairy or magician of our friends little enough in a moment to transport *Babiole* to the Bois de Boulogne to pay her court to *Bagatelle*. But at present, one hardly knows whither to turn for favours of that kind. Our age, they say, merits them no longer; our faith has waned. But at least without subjecting *your* faith to too great a test, you will, I hope, believe me the most zealous, the most devoted of your servants.[20]

Or again:

> Admit that you have served me ill by showing my last letter to Fontenelle. Not that I fear his judgment more than yours, but his will have free scope, and yours is restrained by friendship. Old as he is, he will see clear; young as you are [she was at that moment forty-four] you will be blind. Across your eyes the bandage of friendship, which nowadays I prefer to that of love, will protect me from all I might have to fear from your judgment. You wear

that bandage tight, and I reap the benefit thereof more than anyone I know. Pray, therefore, only lift it up, the better to see the sentiments, with which I wish you a good night.[21]

It was conventionally artificial and insincere. Indeed sincerity would have spoiled the pretty fiction. Take, for example, the badinage of such a paragraph as this:

I no longer know how to deal with you, Madame — you reject the simplest truths, because they are favourable to you. As for compliments, we have long since banished them from our correspondence; and if you will hear of nothing but your faults, you must apply to someone who knows of any in you. To be sure, we like better to be told of what we wish to deserve, or, by self-deception, fancy we deserve, than of what we really do deserve. An ancient writer (I have forgotten which) said to Trajan: *Flattery is long since exhausted towards your predecessors; all that remains for us in regard to you is that we dare be silent.* This then is my policy towards you.[22]

But step beyond the sphere of their correspondence with its perfume and shaded candles into the reality of every day, and the tone changes. Writing to Huntingdon, he speaks of her dryly as having "good sense, that is, good female sense." [23] Or consider the following. His son, then in Paris, had informed him that the Marquise's mother, Madame de Curzay, had fallen seriously ill. She was a fat, burdensome old woman with a lurid past, as we have seen, and was Chesterfield's senior by four years. He disliked her cordially. "If old Curzay," he replied, "goes to the Valley of Jehosaphat, I cannot help it; it will be an ease to our friend Madame Monconseil, who I believe maintains her, and a little will not satisfy her in any way." [24] But re-enter the noble world of the correspondence:

Madame, [he writes] I have doubly lamented your silence, knowing as I did, only too well its cause. Your disciple [Philip Stanhope, Jr.] had informed me of it, and, to do him justice, with all that feeling that the liveliest sense of your kindness must inspire. He had told me of your mother's illness, and consequently of your fears. I would assure you of mine as well, did I not believe that you are fully persuaded of them. The ties of blood are not always those of friendship; but friendship founded on mutual merit, esteem, and confidence becomes more lively and tender when it is cemented by the ties of blood. This was your case; and as you feel all you ought with more than ordinary delicacy, I guessed at your sorrow, before you expressed it in the last letter you have honoured me with. . . .[25]

And later,

The joy I have felt at your mother's recovery has promoted my own; for it was very sincere, and nothing is more salutary than joy, especially for me, when you are so nearly concerned in it.[26]

A charm of the gallant correspondence was its variety. There were no routine ingredients of so much gossip, so much news, so much flattery, so much moralizing, followed by the machine-made ending; but a constant play of whim and wit and unexpectedness interwoven in an ever-changing pattern, or better still, perhaps, resembling a brilliant improvisation on the spinet. Of this delightful pastime, the butterfly species among literary kinds, Horace Walpole remains the supreme master. Perhaps his feminine, his almost girlish, qualities account for this. Chesterfield was too masculine to rival the other's feline lightness, but his letters are none the less superb examples of this forgotten art. He discusses books and people and politics, the decoration of houses, the raising of melons, the education of his son, to the accompaniment, as it were, of a good-humored and sprightly obbligato. Nothing is labored or very serious or very long — which is perhaps the only possible recipe for letter writing. There is, besides, not the faintest hint of effort to suggest a thought of future publication; the artificiality is wholly spontaneous. Nor, unlike the correspondence with his son, do the letters resemble each other, but are always distinct and individually colored.

The Marquise de Monconseil must have enjoyed them; in any case she preserved them. It was not a burdensome correspondence: at its liveliest a letter every month or six weeks perhaps, but finally with ever-lengthening intervals of months or even years. She was not deceived in him. That quality which Lady Suffolk, Dean Swift, and Samuel Johnson felt, that coolness of heart, was equally manifest to her. His noblest protestations had never a golden ring. Unconcernedly enough she rallied him about it and evoked a brief apology which he called his confession of faith on the subject of friendship. It is worth remembering.

Although you will not allow that I have much feeling as a general thing [*quoique vous ne vouliez pas m'accorder des sentiments en général*], do me the justice to make an exception in your favour. It is true that I am not a commonplace friend; if I were, my friendship would be unworthy of yours. First of all, I must know people very well. I do not want a friend without feeling, simply because he has wit, just as on the other hand, I do not care for a sentimental friend without common sense. There must be feeling on both sides to carry it on. From this my confession of faith regarding friendship, judge, Madame, if you are not the first article of it.[27]

No one could take exception to this, nor could anyone assert that Chesterfield's letters to Madame de Monconseil and other friends are wanting in cordial expressions. But the fact remains that he did not succeed in convincing people. No verbiage or *savoir-faire* helped him in this respect; he gave the impression of head rather than heart, of calculation rather than impulse: a character that has clung to him ever since. It may be that he was one of those frozen unfortunates who from reserve and pride convey always a false picture of themselves; but the possibility is doubtful. Cold and warmth, egoism and outgoingness, are generally to be felt in spite of outward manner. The likelihood is that his emotions, when present, were perfectly controlled; that his friendship could be steady and loyal, but never ardent or unreserved; and that, if contemporaries suspected water in the wine of his sentiment, the contemporaries were right.

Of course, as regards his correspondence with the Marquise, one thing is obvious: he was paving the way in Paris for his son. She was to serve young Philip as introduction to that exclusive world, as guide through its labyrinth, as his patroness and polisher. She was eminently qualified to this end by her experience in intrigue, by the worldliness of her training, by her slightly equivocal reputation. She belonged to Madame de Tencin's genre. Other French matrons might have felt qualms about young Philip's apprenticeship to the world and the flesh in Paris, but Madame de Monconseil stood above such weakness. Therefore, in part at least, the Earl courted and flattered her. The services she would render his boy were worth a good many letters. When that need was past, the correspondence sagged sharply.

There is no reason why this should not have been so. The conventions of society sanction the give and take of good offices. He repaid her in favors to her friends, in small gifts, above all in compliments; he balanced the ledger. But the fact remains that the correspondence, for all its tributes to friendship, for all its high-flown gallantries, retained an ulterior object in view. Chesterfield's ambitions for his son color it.

We may disregard this point, however, and continue thankful for the aroma, the atmosphere and charm of that lost world which has been here preserved for us. It is conversation in a salon on the Rue de Verneuil between two people of a vanished social order; and no modern device — record or film — for transmitting to posterity the voices and features of the past could succeed as perfectly as these random letters in perpetuating the accent and cachet of an epoch.

Turning from the Marquise de Monconseil to Marie-Anne du Boccage, we find a different tone. She was perhaps less a woman of the world than the former and certainly much more of a bluestocking. Like Montesquieu, Voltaire, and most of the French progressives before the Revolution, she was strongly Anglophile in sentiment, and had translated Milton's *Paradise Lost* and Pope's *Temple of Fame* into French verse. In addition, she wrote an epic in ten books on the discovery of America, called the *Columbiade*, was the authoress of numerous poems, of a play called *Les Amazones*, and of two pleasant volumes of travel, published in 1770.[28] "She has good parts," wrote Chesterfield to Dayrolles, "and makes no intellectual parade" (*n'affiche pas le bel esprit*).[29] She was just forty when, together with her husband, Ficquet du Boccage, and the learned Abbé Guasco, she visited England in 1750, and dined at Chesterfield House. Healths were drunk to Voltaire and Montesquieu; the dinner sponsored by the Earl's French cook proved entirely Lucullan. She admired her host's learning and library, his paintings, the architecture of his new house, which she termed a palace, his grace of manner and refinement of life. "After having with great honour filled the most important places in the state," she wrote of him, "[he] is so far from regretting them, that in an agreeable retirement he enjoys himself and his friends with the highest relish." [30]

Somehow one thinks of that evening at Chesterfield House as

representing the culmination of his life. Picture him at table with his guests, wineglass in hand, the diamond of the Duchess of Marlborough on his finger. He is so perfectly at home in the world: rich, honored, gifted, serene, the London Richelieu, as Lady Denbigh called him in reference to the witty marshal.[31] He and these French people, with whom he feels at one, are the ultimate product of their age. No uncouth emotion ruffles the placidity of good form; no indiscipline of attention or ill-bred assertiveness interrupts the play of thought. Ideas meet and blend and pass, like a stream of courtiers. Characteristically the glasses are emptied to those field marshals of the ideas of their century: Montesquieu . . . Voltaire . . .

Chesterfield escorted the French travelers to Vauxhall and Ranelagh,[32] and in general saw much of them during their two months in England. When the party sailed for Holland, he gave them a letter of introduction to the faithful Dayrolles.

Thenceforward for a couple of years Madame du Boccage remained one of his favored correspondents. It was the period of young Philip's Parisian visit, and she would be useful to him. But, as we have already observed, the line he followed with her was different from that with the Marquise. It was the literary line. His compliments to the Monconseil pale by comparison. "Madame," he notes in a letter to Huntingdon, "both as a woman and poetess, relishes a little flattery," [33] and he stopped at nothing.

Dense, stupefying, the incense rose. Each word was a caress. Her letters equal the best of de Sévigné's; they excel La Rochefoucauld's or La Fayette's or de Coulanges's. If she writes to him in English, her style is superior to many a lettered Englishman's; she has stolen the strength and energy of the language and added the grace of French. Does she intend further translations of English, such an honor is undeserved; the French stage is "too nice, too chaste, to endure most of the English performances; there are not six English plays fit to appear in their present form on the French stage." "Do you intend soon," he wrote, "to give us something of your own, to comfort me for the present stagnation of my mind, which is languishing for want of food? I do not reckon your charming epistle on Vauxhall and Ranelagh as one of your works; it is but a relaxation for such talents as yours to prepare for some more considerable performance. Pope's *Essay on Criticism* would be an object worthy of your attention, in case you should choose to translate, but I advise you by all means to exercise your own genius. . . . You are one of the few who are not allowed to be lazy." [34] He sent her the busts of Shakespeare, Milton, Dryden, and Pope, "who, if they knew you, would esteem it an honour to be placed in your house." And he added, "I beg you will show some kindness to Dryden, who is jealous of the preference you have given to Milton and Pope. You may give Shakespeare what reception you think proper, as he sometimes deserves the best, and sometimes the worst." [35]

If with Madame de Monconseil he was the veteran man about town, with Madame du Boccage he became the courtly philosopher and literary critic. Some of his most revealing opinions on books and authors are to be found here. But meanwhile young Philip Stanhope enjoyed the du Boccages' hospitality. When his Parisian apprenticeship was over, the letters stopped.

Similarly, it is impossible not to conclude that Lord Chesterfield had his son's interest in mind in his correspondence with Francis Hastings, tenth Earl of Huntingdon. He was a young man of high birth, some three years older than young Philip, and would eventually occupy a prominent position both at court and in parliament. One winces a little at the language used by the Earl in recommending his illegitimate boy to this young grandee's patronage. Philip at that time was eighteen and Huntingdon twenty-one. "Let me most earnestly recommend him, my dear Lord, to your countenance, favour, and if he deserves it, friendship. Consider him as one absolutely belonging to you, and whose character you may establish in the world by the force of your own. I have pointed you out to him as his patron and his model. . . ." [36] And again, some months later: "You make me very happy, my dear Lord, in the friendship and protection which you promise me for my boy . . . look upon him eventually as your dependent, your client, your creature, for those are my instructions to him." [37]

But another consideration than Philip Stanhope's interest played a part in the Earl's relations with Huntingdon. The young gentleman was nephew of Lady Fanny Shirley and son of the formidable Selina Huntingdon of Methodist fame, Chesterfield's religious old friend. He had seen him grow up and had a real affection for him. [38]

Above all, a young man in the process of education irresistibly attracted Chesterfield. He valued himself as an expert on the subject; and, indeed, a very good case could be made for the thesis that among thinkers in this field during the eighteenth century, he deserves high rank. It should be repeated here that it was not merely his son for whom he opened the storehouse of his experience, but his godson, Lord Huntingdon, and others. Even before the publication of the famous letters, the younger generation had apparently identified him with a certain attitude or tendency. George Selwyn, writing to Lady Carlisle in 1768, wished that a young friend of his at his outset in life had imbibed sentiments of honor and delicacy in love affairs *instead of admiring . . . Lord Chesterfield's affected system.*[39] Certainly the Earl enjoyed the company of young men and no doubt passed among them as an oracle. There can be no doubt, besides, that in addition to his real interest in education and to his feeling of competency regarding it, there was a good spice of vanity in unrolling his experience and laying down the law to young auditors. "Consider," he wrote, "that it is not Lord Chesterfield who pretends to advise Lord Huntingdon, but it is an old fellow in his grand climacteric, who having lived long in the world, in Courts, and in business, communicates the result of his experience to a young man of five and twenty who wants nothing but experience." [40]

For all these reasons, he delighted in Huntingdon, who, on his side, regarded Chesterfield as a foster father.[41] Even if Philip Stanhope's career had played no part, the correspondence would have still taken place. Indeed, it continued long after Philip's bubble had definitely burst.

Admirers of Lord Chesterfield may be excused for regretting that these letters were ever published. They disprove so much — for one thing the contention that the moral obliquity of the advice to his son was a desperate effort to impose *savoir-faire* on an exceptionally uncouth boy. All that is objectionable in the correspondence with Philip is implicit in that with Huntingdon. As the latter was older and independent and a great lord and certainly not uncouth, the harping on airs and graces was left out, but the low morality, the calculation and cynicism of the more famous collection remains. The letters to Huntingdon reveal another and unsavory aspect of Epicureanism, however elegant and cultivated. It is the point where the animal in human nature, uncoerced by any transcendent ideal, peers out through the mask of good breeding. An elderly man in the late fifties invariably makes a shabby appearance when he assumes the tone of smoking-room fellowship with youth in matters of sex. Chesterfield's attempt to be a guide and a sympathetic confidant to his son and to Lord Huntingdon in such affairs was both sordid and pathetic. And all such excuses made for him, as that of frank speaking, or the conventions of the world, or eighteenth-century standards, or truth to the facts of life, are beside the point. If nineteenth-century estimates were Mid-Victorian, so also was the judgment of his own age upon this trait in him. It was simply one of the areas left undrained and noisome by his rationalistic philosophy.

"As for mistresses," he cajoled, "I do not presume to stint you, the more the better, provided they are such as neither endanger your health nor your character, and Paris abounds with such, as well as with their opposites. Singing, dancing, and theatrical girls with *id genus omne* are villifying and dangerous, though much the fashion. You will not, I am sure, see better and approve of them, and yet follow worse." [42] But when Huntingdon, with patrician indifference to his canny old friend's advice, followed the fashion and patronized an opera singer, the Earl affably agreed. "Depend upon it," he simpered, "neither the sly insinuations of envy nor the open attacks of malice shall ever make me entertain an opinion injurious to the many virtues and particularly the chastity of Mademoiselle Lany. Her profession of dancer at the Opera, and her rank of dancer, are to me more than sufficient pledges of her innocence and purity. . . ." [43] And more seriously in a later letter: "If (as I suppose was the case) Mademoiselle Lany prevailed with you to pass this winter at Paris, the cause was at your age a very justifiable one; I believe I should do the same at mine, without half so many or so good reasons for it, as I dare say you had. Her situation and degree of character made your connection with her for a time not unbecoming. It is the duration of those connections that makes them disgraceful. . . ." [44] But unable wholly to suppress his distaste for the low station of this inamorata, he remarked to his son that he "would have thought that Lord Huntingdon, at his age, and with his parts and address, need not have been reduced to keep an opera whore in such a place as Paris, where so many women of fashion generously serve as volunteers." [45]

There is no use laboring this point any further. We could amplify it considerably with still more discreditable examples. It is merely another instance of adaptation. The courtly friend of the Marquise's, the engaging pundit of Madame du Boccage, becomes now the paternal roué and confers a smiling blessing on his noble young friend's peccadilloes.

But there is more than the sexual swagger to be regretted in this correspondence. The whole tone is false. Surely it was unnecessary, even according to the polite canons of the day, for a man of Chesterfield's age, rank, and eminence to be quite so dulcet and ingratiating with an untried young fellow in the twenties, even if he had the title of earl. Flattery injected at every turn into the veins of such a youth was not only insincere, but harmful. Will he dissuade Huntingdon, for instance, from extending his travels to Greece and Egypt, the advice is dished up like this: "The wild Arabs in Egypt and the ignorant slaves of Greece are infinitely below your notice, and unworthy of the time they would take up. The broken pyramids and ruined temples of those desolated countries are below your attention except in copper plates, etc." [46] Or again, "Leave pyramids, temples, sculpture and paintings to minds much below yours." [47] A young earl is a very great person, but the assurance that the ruins of Greek and Egyptian civilization are below his notice does not tend to improve him. Does Huntingdon express his opinion of certain French authors, it flatters and confirms that of Chesterfield, who can now assert with pride that his own opinion "has long been exactly the same." [48] Does Huntingdon send him some verses he has written, the Earl replies: "I would not commend your verses to you if I thought it possible that you could suspect flattery or even common civility to have any share in the commendation. . . . You are as much above making bad verses as you are above valuing yourself upon making good ones." [49] Is it a question of conveying the plain piece of information that Philip Stanhope is studying German at Hanover, the Earl tricks it out as follows: "Your little servant Mr. Stanhope is now at Hanover completing his German; your good opinion of him flatters my hopes that he may some day or other deserve your patronage and protection." [50] Does Huntingdon present Lady Chesterfield with a *corbeille* for

her dressing room, the Earl declares that she "is too much con-
founded with the repeated marks of your remembrance to tell me
what she would have me say to you in return. . . ."[51] Granting
that we are dealing here with an age of formality and with an arch-
interpreter of the graces and with the conventions obtaining between people of rank, this sort of thing is still overdone.

But take a step further. Lord Huntingdon is treated to the same
hints as Philip Stanhope in regard to making use of people. Not to
give, but to exchange; not to give, but to get; not to enjoy and to
love for friendship's sake, but always, under the shadow of an after-
thought, to exploit and to plan: is not this the miasma that haunts
Chesterfieldianism? And in comparison with this, as a corrupting
force, the sexual immorality, of which so much stir has been made,
is seen to be merely trivial. Nay, under this scheme, even one's
mistress will be chosen as a social asset; and fornication, santified by
a coronet, will be used to enhance the prestige of a fine gentleman.

"It may be of great use to you," he wrote, "to form certain connections with such young Englishmen abroad as are likely to make
some figure in the world, either from their parts, their rank, or their
fortune. *For between you and I whatever connection you form, you
must govern though they must not think so.** The Marquis of Rockingham, whose father is lately dead, has a very great estate and
great interest in Yorkshire, two circumstances that will give him
weight let his parts be what they will, and I do not know what
they are; as such he is worth your laying hold on, and you may
certainly get him."[52] And later when Huntingdon was Master of
the Horse to the Prince of Wales, the subsequent George III, and
was being royally snubbed by him, what a technique Chesterfield
prescribed of supple courtliness! "As the stake you play for is a very
great one, mind your own game without interruption. . . . You
must win at last. Speak to him if he will not speak to you; though
he be cold, be you officious; and, above all, take care not to complain to any one mortal living of this improper behaviour. . . ."[53]
The Prince's brothers were to be treated coldly so as not to stir his
jealousy; his mother and his mother's favorite, Lord Bute, were
also to be propitiated. It was a breviary of ruse and obsequiousness.

Aside from these aspects, the letters to Huntingdon are infinitely

* Italics not in original text.

diverting and full of color. The social vignettes sparkle and charm. The turns of worldly or literary observation are particularly shrewd.

It is amusing to turn to Richard Chenevix, the Bishop of Waterford. Chesterfield's chameleon talents of which he boasted [54] are nowhere more evident. Here he shifts to gravity, decorum, and even occasional piety, but, let it be at once observed, without any mawkishness whatever. A cheap hypocrisy was entirely foreign to his essentially virile attitude. With Chenevix he used the language befitting the office and age of the person addressed; nor is there any more reason to question the sincerity of his statements in this connection than in that of Lord Huntingdon. What may be criticized is the habit, grown unconscious, of becoming all things to all men in the Chesterfieldian sense. It is the perpetual changing of roles, the actor's art, that breeds misgivings; but the great actor loses himself with equal honesty in every role. Samuel Butler remarks truly enough that no man is a great hypocrite until he has left off knowing that he is a hypocrite. And this, with reservations, may be applied to Chesterfield, rather than the charge of conscious dissimulation. Consider the following examples:

On November 11, 1752, he wrote Chenevix from Bath regarding the education of the Bishop's son:

> If you would have him a very learned man, you must certainly send him to some great school; but if you would have him a better thing, a very honest man, you should have him *à portée* of your own inspection. At those great schools, the heart is wholly neglected by those who ought to form it, and is consequently left open to temptations and ill examples; paternal care and inspection, attended by proper firmness and authority, may prevent great part of that mischief.

Five days later he wrote to his own son, whom he rarely saw and who was finishing his education in Paris under the sophisticated wing of the Marquise, a sermon in praise of vanity as one of the most useful principles in human conduct. The change of tone will be noted.

> I began the world [he says] not with a bare desire, but with an insatiable thirst, a rage of popularity, applause, and admiration.

. . . To men, I talked whatever I thought would give them the best opinion of my parts and learning, and to women, what I was sure would please them — flattery, gallantry, and love. And, moreover, I will own to you . . . that my vanity has very often made me take great pains to make many a woman in love with me, if I could, for whose person I would not have given a pinch of snuff. In company with men, I always endeavoured to out-shine, or, at least if possible, to equal, the most shining man in it. . . . By these means I soon grew in fashion; and when a man is once in fashion all he does is right. It was infinite pleasure to me, to find my own fashion and popularity. I was sent for to all parties of pleasure, both of men or women, where, in some measure, I gave the tone. This gave me the reputation of having had some women of condition; and that reputation, whether true or false, really got me others. With the men I was a Proteus, and assumed every shape in order to please them all: among the gay I was the gayest, among the grave the gravest . . . accordingly I was soon connected with all the men of any fashion or figure in town. To this principle of vanity, which philosophers call a mean one, and which I do not, I owe great part of the figure which I have made in life.

Then turn back once more to the letter of November 11:

I have both philosophy and religion to submit to my fate [his growing deafness] without either melancholy or murmur; for though I can by no means account why there is either moral or physical evil in the world, yet, conscious of the narrow bounds of human understanding, and convinced of the wisdom and justice of the Eternal Divine Being who placed them here, I am persuaded that it is fit and right that they should be here.

Chesterfield means what he says in each instance. The son of his former domestic chaplain would be bred up a plain worthy man; while Philip Stanhope, his own flesh and blood, was destined for courts and parliaments. Therefore, honesty and parental supervision for the one; finesse, Paris, and the Marquise for the other. And similarly he could exult in the fine women he had seduced; but at the same time, with equal sincerity, he could wonder at the existence of moral evil. All these apparent inconsistencies can be explained, if we make sufficient allowances for a bygone age and interpret the letters with sufficient charity. The trouble is that Chesterfield's apologists are forced to do so very much explaining.

Taken by themselves, however, the letters to the Bishop are all one could wish. But it is worth noting that they are apt to be much shorter than those to other friends. A real affection and respect permeate them; but they give the impression also of restraint. The Earl has not so much to say to the Bishop as to Lord Huntingdon. And yet the role was here a profounder one and gives a deeper insight into the mind of the actor. That serene resignation which served him so well is nowhere better expressed. The contempt he affirms here for the pleasures of the world [55] may contain a certain degree of alloy; but for all that, its proportion may be less than in those passages where he thrusts the world upon his son. Who knows? In any case he *practiced* his cheerful, hopeless philosophy.

There is a mixture in these letters of habitual patronage, the deference due a bishop, and simple affection as between man and man. Gradually, as time and old age drifted between them, the communications grew shorter — but at least the habit of friendship lingered to the last. "Do you grow fat?" he wrote him once. "Are Mrs. Chenevix and your children all well? Are you as cheerful and as happy as your good conscience ought to make you? I hope them all; for upon my word, nobody loves and values you more than your faithful friend and servant." [56] The actor here is off-stage.

If anywhere, it is in the letters to Solomon Dayrolles that Chesterfield appears in his dressing room. With other correspondents, he can be described under different rubrics: public-spirited statesman with Faulkner and the Dublin citizens; genial old clubman with Huntingdon; pious, or at least philosophic, nobleman and patron with Waterford; prince of gallantries with the Marquise; pedagogue with his son. But in the case of Dayrolles, more than anywhere else, it would be difficult to classify him. He is not at the slightest pains to be anything at all. If an occasional turn of phrase recalls this role or the other, it is a kind of mechanical lapse and is not sustained.

But the strange thing is, that his personality therewith grows vague, elusive, and hard to define. In the letters to Huntingdon, for example, his features emerge from the page and, so to speak, impose themselves upon our imagination. But here, where he is most relaxed, most at his ease, he fades out. It is as if the personality of the actor became definite only in connection with his various parts, that his essential qualities were made vivid on the stage, but that behind the scenes he lost in impressiveness and individuality, indeed, became a trifle commonplace.

Solomon Dayrolles belonged to the numerous category of people who rise in the world by being agreeable to great men. This does not mean that they are necessarily toadies and parasites, but it does mean that they learn to adapt themselves to the characteristics of their patrons. He was the nephew of James Dayrolles, for many years British Resident at The Hague, and, through Chesterfield's influence, was appointed to the same post in 1747, after serving the Earl as his secretary in the embassy to Holland of 1745 and as his Usher of the Black Rod in Dublin. From The Hague, he was sent as minister to Brussels, and thence retired to his country place in England, as Solomon Dayrolles of Henley Park, Esq. He must be regarded as a successful minor diplomat who had come up from obscure and apparently recent French origins.

Horace Walpole, who was hostile to Chesterfield and everything pertaining to him, gives the following account of Dayrolles at the time of his appointment to The Hague: a probably false account except in the reflection it affords of the new Resident's social position from the standpoint of aristocratic London.

> I have no other event to tell you [he wrote Mann] but the promotion of a new brother of yours. [It will be recalled that Mann was British Resident in Florence.] I condole with you, for they have literally sent one Dayrolle resident to Holland, under Lord Sandwich. . . . This curious minister has always been a led-captain to the Dukes of Grafton and Richmond; used to be sent to auctions for them, and to walk in the Park with their daughters, and once went dry-nurse to Holland with them. He has belonged, too, a good deal to my Lord Chesterfield, to whom, I believe, he owes this new honour; as he had before made him Black Rod in Ireland, and gave the ingenious reason, that he had a black face. . . . Dayrolle is a kind of cousin to him; Dayrolle's father was clerk to old Stanhope [the Honorable Alexander Stanhope, youngest son of the first Earl of Chesterfield, who died in 1707] at the Hague, who lay with his wife. From thence sprung this goodly resident.[57]

Libelous as this is, it conveys perfectly a certain nuance of the sort of relationship between Chesterfield and Dayrolles. Solomon just managed to belong within the magic circle of the gentry; Chesterfield was a great nobleman. As far, therefore, as position went, Solomon did not require special treatment. Naturally, in any case, the Earl would have been too well-bred to flaunt his superiority, but with Dayrolles he could give himself up to the luxury of friendship with a man who was agreeable and grateful and attached and with whom he need not stand on any formality. In point of fact, we first meet Dayrolles in connection with four dozen shirts that Chesterfield directed him to procure in Holland at so many shillings per ell, and then forward to England.[58] During the course of their long correspondence, he was often engaged upon one errand or another: attended auctions for the Earl, sent dress material to Madame de Monconseil, purchased "brochures and flourished ruffles" for his patron, sent him melon seeds or paintings or statuary, looked him out the right sort of claret, gave him on request a watchdog for his new house, services which Chesterfield would never have dreamed of asking Lord Huntingdon, and which were certainly akin to those mentioned by Walpole as rendered to the Dukes of Richmond and Grafton. Moreover, Dayrolles was used as link in the benevolent espionage system maintained by Chesterfield upon his son and befriended the latter at the court of Brussels. When first appointed to The Hague, he served in a measure as his lordship's personal agent with William of Orange[59] and kept the Secretary of State informed regarding the maneuvers of the Earl of Sandwich.

This was one side of the balance. On the other, Chesterfield had him appointed to various posts, saw to it that his salary was paid, offered him his own purse in moments of embarrassment, coached him in matters of diplomatic policy, of love and matrimony, and the like. There can be no doubt of the Earl's strong affection for his protégé. An accent of tenderness by no means frequent in his writing is unmistakable here. "I love to write you," he confided, "because I know that you love to hear from me."[60] Or, "Upon my soul I long to see you for two reasons, which I have not for longing to see many people; they are, that I love you, and that I know you love me. I shall keep a little room for you at Blackheath, where I will refresh you with the best ananas and melons in England."[61] Or, with the playfulness of real intimacy, "Have a good time, fear God, and drink cool as often as you can."[62] Or, dropping the flourish of a conclusion, he will end a letter simply with, "Good-night, dear Dayrolles."[63]

It was a matter of course that he should become godfather of this henchman's first-born son and should at once concern himself with the child's education. He consented, moreover, to act as guardian in the event of Dayrolles's death, and, replying to the latter's thanks, declared, "I owe you much more than that in return for your constant friendship and attachment to me, in all times and upon all occasions, since our first acquaintance. With regard to myself, I might have added the epithet *singular;* for I have not met with the same return from many others, for whom I have done much more. I forgive them, because it is the general way of the world; but then that reflection endears those to me the more, who have virtue enough to deviate from it." [64]

Without knowing the exact difference in their ages, we may assume that the Earl was from ten to fifteen years older, and his attitude was that of an older friend; but this did not prevent him from sharing his most intimate concerns with Dayrolles. He discussed with him the reasons for his retirement, his hopes and disappointments in regard to his son, consulted with him on that subject, gave him his frank opinion about contemporaries, exchanged gossip without reserve.

One would like to know more about Dayrolles himself than can be gleaned from the brief snatches of his letters printed by Mahon or inferentially from Chesterfield's correspondence.[65] He seems to have been a lively, swarthy man, an endlessly obliging good fellow. To judge from a letter to Newcastle, he was hotheaded and a warm partisan. We have, moreover, a glimpse of him in Ireland dancing the minuet with a fine lady and spraining the muscle of a leg, so that he was forced to leave his partner and hop off to the side lines.[66] He kept Chesterfield abreast of the scandals in smart society at The Hague,[67] and in general fitted himself to his penchants and interests. But there is no reason to believe that on his side there was any lack of grateful affection. He piously saved his patron's letters and assisted Maty in their publication. It will be recalled that he stood by Chesterfield's deathbed and that his name was the last ever uttered by the dying Earl.

The relationship of patron and client exists today, as it always has existed, but the leveling of class distinctions has deprived it of what might be called its recognized status. Watchful equality deprecates the implication. But, at any rate, it was here that Chesterfield drew closer than anywhere else to an unselfish intimacy.* He was not bent on molding Solomon, nor on getting anything out of him, nor needed he to care what Solomon thought of him. It was a welcome relief from the effort and conventions of formal life.

These letters are, therefore, rich in biographical fact. Paradoxically, however, as we have already stated, the author of them eludes us. There is nothing very distinctive about the Chesterfield we find here. We must console ourselves with the thought that a four-square personality, always itself and making the same impression everywhere, would hardly have bequeathed to us Chesterfieldianism, the supreme interpretation of *savoir-faire*.

The colors and the gold of Indian Summer are transient. The leaves continue to fall; the days shorten. In terms of human life, it means the passing of old, familiar faces, an increasing loneliness. Chesterfield's brother, John Stanhope, did not live to enjoy his new post at the Admiralty Board. "By the death of poor John," wrote the Earl to Dayrolles, "you have lost a true friend, and I a most affectionate brother and friend into the bargain." [68] Though never effusive, Chesterfield seems to have loved and to have made a companion of him. Even as far back as the first embassy to Holland, he had taken him with him as his secretary. One of the consolations of his retirement had been that he had been able to secure John Stanhope in a good position.[69] "Like his brother and sister," commented the usually caustic Walpole, "he had a great deal of wit and good-breeding." [70]

Even more impressive, as denoting the end of an entire epoch, was the death on December 15, 1751, of Henry St. John, Lord Bolingbroke. With him was identified most of Chesterfield's past: his boyhood, the tempests of his early days in parliament, the first Parisian experiences, the days of *The Craftsman* and the long period of opposition to Sir Robert Walpole. With him too was identified a host of names, the Dukes of Ormonde and Marlborough, the Old Pretender, the Bishop of Rochester, the great circle at Twickenham: Swift, Pope, Arbuthnot, Gay, all the vanished faces. He had admired Bolingbroke more than any other man, for his versatility, his splendid manners, the magnificence of his prose style. He never saw through the shallowness of this paragon, the tinsel and the in-

* One thinks also of Scarborough, but none of that correspondence remains.

sincerity. There was too much blaze for that. Nor did he suspect his admired friend of disloyalty to himself.* He watched him die with the pain that must ever attach itself to the mystery of human suffering and the passing of a brilliant life. For Bolingbroke died horribly.

"I often see our mutual friend Bolingbroke," Chesterfield informed the Marquise on August 1, 1751, "but I see him with a great deal of pain. A humour he has long had on his cheek proves to be cancerous and has made rapid progress of late. Hitherto it is not attended with pain, which is all he asks, for, as to the rest, he is resigned. Truly, a mind like his, so far superior to the generality, would have well deserved that nature should have made an effort in his favour, as to the body, and given him an uncommon share of health and duration."

But he was not spared disfigurement or suffering. Four months passed and he still lingered, clinging in hope to the poor quack medicines of the day, terrified of that future life which his skepticism had hitherto questioned,[71] until at length, stricken insensible by the torture, he died. "Are you not greatly shocked," wrote the Earl once more to Madame de Monconseil, "but I am sure you are at the dreadful death of our friend, Bolingbroke? . . . What a man! What extensive knowledge! What a memory! What eloquence! . . . The world will do him more justice now than in his lifetime."[72]

As so often in his prophecies, Chesterfield was wrong. The fame of Bolingbroke has diminished rather than increased with the passing of time. But at the moment, to those who remained of his circle in London, it seemed that one of England's chief glories had departed.

Meanwhile Chesterfield House had received the finishing touches, and could now be formally dedicated to the beau monde. It was upon this stage that his lordship had designed to act out the closing phases of his life: a splendid setting, symbolic, as we have seen, both of his exalted rank and versatile mind. Here, as the years went by, would assemble all that was fair, witty, and distinguished in the successive London seasons, revolving around him as presiding genius of the polite world. He would impose the tone; he would rejoice in his sovereignty. The years might pass and he grow old

---

* "Lord Bolingbroke, in confidential communication with Lord Marchmont, spoke slightingly of Lord Chesterfield's talents as a minister," etc. *Marchmont Papers*, vol. ii, pp. 289–290, note by Rose.

with them; but he would be amused, he would remain central in what gave life its chief significance and flavor: the social interplay of well-bred people. He could look with composure down such a stately avenue of gorgeous autumn; indeed, he might never live to see the coming of winter at the end of it. Therefore, he made ready a great reception at Chesterfield House.

What would we not give to have been there, to stand at least on one side of the doorway that February evening as the coaches rolled continuously into the courtyard! Steps are let down; footmen caper; horses prance. Up the great stairway inside, plumes and satins, ribbons and stars, wigs of the latest cut, ascend with slow dignity. And, as goal of the procession at the end of the state room, a short, elderly, toothless man with massive head and shoulders, and a tall, elderly woman wearing many jewels. He is exquisitely affable. The French almond-shaped eyes look out beneath the somewhat owlish arch of the brows with an inscrutable twinkle. He smiles often and charmingly, but he never laughs.

A slender, handsome exquisite, with an eye for everything, drifts up, makes his bow. Without knowing it, the two greatest letter writers of England exchange compliments, for the quizzical, languid gentleman is Horace Walpole. The house, he notes, "is really most magnificent." It amused him to observe in the hallway the gilded bronze lantern which had once hung in his paternal hall at Houghton, and had stirred much "Patriot" wit in Sir Robert's day. But, as always, it was the people that most attracted him: those magnificent beauties Elizabeth and Maria Gunning, for instance, the Duke of Hamilton at faro at one end of the room, but his eyes on Mrs. Elizabeth at the other: an inattentiveness that cost him a thousand pounds. Two nights later he would marry her with a bed curtain ring at Mayfair Chapel. . . . Meanwhile the Earl of Coventry went dangling after her sister, the glorious Maria. The archannalist drifted hither and yon making mental notes for the sake of his dear, distant Horace Mann.[73]

It was an immense assembly, a great success. Chesterfield House had been launched with tremendous éclat. A month and a half later the Earl suddenly grew aware of a difficulty in hearing. He had no cold or other illness, but he had become deaf. Memories of his father began to haunt him, the dreary, comfortless man cut off from the world. The horror dawned slowly upon him; he turned from remedy to remedy, hoped for warm weather. His deafness grew.[74] In a month all London had heard of it. Lord Westmorland, writing to Lady Denbigh from Paris, declares that Lady Primrose and Lord Huntingdon arriving from London report Lord Chesterfield to have grown extremely deaf, and that "despairing of recovery he talks of retiring and shutting himself up from the world." [75]

But there was no need of that, for he was already shut up from the world. Deafness meant this for him. The quick uptake of wit, the shades of voice with its many nuances, the easy play of society, which of all things he most loved, was over for him. Chesterfield House had in a measure been built in vain. It was to have been a stage, and now would remain largely a monument.

Added to this, a fall from his horse in the Park left him shattered.[76] The horror went on growing. He perceived that winter had come. He was an invalid and broken. He longed for sleep to free him from thoughts of his deafness.[77] He would try every remedy, "just as he took a chance in every lottery, not," as he phrased it, "expecting the great prize, but only to be within the possibility of having it." [78] "May your latter end, my dear Lord," [79] he wrote Huntingdon, "be not like unto mine." And to Madame de Monconseil: "In vain I philosophize and endeavour to supply my loss by reading, walking, or at table; at our age we feel a terrible void when we can no longer enjoy the pleasures of society. In the dissipation and tumult of youth, one does not fully appreciate them; it is at my age that they become the real and almost the only blessings, and it is just at this point that I see myself deprived of them. I confess to you that I am exceedingly depressed, in spite of all that my reason or my friends can offer by way of consolation." [80]

But these were passing clouds, the involuntary shrinking of the spirit. On the same day that he poured out his heart to the Marquise he put up a bold front to Solomon Dayrolles. "I comfort myself with the reflection," he wrote, "that I did not lose the power, till after I had very near lost the desire, of hearing. I have been long and voluntarily deaf to the voice of ambition, and to the noise of business, so that I lose nothing upon that head: and when I consider how much of my life is past, and how little of it, according to the course of Nature, remains, I can almost persuade myself that I am no loser at all. By all this, you see that I am neither a dejected nor a sour deaf man." [81] Not like his father at least! And statements of this sort are henceforward more usual than repinings.

The steel of his philosophy underneath the velvet makes itself increasingly evident. It is at this point that the hero in the old worldling, the indomitable stamina of his breed, comes to the fore, and almost compensates for his many shortcomings. The lines of Henley's "Invictus" begin to apply to him: his head is still unbowed.

And yet, how chill a philosophy! "At every age," he informed the Marquise, "one must cherish consoling or agreeable illusions. In youth, they come of themselves; in old age, one must search for, or even invent them, and in spite of all that, boredom accompanies them. To avoid infecting you with mine, I bid you good-night, Madame." [82]

The bubble, ambition, had burst; the bubble, society, had followed. He took to quoting the famous lines of Pope:

> Learn to live well, or fairly make your will;
> You've play'd, and lov'd, and eat, and drunk your fill:
> Walk sober off; before a sprightlier age
> Comes titt'ring on, and shoves you from the stage:
> Leave such to trifle with more grace and ease,
> Whom Folly pleases, and whose Follies please. [83]

But after all not quite yet. For him, indeed, the beloved world might be over, but he could still live vicariously. He could still cherish hopes, if not for himself, at least for another. His triumphs might be renewed, his failures might be retrieved; the summits of success he had never reached might conceivably be attained by this younger other self whom he loved. The man who hopes still retains a stake in the world. Chesterfield had still his son.

It was in these years of increasing deafness and invalidism that the obscure tragedy of that hope reached its climax and sank to its ignominious conclusion. In the course of it, all that was best and worst in him, the very quintessence of his nature, appeared. Few have been able with pen and ink so to transmute their personalities into literary form as did he in the letters to his son. Retrospectively considered, in the light of such achievement, the whole of his career, his experience, his philosophy, forms merely a setting for this central, vivid episode.

But before reviewing the story of that supreme relationship with its vain illusions and ultimate frustration, it will be well to complete the background by glancing briefly at the concluding phase of his life.

CHAPTER XVIII
Falling Leaves

I T WILL BE RECALLED that in 1747 an obscure writer, by the name of Johnson, had dedicated the Plan of an English dictionary to Lord Chesterfield, at that time Secretary of State.* He had been accorded a gracious interview by the Earl and had received a gratification of ten pounds. It will be recalled, moreover, that the dedication had served its author as a pretext for delay in composing it, rather than as an opportunity of rendering homage to an eminent statesman. After that, seven years elapsed; no dictionary appeared. Johnson, indeed, had become known to a wider public, on the score of his satire *The Vanity of Human Wishes*, the unsuccessful play *Irene*, and the respected, though in its periodical form the little-read, *Rambler*. But these publications were not of a nature to suggest lexicography, nor to rouse sanguine hopes of the dictionary's completion.

However, toward the end of 1754, Chesterfield's "worthy friend," Mr. Dodsley, the publisher, informed him that this half-forgotten work was nearly finished and would appear in the course of the winter. Whereupon, recalling the prospectus and dedication of seven years before, the Earl published two kindly essays in *The World* magazine praising the work and its author.[1] He assumed that everyone who could afford it would buy the dictionary; of the Plan he declared that "nothing could be more rationally imagined, or more accurately and elegantly expressed." In reference to the confusion of English at that time for lack of a competent standard, he affirmed that recourse should be had to the Roman expedient of electing a dictator, and "upon this principle," said he, "I give my vote for Mr. Johnson to fill that great and arduous post. And I hereby de-

*See *supra*, pp. 242 f.

clare, that I make a total surrender of all my rights and privileges in the English language, as a free-born British subject, to the said Mr. Johnson, during the term of his dictatorship. Nay more; I will not only obey him, like an old Roman, as my dictator, but, like a modern Roman, I will implicitly believe in him as my pope, and hold him to be infallible while in the chair."

According to Horace Walpole, these papers contributed a great deal to the reputation of the dictionary; [2] and well they might, for Chesterfield, at that time, as an arbiter of taste, stood at the summit of both the polite and the literary world. But Johnson, remembering his days of misery, his long struggle up from the depths, with a heart still desolate for the wife he had lost; remembering too, perhaps, the oversanguine hopes that the gracious interview had once kindled and how they had faded, and what the favor of this great man would then have meant, seized his pen and wrote, not a letter which had any just bearing upon facts, but a requiem of those hopes, an elegy of disappointment.*

To the Right Honourable the Earl of Chesterfield [he wrote].

My Lord, I have been lately informed, by the proprietor of *The World*, that two papers, in which my Dictionary is recommended to the public, were written by your Lordship. To be so distinguished is an honour which, being very little accustomed to favours from the great, I know not well how to receive, or in what terms to acknowledge.

When, upon some slight encouragement, I first visited your Lordship, I was overpowered, like the rest of mankind, by the enchantment of your address, and could not forbear to wish that I might boast myself *le vainqueur du vainqueur de la terre;* that I might obtain that regard for which I saw the world contending; but I found my attendance so little encouraged, that neither pride nor modesty would suffer me to continue it. When I had once addressed your Lordship in publick, I had exhausted all the art of pleasing which a retired and uncourtly scholar can possess. I had done all that I could; and no man is well pleased to have his all neglected, be it ever so little.

---

* *Cf.* Plan of the Dictionary, *Works of Samuel Johnson*, Oxford, 1825, vol. v, pp. 1–22. There can be little doubt that Johnson expected more from Chesterfield than he received. "I found that my design had been thought by your Lordship of importance sufficient to attract your favour. . . . I imagine what the world will expect from a scheme, prosecuted under your Lordship's influence."

Seven years, my Lord, have now past, since I waited in your outward rooms, or was repulsed from your door; during which time I have been pushing on my work through difficulties, of which it is useless to complain, and have brought it, at last, to the verge of publication, without one act of assistance, one word of encouragement, or one smile of favour. Such treatment I did not expect, for I never had a Patron before.

The shepherd in Virgil grew at last acquainted with Love, and found him a native of the rocks.

Is not a Patron, my Lord, one who looks with unconcern on a man struggling for life in the water, and, when he has reached ground, encumbers him with help? The notice which you have been pleased to take of my labours, had it been early, had been kind; but it has been delayed till I am indifferent, and cannot enjoy it; till I am solitary, and cannot impart it; till I am known, and do not want it. I hope it is no very cynical asperity, not to confess obligations where no benefit has been received, or to be unwilling that the Publick should consider me as owing that to a Patron, which Providence has enabled me to do for myself.

Having carried on my work thus far with so little obligation to any favourer of learning, I shall not be disappointed though I should conclude it, if less be possible, with less; for I have been long awakened from that dream of hope, in which I once boasted myself with so much exultation,

My Lord,
Your Lordship's most humble
Most obedient servant,
SAM. JOHNSON.*

Chesterfield was delighted with this letter as a work of art, kept it on his table, and pointed out to Dodsley the felicitous turns of expression. It was an instance, declared Boswell, of his "glossy duplicity." But that is nonsense. With an objectiveness of which Johnson and his biographer were alike incapable, he appraised the letter for what it was: a superb expression of hurt pride and rugged independence. He had committed no wrong, and, indeed, had performed all that could normally be expected of him in the affair. From his perfectly balanced temper, even so shrewd a thrust glanced off as from polished steel. Dodsley came nearer to the truth when he exclaimed, "Pooh! Do you think that anything Johnson could say would hurt Lord Chesterfield?" [3]

* Dated Feb. 7, 1755.

These are the facts and *all* the facts of this celebrated episode, which must have seemed negligible to the Earl, but upon which so much has been embroidered.* For, by a singular fatality, no other event in Chesterfield's life has become more widely known or has served more generally to stigmatize him in the public mind. It matters not that, with reference to this particular case, Johnson was not only peevish, dishonest and unjust, but ungrateful as well, and that the other behaved generously and courteously. The story has been too good to drop. If it did not occur as represented, it ought so to have occurred. And thereby hangs a moral.

As in an earlier chapter, for the sake of contrast which would more clearly set off Chesterfield's qualities, standards, and limitations, we ventured to bring him into another focus, that of John Wesley and of the Great Revival, so the Johnson episode provides a similar opposition of personalities; and it is this, disregarding the rights and wrongs of the case, that the popular mind instinctively has seized upon. If Johnson had not become a prototype of sturdy honesty, of the warm heart and impetuous nature, a protagonist of John Bull's stout and endearing prejudices, nothing would be remembered of so trivial an occurrence. In point of fact, the qualities he here exhibited were, except for his rhetoric, fairly discreditable. But it was necessary that the champion of all the virtues which are beloved by the mass of humanity should triumph over the representative of passionless correctness, aristocratic place, and worldly acumen; and therefore triumphed he has and will continue to triumph on the score of his magnificent letter, despite all the protests of historical accuracy.

What is the truth of this question? It is merely that the Johnson anecdote has served mankind as a somewhat faulty pretext to display its love and tenderness for certain human qualities associated rightly in the main with Samuel Johnson, and to express aversion toward certain other qualities — emotional coolness in particular — associated rightly for the most part with Lord Chesterfield. There is that much pith and justice in the story.

The Johnson articles in *The World* were merely two of a series of essays published by the Earl in that magazine during the years 1753-1756: in all, some twenty-three papers. This scribbling, as he termed it,[4] was the chief of the pastimes with which he attempted

* E.g., the entirely fictitious Colley Cibber episode.

to compensate for the failure of his ambitions and the loss of social pleasures during the latter part of his life. We have already noted the political essays written during his period of opposition and published in *Fog's Journal, Common Sense,* and *Old England;* * but in addition to these he had written others on the subject of manners, fads, foibles and crotchets of the day, in the style of Addison. His essays in *The World* continued this genre. Altogether forty-five contributions to periodicals are preserved in his collected works — a sufficient number to place him among the essayists of his age.

The titles of some of the nonpolitical articles will give an idea of their nature. We find him descanting "Upon Common Sense," "Upon Dress," "Upon Ladies Going out of Town," "Upon Coxcombs," "Upon the Taste for French Fashions," "Upon the Danger of Reading Romances," "Upon Ladies Painting," "Upon People of Fashion," "Upon Decorum," "Upon the Italian Opera," and the like. But, just as in his correspondence we have distinguished a variety of roles, so here in his public performance we find a new costume, a new mask.

It was the convention established by the earlier essayists of the century; he followed it adroitly in style and treatment. Common sense is the staple of this tradition, British common sense, imbued with a "marketable morality" as one writer expresses it, and presented sometimes with homely plainness, and sometimes with graceful badinage. It extols decency, thrift, sobriety, and moderation as the essentials of living; deprecates the *outré* and the exotic; and, while turning its back upon any altitude of thought or emotion, clings to a respectable level of tradition. One example of Chesterfield's adherence to the manner of this school will sufficiently indicate his conventionality as an essayist. We have already seen that, if there was any man in England notoriously identified with the French spirit in thought and behavior, it was he. French authors formed the major part of his reading; among moderns, Voltaire chiefly delighted him; it was to Paris that he looked as the supreme training school of his son; it was the French he bade him copy; as for himself, his manners, even his cuisine, were French. We should therefore expect under such titles as "The Taste for French Fashions" and "A Trip to Paris" at least a cosmopolitan attitude. But no sturdy Briton could have expressed himself more insularly.

* See *supra,* p. 166.

It is amusing to discover such phrases as "the absurd and ridiculous imitation of the French, which is now become the epidemical distemper of this kingdom," or "I behold with indignation the sturdy conquerors of France shrunk and dwindled into the imperfect mimics, or ridiculous *caricaturas*, of all its levity. . . . Our clothes, our furniture, nay our food too, all is to come from France," or again: "Methinks there is something very mean in being such avowed plagiaries, and I wonder the British spirit will submit to it."

And at the very time when his son was being groomed to all the finesse of Paris, he writes in the character of an English country gentleman to complain that since a recent visit with his family in that city, "My meat too is so much disguised in the dressing by a French cook, as my wife and my daughter are by their red, their pompoons, their scraps of dirty gauze, flimsy sattins, and black callicoes; not to mention their affected broken English, and mangled French, which jumbled together compose their present language." [5] It may be true that such articles were addressed to the middle classes and were intended to have no application to aristocrats like Bolingbroke, Lady Hervey, Miss Pitt, Lord Huntingdon, or the Earl himself, among others. It may also be true that his contentions were just and that he sincerely deplored a superficial imitation of the French. But the point is that there was nothing distinctly himself in these essays, nothing in the least original; he was expressing once more in graceful fashion the platitudes of the essay type; he was writing as an essayist was expected to write, not as Lord Chesterfield. If, for instance, he had written in praise of the French, or had endeavored to interpret to his fellow countrymen, as he could so well have done, the French genius for grace, clarity, and social intercourse, this would have been consonant with his own experience, and would have rendered a service to British culture.

We have already called attention to a similar characteristic in the political essays. Here Swift is the model. It is the ingenuity of Swift that informs the most trenchant of all his periodical writings: the essay on "The Waxwork Army." And although the satire here rivals that of his master, it is still an imitation.

We are dealing, of course, with an age of types and conventions, nor have we a right to expect of any eighteenth-century essayist that sometimes too obvious effort for originality which marks a later period. But, after all, true genius expressed itself then as now with its own individual stamp, and of this quality, in Chesterfield's periodical work, I am unable to find one trace.*

Perhaps, among his formal writings, the "Characters" [6] of men and women he had known, which remained unpublished during his lifetime and were also a product of his later years, bring us closer to the mind of their author. Here again he is following a beaten track, the one especially associated with La Bruyère; but the cool objectivity of this type, its affectation of impersonal analysis, harmonized peculiarly with Chesterfield's temperament.

These appraisals of contemporaries, which include some twenty names, are possibly fragments of unwritten or lost memoirs. They are historically valuable, but save for their author's tribute to Scarborough and Arbuthnot, their icy detachment excludes any sense of artistic portraiture. They are exercises in anatomy which produce no illusion of life. They betray the characteristics of the writer rather than of the personalities described — the cool mind, the passionless temper. These were not Chesterfield's greatest qualities. If his memoirs had appeared, we may surmise with reasonable probability that they would have been elegantly expressed, but of so impartial a nature that very little would have been added to our knowledge of him, however much they might have contributed to the history of his times.

But fugitive pieces, like the essays and the "Characters," should not be taken too seriously. Most of them were intended primarily to divert the writer himself, to entice his thought away from the interminable hours and from the silence that deepened around him. He had no literary ambition, but enjoyed the niceties of language and the neat craftsmanship of composition. He wrote for the distraction of it and destroyed far more than he published.[7] But at times even this turned stale. "Adieu!" he broke off at the end of one of the later letters to his son — and the suppressed yawn did not cover up the sigh — "Adieu! I am going to the ball, to save my eyes from reading, and my mind from thinking." [8]

The resources of a man of action and of the world are at best reduced when these outlets are closed to him. Be he ever so learned or mentally alert or of good courage, books, meditation and an ear

---

* Roger Coxon in *Chesterfield and his Critics* is inclined to rank the essays much higher than does the present writer, and should be consulted on this point.

trumpet do not compensate for the loss of his primary interests. But in Chesterfield's case, there was a special curtailment owing to the limitations of his type of mind. His opinions on history and literature make it abundantly evident what these were. Although the fine library at Chesterfield House contained the great books of the western world, together with others more ephemeral, their owner's preferences were strictly bounded and predetermined. Other retired statesmen have found solace in religious or philosophical speculation, in the sublimities of the sages or poets who have ennobled human life, or, on a lower plane, in the graceful fictions of imaginative writers; but from this Chesterfield was debarred by the intense practicality of his realism. His well-known opinion of Dante — that he was not worth the pains necessary to understand him — illustrates this attitude. Homer, Virgil, and Milton, in spite of their great passages, were bores who required a good deal of snuff. Shakespeare was an uncultivated genius whose beauties are disgraced by extravagance and nonsense. Petrarch was a singsong, lovesick poet "who deserved his *Laura* better than his laurel." [9] We may agree or not with these strictures, but they serve to distinguish the sort of mentality that could make them. He had no interest in the transcendental, the fanciful, or speculative. His favorite reading was historical, but here again he read with the a priori prejudices of the rationalist. In particular, he suspected the honesty of any ideal enthusiasm; and, as the history of Europe has been largely influenced by just such currents, a preconception of this sort will inevitably close the mind to any but a one-sided and, on the whole, a rather puerile interpretation. Thus, Mahomet was a "famous imposter"; the Crusades were "the most immoral scheme, that was ever contrived by knaves and executed by madmen and fools, against humanity"; the Popes were old cheats; Peter the Hermit was both a knave and madman; Ignatius Loyola was a madman with mad and wicked designs; Rome, once the capital of the world, was now the capital of imposture; the great Fénelon, Archbishop of Cambray, was a time-server and a pimp; the Reformation rose from the disappointed avarice of Luther, who was enraged that his order, and consequently himself, had not the exclusive privilege of selling indulgences.[10] Admitting the immaturity of historical studies at that time, it must still be allowed that such opinions are the result, not of misinformation after a painstaking investigation of what sources there were, but of a *parti pris* derived from religious skepticism. Far from being the expression of independent thought, they are commonplaces belonging to the school of Voltaire.

On the other hand, Chesterfield's preferences are no less illuminating than his aversions. They were so inevitable that it is hardly necessary to enumerate them. In literature they were Pope, Addison, and Swift, Crébillon the younger, Marivaux, La Bruyère, La Rochefoucauld. In history and practical philosophy they were Bolingbroke, de Retz, Montesquieu, Cicero, and Locke. Above all, dominating both fields, stood Voltaire. There was no one kind of writing in which he had not excelled; his *Siècle de Louis XIV* showed how history ought to be written; the *Henriade* gave Chesterfield more pleasure than any other epic poem he had ever read. His remarks on this subject contain a sort of profession of faith regarding literature, which briefly sums up the entire matter. "I am grown old," he declared, "and have possibly lost a great deal of that fire, which formerly made me love fire in others at any rate, and however attended with smoke, but now I must have all sense, and cannot, for the sake of five righteous lines, forgive a thousand absurd ones. . . . The *Henriade* is all sense from the beginning to the end, often adorned by the justest and liveliest reflections, the most beautiful descriptions, the noblest images, and sublimest sentiments; not to mention the harmony of the verse, in which *Voltaire* undoubtedly exceeds all the French poets." [11] There can be no cavil upon a question of taste; but as to the supreme excellences of the *Henriade*, it would be difficult at present to find anyone who would agree with this verdict.

Hence, as we picture him in his splendid library during the long evening of his life, it is difficult to avoid the impression of something more than deafness, age, and infirmity that hemmed him in. We could wish him a more ample refuge than the philosophy of Voltaire; a wider horizon than that presented by Bolingbroke, Crébillon, and Pope; richer resources than the snuffbox of common sense, tinctured with disillusionment, could provide.

But granting this, together with its implications, the limit of criticism has been reached. Otherwise there can be little but admiration for the last period of Chesterfield's life. Here something heroical emerges that compels respect and implies a challenge.

When the dust of ambition had cleared away, there remained a shrunken old man, confronting the approach of death, or rather the painful decline of life, gallantly and serenely. Without hope as without fear, utterly tired of living, convinced of human futility, he met disappointment, ill-health, loneliness and the irony of the universe with a debonair acquiescence. Above all, not to whine or wince; above all, to look the facts of life in the face, through eyes undimmed by any tear of self-pity or sentiment; above all, with a whimsical epigram, to decline sympathy and disarm compassion. If there was Stoicism in this, an Epicurean grace concealed the outlines. He kept himself occupied with an infinity of pleasant trifles — from cultivating melons at Blackheath [12] to acknowledging in courtly French the honor of his election to the Académie des Inscriptions et Belles-lettres at Paris.* "I make the most of everything I can," [13] he wrote; and the statement was more than a phrase; he practiced it. As the crowning moral of the art of living, no better philosophy could be devised.

There are many pleasing glimpses of him scattered up and down those twenty years. The turmoil and factions of the past had been forgotten. Like other old men, he lived to become memorial of other days and ways. As to us the Victorian era, so, to the England of George III, the age of Pope, Swift, Gay, Addison, and Steele, Walpole's ministry, the Hanoverian advent, Marlborough and his victories, the Old and Young Pretenders, the excursions and alarms and freer manners of that receding time, were grown vaguely romantic, venerable, or picturesque. And with all this Chesterfield had been connected, sometimes in a distinguished role. The world of younger men cared nothing for outworn rivalries. His reputation for wit and social address was already becoming traditional. A halo of great friendships and contacts surrounded him. [14]

Young Edward Jerningham, one of the fashionable poetasters of Horace Walpole's circle, reflected the sentiment of his generation in a poetical address to the Earl of which the following is illustrative:

> Though deafness, by a doom severe,
>   Steals from thy ear the murmuring rill,
> And Philomel's delightful air;
>   I e'en deem this but a passing ill.

* This was in 1755. *Cf.* Maty, *op. cit.*, vol. i, part ii, pp. 274 ff.

Ah! If anew thy ear was strung
Awake to every voice around,
Thy praises by the many sung
Would stun thee with the choral sound.[15]

And Chesterfield's reply is equally illustrative of the humor and facility which he retained to the end of his life:

Accept, then [he wrote], my humblest thanks, in humble prose, for your very good verses upon a very indifferent subject; which, should you be reproached with, you may very justly make the same answer that your predecessor, Waller, did to King Charles after the Restoration. The King accused him of having made finer verses in praise of Oliver Cromwell than of himself; to which he agreed, saying that fiction was the soul of poetry. Am I not generous to help you out of this scrape at my own expense? . . . I have truth and impudence enough to say, *Tu m'aduli ma tu mi piaci* [You flatter me, but you please me]. . . . What am I to suppose you are now doing in Norfolk? . . . If you stray among the hills, vales, and purling streams, it is to make your court to the muses, who have long had such an affection for you, that (I will answer for it) they will meet you wherever you please to appoint them. If to those nine Ideal Ladies you add a tenth, of real good country flesh and blood, I cannot help it; but God forbid that I should advise it. In all events, I believe you would be equal to the ten. . . . I desire my respects to Lady Jerningham; but not one word of the tenth muse.

Young Jerningham reverently preserved this letter.

Even Horace Walpole, son of Chesterfield's old enemy, softened to him at the end, visited him frequently, and in 1770 entertained him at breakfast at Strawberry Hill. Verses from the archdilettante's pen and set up on his famous press were presented as a souvenir:

Few paces hence, beneath yon grottoed road,
From dying Pope the last sweet accents flowed.
O Twiknam! would the friend of Pope but bless
With some immortal strain thy favour'd press,
The happier emblem would with truth depose,
That where one Phœnix died, another rose.[16]

And when in turn this second Phœnix expired, Walpole lamented that he would no longer have his lively sayings to retail.[17]

By an odd chance, which gives a curious balance to his correspondence, the figure of Lady Suffolk, the Mrs. Howard of the

Young Court forty years before, re-emerges briefly in the last letters. She too remained, an almost legendary survival of that lost
time, placid and elegant as ever, chatting with the omnivorous
Walpole about ghostly scandals of half a centruy ago. For her
the worn-out old nobleman of seventy-three revived the badinage
of Leicester Fields; and, like a veteran actor who can never forget
his maiden part, recaptured the antiquated spirit of that vanished
stage. His relations with Lady Suffolk had always been on a tone
of polite jesting; it was the special costume in her case. He addressed her now from Bath in the character of his footman, Thomas
Allen. The lady, unable to sustain the comedy unaided, called in
the pen of Horace Walpole to her assistance, and answered in the
person of her maid, Mrs. Wagstaff. The Earl, alias Thomas Allen,
replied.[18]

Or he corresponds with his quondam associate, enemy, and now
long since forgiven contemporary, the Earl of Bath, to whom he
complained that he had grown very lean and very deaf. Whereupon
the other replied that he could lend him some fat and would be
glad at any time to lend him an ear.[19]

Or, writing to Lord Huntingdon, established at the Prince of
Wales's court, but on temporary absence in the country, the in-
corrigible old gentleman suspects that "the squire's or the curate's
plump daughters, or even the cherry-cheeked milkmaid," rather
than a love of rural solitude, accounts for it.[20]

More intimately and most delightfully of all, however, he appears in his relationship to his godchild and heir, Arthur Stanhope's son, the Earl of Chesterfield soon to be. It lent the glow
of tenderness and gentleness to his old age. The new Philip filled
a place left vacant in Chesterfield's life by the growth of his own
son to manhood and by the failure of the hopes he had entertained
for him. Long accustomed to the role of mentor, he would have
found himself lost without it. He adopted his godson, assumed entire charge of his education, and at the earliest possible moment
began writing him letters which in themselves form a collection
inferior to the more famous series only because they extend no
farther than boyhood.* But there is one significant difference. The

---

* At the time of the Earl's death in 1773, his godson was eighteen years old.
On the relationship between the two, *cf.*, in addition to Carnarvon, Sidney L.
Gulick, Jr., in his excellent introduction to *Some unpublished letters of Lord
Chesterfield*.

vicarious dreams he had cherished in the case of his son, the inexorable program he had laid out for him, have now somewhat faded. Indulgence has replaced them, an old man's selfless affection for childhood. The subject of his letters to "Sturdy," as he nicknamed his godchild, is in general worldly enough. He deals with manners: he discusses the importance of the *suaviter in modo, fortiter in re;* but the tone has changed.

He yearned over the little boy with an almost maternal devotion. "What pity it is," he mused, "that this native truth and innocence should ever be warped! But it will in time . . . a man must live with men, and if he is too open and sincere, he will infallibly be the bubble of most of them. *But I shall not teach him this piece of worldly prudence, which will come of itself soon enough.*" * Fifteen years before, when writing to the older Philip, he had had no such scruples.

There is also more tolerance and kindness in the letters to his godson; the emphasis shifts more frequently from the advantage of getting to that of giving. "Let us then," he enjoined, "not only scatter benefits, but even strew flowers for our fellow-travellers in the rugged ways of this wretched world." [21] The ethical note is more prominent, more earnest.

With the infatuation of age, he extolled this child as he had never extolled his son; if he did not love him as much, at least he spoiled him more. "Your parts," he wrote in his last letter, "have not only answered my hopes, but my most sanguine wishes; I esteem, I admire you, and you are esteemed and admired by others, in your now little sphere." [22] He had never expressed himself in that way to the earlier Philip Stanhope; and yet, save for his title, the fifth Earl of Chesterfield proved no less a nonentity. The portrait of him by Russell at the age of fourteen is that of a solid, pugnacious, and very commonplace youth, in spite of the Shakespearean costume he wears and the Anacreon, Horace, and Cicero which lie before him on the table. [23]

But the boy need not concern us. It is the old man's fondness for him which is the arresting, charming thing, which reveals unsuspected, incongruous qualities. There are repeated invitations to Philip to dine with him, to bring his schoolmaster Mr. Dodd, and his chum, young Ernst, along. He called the latter "a very well-

* To A. C. Stanhope, Sept. 15, 1763. Italics not in the original.

bred pretty boy," conceived an affection for him, and even wrote
to him.[24] Or we find him at dinner with Philip and the lad's sister,
Margaret: the two children no doubt a little overawed by the
footmen and the magnificence, confronting the venerable wig and
glittering star and the shrewd old eyes of their great kinsman.[25]
Or he chuckles over the present of a haunch of mutton from Master
Stanhope, aged nine, accompanied by a note in doggerel French
and Latin, which he sent on to the boy's father: *Le petit progredi
rogat sa Grandeur d'accepter partem d'un ovis, que son charissimus
pater lui a envoyé.*[26] Or he recruits an audience of the first quality to
attend some theatricals presented singlehanded by young Stanhope
and young Ernst, calling themselves the Chesterfield Company, at
Mr. Dodd's house in Southampton Row. Lord Chesterfield, Count
Braht, the Marquis de Guerchy, Sir Thomas Robinson, Sir Richard
Temple, Sir Alexander and Lady Grant, the Bishop of Chester,
Lady Harrington and her daughter, Lady Catherine Stanhope and
her daughters, Mr. Lovel Stanhope, among others, were present.
There were scenes from Shakespeare, Terence, Dryden, Corneille,
and Foote. There was a prologue by Master Stanhope and an epi-
logue by Master Ernst, "the whole to conclude with a concerto
upon the harpsichord by Mr. Ernst."[27] How the audience applauded, and how bored they must have been! But we can imagine
Chesterfield's arch looks and beaming face.

Of course he repeated the same mistakes in the education of
Philip minor as of Philip major. He blundered in the choice of tutors
for both of them. (Mr. Dodd, his selection for the younger Philip,
died subsequently on the gallows for forging his pupil's name to
a note.)* He sent each of the boys in turn to so unlikely a school of
manners as Leipzig; and kept them both under a system of espionage that had little to commend it. He advised fashionable mistresses.[28] Chesterfield, who, unlike Lady Huntingdon, as he declared,
had no faith in sudden conversions,[29] remained unconverted to the
end. He could not learn new tricks. An imaginary dialogue between
the Duke of Buckingham and Sir John Cutler, found among his
writings after his death, concludes on the following significant
note:

---

* In the case of his godson, however, he chose a Swiss gentleman to act
as governor during the former's foreign travels, one Georges Deyverdun, and
not, as in the case of his son, an English parson. *Cf.* Gulick, *op. cit.,* p. 8.

Sir John. . . . If we were both of us, after our experience, to begin the world again, I believe we should ——
Duke. Do exactly as we did before, for though experience often informs our minds, it can never change our natures.[30]

And the fable can be applied to him. But it is equally true that in his case old age brought with it, if not conversion, at least a refinement toward his higher self. "The heart never grows better by age," he once wrote: "I fear rather worse; always harder." [31] He disproved his own apothegm.

Together with title and estate, he left Philip Stanhope, then on his travels, a legacy of advice, a last letter to be delivered on his return.[32] It is the most complete, the truest expression of his philosophy. He had found no answer to the problems of life, save fortitude, prudence, and self-control; he had rejected the comfort of any transcendental faith; but such as he had he gave. Being what he was, anything else would have rung false. There is a yearning quality in this letter which touches the heart. His essential paganism would have reached higher if it could.

"These are not the dictates," he wrote, "of a peevish, sour old fellow, who affects to give good rules when he can no longer give bad examples; but the advice of an indulgent and tender friend (I had almost said parent), and the result of the long experience of one, *hackneyed in the ways of life.*" And after counsels, which repeat those to his son, he concludes, "Yes, I have been young, and a great deal too young. Idle dissipation and innumerable indiscretions, which I am now heartily ashamed and repent of, characterized my youth. But if my advice can make you wiser and better than I was at your age, I hope it may be some little atonement. God bless you." [33]

During these latter years, now and then, gusts of the active world he had abandoned disturbed the monotony of Chesterfield House. More than once his political judgment and talents as a mediator were called upon by the Duke of Newcastle, his aged but still bustling relative. In 1757 he took part in the reconciliation between Newcastle and Pitt; between Newcastle, the Princess of Wales, and Lord Bute.[34] Now that he desired nothing, competed for nothing, all factions could turn to him, cite his opinions, avail themselves of his diplomatic address. We find Lord Hardwicke quoting him with approval in 1756.[35] He was Newcastle's political confidant until the Duke's death in 1768.[36] Though at a distance, he remained constantly interested in public affairs, which for the most part he believed were going to the dogs.

We have already commented upon his habit of gloomy, and usually unfulfilled, predictions. They were numerous toward the end of his life. He believed that the great days of English trade were past. He wondered whether he or England would be dead first. He was certain that Britain was undone, both at home and abroad; it was no longer a nation; he had never seen so dreadful a prospect. In 1762, despite recent victories abroad, he feared that the country was not so well prepared to repel invasions as to make them; and, dreading an attack of the French and Spaniards, exclaimed: "*What will it avail us if we gain the whole world, and lose our own soul?*" In the same year, he prophesied the approaching end of the Jesuits and the Papacy.[37] In 1766, for once correctly, he apprehended the loss of the American colonies within a few years. Good Whig as he was, and opposed to autocratic pretensions of the Crown, the policies of George III alarmed him. In particular, he regarded the Stamp Act with abhorrence.[38]

Much has been made of his sagacity in predicting the French Revolution, although that honor was shared by a good many others, but the prophecy had two parts, of which only the first was justified. After foretelling the Revolution, he added, "I am glad of it; the rest of Europe will be the quieter." [39] On the whole, it must be allowed that the proportion of fulfillment to the number of these forecasts was not very high.

Poor Chesterfield, at the end of his life, seems to have been harassed by Cupid, who insisted on aiming his darts at the Earl's elderly male relatives. They turned to him in their quandary, and put him to no little trouble. It was all the more annoying in the case of his brother, Sir William Stanhope, because a son born to that gentleman would have destroyed young Sturdy's chance of the title. But marry he did, though past sixty, a young woman twenty years old,* "whom," growled Chesterfield, "he had by God's good providence found of a retired disposition, and who had been bred up prudently by an old grandmother in the country." [40] The happy couple departed for Italy. Upon their return, their chaise stopped

---

* Anne Delaval. She was his third wife; they were married Oct. 6, 1759.

at Blackheath, and Sir William, emerging, made his wife a low bow. "Madam," said he, "I hope I shall never see your face again." "Sir," she replied, "I will take all the care I can that you never shall." [41] And entering Babiole, Sir William poured his woes into the Earl's disgusted ear trumpet. He had to act as go-between in the case, and lamented afterwards that "he would much rather negotiate the most difficult point of Imperial law with the whole Diet of Ratisbon than negotiate any point with any woman." [42] It tried his diplomacy to the utmost. In the end, the contestants were separated: "the only solid and lasting peace between a man and his wife," declared the gratified mediator.[43] At least Sturdy had been saved.

Then Arthur Stanhope grew amorous, and appealed to Chesterfield for advice, which his lordship gave him in no uncertain terms.[44] But the inflammation continued. "I cannot help telling you," wrote the exasperated nobleman, "that I plainly perceive that you are resolved to marry again: but for God's sake be cautious. Consider that your own happiness entirely and your children's in a great measure depends upon it. If you want a woman, follow the sacred example of the ancient Patriarchs, and take a handmaid." Counsel in vain. Arthur Stanhope, aged sixty, married a girl of twenty-five,[45] and died not long after.

But all this — correspondents, attachments, political dabbling and vexations — were in a sense only pastime, the hobbies and duties of one whose personal interests were over. According to the season he journeyed from London to Bath and back to London, "never free from ills of one kind or another," [46] following cures in which he had no confidence. And no wonder he had none. He tried the urine of hares, "so long and so often," he wrote, "that whether male, female, or hermaphrodite, I have probably had some of every gender." He tried the galls of hares. He tried the Bath waters in every fashion; bathed his head, pumped it; dropped water into his ears, douched them, blistered them — all in vain.[47] He had, as he said, three nurses — an ass, a cow, and a milch goat — and feared that the latter might make a satyr of him.[48] But pains, deafness, and weariness of the flesh hung on. Their counterpart was loneliness and weariness of the spirit.

He has been compared most unjustly with his old acquaintance and contemporary, the Maréchal de Richelieu, that perennial wit and man about town, lingering on from one Parisian generation to the next.[49] But Richelieu was a coxcomb and butterfly, whose career had been founded and sustained only by social prowess and immeasurable rapacity. He belonged merely to the genus clubman, *bon viveur*, and corrupt courtier. Beneath Chesterfield's veneer there was a depth and a resonance of which such as he could know nothing. A Richelieu may encounter illness and disappointment, but he lacks philosophy enough to be conscious of disillusionment. The rewards, pleasures, and passions of the world remain for him alone desirable, even when he can no longer taste them. But with Chesterfield this was not so. Something not quite French, after all, the eternal note of sadness haunting the North, reappeared in him at the end. He discovered that life, as he knew it, had been only a shadow play of light and color against the darkness of inscrutable mystery. What was the sense of it all? He did not know. What, if anything, lay beyond? He could not guess; he had no theory. But at least he felt impatient of illusions, weary of the empty farce, and at times gazed wistfully beyond it. We can hardly imagine Marshal Richelieu writing the following lines: "When I reflect back upon what I have seen, what I have heard, and what I have done myself, I can hardly persuade myself that all that frivolous hurry and bustle of the world had any reality; but they seem to have been the dreams of restless nights." [50] In one of the first letters to his godson,[51] he bade him learn the following bitter lines from Dryden's *Aurengzebe:*

> When I consider Life, 'tis all a cheat;
> Yet fool'd with hope, men favour the deceit,
> Trust on, and think tomorrow will repay;
> Tomorrow's falser than the former day;
> Lies worse, and when it bids us most be blest,
> With some new hope, cuts off what we possest.
> Fond cozenage this. Who'd live past years again?
> Yet all hope pleasure from what still remain;
> And from the dregs of life, think to receive,
> What the first sprightly runnings could not give.
> I'm tired of seeking for this chemic gold,
> Which fools us young, and beggars us when old.

"When one is in the world," he remarked on another occasion, "one must make the best of it; but, considering what that best is upon the whole, I doubt it is only making the best of a bad bargain." [52] Nor is it possible to associate a man like Richelieu with such a judgment as the following upon the objects of former ambition: "I know their futility," wrote the Earl, "and I know now that one can only find happiness within oneself." [53] For it must be admitted that, at the end of his life, Chesterfield, the veteran man of affairs, wit, Epicurean, and social arbiter, rose in stature above all this, freed himself from those shackles. It should be repeated that there was nothing obvious in the process; none but his intimate friends would note the difference; to the world in general he would appear simply a deaf, gracious, and witty old nobleman, the logical conclusion to his former self. And this in more than one sense he was. It was not that his familiar qualities disappeared or were suppressed, but that new elements, latent in him, emerged, and that these give dignity and greater significance to his character.

It is essential for our purpose to note this. If he had been merely a Richelieu, we would have been wasting our time with him. Whatever the usual level of life, and however generally most of us pursue material objects, we have still enough complacency, for the most part, to condemn an unabashed and satisfied sensualism. A man of the world on that footing is not worth the trouble of an analysis. It is Chesterfield's distinction, and it constitutes his importance for us, that he lived to perceive his life's futility; that endowed with a great mind and with great talents, he advanced as far as they could take him above the merely carnal plane. A supreme man of the world, he looked across the world and pronounced it a wilderness; but beyond this point no exercise of reason, however talented, could carry him.

Did he find within himself that happiness of which he had written? No, unless the term be diminished to mean no more than calm endurance. Of this there are many reflections in the last letters, but of little more. To live without too much pain and to die without fear [54] was become the primary object. Even his epigrams savored of death. Shortly before the end, he referred to his afternoon drive as the rehearsal of his funeral. Horace Walpole relates that when "asked how his contemporary, Lord Tyrawley, did, he said, 'To tell you the truth, we have both been dead this twelvemonth, but we do not own it.' " [55]

Throngs of new faces now filled the Pump Room and the West

End; except for a handful of derelicts like himself, he stood practically alone; the brilliant friends, the fair women, he had known were
gone. Every day brought with it a new *memento mori*. There was,
for example, the illness of his old servant, White, who had lived
with him forty years. "We were young and healthy together," he
wrote; "we are old and crazy, and seem to be tending to our last
stage together." He began speculating which of them would go
first, and believed, as he put it, that they would *start fair*.[56] And we
find him at Bath, crawling out frequently to visit the palsy-stricken
Harte for compassion's sake; and, skeptic as he was, rejoicing that
the old dominie had grown extremely devout, "because that is always a comfort to the afflicted." [57] He could not draw upon such
comfort himself; but he welcomed it for others.

On a day of late summer at Blackheath, burdened by the sense of
finality in everything, he penned the following lines, which are
among the most eloquent and saddest he ever wrote: "I feel the
beginning of the autumn, which is already very cold: the leaves are
withered, fall apace, and seem to intimate that I must follow them;
which I shall do without reluctance, being extremely weary of this
silly world." [58] It expresses the closing mood of his life; with a shrug
of lassitude, the Prince of Vanity Fair turned away.

One cannot help recalling, in contrast to this bleak acquiescence,
the humble faith with which Johnson met his death some years
later, or the exultant joy of Wesley's final hours in the bare little
room near City Road, when, "lifting his hand . . . like a soldier in
the moment of victory, he exclaimed, 'The best of all is, God is
with us.'" But they were men of a different stamp; they served
other masters and received throughout their entire life other
rewards.

Not long before Chesterfield's death, Voltaire at Ferney wrote
him a letter which may be considered the truest as well as the
noblest estimate that has ever been made of him. It was curiously
fitting that he should receive the supreme accolade from the greatest
Frenchman of his times, the one who more than any other expressed his own attitude and convictions. It was the hail and farewell of kindred spirits, veterans of life, on the threshold of the
unknown.

"Your lot has been and still is," wrote Voltaire, "one of the most
desirable in that great lottery, where the prizes are so few, and

where the great prize of constant happiness has never yet been drawn by any one. Your philosophy has never been disturbed by dreams [*par des chimères*] which have sometimes troubled fairly able minds. You have never been in any sense an impostor nor an impostor's dupe, which to my thinking is no common virtue, and adds to that shadow of felicity, which may be enjoyed in this short life." [59]

Yes, however we view him, Chesterfield had been no hypocrite at least; he had remained true to himself; he had looked at life steadily, and had followed Reason, the only star he could see.

As he had desired it, the end came without pain and without fear.* He had long felt "a gradual decay, though a gentle one," [60] an intolerable weight and tedium of living. Dysentery was the immediate cause of his death, which occurred on March 24, 1773.

It was a lonely, unattended deathbed. His godson was abroad; his son was dead; neither Lady Chesterfield † nor any other relative seems to have been present. But there clings to the final scene a reminiscent quality, faint as the odor of withered leaves. A half hour before he died his *valet de chambre*, opening the curtains of his bed, announced: "Mr. Dayrolles." The Earl summoned his strength to speak for the last time: "Give Dayrolles a chair."

Mors donata, non vita erepta.[61]

---

* This, at least, is according to Maty, who was probably the best informed. But a month or two earlier, Mrs. Montagu recorded that he had been suffering terribly from an inflammation of the neck of the bladder. She adds: "He endured all his pain with great patience and unalterable good humour." Mrs. Montagu's *Letters* (ed. R. Blunt), vol. i, p. 250. Some details relative to Chesterfield's last illness are contained in the letters to his godson and in his *valet de chambre* J. Walsh's addenda to them. *Cf.* Gulick, *op. cit.*

† S. Tytler(*The Countess of Huntingdon and her Circle*, p. 85) states, I know not on what authority, that Lady Chesterfield refused to leave her husband's deathbed. This is very likely true in a general sense; but the Earl's death seems to have occurred unexpectedly at the last. Maty makes no mention of her as present.

PART SIX

The Ordeal of
Philip Stanhope

CHAPTER XIX
Kindergarten

THE PRECEDING STUDY may in a manner be regarded as the pedestal of a monument. If we have hitherto all but ignored Philip Stanhope, Chesterfield's inglorious and yet famous son, it has been merely for the sake of perspective and to give to the subject its culminating importance. By a queer twist of destiny, the series of intimate letters to this obscure youth remain as the Earl's one imperishable achievement; all the rest has been swept away. "There will be a thousand things in my letters," he once wrote him, "which I would not have any mortal living but yourself see or know." [1] It is precisely this most secret area of his life which has become world-famous.

Fundamentally perhaps it is not so odd after all, but is merely the illustration of that spiritual law whereby those things, however obscure and unimportant, which have claimed our whole heart receive a reality and permanence denied to more spectacular but conventional objects. Chesterfield toiled over his letters in order to fashion a certain individual whom he loved. For that purpose he poured himself out, and insensibly a great book came into being. To believe intensely and to identify oneself with that belief seems to be as good a recipe for any kind of immortality as can be formulated. Chesterfield's skepticism admitted one exception; he believed absolutely in his own acumen, in his knowledge of human nature, in the validity of his own experience, in the infallibility of his common sense, in the power of reason to understand and direct life. And because he believed as intensely as he did, he remains the perpetual interpreter of that form of rationalism.

To return to Philip Stanhope. His story deserves the leisure and method of the novelist. By turns it is poignant, grotesque, comic, sordid, and tragic. It is the story of a great love, blinded by ambition, deformed by a theory, which marked him as its object and victim. To a disciple of reason, any emotion is suspect; it does not do to let the heart command. Chesterfield's education of his son was merely the rationalization of his love. It rendered it respectable. The tragedy of Philip Stanhope resulted from that process.

From the outset, a goal was selected and a system established. While the child was in swaddling clothes, his father had already destined him to parliament and the foreign service,[2] as a choice of profession which may be accounted for by two reasons. In the first place, underestimating the obstacle of Philip's birth, paternal pride could not stomach the idea of anything less than the highest, the most brilliant and glittering, for him. And, secondly, the diplomatic and political career was the one Chesterfield himself had followed, and which he would now retrace in the person of his son. It was the only career he himself knew and valued. He might write about the "coarse ropes and dirty pulleys" of public life, but he bent every nerve to teach Philip the use of them, and to gain him a hearing upon the stage he had abandoned. The art of the diplomat, its blandness and subtlety, exerted an enduring fascination for him. It was not without reason that he once wrote of his son as his other self. The vicarious element unquestionably played a considerable part in the selection of Philip's profession, as it did throughout the entire relationship with his father, in all the pleasures, amours, and triumphs that Chesterfield imagined for him in vain. The truest answer to the question of what we would do with our lives could we live them over again is to be found in the plans we make for those who are dearest to us. Of Chesterfield, it can be stated with confidence that he would have followed the same course.

Similarly, in the system of education chosen to attain this objective, the Earl followed in general the plan which had been used in his own case. With no apparent relish, he conceded to Philip three or four years at Westminster School instead of the exclusive private instruction of his own youth; but he lopped off at the other end the years at the university. Conventionally progressive, it was inevitable that he should hold by the tradition of Halifax, Locke, and subsequent *esprits libres*.

Among lost or rather neglected masterpieces, Locke's contributions to the science of teaching — *Some Thoughts Concerning Edu-*

cation and *The Conduct of the Understanding*[3] — occupy an undeserved place. The famous *Essay* has unjustly eclipsed them. On the score of style as well as content, by virtue of vigorous thought and intellectual honesty, they should be among the chosen books of any educated man. In them the founder of rationalism and of modern psychology, the presiding genius of the eighteenth century, is seen to be also the legislator of modern education. Though certain tenets, such, for example, as the emphasis on parental authority, have been outgrown or abandoned, our practice in general has not yet overtaken the prophetic reach of Locke's vision two hundred and fifty years ago. It was this progressive, humane method which Chesterfield adopted for the education of his son.

The term adopted can be used in a literal sense. The first of the two tracts we have mentioned, *Some Thoughts Concerning Education*, became one of the Earl's textbooks. He both quoted from it and recommended it earnestly to Philip Stanhope.[4] No more than a glance through this treatise is required to recognize the extent of Chesterfield's indebtedness. Principles and details are alike retained.*

Beneath the teaching both of master and disciple, there lay an assumption which has become increasingly orthodox among modern psychologists. It was the belief in the molding power of environment on character rather than in the influence of heredity. For Locke, a child's mind at birth was like "wax to be moulded and fashioned as one pleases,"[5] and though he subsequently qualified this statement by observing that "in many cases, all that we can do, or should aim at, is to make the best of what nature has given,"[6] for all practical purposes, he assumed a *tabula rasa*, over which, within limits, the educator had a free hand. Chesterfield affirmed a similar creed.[7]

Equipped with such an object and such a system, directed by a will of steel, he set himself to produce a work of art. He thought of the education of Philip Stanhope in terms of authorship or painting or architecture. It became a standing joke between them to describe the boy as a small quarto which he had once published, but intended to reissue in progressively corrected editions.[8] Or Philip

---

* The only essential difference is in regard to the learning of Greek. Locke did not regard it as necessary for the gentleman, while Chesterfield considered it a valuable accomplishment.

was a canvas upon which his tutor, "Raphael" Harte, had drawn outlines that at length awaited only the coloring of Titian, and the graces of Guido. Or he was an edifice provided with a solid Tuscan foundation upon which "the Doric, the Ionic, and the Corinthian orders would rise gradually with all their beauty, proportions, and ornaments." [9]

What then went wrong? For obviously Philip Stanhope, as a work of art, was a failure; nor did Chesterfield's godson and heir, who succeeded him as fifth Earl and upon whom the same system was tried, cut any remarkable figure in the world. The answer to this question involves not only Chesterfield and his son, but the central problem of education itself; nor can it be evaded on the usual pretext that Philip was a dolt out of whom nothing brilliant could be made. To begin with, it must be pointed out to the credit of Locke, that although Chesterfield followed his system in the main, pride and impatience introduced some modifications. If education, as described by Locke, may be compared to the art of gardening, the process employed by Chesterfield more nearly resembles the science of the hothouse. That is, the tempo of everything has been accelerated; pressure has been imposed, and this, from Locke's standpoint, was the antithesis of everything he recommended. At the age of five, Philip Stanhope was already being lectured about the composition, cities, and resources of the United Provinces, whither he was being taken by his mother on a visit. His schooling had begun. At thirteen, he must have the knowledge of sixteen; [10] he had reached the fifth form and the Earl could almost speak of a prodigy. Pay attention, work, reason, observe, reflect, memorize: this, to the tune of threats or cajolery, continued to be dinned in his ears from the outset. It may, therefore, not impertinently be questioned whether the boy's eventual dullness bore no relationship to this early cramming. In such an important respect, at least, Chesterfield parted company with Locke.

But the system itself had inherent deficiencies that went still deeper. Aware that appeals to the reasonableness of effort, labor, self-discipline, and noble conduct were not enough, but that an emotional dynamic was necessary, both Locke and Chesterfield enlisted for this purpose vanity, ambition, pride — in a word, egoism. And this, in the last analysis, means the negative pole of life, to which outgoing love stands in the positive, the creative relationship. There is no use proclaiming, as both of these writers proclaim, the necessity of a spotless moral character, the sovereignty of truth, the value of virtue; there is no use doffing one's hat to a vague and incomprehensible Deity, and then, after these fine gestures have been made, to call in selfishness as the impresario of life. Chesterfield is perpetually assuming that Philip Stanhope is above reproach in regard to ethical matters; he refers him to his own reason, and to his tutor, Mr. Harte, as sufficient guides, though every now and then, in addition, he strikes out a shining and unexceptionable passage on the subject of ethics or religion.[11] But such an assumption is impossible, if reason and Mr. Harte and the foreign service are all poor Philip has to make the discipline of right living appeal to him; and it is especially impossible if, when worldly success has been established as the supreme goal and ambition as the driving force, flattery, dissimulation, and adultery are not only permitted but urged on him by his father as means to the end. This would appear to me obvious, were it not for Chesterfield's apologists, who have argued that flattery is harmless, and that adultery, though regrettable, was especially at that time the way of the world.

The problem of finding an adequate incentive, of establishing it as the mainspring of effort, is the central problem in education. Methods of teaching, libraries and laboratories, intellectual proficiency, all the paraphernalia of learning, are secondary to this primary issue, and must fail if it is not achieved. Chesterfield's famous contemporary, William Law, pointed to this defect of Locke's system in some of the most forceful pages of the *Serious Call*.[12]

But another kindred fault is peculiar to Locke's method. It would be almost a contradiction in terms, it would be certainly incongruous, if in the neat and formal garden of his system any nook or tanglewood had been left for the fancy or emotions. Poetry and music are alien there; legend and romance are banished; heedless sentiment is taboo. The hedges are exquisitely trim, the corners are sharp, the gravel walks are sometimes harsh and long and relentless. The prim custodian, reason, hovers always in sight. The air is clear in that garden, there is no mist; but the flowers are without aroma, the trees without shade, the birds without song. Altogether one would not like to spend one's life shut up there, like Philip Stanhope, drilled by his father's avid Graces.

A final query imposes itself regarding Locke's program. It was one of its cornerstones that the paternal will must be absolute — without exception and without appeal. Chesterfield, in the most silken, but vise-like manner, made that plain. "I shall always love you as you shall deserve," he would say; or "I always made you feel the weight of my authority, that you might one day know the force of my love." [13] Admitting a perfect parent, this is well enough. Otherwise, who is to educate the educator? Otherwise, paternal autocracy, though well-intentioned, may lead to failure. Did it not mean failure in this case? What did it avail poor Philip that he was deprived by his father's ambition of hearth, home, and country in order to be made a polished man? But as we ponder the monotonous annals of his life — from lodging to lodging, from capital to capital, over the endless highroads of Europe — and as we study his failure, we are sometimes consoled by the thought that he would have been horrible as a success.

The great correspondence opened, as we have already noted, when Philip was five. It began with a sprightly little lecture on the geography and composition of the United Provinces; and this set the tone for the next twenty years. It is unlikely that the lad ever thought of his father save as a preceptor, a never-failing fountain of instruction, exhortation, and advice. The pretense of familiarity was demanded by the system, and received lip service, but it remained pretense.

He was known as "Frisky" in those days, a chubby, lively little boy who lived with his mother, Madame du Bouchet, and from the outset was surrounded with attendants adequate to a future paragon. There were Lisette and a valet and Miss Pinkerton and Miss Williams. As head tutor, there was Michael Maittaire, seventy years old at the time, a scholar eminent enough to find a place in Pope's *Dunciad*,[14] and, associated with him, Mr. Martin for Latin and Monsieur Pelnote for French. Above them all, throned on the Olympus of Grosvenor Square, Argus-eyed and anxious, sat the Earl, superintending operations. Every week or so he sent his coach to fetch the boy, scrubbed and dressed, a very small pea in a large pod, for an interview with him; put him through his paces and made much of him. The Duchess of Kendal, Melusina's mother, was living then, and Chesterfield spent some time at Isleworth; moreover the semiannual visits to Bath had long since begun; but no absences interrupted the archpreceptor's supervision. It is thanks to them that we have the letters.

Frisky at six had begun Latin and Greek,[15] and was deep in Latin and Greek mythology, with which his father acquainted him from letter to letter. In addition, the Earl instructed him in the lives of famous men, such as Demosthenes and Cicero, drilled him in geography ("Nothing will amuse you so much as studying maps"), [16] lectured him on Roman history, on morality as derived from Roman history, on the difference between prose and poetic diction, and coached him about letter writing and spelling. In addition to these subjects (already a full curriculum for six) he was being instructed in French, his maternal language, in English, and in dancing.

The letters of this period are charming and deserve a more prominent place than they have often received in editions of Chesterfield, but they are not letters; each is a perfect little essay or chapter on a given subject: mythology, history, or style. If the loose-leaf notebook had been invented at that time, they could have been bound up together for schoolroom purposes. One letter takes up the thread of the last, and the next maintains the sequence. In addition, some of them were pensums. Frisky was to look up such words in the dictionary as he did not understand; or he must learn by heart enclosed epigrams, or must translate an occasional French letter into English,[17] or must translate Latin passages, or must work out exercises in metrics.

It is not difficult to imagine the arrival of such a letter from his lordship, the reverence with which it was handled by the tutors, the way it was served up to Frisky as a privilege and treat, the care with which it was preserved as coming from so titled a pen. Only, one wonders if Philip's heart leaped up at the prospect of another task, however graciously imposed. Probably no notion of rebellion against such an august parent would ever cross his mind; but surely on occasions he may have indulged a sigh. "Translate the following into English," ordered the Earl, writing in French: "My dear Papa: It is true that you praise me, but it is equally true that you make me pay for it, for you make me work like a galley-slave to achieve it. No matter, one cannot purchase glory too dear. So Alexander the Great believed, and so also believes Philip the Small." [18] And Frisky, laboring with his quill, set to work.

By seven, he was reviewing his Latin and Greek grammar, and Maittaire would acquaint him with Horace, Virgil, Terence, and Martial. The study of history was continued in greater detail along with other subjects; but a new string had been added to the lyre: the lectures on good breeding had begun; the beau monde was now made to dangle before the child's consciousness.[19] Thereafter he would hear enough about it. In the meantime let him beware of the English, who were either boobies or puppies, and let him emulate the polished and easy carriage of the French. Philip Stanhope turned out egregiously awkward to be sure, but had he shown himself a veritable Ganymede, it is probable that there would still have been many a letter on politeness. It was a passionate topic with the Earl.

By this time we may suppose that the boy's education had been in progress three years, and we begin to learn that he was inattentive. The screws, therefore, began to be applied at that point, gently and with all the tact enjoined by Locke, but unremittingly. No hint of chastisement; at most and rarely, the insinuation, more dreadful by its vagueness, of parental wrath, a steady pressure and constant iteration in varying keys. "There is a figure of speech called Irony," remarked the Earl; and, as an example of it, imagined the case that he should praise Philip's attentiveness and memory: "Would you not plainly perceive the irony," he added, "and see that I laughed at you?"[20] This might be called the playful touch. It was followed up in subsequent letters with little homilies or random allusions, all charming and good-humored, but the probe never stopped. Small wonder that the mind of a seven-year-old child faced by Horace, Virgil, Terence, and Martial, set to translating passages from Cicero and Seneca,[21] lectured on metrics and history, should endeavor to shirk the jumps. The pressure was kept up. Finally, in spite of inattention, they managed to cram a prodigious amount of learning into him.

The casual reader, dipping here and there into the letters, will be charmed by the Earl's gentleness. It is only when the collection is read consecutively and as a whole that the relentless character of the system becomes apparent. A drop of water is pleasant enough, but many drops wear away stone, or, used as a torture, will wonderfully soften a victim's skull. The waistcoat that was to give such an elegant figure to Frisky was of the finest brocade; but the endless lacing of it, knot by knot through the years, must have been painful.

By seven and a half Philip was being instructed in the figures of rhetoric — the first boy, exulted his father, who had ever been taught them at that age [22] — and this led to an analysis of poetic diction. As a reward for his labors, the precocious child asked for an amber-headed cane and a pair of shoe buckles, which were readily accorded, together with an approving sermon on modesty as opposed to bashfulness. Equipped with cane and buckles, he was urged to unite modesty to a polite and easy assurance.

By eight, the boy had advanced to Rollin's *Ancient History*, had made progress in Greek, and to his father's satisfaction protested against the nickname Frisky in favor of another inexpressibly vile, namely, Polyglot. In token of approval, the delighted Earl sent him, by way of treat and amusement, a "Historical, Chronological and Geographical Dictionary." [23]

Thus, step by step, Philip toiled on. His studies grew constantly more difficult. There was always more Latin to translate and pen-sums to write out — for instance, whether ostracism was right or wrong, together with reasons for the opinion given; recapitulations of Rollin, [24] ceaseless study of diction, the analysis of words. Now and then the eager father would impose a novel task, for example: "Write down, and learn by heart, every day, for your own amusement, besides what you do with Mr. Maittaire, ten words of Greek, Latin and English, out of a dictionary or vocabulary, which will go a great way in a year's time, considering the words you know already." [25] If learning, virtue and manners are the three strings of Chesterfield's lyre, [26] the first was kept chiefly resounding at this period with an occasional twang from the second and a gradually increased thrumming of the third.

That the child survived these increasing demands is perhaps owing to the fact that from the outset his tutors conspired with him. It was to their credit and profit as well as his own that he should put his best foot forward. Perhaps, too, they felt sorry for him. Usually they made their court to the Earl by praising him, but they did more. Now and again Chesterfield suspects that a help-ing hand had been given in some task or other, [27] or he forbids any-one to help, or he points out sarcastically that he had no doubt but that Philip in a short time would be able to write as well as "the person (whoever he was)" that wrote the manuscript which had been sent to him as his son's.[28] With the best will in the world — and Philip labored to please — the boy was forced by the rigor of the standard imposed on him to take whatever means he could find to satisfy it. This, as we shall see later, involved subterfuge and the dissimulation so eloquently recommended by his father.

It is unnecessary to follow him through the steps of his Westminster drilling with the new staff of instructors: Mr. Fitzgerald, Monsieur Coudert,[29] Mr. Morel, under the general command of Dr. Nichols, and reinforced during vacations by some of the old staff, Maittaire for Greek and Monsieur Desnoyers for dancing.[30] If we may judge from the infrequency and shortness of his letters, Chesterfield himself had less interest in this phase of his son's training than in any other. He could not follow him in imagination to Westminster School as he could elsewhere, nor live over again with Philip an experience of boyhood he had never known. That he sent him to Westminster at all was in the nature of a makeshift to fill in time between eleven and fourteen.* He was impatient to have the Tuscan foundation of his work of art finished and out of the muddy schoolroom stage, so that he might begin to rear, and with a master's hand adorn, the Corinthian superstructure.

For now the supreme period of Philip's training was about to begin. He would leave the provincialism and boorishness of England behind him and launch out upon the variety, the French-colored variety, of Continental life. He would commence that process of infinitely shifting contacts which would polish him to the desired smoothness of worldly address. Here Chesterfield's fancy would indeed accompany him with an almost breathless interest, would hover about him sylphlike from morning to night,† would relive in Philip's person, and greatly extend, his own too brief experiences of European travel. There are no indications that the Earl ever visited any foreign countries except Holland, Belgium, and France. Through Philip's eyes he would now view courts and capitals which political life or ill-health had prevented him from knowing. In this other self of his, he could now visit Potsdam and talk with his hero, Frederick of Prussia; he could attend the court at Turin; he could taste the heady frivolities of a Venetian carnival;

---

* Philip entered Westminster in 1743, and left it in 1746.
† Chesterfield makes use of this figure himself. July 6, 1748.

he could bask in the respectable antiquity of Rome, and could collect objects of virtu in Florence. Above all, at last, he could actually reside in Paris. . . . There can be no other interpretation of the gusto of the great letters which were now also about to begin. The repressed imagination of the archrealist found its wings here.

But he could do all this fully on one condition. Philip must become a man of taste, a man to be given the freedom of such amenities. The English and Westminster crust must be scraped off. He must become really another self — alert, insinuating, vivid, popular — if the vicarious illusion was to be complete.

CHAPTER XX
Lausanne, Leipzig, and Berlin

INTO PHILIP STANHOPE'S LIFE there now entered a person who had been appointed by the Olympian parent to supervise and direct him during the next four years. This was the Reverend Walter Harte, M.A., of Oxford. He had been recommended to Chesterfield by his friend Lord Lyttelton,[1] though a recommendation from one whom the Earl regularly held up as an example of inattention and awkwardness[2] might have been considered ill-omened.

Anyone familiar with the academic profession has encountered many Hartes. He was an unworldly, bookish, easy-going man, lovable, affectionate, probably a little owlish, and conventional in an Oxford clerical sense. The stains of snuff or soup would be visible on his waistcoat; he would be apt to forget names or appointments, and would love to mull over choice Latin passages. He had a pretty vein of poetry in youth; and had even composed verses to young ladies;[3] but his muse grew ponderous with age. In the end, he produced a life of Gustavus Adolphus and a work on agriculture, two subjects for which one would imagine him to have been wholly unqualified.

There was a mutual affection, perhaps also a tacit alliance, between him and the hard-driven Philip. He made up for his lack of graces in kindness and a warmth of heart of which the boy had probably some need during his years of wandering. But from Chesterfield's standpoint Walter Harte remains an enigma. In accordance with Locke, who emphasized the choice of a governor, he had searched out a tutor for his son with the greatest care. Harte had already been selected at least a year before the Continental journey began. Chesterfield had no illusions in regard to his social accomplishments; he had chosen him for his probity and his learning. Harte would finish the Tuscan foundation of virtue and classics in the most thorough, solid fashion. But if manners occupied so important a place in the Earl's program, if he was already aware of Philip's deficiencies in that respect, if, indeed, he sent him out of England so that he might counteract these by the polish of the Continent, why did he thrust him into the intimacy of so plain a person as Harte? We can only exclaim with his lordship's brother, Sir William Stanhope, who liked the boy: "What could Chesterfield expect from him? His mother was a Dutch woman, he sent him to Leipzig to learn manners, and that, too, under the direction of an Oxford pedant!" [4] And Maty majestically laments that this was the fundamental error in the plan of Stanhope's education and the source of all the future mistakes in his conduct.[5]

There is no satisfactory explanation for Harte's appointment except that Chesterfield's vaunted good sense went badly astray, and that, too, in the one case where it most concerned him to use it. Probably he believed that the distinguished entree he provided for his son in each of the cities visited, combined with his own admonitions and the final polishing in Paris, would more than counterbalance the tutor's example. But he judged wrongly, and one would imagine that a far less experienced worldling than he would not have made the same mistake. Years later when he was pondering the education of his godson, he declared, perhaps with a glance at Harte, that the best governor was a very useless and a poor governor, a very pernicious animal to have about a young man.[6] Yet he seems never to have learned his lesson. To be sure a Swiss man of letters was chosen to accompany his godson abroad, but the latter followed approximately the same course of training. Like most other men, as he grew older, Chesterfield, for all his wisdom, tended to follow established grooves, from which it was difficult to dislodge him.

Sometime in the late summer of 1746, Harte (after a memorable interview with the Earl, we may be sure) set out with Philip for Lausanne, which had been appointed as the first halting place in their travels. After a hard journey up the Rhine from Frankfort to Heidelberg to Schaffhausen, which included the breakdown of their coach and roughing it in farmhouses, they crossed Switzerland to Bern, and then down to the vineyard-terraced slopes of

Lake Geneva. In Lausanne they found a packet of the Earl's letters waiting for them, and took lodgings in the house of a Monsieur Brenles. Here too, as elsewhere, the way had been smoothed and doors stood open. Monsieur de Bochat, Professor of History and Civil Law at the University of Lausanne, read lectures to the fourteen-year-old Philip. Madame de Bochat, a Madame de St. Germain, a Monsieur Pampigny, evidently people of note, countenanced him. It would be his own fault, as his father more than once pointed out, if he did not acquire the allures of good company.

At this point the great, the typical letters begin. The grubby schoolboy had come out of the egg and stood ready to be scraped, brushed, manicured, and groomed. Harte was of no use here; Chesterfield must take a hand, must prepare his other self for the magnificent world. He trimmed his pen with gusto and launched out upon the absorbing passion of his life.

He used home truths to begin with. Among the letters awaiting Philip in Lausanne were several calculated to jerk him up to attention. "I do not so much as hint to you," wrote his lordship, "how absolutely dependent you are upon me: that you neither have, nor can have a shilling in the world but from me; and that, as I have no womanish weakness for your person, your merit must and will be the only measure of my kindness." [7] In another place he adds that he has, thank God, discovered no vice of the heart and no peculiar weakness of the head in Philip, but he has discovered laziness, inattention, and indifference.[8]

It was upon this theme, with endless variations, that many of the subsequent letters would turn. With alertness and energy as the driving force of success, its instruments, which are learning, manners, and the knowledge of the world, formed the logical divisions of the future homilies. "My long and frequent letters," he asserted, "which I send you in great doubt of their success, put me in mind of certain papers, which you have very lately, and I formerly, sent up to kites, along the string, which we called messengers; some of them the wind used to blow away, others were torn by the string, and but few of them got up and stuck to the kite. But I will content myself now, as I did then, if some of my present messengers do but stick to you." [9] This might be regarded as an introduction to the correspondence as a whole.

It was the year of Chesterfield's incumbency as Secretary of State, and the press of affairs cut down the frequency and length of his essays to Philip; [10] but none the less it is probable that many letters from this period have been either lost or, perhaps even more likely, suppressed. One gathers somehow that the winter at Lausanne was none too successful, and that there may have been certain communications from the Earl which were unpleasant to preserve or discreditable to publish. There are other lacunae of the same kind later on, where scorching letters from London, mentioned by Chesterfield to correspondents such as Dayrolles and the Marquise de Monconseil,[11] have disappeared. The small number of those remaining from the Lausanne period may not without reason be ascribed to editorial qualms rather than accident.

A youth of nineteen, Edward Eliot, the son of a rich and politically powerful county family,* and therefore most eligible as a friend for Philip, seems to have joined him and Mr. Harte in Lausanne and later to have accompanied them to Leipzig. From him indirectly [12] are derived curious footnotes regarding young Stanhope during the first year of his Continental sojourn; and we can piece still more together from Chesterfield's remarks to Dayrolles. It appears that the English schoolboy fresh from Westminster kicked over the traces for once, and under the too mild governance of Mr. Harte made something of an ass of himself. It is horrible to imagine what would have happened had Chesterfield heard of the following episode.†

One evening Philip and Eliot were invited to an assembly of the local elite, ladies and gentlemen of the first importance, among them some of the Bernese aristocracy, who are as proud as any in the world. Of these, a group of portly senators were engaged at cards, and absorbed to such an extent that they paid no attention to young Stanhope, who stood behind them looking on. They did not observe that he had snipped the strings of their breeches and attached their full-bottomed wigs to their chairs. He left the room shortly afterward, and re-entered it crying, "Fire! Fire!" whereat

---

* He was born in 1727, the son of Richard Eliot of Port Eliot; was created Lord Eliot in 1784; died in 1804.

† In Charlemont's narrative it is given as happening at Bern, but it occurred more likely at Lausanne. (*Hist. MSS. Comm.*, MSS. of Lord Charlemont, pp. 326–330, Lord Charlemont to Lord Bruce, July 17, 1744.)

the cardplayers started up and displayed their scalps and their bottoms equally unveiled.

About the same time, Lord Chesterfield, lost in a pleasant reverie, was writing: "Let us discuss your amusements and your pleasures. . . . May I ask you what they are? Is it a question of a friendly little card game in good company, or of agreeable little suppers where gaiety and decorum are at one? Are you paying court to some beauty, your attentions for whom will aid in refining you? Make me your confidant in this matter, you will not find me censorious. Nay, rather I desire the post of minister of your pleasures; I will point them out to you, I will even co-operate in them." [13]

It is hard to imagine any crime that Philip could have been guilty of which would have distressed his father to such an extent as the prank we have described. There was enough dynamite in it to have blown him and Mr. Harte beyond the reach of any reconciliation. One would like to know how it was smoothed over and hushed up, what appeals were made on behalf of the boy's youth, and what agitated hours the Reverend Mr. Harte put in. It behooved him in this instance to connive with his pupil in hoodwinking his patron, and, as far as we know, not a whisper of the abomination reached London.

There are other evidences of the schoolboy in Philip that winter, in spite of Professor Bochat's lectures on law and Lord Chesterfield's lectures on *savoir-faire*. He had a handsome face, but, being fat, short and clumsy, found the streets of Lausanne rather steep.[14] "They will keep you warm," consoled his father. He had shed the soberer clothes of Westminster and now blazed out precociously "in a scarlet coat laced with gold, a brocade waistcoat and other suitable ornaments." [15] Chesterfield probably advised him to pass as his ward, nephew, or even more distant relative;[16] but the boy's vanity would not permit it, and he swaggered on the score of his father, the British Minister of State. Indeed, he became so forward on that point, that the riding-master at the manège, tired of the constant phrase, "my father, Lord Chesterfield," observed brutally one day, "Oh, is Lord Chesterfield your father? Well then, apparently, Lady Chesterfield is your mother": one of those crushing retorts that are monumental in life.[17]

One gathers from all this that Philip may not have been popular in Lausanne, despite the flattering comments upon him of Madame de St. Germain and Monsieur Pampigny recorded proudly by the Earl in one of the few letters from that period which have been preserved. According to them, he was not only *décrotté*, but tolerably well-bred; the English crust of bashfulness, shyness, and roughness ("of which, by-the-bye," commented the Earl, "you had your share") was pretty well rubbed off.[18]

Then something happened — some escapade of which Solomon Dayrolles in Holland got wind through Madame de Bochat. The Earl thanked him disconsolately for his account, though he couldn't say that it gave him great comfort, and in another letter he remarked significantly: "I have not yet mentioned, either to the boy or Mr. Harte, anything of what Madame de Bochat writ to you, that they might not suspect from whence it came or endeavour to fish it out. But as soon as they are got to Leipsig, they shall hear of it with a vengeance, but so, as that it shall be impossible for them to guess from whence I had it." [19] Probably this refers to some party of pleasure where the spring had gone to Philip's head. Harte wrote a satisfactory letter with the assurance that there had been no gaming involved.[20] But from Chesterfield's standpoint the two wanderers left Lausanne under a cloud.

They proceeded by command up through Germany to their next station at Leipzig; and confidential reports from Monsieur Brenles and the de Bochats followed, which somewhat allayed paternal anxiety. De Bochat forwarded another confidential report to Professor Mascow of the University of Leipzig, with whom Philip was to lodge; the Earl warned his son that he would have a hundred invisible spies about him in Leipzig who would keep him informed of everything he did or said. Thus primed, the boy and his tutor journeyed on north through Switzerland to Munich, where Philip was presented at his first court, then up through Germany, reaching Leipzig at the end of September. Here another packet of the famous letters awaited them, and probably the thunderbolt mentioned to Dayrolles.[21]

What it was, we do not know; but Philip's overt sowing of wild oats was over; he had had his fling — a rather short one after all — and now settled down to the grind that had been devised for him.

Two months later his father was happy to state that he was really working hard and had barely the time to eat, drink, and sleep.

Leipzig represented the last stages of the cramming process to which Philip Stanhope had been subjected from the age of four or five. Being now fifteen years old, he was engaged in studies which would occupy the closing terms of a modern undergraduate course or would be even included in postgraduate work. He would be studying Grotius, *De Jure Belli et Pacis*, the *Institutes of Justinian*, and the public law, history, and constitution of the Empire. He was to make himself an absolute master of the German language and of German history, including the contemporary situation of the German states. These studies, together with French and later on Italian, the whole of modern history from the fifteenth century down, and modern chronology and geography, would form, so to speak, his major subjects; but they by no means exhausted the list. He would continue the study of Greek and Latin with Harte, and would devote some time to rhetoric, logic, geometry, and astronomy.[22] Nor, with the exception of philosophy and mathematics, were these subjects to be undertaken in a superficial spirit. All modern languages were to be spoken "as purely and correctly as the natives of the respective countries"; and all the principal modern languages were to be learned. His study of history and international law was confined to no mere textbook summaries, but involved highly technical treatises, such as Bougeant's *Histoire du Traité de Munster*, Adamus Adami on the Treaty of Westphalia, the *Corps Diplomatique*, and the like, not to mention more general writings such as the *Letters of Richelieu*, the *Memoirs of de Retz*, and the diplomatic essays of Caillières and Pecquet.[23] He was to be prepared to answer such minute questions as the number of companies and men per company in the Saxon regiments, the amount of the daily pay of a Saxon foot soldier, dragoon, and trooper, the various ranks in a general staff, etc. He was to attend carefully to and retain all the subtleties and minutiae of imperial law as expounded by the learned Professor Mascow. Already well versed in Greek and Latin, he was to complete his mastery of them as a sort of cultural crown. He would read them for his amusement, as a relaxation from more serious studies. And if, after all this, there should be any leisure, almost every letter contains suggestions of useful books to be perused on the side.

Hence, "for God's sake, my dear boy," exclaimed the Earl, "do not squander away one moment of your time." [24] Not even the calls of nature should tempt Philip to interrupt his studies, but like a gentleman of the Earl's acquaintance, he is urged to keep a Latin classic in his pocket in order to make the most of such intervals.[25]

In short, he was sent to Leipzig, one of the centers of European learning, chiefly to complete his stock of knowledge. The importance of German as a language, in view of England's Hanoverian monarchs and the connections with Hanover and the Empire, was an added incentive, all the more so as few English diplomats had the slightest notion of it. But learning and German were by no means all. More insistent now, and at times eclipsing every other objective, is the necessity of understanding people and the arts by which they are influenced. "Search, therefore," commanded Chesterfield — and it should be again recalled that Philip was only fifteen years old — "with the greatest care, into the characters of those whom you converse with; endeavour to discover their predominant passions, their prevailing weaknesses, their vanities, their follies, and their humours, with all the right and wrong, wise and silly springs of human actions, which make such inconsistent and whimsical beings of us rational creatures. A moderate share of penetration, with great attention, will infallibly make these necessary discoveries. This is the true knowledge of the world; and the world is a country which nobody ever yet knew by description; one must travel through it oneself to be acquainted with it." [26]

Indeed, soon a new theme begins to emerge in the counterpoint of the letters, the idea that the arts of the world are more important than learning, necessary as that may be.[27] In other words, book knowledge, which had been hammered into Philip during his whole life and for which he had acquired a real fondness, is increasingly left to take care of itself, while *savoir-faire* is spurred forward.

Leipzig, as Chesterfield admitted, was not the haunt of manners. His son would contract a little German dirt; but he felt that it was more easily rubbed off than English dirt; [28] and then he counted on his own powers of eloquence and persuasion measurably to offset it. Philip, therefore, mere adolescent as he was, began his strange and somewhat terrible instruction. The worst of it was that, taken bit by bit and adage by adage, it was all so true, so wise, so penetrating, but that the total effect of it must be to corrupt every generous impulse.

He was instructed to beware of making confidences, to have a real reserve with everybody, while pretending to have no reserve with anyone; to adapt himself to every company; to find out and flatter the prevailing weakness of the people he desires to gain; to realize that scarce any flattery is too gross for women to swallow; to sacrifice to the Graces and remember that the mind is almost always the dupe of the heart; to smile often, but never to laugh; to cultivate an ease of manner equal to any emergency; to understand that only at courts can a person be smoothed up to the highest polish [29] and that progress can only be made in the best companies; to study the *Maxims* of La Rochefoucauld and the *Characters* of La Bruyère.[30]

Nothing was too small for the intent father's interest, the care of Philip's teeth and mouth, his dress and diet, the cleanliness and manicuring of his nails, the fine art of carving, his handwriting.[31] "Consider seriously, and follow carefully, I beseech you, my dear child, the advice which from time to time I have given, and shall continue to give you; it is at once the result of my long experience, and the effect of my tenderness for you." [32]

But no more here than elsewhere did Chesterfield rely on theory, as distinct from what might be termed clinical practice. The Duchess Dowager of Courland held a kind of court in Leipzig, to which Philip was presented by the Count and Countess Flemming.[33] More useful still, he could visit Dresden in his vacations and enjoy the civilities of the British minister to Saxony, Sir Charles Hanbury Williams, an admirer of Chesterfield's who showed his respect for him by kindness to his son. Sir Charles presented Philip at the Dresden court to the Elector, who was at that time King of Poland. In short, whatever Leipzig and Dresden could provide of great and fashionable stood open.

There was no economy used in turning him out on a proper footing. If he had been heir to his father's title he could not have been treated more handsomely. Served by two liveried footmen, one to dress him and curl his hair, the other to ride behind his coach; lodged at the house of one of the most considerable men in town, and finally attended by an English cleric, he would appear to German eyes a young man of dignity and importance. Chesterfield would not curtail his ideal other self by parsimony. The boy might be illegitimate, but in every other respect he should surpass or equal the noblest of them. Not the rich Edward Eliot, nor Philip's schoolfellow from Westminster, Lord Pulteney, the son of the Earl of Bath, who joined him in Leipzig, should make a finer showing. As in the old Cambridge days the Witty Club had stood modishly aloof from the rank and file of the university, so now the present Philip Stanhope would be equipped with funds and introductions to move in circles far above the guzzling collegians at Leipzig. For the sake of German only, he was permitted to associate with them at a sort of ordinary maintained for young men of fashion in the neighborhood of his lodgings; but the Earl rejoiced to learn that his son perceived "the indecency and turpitude" of such of these students as "disgraced and fouled themselves with dirty whores and scoundrel gamesters." [34] The boy complained also that most of the eating club lacked the tone and graces of good company, though one suspects that such criticism may have been partly inspired by the distaste for soup and potatoes which sufficed the less pampered natives. But his father permitted no change of boarding place. Philip's stomach had to pay the price of a new language.

The creation of a paragon is apt to be hard on the paragon. Young Stanhope hovered perpetually between Scylla and Charybdis. If he cultivated too much the solid virtues with Harte and Mascow, if he indulged his fondness for old books and classical authors, he came out short in regard to the "lesser talents, the *leniores virtutes*" upon which his father kept insisting. If he neglected his studies, on the other hand, he would certainly bring down upon himself a brilliant sermon on inattention. Over every moment and every movement of his life, he was aware of the invisible presence of his father, a smiling, graceful presence, speaking invariably the language of ambition and common sense, but his master absolute and demanding implicit obedience. At all times he felt himself under observation, and the Earl took good care to remind him that such was the case. Again and again, at Leipzig, at Turin, at Hanover, at Paris, reference is made to the spies, the informants who would report back to London Philip's slightest indiscretions. There had been a recent illustration of this in the thunderbolt following

Lausanne; there was to be a second illustration of it at Leipzig. Chesterfield exaggerated, of course; he did not have so great a number of agents supervising Philip's behavior as he claimed, but he had acquaintances in most places who informed him, some truthfully, some falsely, about the boy, and he made the most of this to maintain an attitude of knowing everything.

It was bad training. It could not but create and justify a reaction of subterfuge, pretense, and conspiracy. The Reverend Mr. Harte, feeling himself also under surveillance, would inevitably sympathize with Philip and, as far as possible, make common cause with him. Loyalty and obedience must be based on confidence. The latter may be betrayed; but that risk has to be taken, and Chesterfield would not take it. He urged his son repeatedly to confide in him, imposed himself as a friend, promised that he would abet rather than censure his pleasures. But the pleasures had to meet his approval; the friendship had to be on his own terms; the confidence was one-sided. While honestly desiring it, he made confidence impossible by announcing an espionage system which implied no real confidence at all. Here, as so often, an ounce of foolish chivalry, an act of simple faith, would have been wiser, would have availed far more, than all the cautious common sense that cynicism inspired.

As it was, Philip went everywhere attended by his father's magnificent shadow. The trifles as well as the essentials of his life were to be submitted to Chesterfield House. The question, for example, as to whether he, like his older friend Eliot, should cut off his hair and put on the wig of manhood, or whether his native locks should continue to be curled and powdered, had to be decided by the infallible Earl. Philip, eager to copy the bigger boy and to be really grown-up, had complained of headaches and pimples on the head. But Chesterfield pronounced against him: "I can by no means agree to your cutting off your hair. I am very sure that your headaches cannot proceed from thence. And as for the pimples upon your head they are only owing to the heat of the season; and consequently will not last long — Mr. Eliot's hair grew so ill and bushy, that he was in the right to cut it off. But you have not the same reason." [85]

It is interesting to catch the reflection of Philip's letters in the replies of his father, and to note how he tuned them to meet the

Earl's desires, while on the other hand his good ally, Mr. Harte, loyally co-operated with glowing reports to London.[36] When some troublemaker among the spies sent home derogatory information that brought down an avalanche of reprimand, entreaty, and argument, it required brisk work on the part of both pupil and tutor to allay the storm. This was the case after Philip had visited Dresden, and Sir Charles Hanbury Williams had sent home the disastrous word that he enunciated badly, that he spoke "quick, thick, and ungracefully." The deluge followed. Chesterfield congratulated both himself and his son that he was informed of this dreadful thing in time (as he hoped) to prevent it. He was infinitely obliged, and he felt sure that Philip would be infinitely obliged to Sir Charles for this information. "Good God!" he exclaimed, "if this ungraceful and disagreeable manner of speaking had, either by your negligence or mine, become habitual to you, as in a couple of years more it would have been, what a figure would you have made in company, or in a public assembly?" Let him read what Cicero and Quintilian have to say about enunciation, what stress they lay upon the gracefulness of it. Suppose Roscius had spoken "*quick, thick,* and *ungracefully*" (how those adjectives rankled!), would Cicero have thought him worth the oration which he made in his favor? From now on he is to read every day aloud to Mr. Harte, who is to correct him every time he speaks too fast, misses the proper stops, lays a wrong emphasis. From now on, he is to open his teeth when he speaks, and is to pronounce every word distinctly. He is to beg Mr. Harte, Mr. Eliot, or anybody else he speaks with, to remind and stop him, whenever he falls into a "rapid and unintelligible mutter." But that was not the whole of it. Another of the spies who had seen Philip lately reported that he was awkward in his motions, negligent in his person. The Earl was sorry for both and so would he be when it was too late. "Awkwardness of carriage is very alienating; and a total negligence of dress and air is an impertinent insult upon fashion and custom." Let him be sensible of his good fortune that he has one, like his father, who interests himself enough in him to inquire into his faults and inform him of them.[37]

After that, Philip and Mr. Harte laid their heads together. Philip labored, but he also stopped the mouth of lions, such as the potential informant Count Pertingue, who, upon returning to England a few months later, corroborated the flattering statements of Mr.

Harte. The Earl expanded with delight. Mr. Harte, he announced, had reported that Philip was doing well in every respect: he had nearly attained the goal of Greek and Latin; when he read aloud, he enunciated very properly and distinctly; he sought for praise from the praiseworthy; Count Pertingue confirmed all this and added that Philip was also a favorite with the Count du Perron, who hoped to be useful to him in Turin. "God bless you," said the Earl, "and may you continue to deserve my love as much as you now enjoy it." [38]

Glimmering through all this, of course, disguise, distort, rationalize it as he would, but breaking through in spite of him, shone love. Even when there were no letters to answer, he still wrote, driven on, as he put it, by his fears, his hopes, and his doubts. "When I have wrote you a very long letter upon any subject," he declared once, "it is no sooner gone, but I think I have omitted something in it, which might be of use to you; and then I prepare the supplement for the next post: or else some new subject occurs to me, upon which I fancy I can give you some informations, or point out some rules which might be advantageous to you. This sets me to writing again, though God knows whether to any purpose or not. . . . But, whatever my success may be, my anxiety and my care can only be the effects of that tender affection which I have for you; and which you cannot represent to yourself greater than it really is." [39] There is no mistaking the accent of this. It is yearning, elemental love.

An absorbing relationship like this eclipses every other. It is almost with a shock of surprise that we meet an occasional reference to Philip's mother, Madame du Bouchet. One gathers that he was a somewhat negligent son, that he was absorbed by his father to such an extent as often to forget his father's obscure mistress. The Earl occasionally urged him to write to his "Mamma," commands him to send her a gift, such as a tea set from Dresden,[40] or reports that she is anxious for lack of a word from him. But the solicitude seems to have been largely on Chesterfield's side. When a boy's father is peer of England, a great officer of state, the source of every material benefit, the monopolizer of every hour, and when his mother is simply a nameless dependent without authority, it requires a depth of feeling that Philip had never been given the leisure to cultivate for him to remember her often. There were too many tutors, too many studies, and too many lectures on good form to allow him the sentimental luxury of a mother. To meet the natural craving for some object of affection during the Leipzig period, his bullfinch, Matzel, served as a substitute.

It is worth pausing a moment to sigh (a little in the manner of Sterne) over the memory of Matzel. He represents so perfectly the rigid diet of the affections upon which Philip Stanhope was kept. When at length he fell victim to a cat, and that small outlet was stopped, the boy probably grieved a while. But Sir Charles Hanbury Williams wrote an ode on the occasion;[41] and Lord Chesterfield did not miss the opportunity of giving Philip a lesson by remarking that "the unfortunate Matzel . . . spoke *his* language very distinctly and gracefully."

Meanwhile, considering everything, the Earl was pleased and upon reviewing the year at Leipzig pronounced it a success. It had been much better, he informed Dayrolles, than he had expected.

"We are absolute masters," he triumphed, "of Latin, Greek, French, and German, the last of which we write currently. We have *le droit public de l'empire,* history and geography, very ready, so that in truth, now we only want rubbing and cleaning. We begin for that purpose with Berlin at Christmas next; Vienna at Ladyday; and the Academy at Turin, at Midsummer; for a whole year. Then to Paris, *et si cela ne nous décrotte pas, il faut que le diable s'en mêle.*"[42]

The long succession of letters, if viewed as a whole, is not to be described as a straight line, but as an alternating rise and fall of interest on the part of their author. The pulse beat quickens at various points of Philip's career, when some important event is at hand. During the autumn of 1748 Chesterfield was looking forward to Berlin. This was to be his son's "first step into the great world."[43] All that had preceded it — the trivial good company at Lausanne, the Duchess of Courland's little court, even the court at Dresden — had merely been tentative, practice flights; the debut at Berlin was of real importance. For this a special effort in coaching was required, and Chesterfield exerted himself to provide it. Some of the most searching, the most beguiling letters of the entire collection are to be found at this point. The pursuit of learning fades into the background; the masterly essays on manners and the knowledge of the world begin. For it was crucial that upon entering the beau monde Philip should not trip over the threshold.

He was now sixteen, and his father could go a little deeper into the tricks of the trade. His analyses of human nature could become a little more subtle and a little more cynical. He could let Philip more completely into those secrets upon which he prided himself, and for which he had paid the price of his own illusions. It is now that he especially sponsors and defends La Rochefoucauld's thesis of enlightened selfishness; that he dissects the nature of women; that he probes most the various types of human vanity. "Women," he lectured, "are merely children of a larger growth. . . . A man of sense only trifles with them, plays with them, humours and flatters them, as he does with a sprightly forward child. . . . No flattery is either too high or too low for them. They will greedily swallow the highest, and gratefully accept the lowest; and you may safely flatter any woman, from her understanding down to the exquisite taste of her fan. . . . But these are secrets, which you must keep inviolably, if you would not, like Orpheus, be torn to pieces by the whole sex. . . . They have, from the weakness of men, more or less influence in all courts. . . . It is, therefore, absolutely necessary to manage, please and flatter them: and never to discover the least mark of contempt, which is what they never forgive. . . ."[44]

The subject of dancing occurs to him, and he pictures the beloved Philip treading the mazes of a minuet. Or he wonders if his son carves "adroitly and genteely, without hacking half an hour across a bone; without bespattering the company with the sauce, and without overturning the glasses into his neighbour's pockets." He would have him *omnibus ornatum excellere rebus,* and thought nothing above or below pointing out to him.[45]

He began to discourse upon the chief qualities of a diplomat, and declared that a foreign envoy's principal business is that of a spy, "to get into the secrets of the courts at which he resides." This he accomplishes by engaging manners and an insinuating behavior, which render him welcome in the best society and domestic in the best families, where he can elicit confidences or profit by careless remarks. "Here women may be put to some use," added the Earl, with a thought perhaps of his intimacy with Lady Yarmouth. "A King's mistress, or a minister's wife or mistress, may give great and useful informations; and they are very apt to do it, being proud to show that they have been trusted." [46]

He re-emphasizes the need of keeping only good company, and defines in detail what good company is. He draws up lists of points on good manners in one letter, or philosophizes the subject in another. He writes essays on the Graces and illustrates them from the lives of the great masters of *savoir-faire* he had known, such as the Duke of Marlborough; or from his own life, coloring it to suit the purpose. He discourses at length about the use of money. [47]

The letters are frequent, solid, and deeply pondered. They are often two thousand words long. What a strange contradiction in personality it seems: the Earl of Chesterfield shutting himself up for hours, quill in hand, to dream and scheme and build castles in the air and cover reams of paper for the fat little youth over in Germany! Behind all this there was love, indeed; yes, and the joy of the literary artist in the fine turns of expressions, the lucent phrase, the astute observation. But more than anything else, it was his own life — richer and younger and freer than before — that he was living over.

Thus, duly instructed in the foibles of men and the frailties of women, armed cap-a-pie with all the wisdom of his father, chubby young Philip, escorted by his valets and the Reverend Mr. Harte, took coach sometime in January, 1749, and plodded off through the mud toward Berlin. School days were over; he would now at length make his bow to fashionable life.

Chesterfield regarded the court of Frederick II as the "politest, the most shining, and the most useful Court in Europe." [48] Moreover, he considered Frederick himself, who had recently begun his career of glory by snatching Silesia from Austria, without question his greatest contemporary. This opinion continued through the years, while each succeeding victory of the Prussian King defeated one after another of the Earl's gloomy predictions, until at length he hailed him as the ablest prince in Europe, *l'homme de Prusse* whom "he honoured and almost adored," and whom he referred to as Augustus. [49] On the other hand, Frederick, who was not immune to flattery, had conceived a high opinion of Chesterfield. They never met, but each took care that the other should learn of his admiration. Maty records that this understanding between them dates from the Earl's visit to Spa in 1741, where he encountered a Prussian envoy to one of the German courts, who did not fail to report back to his master the encomiums of the English statesman. Naturally also, as Secretary of State, Chesterfield had opportunities to convey dulcet regards to the ears of Frederick. But he had other less official and yet even more convincing channels. It was notorious that private mail entering or leaving Prussia was apt to be inspected by government officials. Hence nothing could be more simple than that his letters to Berlin should contain the most exquisite incense. It was not insincere, but it most certainly reached its address.[50] In return, Frederick invited his admirer to visit him at Potsdam (a visit that the Earl's participation in the ministry of 1745 prevented), and often spoke of him as the best friend he had in England.[51] To Sir Charles Hanbury Williams at his first audience with Frederick, the latter expressed his high esteem of Lord Chesterfield.[52]

Besides the head of the state, there were other important people in Berlin who would sponsor Philip. He carried letters of introduction to Andrié, former Prussian agent in London, and Count Francesco Algarotti, a chamberlain and protégé of the King's. Thus the stage was set and the audience disposed to favor him.

Meanwhile Lord Chesterfield warmed his hands before a January fire and gave his fancy rein. "I often reflect, with the most flattering hopes," he mused, "how proud I shall be of you, if you should profit, as you may, of the opportunities which you have had, still have, and will have, of arriving at perfection; and, on the other hand, with dread of the grief and shame you will give me, if you do not." [53]

Nor, for once, was he disappointed. He did not hear at the time and perhaps he never heard that the hydra of Philip's illegitimacy reared its head upon this first entrance into the beau monde; that sticklers on etiquette were not quite certain as to his eligibility at court, his *hoffähigkeit;* and that Frederick himself with greater honor to Chesterfield than to his son silenced the objectors with a ukase that if it were "Lord Chesterfield's dog, he would have him treated in the most distinguished manner." [54] So, the debut took place under faultless conditions; and the loyal Mr. Harte, rising to the occasion, stole a leaf from his patron's own book and wrote back a glowing account: that Philip had behaved to those crowned heads with the respect and modesty due them, but at the same time without being any more embarrassed than if he had been conversing with his equals.[55] "This easy respect," declared the gratified father, "is the perfection of good-breeding." But for all that, it is impossible not to suspect that at the interview with Frederick a tailor's dummy would have behaved with a like ease and modesty. Not long afterwards the Count du Perron, who had known Philip recently in Leipzig, took off the edge of Harte's rhapsody by admitting to Chesterfield under pressure that when Philip had learned some manners he would be perfect, for one had to allow that he still smacked of the schoolroom.[56] Henceforward, during the next three years, the acquisition of manners would constitute the almost exclusive subject of what might be termed Philip's postgraduate course. The butterfly Graces would be the quarry which the lumbering youth would pursue.

The Earl had sent him an allegorical picture of them by Carlo Maratti with the rubric, *Senza di noi ogni fatica è vana* (Without us no effort avails), and advised him to use it as an icon for his prayers.[57]

The next year in particular he considered decisive, and girded himself, as it were, to flog Philip through this special heat. Threats and promises alternated; the letters stretched to inordinate length.

When a month of polishing at Berlin had supposedly removed some of the Leipzig roughness, Philip took coach, together with the valets and Mr. Harte, and jogged away through the February sleet, over endless roads, for a turn or two of the emery wheel at Vienna. They passed through Prague, and reached the Austrian capital by April. The plan was then to cross the Alps to Venice, study and, if possible, capture some of the Graces at the spring carnival, and thence proceed to Turin, where Philip would spend the summer and autumn at the Academy * presided over by Count Salmour; thereafter it would be Naples, Rome, and Florence, before the finale in Paris.[58]

It is interesting to note that this was precisely the route that Chesterfield had planned for himself long ago after leaving Cambridge and which had been interrupted by the death of Queen

---

* It should be remembered that such an Academy was in no sense scholastic, but was concerned with the exercises of a gentleman — dancing, fencing, riding, etc.

Anne.[59] He would now in a sense accomplish it. Considering the likelihood that he himself never visited Italy or Switzerland or Germany, it is amazing with what ease he followed his son's travels, familiar, as it were, with each new scene, with the customs and climate and leaders of fashion, with the points of interest which should be visited. It was the result of omnivorous reading in many languages, and of a cosmopolitan acquaintance; but it was the result, too, of an uncommonly powerful imagination.

CHAPTER XXI
Italy, France, and England

To review in detail the course of Philip Stanhope's wanderings through Italy, armed with letters of introduction to the right people, escorted by his father's invisible presence, pursued by sermons on good manners, would be only tedious. One thinks of him sometimes in the center of a swarm of gnats — *savoir-faire, tournure, les manières nobles, le je ne sais quoi, le ton de la bonne compagnie, garbo, gentilezza, leggiadria* — each buzzing away continually in his consciousness. Turin was given up for one reason or another; otherwise the program remained unchanged. From noble salon to noble salon his weary pilgrimage went on. Oh, sighed his father, if a well-bred company, at the sight of Philip, could only be brought to exclaim, "What a pretty fellow! How polite, graceful, spirited he is!" he, Chesterfield, hovering sylphlike about his son, would immediately assume his own shape, become visible, and embrace him.[1] But flattering as his lordship's informants were, they never cared to damn their souls to quite such an extent as this. There seemed always to be room for improvement on the side of manners, and sometimes the anxious father feared the worst. "You cannot imagine the grief it would give me," he shuddered, "if you should happen to be called, Muttering Stanhope, Absent Stanhope, Ill-bred Stanhope, or Awkward, Left-legged Stanhope."[2] Distrustful of reports, he wanted to judge of Philip's appearance for himself and ordered him to have a miniature made, for which he waited impatiently. That nothing, however costly, should be lacking to his son's wardrobe, he sent him his own diamond shoe buckles. No expense of gold or thought was too great; nothing else mattered, if only Philip could be turned out upon the world at last a shining, well-bred man. It was at this period that the greatest letters on manners were composed.

The Chesterfieldian system of manners was based on three main principles — the Golden Rule, a study and imitation of the best attainable models, and a practical knowledge of human weaknesses. It combined etiquette with experience, and took as its guide one of the profoundest articles of Christian ethics. But altruism and a spiritual purpose were not its inspiration. It was evolved for the sake not of righteousness but of success. And thus vitiated, the Golden Rule, having lost its sanction, becomes merely gilded. At its best, this means winsomeness, affability, and thoughtfulness, one of the charms of life; but at its worst — and phrase it ever so innocently, there is a worst — it means the subtlest form of heartlessness and deceit. Here as everywhere, the underlying motive is vital. We can easily imagine in that great gentleman, St. Francis de Sales, a courtesy equal, and indeed, perhaps, similar to Chesterfield's; but the total impression would be wholly different. It is the essential chill, the actual meanness, that no such terms as *manières nobles* and *gentilezza* can hide, that distinguishes and in the end discredits Chesterfieldianism.

But though it is easy to reduce the system to its elements and to condemn its motive, it is exceedingly difficult to describe the luxuriant and often lovely variations of its application to life or to convey the grace, versatility, and charm of its literary expression. The letters themselves must be read to be appreciated. Their aroma, wit, and ingenuity, the immortal, iridescent reflection of the age they mirror, can be conveyed in no other way. It is the total effect that is wrong, the spirit that is false; on the other hand the details are always plausible, usually beguiling, often commendable and wise.

It is this curious equivocation in Chesterfield that has raised up for him a throng of worthy defenders armed with quotations from the letters that a seraph would not disavow. There is nothing wrong — on the contrary there is everything good — in patterning ourselves upon the manners of those who are recognized as possessing them; in gaining the affection of our fellow mortals by thoughtful attentions; in banishing self from conversation; in refusing to propagate scandal or gossip; in gaiety and good spirits and dignity of behavior; in lack of self-consciousness; in the avoidance of bad habits.

There is something less praiseworthy in the mask of reserve; in the open features and disguised thoughts, the oft-repeated *volto sciolto, pensieri stretti;* in the emphasis on dissimulation; in paying people with appearances and the steady resolution to make a bubble of the world; in smiling always when one cannot strike.[3]

There is nothing good — on the contrary there is everything wrong — in the calculated practice of flattery; in probing for weaknesses so as to exploit them to one's own advantage; in fashionable adultery; in the profound distrust of every ideal cause and every spiritual issue; in the attitude of compromise between what is and what ought to be.

But all of this springs from the same root and is not separable. All of this constitutes Chesterfieldianism. "Take out the immorality," affirmed Samuel Johnson of the *Letters,* "and it should be put into the hands of every young gentleman." The trouble is that the immorality cannot be taken out. Chesterfieldianism is one thing — a definite, unified attitude toward life; Chesterfield expurgated, filtered, and idealized is nothing at all — a cross between savorless fiction and a patchwork of maxims.

Such was the system with its mixture of good and bad, its secular virtues and expedient compromises, that his lordship injected into the brain of Philip Stanhope at this time in ever-increasing doses.

One dread especially haunted him during his son's Italian training. It was the fear of his contamination by those throngs of young Englishmen who were similarly making the Grand Tour under orders from home and with a like view of fashionable polish. These miserable pests did not have the benefit of parents any more trained, any more presentable than themselves; their fathers had neither the desire nor the ability to educate them, nor to select traveling tutors for them, like the impeccable Harte. They were simply, in a vague fashion, doing the correct thing by touring Italy, and meanwhile followed their low bents by congregating together, joining in turbulent and vulgar pleasures, seeing nothing of the best Continental society, and, indeed, excluded from it, learning no language, no manners, and no sense; cultivating only vices, and losing nothing of their provincialism except their healths. "These unfortunate young persons," as Chesterfield called them, cluttered up the European capitals, and surrounded Philip with unthinkable dangers. He warned him repeatedly of them, and gave Harte strict orders to prevent his son from being contaminated by them. The following passage will illustrate his horror of his fellow countrymen and method of combating them.

I will [he writes] suppose you at Rome studying six hours uninterruptedly with Mr. Harte every morning, and passing your evenings with the best company of Rome, observing their manners, and forming your own; and I will suppose a number of idle, sauntering, illiterate English, as there commonly is there, living entirely with one another, supping, drinking, and sitting up late at each other's lodgings; commonly in riots and scrapes when drunk; and never in good company when sober. I will take one of these pretty fellows, and give you the dialogue between him and yourself; such as, I dare say, it will be on his side; and such as, I hope, it will be on yours.

Englishman. Will you come and breakfast with me to-morrow; there will be four or five of our countrymen; we have provided chaises, and we will drive somewhere out of town after breakfast?

Stanhope. I am very sorry I cannot; but I am obliged to be at home all morning.

Englishman. Why then, we will come and breakfast with you.

Stanhope. I can't do that neither; I am engaged.

Englishman. Well, then, let it be the next day.

Stanhope. To tell you the truth, it can be no day in the morning; for I neither go out, nor see anybody at home before twelve.

Englishman. And what the devil do you do with yourself till twelve o'clock?

Stanhope. I am not by myself, I am with Mr. Harte.

Englishman. Then what the devil do you do with him?

Stanhope. We study different things; we read, we converse.

Englishman. Very pretty amusement indeed! Are you to take Orders then?

Stanhope. Yes, my father's orders, I believe I must take.

Englishman. Why hast thou no more spirit, than to mind an old fellow a thousand miles off?

Stanhope. If I don't mind his orders he won't mind my drafts.

Englishman. What, does the old prig threaten then? threatened folks live long: never mind threats.

Stanhope. No, I can't say that he has ever threatened me in his life; but I believe I had best not provoke him.

Englishman. Pooh! you would have one angry letter from the old fellow, and there would be an end of it.

Stanhope. You mistake him mightily; he always does more than he says. He has never been angry with me yet, that I remember, in his life: but if I were to provoke him, I am sure he would never forgive me; he would be coolly immovable, and I might beg and pray, and write my heart out to no purpose.

Englishman. Why then, he is an odd dog, that's all I can say; and pray are you to obey your dry-nurse too, this same, what's his name — Mr. Harte?

Stanhope. Yes.

Englishman. So he stuffs you all morning with Greek, and Latin, and Logic, and all that. Egad, I have a dry-nurse too, but I never looked into a book with him in my life; I have not so much as seen the face of him this week, and don't care a louse if I never see it again.

Stanhope. My dry-nurse never desires anything of me that is not reasonable, and for my own good; and therefore I like to be with him.

Englishman. Very sententious and edifying, upon my word! At this rate you will be reckoned a very good young man.

Stanhope. Why, that will do me no harm.

Englishman. Will you be with us to-morrow in the evening then? We shall be ten with you; and I have got some excellent good wine; and we'll be very merry.

Stanhope. I am very much obliged to you, but I am engaged for all the evening, to-morrow; first at Cardinal Albani's; and then to sup at the Venetian Ambassadress's.

Englishman. How the devil can you like being always with these foreigners? I never go amongst them, with all their formalities and ceremonies. I am never easy in company with them and I don't know why, but I am ashamed.

Stanhope. I am neither ashamed nor afraid; I am very easy with them; they are very easy with me; I get the language, and I see their characters, by conversing with them; and that is what we are sent abroad for, is it not?

Englishman. I hate your modest women's company; your women of fashion as they call 'em; I don't know what to say to them for my part.

Stanhope. Have you ever conversed with them?

Englishman. No; I never conversed with them; but I have been sometimes in their company, though much against my will.

Stanhope. But at least they have done you no hurt; which is probably more than you can say of the women you do converse with.

Englishman. That's true, I own; but for all that, I would rather keep company with my surgeon half the year, than with your women of fashion the year round.

Stanhope. Tastes are different, you know, and every man follows his own.

Englishman. That's true; but thine's a devilish odd one, Stanhope. All morning with thy dry-nurse; all the evening in formal fine company; and all day long afraid of old Daddy in England. Thou art a queer fellow, and I am afraid there is nothing to be made of thee.

Stanhope. I am afraid so too.

Englishman. Well then: good-night to you: you have no objection, I hope, to my being drunk to-night, which I certainly will be.

Stanhope. Not in the least; nor to your being sick to-morrow, which you as certainly will be; and so good-night too.[4]

The best company in Rome — the Cardinal Albani, the Princess Borghese, the Venetian ambassadress, the Duc de Nivernais, ambassador of France. There were other introductions no doubt, but these were enough. Not for nothing had Chesterfield supplied the Duc de Nivernais's father, the Duc de Nevers, with a magnificent stallion and an Arab riding horse; * not for nothing had he corresponded for years with these great French lords; a *quid pro quo* could now be expected. He asked the Marquis de Monconseil to suggest to Nivernais that he consider Philip, who was presented to him in the guise of a nephew, as a little Frenchman of his suite, that he domesticate him in his anteroom, and make him his page, so that he might have an opportunity to study the character of a well-bred man from the finest possible model.[5] And Mr. Harte, to the Earl's great satisfaction, wrote back that there were very few English in Rome, and that Philip was frequenting the best foreign companies.

His lordship indulged himself at this time in the fondest dreams; the vicarious pleasure he took in Philip's progress deepened toward the sensual. He began to ogle the boy about women. Was he gallant? Did he make love handsomely? Was he concerned to soften by his cares and his attentions the rigors of some proud princess? [6] Had any woman of fashion and good breeding taken the trouble of

---

* While Philip was in Rome, Chesterfield also corresponded with Madame de Monconseil in regard to a rolling chair for gouty invalids, which he promised to procure for this nobleman. To Madame de Monconseil, Dec. 4, 1749.

abusing and laughing at him amicably to his face? Had he found a good *décrotteuse?* In his youth, said the Earl, a fine woman in Paris had taken that trouble with him, had accepted him as her novice, and prescribed a fashionable amour as the best polisher. He points out that "the gallantry of high life, though not strictly justifiable, carries, at least, no external marks of infamy about it"; that "neither the heart nor the constitution is corrupted by it; neither nose nor character lost by it, and that manners are possibly improved." [7] He declares that the Roman ladies are no highbrows and will not fall upon Philip's neck because of his knowledge of Greek. The idea of the dear boy's conquest of some fashionable woman, and of the incentive that that would give him to perfect his manners, warmed the Earl to poetry. He put together verses that should be set to the music of a somewhat jerky minuet.

> Would you engage the lovely fair?
>   With gentlest manners treat her;
> With tender looks and graceful air,
>   In softest accents greet her.
>
> Verse were in vain, the Muses fail,
>   Without the Graces' aid;
> The God of Verse could not prevail
>   To stop the flying maid.
>
> Attention by attentions gain,
>   And merit care by cares;
> So shall the nymph reward your pain,
>   And Venus crown your prayers. [8]

On the strength of all this, he henceforth laid aside the former salutation "dear boy" and wrote "my dear Friend." It was a symbol of intimacy.

But what in sober fact did occur at Rome differed a great deal from the proud father's lyrical hopes. Mr. Harte had lied, or at least he had equivocated. There may not have been many English in Rome, but Chesterfield's "dear friend" went hand and glove with those who were; Philip may have frequented the best companies, but he frequented others also, which, from his father's standpoint, were undoubtedly the worst. Alas, in the real as distinct from the imaginary dialogue between Stanhope and the Englishman, he had not shown himself so virtuous and reserved.

This was not all. While Chesterfield inhaled the frequent thought of Philip languishing, not in vain, for some proud princess, alluring her with manners which had suddenly become distinguished, dazzling her perhaps a little with the gleam of the paternal buckles on a neatly shod foot — some whimsical fine woman who would initiate him into the necessary mysteries and turn him out a complete little gentleman — while he pondered these things, Philip was actually dancing attendance on a young girl of no name, fortune, or position, the illegitimate daughter of a wealthy Irishman called Domville, but going by the name of Eugenia Peters. She was accompanied by a vulgar, underbred woman, ostensibly her mother, but probably a governess. Though exceedingly plain, she had been carefully educated, sang well, and played perfectly on the harpsichord. "As they were Englishwomen," wrote Lord Charlemont long afterwards, "we frequented their lodgings, while some of the unoccupied among us, of which number Stanhope, in spite of his father's earnest and gallant exhortations, was one, persuaded themselves that they were smitten by the accomplishments of the amiable Eugenia." [9] It was at the lodgings, then, of this obscure, deplorable female, and not in the anteroom of the Duc de Nivernais, that Philip frittered away his precious time; it was for her that Lord Chesterfield's diamond buckles gleamed. Where was "Raphael" Harte, the blameless and trusted? [10] Where the intelligence service? What of the *garbo*, the *gentilezza*, the *leggiadria*?

Of course, Stanhope amounted to something at the lodgings of Eugenia Peters; he was a very eligible young man. He did not have to be on a perpetual *qui vive* in regard to behavior and language, but could relax a bit and romp a little and crack jokes and laugh; in short, he could be young there. At his ease, with legs stretched out, diamond buckles and all, he could listen to Eugenia at the harpsichord, and admire the whiteness of her neck and the curve of her elbow. She was not a proud princess who terrified him with her titles and *savoir-faire* and mocking eyes, but a simple little Irish girl who warmed his heart.

At the French embassy, he was nothing at all: an awkward, hideously shy Tony Lumpkin, set down shivering among a horde of grandees. Wicked as it was of him, forgetful as he showed himself of the "duties of man, son, pupil, and citizen," one can understand, and in a measure, perhaps, even seek to excuse him. It might be suggested that he craved not a salon, but a sense of peace and home, and that he may have felt desperately cold and lonely at times in the ever-changing caravanseries of his life. Perhaps, had he heard of them, even Lord Chesterfield might ultimately have condoned such delinquencies, if they had stopped at this point. He would have reflected that Lord Charlemont and Lord Bruce were among these English at Rome, and that they might prove a valuable connection for Philip later on.[11] If he had learned that Philip had seduced the amiable Eugenia, he might have felt still more inclined to leniency, because young men must begin somewhere, and Philip might have begun worse. Besides, he did indeed frequent the best foreign companies.[12] But what he could never have forgiven at all, had he known of it, was what actually happened: that, instead of an amour, a passing amusement, the unbelievably asinine Philip fell in love with the girl, that he became sentimentally involved, that when they separated he remained loyal to her. This was bourgeois, vulgar, and weak; above everything else, it was unintelligent, and for such offenses there could be no forgiveness. With such negligible persons, it was legitimate to satisfy one's lust; but it was never permissible to lose one's head nor one's sense of social distinctions.

No defense can therefore be made of Philip's behavior on this score. He probably enjoyed Rome; * and perhaps the Eternal City left him with memories the sweeter for being innocent and moon-struck, the sweeter too for not having been shared with his would-be confidant, the Olympian at Chesterfield House. Philip was too humdrum and heavy a mortal to indulge the poetic vein; but nevertheless he had had his own modest Arcadia.

Meanwhile the supreme moment of his education approached, the grand climax of the years, which should put a final cornice upon the Corinthian superstructure. Having finished with Rome, and having examined the curiosities of Naples under the auspices of the well-bred Monsieur and Madame Fogliani and of the social leader, Comte Mahony,[13] he was journeying north toward Paris. His sojourn there, affirmed his father, would be of infinite consequence to him; the letters henceforward would be calculated for that meridian.[14]

About this time, Chesterfield was engaged in debate with the

* His father noticed it. He wrote unsuspectingly, "You seem to like Rome. . . ." March 8, 1750.

Marquise de Monconseil about Philip's Parisian plans. For several years now in his letters to the Marquise, he had styled the boy her pupil, her *galopin*, her creature, who would be chiefly under her direction in Paris, and had thus endeavored to build up a real interest in him on her part. "It is not," he insisted, "to make you a stale compliment, that I protest to you my belief that his success in the world depends more on you than any other thing." [15] They were engaged then in settling the final arrangements.

After some polite argument they decided that he should live at de la Guérinière's fashionable academy for young gentlemen, in order to perfect himself in such exercises as riding and fencing. Supplementary instruction would be provided for the afternoons. The evenings would be devoted to society under the direction of Madame de Monconseil and Chesterfield's other friends in Paris.

Philip would be eighteen by then and would receive his manumission from Mr. Harte, who, after establishing him at the academy, would return to England. He would be left in Paris "upon the foot of a man of fashion," with his own coach, a *valet de chambre*, a footman, a *valet de place* ("One more servant than I had," observed his father). He would be given an ample allowance for charity, clothes, theaters, and even for cards at low stakes.[16] A "cargo of letters" would be awaiting him there "to wits, scholars, and fair ladies." [17] This was the moment to which Chesterfield had been looking forward from the beginning, for which he had planned with infinite attentions and civilities — the arrival of his son in the polite capital of the world, the city of his soul.

Looking back now over Philip's ledger, he felt on the whole satisfied. In the credit column stood French, German, Italian, Latin, Greek, Logic, Ethics, History, the *Jus Naturae*, the *Jus Gentium*, and the *Jus Publicum*. Being ignorant of Eugenia Peters, he noted only on the debit side, faulty English, Enunciation, and Manners. This he declared to be a very true account and a very encouraging one. A man who owed so little as this could clear it off in short order.[18]

He had every confidence in the emery wheel of Paris. "It is with the greatest pleasure," he wrote, "that I consider the fair prospect which you have before you. You have seen, read, and learned more, at your age, than most young fellows have done at two or three and twenty. Your destination is a shining one, and leads to rank, fortune, and distinction. Your education has been calculated for it; and to do you justice, that education has not been thrown away upon you." [19]

This may be regarded as Philip Stanhope's diploma. At seventeen and a half, he had finished, to his father's satisfaction, a course far more rigorous than that usually covered by the modern undergraduate.

Moreover, to his lordship's additional gratification, the long-awaited [20] miniature arrived. To establish the artist's competence, he had had one painted at the same time of Mr. Harte, who would not have changed in the last three years, and when this proved "by far the most like he had seen in his life," he drew the happiest conclusions regarding Philip's likeness. One can picture him in the little blue boudoir at Chesterfield House, with the miniature before him, studying it. Here actually was his boy, flesh of his flesh, the center of unnumbered hours. He looked at the face with loving, prejudiced eyes, found that it had spirit and finesse, lingered over every feature, attempting to pierce beneath it to the mind. He had to admit that Philip was fat and short, but he really believed that the exercises at de la Guérinière's would make him shoot up to a good size.[21] The miniature pleased him. No cloud disturbed the serenity of the prospect, as the boy and Mr. Harte turned north.

It seemed to Chesterfield that they took their time about it, that they even dawdled en route. He was forever announcing to the Marquise the proximate arrival of her *élève* and *galopin*, but Philip lingered in the south. He visited Florence, Siena, Turin, Milan, Genoa, then crossed to the Riviera, and stopped for a while at Montpellier. They had been due to reach Paris in October, and were two months late. The letters at this time were bursting with Paris — last-moment counsels, introductions, warnings suited to the momentousness of the event.

At length Philip, Mr. Harte, and the valets toiled along north through the late autumn weather, and probably on a dark December afternoon rattled over the cobblestones of the Daedalian city.

On December 24, 1750, Chesterfield could at last exclaim with infinite elation: *Vous voilà à la fin Parisien!*

It is pleasant to reconstruct, by conjecture and from casual reference, Philip Stanhope's arrival in Paris, that Paris of the mid-eighteenth century, so much smaller, more haphazard and ancient than the modern city of the Buonapartes and Haussmann. Probably, before he moved to the academy, he and Harte stopped at the Hôtel de Luxembourg, Rue des Petits Augustins, which had been patronized by his father. There Chesterfield's friend, the Abbé Guasco, immediately waited upon him.[22] From there he launched out forthwith upon a series of calls: on Lady Hervey, the beautiful Molly Lepel of long ago, who was spending the winter in Paris; on Lord Albemarle, the British ambassador, and Mr. Yorke, son of the Lord Chancellor, who was attached to the embassy; on the Marquis de Matignon, to whom both the Earl and Lord Bolingbroke had written about him; on the President Montesquieu; on the Maréchal de Coigny; on Madame de Berkenrode, the Dutch ambassadress, Chesterfield's former flame; on Madame du Boccage; on the Marquise de Monconseil; on the Abbé Sallier. The first few days were exceedingly busy.

Meanwhile Harte lingered on for a fortnight and then returned to England to make a final report and to reap the fruit of his labors. He was established for life. The rich Edward Eliot gave him a living in Cornwall,[23] and Chesterfield had squeezed out of the government an appointment for him as prebendary of Windsor.* With his livelihood assured by two such sinecures, he had nothing more to do than write and mull over books, and later to nurse his health at Bath: a situation to be envied by the whole fraternity of the pen.

Arrived at Chesterfield House, he abounded in praise of Philip. The latter, it appeared among other things, was "exceedingly careful and jealous of the dignity of his character," and "had acquired a most correct and extensive knowledge of foreign affairs." All this was worth a prebend of Windsor. But other good reports, as might be expected from so courtly a band as the Parisian circle, came in. Certainly, after the first interview, they could not dash cold water over his lordship's eagerness; and the favorable accounts were, therefore, unanimous. Madame de Monconseil, Madame du Boccage, Lady Hervey, Lord Albemarle, the Marquis de Matignon, among others, wrote back punctiliously in just the style one would

---

* This was not easily obtained. *Cf.* letter to Dayrolles, April 27, 1750: "It is very true, that, after a series of difficulties, which, I believe, were never made before upon so trifling occasion, Mr. Harte has at last got a prebend of Windsor. I am most extremely glad of it; for, that debt being paid, I owe no man living anything."

expect of them. They assured the Earl, to his great satisfaction, that Monsieur Stanhope would soon be entirely like a Frenchman; they ventured to promise that he would succeed; they praised his great fund of knowledge and the modesty with which he concealed it; they extolled his face, which was handsome, though small, and his manners, which were entirely correct, though still lacking a trifle in grace; but they averred that he would soon acquire the requisite tone, that he was making progress daily by frequenting the proper company.[24] Chesterfield was delighted; for once he had no criticisms to make. It was only later, after the first compliments had been presented, that the polite informants began to hint this and hesitate that, and the sad truth once again gradually emerged that, for all the panegyrics, our manners still lagged, and the original homespun remained unchanged.

There can be no question that at this time Philip did his best. Since, as his father declared, his chief point at Paris was to become entirely a man of fashion,[25] he slaved away at it day and night. Let the average reader imagine himself in such a situation — exposed day by day to a battery of critics, for whom behavior was alike the finest and the most important of the arts; for whom the simplest gesture, such as the handling of a snuffbox or a cane, the pointing of a foot, the tilt of an elbow, had a deep significance; for whom manner was more important than matter, who regarded a modulation of voice, sweetness of expression, and clear utterance as essential; to whom the turning of a phrase or compliment was the hallmark of good breeding; who had been subjected to a discipline of acting far more rigorous than that now required of any actor — and let the reader imagine himself a fat, awkward young fellow, rather short, and with legs none too shapely, entering, let us say, the crowded drawing room of the Marquis de Matignon, encountered by the cool appraisal of a myriad French eyes, a babble of French voices, an expanse of "proud princesses," a kaleidoscope of splendid costumes! That he was a foreigner would not help him before the native disdain of everything foreign, nor would the fact of his illegitimacy, which would soon be whispered about. One would suppose, moreover, that his self-consciousness would not be lessened by the knowledge that Lady Hervey, Madame de Monconseil, Madame du Boccage, and the rest, had been appointed by his father as special critics to analyze and correct any false move he made. Indeed, the Earl repeatedly ordered him to beg them for such lessons. "Correct me, I beseech you," he was to tell them, "and chasten me even publicly, when you catch me tripping." [26]

So harassed, Philip, as we have already noted, seems to have striven manfully. He dangled from salon to salon under the appraising eyes of his mentors; though by no means a devoted horseman, he rode every morning at the *manége* to reduce his weight; and he toiled long hours with the dancing teacher, Marcel, who in the distant past had fashioned Chesterfield himself, and to whose lectures he was now to apply himself as diligently as he had formerly done to Professor Mascow's. [27]

We can imagine the poor boy at work with this ancient martinet of the Graces. He would leave the room, and then re-enter it to present himself to Marcel as to a minister of state, the lynx-eyed old gentleman criticizing every flourish, every pose, and every glance. He would again withdraw and once more come in to find Marcel as a woman of fashion, and would put his stout self through another set of curvets and gestures. He would retire a third time, and re-enter to meet Marcel in the guise of a petitioner, perhaps, a tradesman, or some other inferior. This required a different bearing, a different assortment of manners; and so on, through the various roles of society. He practiced with Marcel different facial expressions: how to look tender, respectful, cheerful, unctuous, insinuating. [28] One would particularly have enjoyed watching Stanhope give his round face the insinuating turn. But especially the maestro was desired to pay attention to Philip's arms. "It is they," declared the Earl, "that decide of a man's being genteel or otherwise, more than any other part of the body. A twist, or stiffness of the wrist, will make any man in Europe look awkward." [29]

Chesterfield was urgent about all his son's exercises at this time. Could he manage a spirited horse over the hurdles? Had he been advanced to the use of stirrups? How did his fencing progress? To cut down his fat, he should take a double dose both of the *manège* and the *salle d'armes;* he should diet and walk a good deal in the Tuileries. But above all, what did Marcel say of him? Was Marcel satisfied?

As a result of these labors, Philip did make progress. No less a judge than Lady Hervey herself reported that he danced very genteelly. Marcel was satisfied, and considered him among his better pupils.[30] Madame de Monconseil affirmed he had most surprisingly improved in "air, manners, and address," [31] And yet . . . in spite of everything, the reports still hinted that he was far from perfect.

But if manners were so burning an issue; if they were to become a matter of life and death, the question once more imposes itself as to why Lord Chesterfield waited until Philip was past eighteen before subjecting him to so intense a discipline. The acquisition of manners in the French-Chesterfieldian sense was an art far more difficult than that of a tightrope walker or acrobat; it required a physical delicacy of a more complicated order. And if professional acrobats usually begin young, there is all the more reason to believe that an aspirant of the Graces should be subjected to continuous training from his earliest years. This had been true of Chesterfield himself under the tutelage of Lady Halifax. It was true of practically every French gentleman; from babyhood on, they were taught the movements of politeness. If Chesterfield found it impossible to keep Philip with him as a child; if he found it expedient to send him to Westminster and then to entrust him three years to a governor as inelegant as Mr. Harte, he ought not, on the score of a correspondence course in manners (for that is precisely what his letters amounted to), to expect the airs and graces of a Parisian dandy. That method, even in the case of a boy far more brilliant than Philip, would be bound to fail. After all, one must make a choice in education; the *omnis homo* is too rare a bird to go searching for. If learning is the chief desirable, we must content ourselves with a merely decent behavior; if the art of pleasing is the primary goal, we should beware of too much *Jus Gentium, Jus Publicum, Jus Naturae.*

The point of Chesterfield's failure in this respect is worth laboring, for it directly concerns one of the most important questions that can be raised in regard to him. We have attempted to show that if anyone, by training and by natural ability, had a right to consider himself wise in the ways of the world, it was he. And yet at this point the doubt arises, though not for the first or last time, as to whether the common sense and worldly wisdom upon which the wiseacres set so high a value, is really very wise or essentially valuable, whether, on the contrary, it is not apt, especially when dealing with human personalities, to be pathetically inadequate.

* * *

There was, however, another exquisite lapidary's wheel that had not yet been tried upon Philip. Marcel and the Marquise, the best Italian and French companies, the Earl's own persuasions, might not yet have availed to bring out an adequate luster; but there remained a final process, so intimate, so pervasive and powerful, that the dullest clod could not but be irradiated and transformed by it. This new emery stone and polishing elixir was, in the flat-footed modern parlance, sex; in the smoother glossary of the eighteenth century, it was gallantry. Until Philip, in other words, had passed through the scintillating experience of a fashionable amour, there was no cause for despair.

We have already noted that Chesterfield began hinting of this and smacking his lips while Philip was still in Italy. He had even composed a sly Ovidian verse, a poetic nudge, on the subject. But when Philip reached Paris, the hints became broader, and the nudges became digs with the spur.

There has been a tendency on the part of the Earl's apologists to take the following line. They argue that Chesterfield, looking squarely at life and accepting the sexual deviations of youth as a necessary part of it, considered an affair with some fashionable woman less harmful to his son's health and reputation than the embraces of a dancing girl or prostitute. And it is perfectly true that he did so consider it. But the implication of this argument is that he regarded such an affair as a necessary evil, or at least a matter of indifference in a relatively imperfect world and perhaps even the subject for an indulgent, companionable smile. Such an implication is false, because of what it conceals, which is the fact that he considered a liaison of this kind as highly commendable, useful, praiseworthy and to be strongly urged. It conceals also the fact that Philip Stanhope does not appear to have been in the least amorous,[32] and that he shrank from the affairs to which his father pointed him. Certainly there is not the faintest indication that a genteel amour was required to save him from worse temptations. As far as one can judge at this distance, his tastes were scholarly and his nature was that of a jovial, lubberly, university don. That much of the excuse for his father's pandering falls to the ground.

But, indeed, there can be no excuse, no defense at all, for this ugly feature of the letters. If the laxity of the age be regarded as a palliative, it should still be recalled that contemporaries repudiated such an attitude as emphatically as have subsequent critics. The truth is that an abscess suppurates at this point. Sexual immorality plays no great part in the letters, but it is not accidental; it represents vividly a still more inclusive evil.

When Philip arrived in Paris, he took with him, as we have seen, a letter of introduction to Madame de Berkenrode, the Dutch ambassadress, a vivacious lady who had captivated Chesterfield at The Hague in 1745. It needed only for the boy to remark conventionally enough that he was in love with her for his father to make, or at least to hint at, certain assumptions. "Are you in love with Madame de Berkenrode still," he wrote, when his son had been hardly a month in Paris, "or has some other taken her place in your affections? . . . A reputable affair befits a gentleman (*un arrangement honnête sied bien à un galant homme*)." [33] A month later, he was again probing, "Do you see your way clear as yet to some genteel affair?" [34] And as Philip six weeks afterwards was still evidently unattached, he began making suggestions. There was that charming young Madame de Blot, for example, who was said to be pretty as a picture, and who none the less had been thus far absolutely faithful to her husband, although they had been married already more than a year. "Fiddlesticks! That woman must be taught the world. Well then, teach it to each other. Effort, insistence, attentions, soft looks, passionate vows on your part, will evoke at least some whim in her, and when that is present, deeds are not far off." [35]

But the progress with Madame de Blot did not seem rapid, and the impatient father turned on another tack which he considered, perhaps, easier. He recalled a Madame Dupin, the wife of a *fermier-général*, who had been handsome ten years before, and who had now a certain following among the wits, such as Fontenelle and Marivaux. True, she was fifty, but was well preserved, and her age would render her less exacting. "She has good parts, reading, manners, and delicacy," he instructed Philip: "such an *arrangement* would be both creditable and advantageous to you. She will expect to meet with all the good breeding and delicacy that she brings; and as she is past the glare and éclat of youth, may be the more willing to listen to your story, if you tell it well. For an attachment [that is, a more lasting amour] I should prefer her to *la petite Blot;* and, for a mere gallantry, I should prefer *la petite Blot* to her; so that they are consistent, *et l'une n'empêche pas l'autre.* Adieu. Remember *la douceur et les grâces.*" [36]

It happened that Philip mentioned with praise a certain Madame de Case, and this was enough to set off the Earl's hope on another scent. Who was the "beautiful" Madame de Case? If she deserved that epithet, she deserved Philip's attentions. "A man of fashion should be gallant to a fine woman." [37] He was delighted to become the factor for his son in purchasing dress materials, such as mohair, for the ladies to whom Philip was supposed to be attentive. [38] Although counting the hours till his return in the summer of 1751, he still gladly permitted him to delay leaving Paris, provided some genteel affair was in progress. [39] Such a longed-for consummation ought not to be interrupted.

Philip hung back from all these allurements. "If only I dared," he faltered, and roused snorts of disgust from Chesterfield House.

What do you mean by your "If I dared!" What keeps you from daring? Dare always when there is hope of success; and nothing is lost by daring even when there is no hope. A gentleman knows how to dare and when to dare; he opens the siege by effort, care, attentions; if he is not at once turned back, he continues steadily on to the attack of the stronghold itself. After certain approaches, success is infallible, and only blockheads doubt of it or do not attempt it. Is it the respectability of Madame de la Valière which keeps you from daring, or does the ferocious virtue of Madame Dupin hold you back? Does the invincible chastity of the fair Madame Case discourage you more than her beauty allures? Pooh! Learn this, that the demurest woman on earth, far from being offended, feels herself flattered by a declaration of love which is made with grace and politeness. Very possibly she will not consent, that is if she has a taste or a passion for someone else; but in any case she will not be angry with you — so that there is no question of daring when there is no danger. But if she is inclined, if she listens and permits you to repeat your declarations, you may be certain that she will laugh at you, if you do not dare everything else. I advise you to start rather with Madame Dupin, who has still more than enough beauty for a young puppy like you. Moreover, she knows the world, has wit and delicacy. Her age does not leave her a free choice of lovers, and I assure you that she will not reject the offer of your very humble service. Therefore, distinguish her by your attentions and soft glances; take the proper occasions to whisper in her ear that you wish it were only friendship and esteem that formed the motive of your regard for her, but that much tenderer sentiments were the real cause; that you suffered in confessing this to her, but that you would suffer still more in concealing it.

I realize that in telling her this for the first time, you will look rather foolish and rather hang-dog, and that you will tell it very badly. So much the better; she will attribute your confusion to the excess of your love, instead of to its true cause — your small experience of the world, especially in such matters. Self-confidence is the loyal friend of the lover in a case like that. Fear nothing, then; be gallant; speak well and you will be listened to. If you are not heeded the first time, speak a second, a third, a fourth time. If the place has not already been occupied, be assured that in the long run it can be taken.[40]

In spite of these inspiring sentiments, however, little Philip would not make the plunge, but stood finger in mouth on the shore entreated by his impatient father. He cast longing eyes at his books, which were so safe and comfortable and unexacting. The Earl prodded him on toward the dizzy, glittering river. "I had much rather that you were passionately in love with some determined coquette of condition . . . than that you knew all Plato and Aristotle by heart." [41] Too late; the snuffy effect of Leipzig hung on; his return to England did not have to be postponed because of some gallant affair. And yet for many years the Earl did not give up hope, but went on suggesting and ogling from time to time. Long afterward, when his son had been finally launched on his diplomatic career, he rejoiced at the rumor that he was in love with a fair Madame in Hamburg, and sent him an extra hundred pounds on the score of it.[42] But this, like all the other affairs that might have been, was probably no more than a will-o'-the-wisp. On the emery wheel of the determined coquettes, at least, Philip never permitted himself to be bound. Likely enough, even while the Earl was buying mohair for his son's prospective conquests, and sending him tips on the art of love, Philip was dispatching furtive letters to the Irish Eugenia he had known in Rome. It would be impossible to romanticize Philip; but one suspects him of a kind of bourgeois loyalty.

*　　*　　*

During the spring and early summer of 1751, Chesterfield looked forward with increasing eagerness to his son's return to England on a visit of inspection and stocktaking. He counted the days, then the hours, and at last the very minutes, and declared that he looked upon their meeting "as a young woman does upon her bridal night." [43] Hopes and fears assailed him in turn. "Good God!" he had written, "how I should be shocked, if you came into my room, for the first time, with two left legs, presenting yourself with all the graces and dignity of a tailor, and your clothes hanging upon you, like those in Monmouth Street, upon tenter-hooks! It would endanger my health." Now, what with conflicting statements from Paris, Harte's panegyrics, and the evidence of the miniature, he was between doubt and expectation. "As fathers commonly go," he mused, thinking perhaps of his own youth, "it is seldom a misfortune to be fatherless; and considering the general run of sons, as seldom a misfortune to be childless. You and I form, I believe, an exception to that rule; for I am persuaded that we would neither of us change our relation, were it in our power. You will, I both hope and believe, be not only the comfort, but the pride of my age; and I am sure I will be the support, the friend, the guide of your youth." [44]

Characteristically, he began to draw up a little curriculum for his conversations with Philip during the latter's stay in England. They would discuss the purity and elegance of the English language, in which Stanhope was very deficient. Another topic would be the constitution of England. A frequent subject of lectures would, of course, be manners, attentions, and address. Clothes would be likewise descanted on. Philip would see a great deal of company of all sorts; he would be expected to do the honors of his father's house and table, and the Earl would check the least inaccuracy or inelegancy. He must look forward to the most critical examination that anyone ever underwent. Whether his visit would be pleasant, therefore, might be doubted, but his lordship felt convinced that it would be useful. [45]

As the appointed time drew close, an almost fluttering quality becomes apparent in the letters. For once the silly, rational pose of paternal affection dependent on filial merit breaks down, and we catch the somewhat pathetic glimpse of a fond, solicitous human heart. Unable to wait longer he confessed to a "weak" impatience and cut down the delay in Paris by five days. Philip's journey from Calais on was visualized step by step in his mind: twenty-four hours to Dover after arriving in Calais; if Stanhope landed in the morning and took a post chaise, he could reach Sittingbourne that same day; if he landed in the evening, he could get no farther than Canterbury, where there was a better inn than at Dover. "I will not have you travel in the night," insisted his lordship, "nor fatigue and overheat yourself by running on four-score miles the moment you land. You will come straight to Black-heath, where I shall be ready to meet you, and which is directly upon the Dover road to London; and we will go to town together, after you have rested yourself a day or two here." [46]

It requires no exuberant fancy to imagine that the Earl, habitually serene, gave no signs of unwonted agitation on that long-desired August day.* Perhaps he read; more likely he strolled, his gaze on the fine prospect of the river, but with an ear alert for a rattle of hoofs and wheels up from the Dover road. At last it came — unmistakable. His son, the hero of his dreams, a figment, indeed, of thought rather than a reality, was at the door. It had been five years. He had last seen Philip as a child, and did not know the young man arriving from Dover in the post chaise. The child had grown into . . . what?

A gasp, hardly suppressed, answers that question. Heroes of dreams are apt to shrink and fade in the light of common day. He expected at least an imitation of a Parisian beau, some trace of dash and fire; but the post chaise delivered up to him, in spite of the five years and mountainous effort, a very English mouse — a short, chubby young man, extremely round-shouldered, awkward, and nervously shifting from foot to foot.[47] Where on earth had he caught such manners, such an air? Even Westminster School and the pedants of Leipzig could hardly account for them. Where was the fruit of so much eloquence and coaching? Not one trace. As to doing the honors of house and table, the notion had become rather an irony, the sooner the better forgotten. A gasp indeed, stifled and covered up with humor but still recognizable, expresses the Earl's reaction to his returning paragon.

Honors of house and table! In those days Lord Chesterfield surveyed his offspring at dinner with a dolorous heart and a rising

* He was to leave Calais on Aug. 22 or Aug. 23, New Style.

sense of horror. Lord Charlemont relates that shortly after Philip's arrival, he was dining with his father in a large and polite company. One dined well at Chesterfield House; the table glittered with silver and was covered with delicacies. Philip, to whom eating meant apparently much more than an occasion for small talk, allowed his gaze to fasten on "an oval silver dish containing a quantity of excellent baked gooseberries, then a rarity, snowed over with a rich covering of whipped cream." Lady Chesterfield served him abundantly, but Philip, longing for more, could not bear to see the courses changed without another helping of his favorite dish. He beckoned the servant who was removing it, and hurrying so as not to delay the next course, placed the silver dish still foaming with cream under his chin and began "to lap it up in hasty spoonfuls." The eyes of the company centered on him. Was it for this that young Stanhope had spent five years on the Continent, had been presented at courts, had been introduced in celebrated salons? Was it to this end that such experts as Sir Charles Hanbury Williams, the Duke de Nivernais, the Princess Borghese, Lady Hervey, and the Marquise de Monconseil, not to speak of their distinguished host himself, had polished and refined him? Was this the easy manner acquired by foreign residence? — then, reflected the company behind arched eyebrows and twitching lips, they thanked God for an English training. Philip lapped on. There are certain trivial moments that search the heart with a white-hot scalpel. Across the anguish of Chesterfield's mind would have flashed his ludicrous hopes, contrasted with this reality. He felt the ridicule and could read (none better) the thought of the company. Never in his life, perhaps, did his self-control undergo a harder test or rise more brilliantly to the occasion. There was but one thing to do. He expressed the unspoken raillery, and by putting himself at the head of the mockers, drew the fangs of the joke. Calling to a valet, who stood at attention behind Philip's chair, he remarked casually, "John, why do you not fetch the strop and the razors? You see your master is going to shave himself." And at every word he twisted the knife in his own wound.

Honors of house and table, indeed! Alas, Ichabod! At another dinner party, Philip, hearing a noise outside and having not yet learned, in spite of all his training, to moderate his curiosity, sprang up to peep out of the window. This was bad enough, but what complicated it was the fact that he had tucked the tablecloth rather than his napkin through a buttonhole, and therefore drew it along with him to the overturning of the soup, the consternation of the guests, and his father's misery. Considering all the letters, all the dreams, the tutors, valets, professors, contacts patiently established, expenditure of gold and time, the humor of moments like this is nothing but the starkest tragedy.

But the long-established hopes of a masterful, resolute man die hard. Certainly they are not to be dismissed because of one fiasco. Love, pride, vanity, the habit of years, combined with sheer stubbornness, held Chesterfield more firmly than ever to his consuming purpose. The pewter must be transmuted; the loutish Philip must become a polished diplomat. No other career was thinkable. On then once more in pursuit of the Graces, our lubberly self mincing forward to the interminable minuet accompaniment of the Earl's precepts.

Chesterfield had intended that his son should remain no longer than a month or six weeks away from Paris.[48] Now, instead of dispatching him back again, he bundled him into his coach and carried him to Bath for an intensive polishing. This time he resolved to do the job himself. The pace must have been hard and furious; it lasted three months. At the end of it he felt gratified with the progress. "He holds himself better," announced the Earl to the Marquise, "enters a room better, does not kick his feet about so much, and has broke himself of many of those pretty tricks he had learnt at school, and had since cultivated in the company of the bears he had the misfortune to meet with in his travels. What gives me some hope is, that he is now sensible of what is wanting. . . ."[49]

One would give a good deal, were it possible (projecting oneself back through time) to overhear a private conference between Chesterfield and his son, a sermon livelier and longer than any letter, diversified, too, by expression of face, gesture, and tone of voice, delivered with all the spirit and address of which he was capable. Reminiscences and anecdotes served as illustrations; ridicule was the rod; the séances may have been painful for Philip, but they were certainly not dull. Or it would be amusing to attend a dance at Thayer's or Harrison's Assembly and observe the triumph in his lordship's eyes, as Philip, pirouetting and posturing with some "determined coquette" annexed for him by his father, threaded agilely the successive figures; for there, at least, he was at ease — he danced well.

An incident which occurred the following spring indicates the tenacity with which Chesterfield clung to his forlorn faith. In an argument with a friend who denied that Philip would ever acquire the manners of the world, as something contrary to his very nature, the Earl bet fifty guineas that he would, and declared that such accomplishments were not a matter of nature, but depended on the will. "If you think I shall win," he hinted to Philip, "you may go halves if you please." And he added wistfully, "I would most cheerfully give a thousand guineas to win those fifty." [50]

CHAPTER XXII
The Candle Snuffer

DURING the four following years, destiny played cat to the mouse of Chesterfield's hopes. It was a tantalizing, cruel process; but if we consider the whole of his life, this culmination would seem to have been inevitable; there were no accidental factors in it; it was a case of attempting the impossible and of reaping what had been sown. Philip Stanhope's ineptitude and illegitimacy were the obvious difficulties; but his father's long and bitter opposition to the King played an equally important role. These were the days when the anxious Earl, yearning over his son's career, must have been haunted by the ghosts of old lampoons and clever witticisms with which he had once amused the "Patriots" at the expense of George II, Queen Caroline, and Walpole.

Since then he had served with distinction in the cabinet, and had retired on good terms with the King to a steady support of the ministry in the House of Lords; but the ridicule and antagonism of ten years was not to be forgotten on the score of some public services and suave courtliness. The old, cruel barbs, the unforgivable insults, still rankled. George Augustus, in the late afternoon of his life, may have grown to tolerate Chesterfield, all the more so that Lady Yarmouth favored him, but there is no reason to believe that he felt a warmer sentiment. It was the past with its feuds and its bitterness that continued now to balk and impoverish young Stanhope's future.

There were first the hopes that centered about Philip's presentation to King George at Hanover in the summer of 1752, after several months of additional polishing in Paris. It was by nature of a trial flight to test the royal favor; and from the reception accorded him much could be predicted. For this Chesterfield mustered all his influence and experience. Philip traveled north primed for every eventuality. Lodgings next to the Duke of Newcastle's house in Hanover were engaged for him; a relative, Mr. Stanhope Aspinwall, one of the Stanhope clan, stood ready to serve him at court; he was instructed what people to cultivate and how to cultivate them; what reefs to avoid and what channels to follow.[1]

But the event was discouraging. The King, who might have raised objections on the score of Stanhope's birth, received him, indeed, but with so wooden a countenance and so formal a manner that no comfort could be derived from the ceremony.[2] On the other hand, in compensation, Newcastle showed himself unexpectedly kind. To Chesterfield's delight, he proposed, unsolicited, the Residenceship at Venice as an appointment for Philip's diplomatic debut. Nothing could be better. The Earl wrote him a letter overflowing with an almost pathetic gratitude,[3] communicated the good news to Dayrolles and the Marquise, regarded this prospect as eclipsing the King's lukewarm reception.[4] Meanwhile, awaiting his commission, Philip should broaden his experience of courts by visiting Dayrolles at Brussels and under his chaperonage frequent the good company surrounding Prince Charles of Lorraine.

But here again the specter of Stanhope's illegitimacy blocked his path. The Imperial Minister, Marquis Botta, vented his indignation upon Dayrolles for daring to present a person of Philip's birth to His Royal Highness, the Emperor's own brother, and thus misleading the Prince into inviting such a person to his table. In vain Dayrolles replied that he could not see why a gentleman who had been well received by the Kings of Sicily and Poland, who had been presented by Lord Albemarle to the King of France, and by the Duke of Newcastle to the King of England, might not have the honor likewise of being presented to Prince Charles of Lorraine;[5] the proprieties had been outraged, and the best Dayrolles could obtain was that Marquis Botta would keep silent on the matter, and that Stanhope should leave Brussels.

Considering Venice, however, such a contretemps, ominous as it was, could be ignored. It was upon the confirmation of this appointment that Chesterfield bent his energy during the following year. And for once everything promised well. There were no other aspirants to the post; Newcastle remained favorable; the

Lady Yarmouth lent her influence.[6] Philip was fetched home from France to attend three or four of the royal levees; the Earl prepared Newcastle with arguments to meet any objection on the part of the King;[7] indeed, he regarded the affair as settled.[8] Only George Augustus himself said nothing. It amused him perhaps to keep his old and now harmless enemy dangling hat in hand and supplicating for a trifle.

For in the end he refused bluntly to appoint young Stanhope, on the ground once more of his bar sinister.

It was a pretext which had not been intended to deceive, nor did it deceive Chesterfield. The bitterness of those days is reflected in his correspondence to Newcastle. He protested that he could but too justly apprehend that Mr. Stanhope suffered chiefly from his relation to him who was with the utmost truth and respect, his Grace's humble, obedient servant.[9] To Dayrolles, he owned that considering his conduct since he had retired from court, the facility he had shown when he might so easily have raised diffi-culties, and considering that he had declared that as this was the first, it should also be the last favor he would ever ask, he had not expected such a refusal.[10] To Madame de Monconseil, he lamented that "her little boy" was not going to Venice; he had believed himself sure of the commission, but at court was anything sure? "Yes, that much is promised there, and little performed."[11]

It had been a sad blow, but inveterate hope rallied to the Earl's comfort. There remained for the future one certain thing which depended merely on the length of his purse and of which neither King nor court could deprive him. This was that seat in parliament, of which he was fond of observing that, like the cloak of charity, it covered a multitude of sins. Let Philip once belong to the House of Commons, and he became of some value, at least, by reason of his vote, nor could his birth be cited officially against him without offending the pride of that supreme body of which he would have the honor of membership. But this was the least of it. Let him take part in the debates; let him (as was by no means impossible, nay, in view of his education, it was likely) shine as an orator there, and his career was established in spite of King, court, and all the bars sinister in the world.

Philip, however, should not hang about until the next parliament, to become imbued with English boorishness. Here were two years which could be excellently devoted to acquiring the coats of varnish which were still lacking, the manners and cosmopolitanism of courts. Therefore his valets once more buckled his valises; the inevitable post chaise appeared at the door, and he rolled off again on his endless travels.

He visited The Hague, and then the courts at Mannheim, Munich, Ratisbon, returned possibly to Dresden, and finally rejoined his father at Spa in the summer of 1754. We find him delighting the Earl by a reported love affair with a Madame Munter in Holland, or engaged in boar-hunting in the Palatinate, or well received at the court in Mannheim (though his father vainly searched the *Gazette de Cologne* for a mention of him),[12] or surviving a horrible journey from Mannheim to Munich, or driving in a race of sleighs in the latter capital, or buried in the snow upon a vain attempt to reach Berlin. We find the familiar type of instructions: Philip must rid himself of his forbidding, gloomy look, and accustom his countenance to smiles and his eyes to softness, he must put on *douceur* and a kind of convent manner.

But now that he is definitely slated for the next parliament, the letters are principally concerned with keeping him up with affairs in England and preparing him as a public speaker.

As the House of Commons is the theatre where you must make your fortune and figure in the world [wrote his father] you must resolve to be an actor, and not a *persona muta*, which is just equivalent to a candle-snuffer upon other theatres. Whoever does not shine there, is obscure, insignificant, and contemptible; and you cannot conceive how easy it is for a man of half your sense and knowledge to shine there if he pleases. . . . Your success in Parliament will effectually remove all *other objections;* either a foreign or a domestic destination will no longer be refused you, if you make your way to it through Westminster.[13]

When they met at Spa, he would pour out to him all his experience of the world.[14] The star of hope was once more in the ascendant. The misadventure at Brussels, the rebuff in regard to the Venetian commission, were past; the future beckoned reassuringly. And as the enchantment of distance, heightened by the passage of time, settled upon Philip, his father's confidence in him increased. "My only remaining ambition," he declared, "is to be the counsellor and minister of your rising ambition. Let me see my own youth revived in you, let me be your mentor, and, with your parts and knowledge, I promise you you shall go far." [15]

But, while Philip wanders from court to court, improving his German and his manners, seeking to assume a smiling countenance, and preserving his father's letters on his future as an orator, we may once more pause to marvel at this astounding training for a parliamentary career. There is no need to ask what sort of preparation for life such fashionable vagrancy could give, this existence in posthouses and post chaises, the crowd of acquaintances, Swiss, German, Italian, Dutch, French, the homelessness, the constant fluidity of everything. What integration, what depth of personality, would be possible in the circumstances? The answer to that is obvious. But as a preparation for parliament, one is bound to confess an absolute amazement at its ineptitude.

Instead of making love to Madame Munter at The Hague, why was Philip not paying court to some woman of influence in England? Instead of perfecting his German, why was he not polishing his English? Instead of dangling at Electoral courts on the Continent, why was he not listening to debates in the House? And one would imagine that fox hunting with Englishmen would be of greater value to his parliamentary career than pigsticking with Germans in the forests of the Palatinate. Why did he not put in these two years under his father's direct supervision making friends at home, rather than drifting, alien and unattached, through the Empire?

There is no reply to this except that once again the Earl's common sense and worldly wisdom seem to have broken down. From first to last, the thought of Continental urbanities, the intricacies of foreign courts, the glamour of distant carnivals, the cosmopolitan ideal of a citizen of the world, dazzled him. And once again, faced with the repeated blunders of this high priest of sense and reason, we are left with a certain skepticism and bewilderment.

Philip was brought into the new parliament through the interest of his old friend Edward Eliot, though Chesterfield paid for his seat.[16] In the spring elections of 1754, he was returned for Liskeard in Cornwall. Probably he accompanied his father back to England in the late summer of that year.

A twelvemonth's blank follows. Certainly he did not hasten from the ranks to become a paladin of debate. On that stage of his career, he clung to the role of candle snuffer with a vengeance, though vigorously prodded, we may suppose, by his eager father. At length, after infinite pains by the Earl to prepare him for his first appearance, on November 13, 1755, in that debate on the Address where the future Lord Mansfield distinguished himself, and where Pitt won new laurels, young Stanhope, notes in hand, delivered his maiden speech.

It was very bad. Stage fright seized him; he forgot his speech, lost his breath and stood in the midst of a vast silence. Then, consulting his notes, with what desperation one can imagine, the words came back to him and he managed to finish.[17] It was not a ridiculous failure, it was simply negligible. But he had failed. All the past, building toward this moment, had been in vain.

His father rallied loyally to him as usual, and wrote a letter which, in view of the circumstances and the disappointment, was the most delicate and the noblest of the entire correspondence. "I hear that you were stopped for some time in your career; but recovered breath, and finished it very well. I am not surprised, nor indeed concerned, at your accident; for I remember the dreadful feeling of that situation in myself; and as it must require a most uncommon share of impudence to be unconcerned upon such an occasion, I am not sure that I am not rather glad you stopped." Chesterfield never lied more gallantly. He added, "I am told that you are much mortified at your accident, but without reason; pray, let it rather be a spur than a curb to you."

But no prodding, no entreaties, no arguments, ever availed to lift Mr. Stanhope out of his seat again. The memories of that ghastly moment of silence were leaden weights. He was finished. His career as an orator ended at that point.

At that point too ended his father's hopes. In spite of the careless smile and brave encouragement, Chesterfield realized now at last that the long effort had been to no purpose, that he too had failed, that his work of art was only a daub. The last of those objects for which he had striven in his life had crumbled irrevocably. The first had been political greatness; he had failed to achieve the summit. The next had been typified by Chesterfield House, the stage of social pre-eminence; deafness and ill-health had sealed the doors. But there had still remained the fortunes of his son, a proud escape for thought and imagination, a renewal of his youth. He had reveled in their magnificence. He now perceived that that too had been an illusion.

He was not a man of theatrical phrase or gesture. It is probable that he only smiled, but there is visible in his writing from hence-forward that subtle difference between a dynamic concern in life and the hobbies of an invalid patrician, intent upon spending as cheerfully as possible his remnant of time.[18]

At this point also the great letters end. From now on the essay disappears; the rich style, the play of thought, the wealth of comment and allusion typical of the earlier years, vanish. The mask of Olympian parent is for ever discarded. We have only letters now of an indulgent, affectionate old man; but they are short, languid and in general undistinguished.

From the habit of an affection no longer rationally explained, he continued to push his son forward at every opportunity. That same year, by an adroit motion for adjournment in the House of Lords, he had saved the King from an embarrassing situation, and had gained favor at court.[19]

In part, no doubt, owing to this, the King concluded that Philip Stanhope's birth did not after all debar him from the foreign service, and in the following year Chesterfield was able to thank the Duke of Newcastle for appointing Philip to the lowest step of the diplomatic ladder. It was a post the very thought of which he had ridiculed in the days of his great plans [20] — the dingy, glamourless little post of Resident at Hamburg — but now he expressed his acknowledgment with tremulous thanksgiving.

> What shall I, what can I, say [he exclaimed] to express my gratitude for his Majesty's extreme goodness to me in the great favour which he has been pleased to do to Mr. Stanhope, and the most gracious manner in which your Grace informs me that he did it with regard to me? I can only beg of his Majesty to add one more and greater favour to it, which is that he will give credit to the sentiments of my heart, which my words can by no means express, and which, God knows, I am now too insignificant and useless to prove by actions.
>
> Your Grace's friendship to me upon many former occasions *ne s'est pas démentie* upon this, and my former sense of them could

not be increased by this, which has completed all that I could wish. I have now nothing left to ask for in the world, and you will never be troubled with me again, but sometimes to remind you of my gratitude, and of the sincere respect with which I shall ever be your Grace's humble obedient servant.[21]

But an aside to Dayrolles about that time gave his real opinion of the Hamburg Residency. "It is an obscure inefficient thing," he grunted, "fit for those who propose to stagnate quietly for the rest of their lives." [22] Beggars cannot be choosers. Old age is the harvest season of life's ironies; Lord Chesterfield's gratitude in behalf of his son for the post in Hamburg belongs to these.

It is significant that in a letter of advice to Dayrolles that same year regarding the education of his sons, he urged him not "so much to consider what you would choose for them as what they are likely to succeed best in." [23] It had taken the fiasco of a life to teach him that lesson.

Meanwhile he attempted to keep Philip in a good humor with himself, realizing that there is no defeat in the world like the consciousness of defeat. He let him know that the King approved of his official letters from Hamburg. He declared to him that if he had had the choice of an advantageous situation and a good debut in it, he could not have wished anything better than Hamburg and Philip's performance there. He schemed to throw the credit for an important negotiation with Russia into Philip's way; but the latter, too slow-witted to react quickly, let the occasion pass. He lobbied in vain to secure him the posts of Munich or Berlin. When the time came to press Newcastle farther, he prevailed on the latter to promote Philip from Hamburg to Ratisbon.[24] When Edward Eliot had refused Stanhope the borough of Liskeard in the next parliament, he persuaded Newcastle to bring Eliot to terms. No doubt by reason of the Earl's industrious "shoving," Philip became envoy to the Diet at Ratisbon, and then envoy extraordinary to the court at Dresden. It was here that Boswell knew him and admitted that although without graces he was "a civil, well-behaved young man." [25]

But though alert for his son's benefit, the parent of these closing letters is no longer the scintillating, masterful personality of the past. He has suddenly grown much older, much softer. "I begin to be sensible of the autumn of the year," he wrote, "as well as of the autumn of my own life." [26] The phrase "God bless you" stands regularly now at the end. "Make this Christmas as merry as you can," he wrote toward the last, together with a present of £200, "considering the little happiness left us, nothing is as unfortunate as melancholy" (*pour le peu du bon tems qui nous reste, rien n'est si funeste qu'un noir chagrin*).[27]

A sort of wistfulness crept into the letters. He wished that Philip would write more fully, in greater detail about himself. A note of chill and loneliness, a yearning to come in out of the darkness and draw up before the fire of mutual affection makes itself now and then apparent. He would share his son's friendships, gaieties. "Admit me to your fireside," he pleaded, "in your little room; and as you would converse with me there, write to me for the future from thence. . . . Have you formed what the world calls connections? . . . Have you either fine or well-bred women there? *Y-a-t-il quelque bon ton?*"[28] Always liberal of funds, he liked to picture his son's household in Dresden — four sedentary footmen and one running one — the German servants would be calling him *seine Excellentz*, and the French, Monseigneur.[29] How the old pride hung on!

Let Philip only admit him to his little room. . . . That would never have done! If he had, it is likely enough that servants and equipage, *seine Excellentz*, and the very Residency itself would have been blown into thin air. There was that much explosive left in Chesterfield. The little room was cozy and warm, no doubt; but it contained what the Earl would have considered more shocking than a Medusa: in other words, a wife, who was neither proud nor cold nor very bon ton, the former somewhat questionable Irish girl Eugenia Peters. And if at the time when he was enjoying the thought of his son's household in Dresden, he could have inspected it in person, Lord Chesterfield would have found it even larger than he thought by two grandsons of whom he had no notion. But this terrible secret was well kept.

In point of fact, one feels that, for all his yearning, he had never passed the threshold of the little room, at the door of which he had knocked so many years. He would enter there only on his own terms, and hence he could never enter at all. The confidential attitude, the gesture of comradeship, the pretense of abdicating authority, remained somehow unconvincing. Philip kept his inner sanctum free from that probing eye. In this respect, then, also,

Lord Chesterfield failed: he did not even win the confidence of that one being whom he loved best on earth. What had been lacking? Not love, but the perception of life's most important values.

On the other hand, though Philip has been held up as an example of treachery and ingratitude, it is hard to avoid the feeling that we, no more than his father, have been permitted a glimpse of his actual self. Could it be that, tired of the everlasting parade, the role he could never fill, the glittering ice palace of his life, he resolved to have one simple, humble place, warm and loving and all his own? Could it be that through the long ordeal of Paris, London, Bath, the German courts, and Paris again, through the ordeal of his father's ambition, which prescribed and furnished even the women he was to love — that through all this he remained loyal to a boyhood attachment? If so, there is something unexpectedly appealing in this forlorn romance. At any rate, we find it difficult to regret that at the end of his homeless life, he learned the meaning of home. It is true that he dared not face Lord Chesterfield, nor tell him the truth. He was no hero. But for this, are we to blame him, or the master who fashioned him?

As to the date of his marriage with Eugenia Peters, nothing so far is known. Lord Charlemont, our only source on this point, suggests that she accompanied him to Hamburg in 1756; and it is amusing to reflect that the gift of a hundred pounds sent him by the delighted Earl on the rumor of an affair with a supposed fine woman of that town,* may have ignominiously lined the purse of Philip's wife; but Charlemont himself is exceedingly vague, and disclaims any certainty.[30] Nor is it possible to learn much regarding the character of Eugenia. One suspects that circumstances later on hardened, and perhaps coarsened, her; but this is largely speculation.

Chesterfield's affection, then, outlived the shipwreck of his hopes; but, as we have already noted, it was rather the relaxed affection of old age. What his son did or left undone no longer interested him as in the past. "He has very good wares in his shop," he wrote Madame de Monconseil, "but he has no talent for exhibiting them to the best advantage, as he should. Finally, in spite of all the care I have taken to polish him, he is still too English." [31]

* *Supra*, p. 357.

It was the news of his son's declining health that revived a last flame of the instinctive tenderness which he had so carefully disowned in the past. There was no attempt now to disguise what he would once have called a womanish concern. Though half-dead himself, his anxiety brooded over Philip. He consulted doctors in London, gave his own opinions as to the nature and cure of his son's malady, concurred enthusiastically in his decision to escape winter by a visit to the South of France.[32] Dr. Monsey's powders, mares' and asses' milk, turnip diets and rhubarb, the differences between rheumatism and gout, figure a good deal in the letters at this point. As one visit to Provence had not proved sufficient, he secured a leave of absence of one year for Philip, agreeing to make up to him a deduction from his salary of forty shillings a day, for the payment of a chargé d'affaires; and bargained for him also the title and pay of Plenipotentiary on his return.[33]

This was in the spring of 1768. But Stanhope never returned from Provence. After an illness of some months, he died of the dropsy in a house near Avignon on November 16, 1768. There is some evidence that he became a Roman Catholic before the end, and was buried by an English priest, one Cyrus Carteret, at Vaucluse.[34] If any circumstances could have added to Lord Chesterfield's desolation upon receiving the news of his death, it would be this apostasy to "superstition."

But such a detail must have been eclipsed by the greater disappointment. It was Eugenia Stanhope, the hitherto unknown wife, who announced both her husband's demise and her own and her children's existence. So, upon the report of death, came knowledge that made even bereavement impossible: the realization of what, from his standpoint, could only be regarded as his son's perfidy, a deception not inadvertent or transient but calculated, a deceit, with all the equivocation it had made necessary, carried out over a period of years. All that he had given, all the thought, the care, the gold, the love, had once more, and now in this deeper, irrevocable sense, proved vain. For, indeed, far worse than the loss of Philip Stanhope must have been the bitter conviction that, in the truest meaning of the term, he had never possessed him at all.

Would he flinch, or lament, bluster, or proscribe? There was not the slightest murmur. A hint only of his bitterness may have revealed itself in that first letter to Mrs. Stanhope, where he agreed with her that, despite Madame du Bouchet's objections, she had done well in complying with her "late husband's" desires as to burial.[35] Something of the frost at his heart lingers in that phrase. But for the rest, he received the undesired woman kindly, if coolly; provided for his grandsons' education, showed them affection, cared for them in his will. In no passage of his life does he show himself greater, more admirable than here.

As to Chesterfield and Philip Stanhope, we can blame neither of them too much; we must pity them both. They were victims of a false philosophy in a world which makes no allowance for such error. Out of the labyrinth of pride and ambition, the little rush light of reason could not guide them, and love perished there.

It was a tragic muddle.

Epilogue

It does not do to be too frank with regard to yourself, or you will find that the world is accepting your own estimate, or accepting it at a discount. — Chauncey Tinker, *Young Boswell*.

The lives of great men are often enlarged by death to an increased influence. They begin a timeless career of universal bearing, magnified by legend, refracted by the personalities of innumerable critics. But many of the great dead would be amazed or appalled by the extent of their influence or the direction it has taken. Could even the prophetic Virgil have foreseen his office in Dante's hell? Or Shakespeare his matchless empire? Or Swift his kindergarten renown? Or Johnson his debt to Boswell? Or Chesterfield the fame of his letters? It is at this posthumous and wider career of the latter that we should glance briefly.

Following his death, there was none of that thunderous praise which Edward Jerningham had declared would stun the Earl could he have heard it. Obituary notices were adequate; they reviewed the events of his life; they gave examples of his wit; but they remained cool, or rather perhaps, vague.[1] His political achievements had long since become hazy in the public mind; at his death, it was primarily for his repartee that people remembered him. He had cultivated his talent for the epigram until, though spontaneous enough, his wit had also become a mannerism, a habitual method of expression associated with him and too often indiscriminately applauded. Years before his death Mrs. Montagu, writing to Lord Lyttelton, had remarked: "Pray tell Lady Hervey that I believe Lord Chesterfield is very well, for he utters an hundred *bons mots* a day, which would be impossible, even for him, if he were not in health." And again later she maintained that his lordship had "snipped his own wit into epigrams, and he always admires everyone who writes a kind of pert jargon."[2] So now at the end, it was not his eloquence nor his diplomacy nor his rule of Ireland that the death notices recalled, but his fame as a jester. Horace Walpole retailed his final bons mots, and exclaimed, "Is it not charming to be so agreeable, quite to the door of one's coffin?"[3] There had been already two anthologies of wit in which he had featured, but publishers now hastened to get out a third collection with the title *Lord Chesterfield's Witticisms*.[4]

Such old friends as Dayrolles and Chenevix grieved no doubt; but the note of public affection and regret is distinctly lacking. The preface to an edition of the *Witticisms* published five years later contains the following significant passage: "[He died] lamented by his friends, but as little noticed by the world as if such a man had never lived. Not a Muse wept over his urn, though many had distilled their incense in his ear, and many had fed at his board. So true it is, that, if we forget the world, we shall be forgotten by it, however great our merits." It could not be otherwise. He had never invited affection, nor, indeed, believed it possible that a man could have more than two or three intimate friends in the course of a life. His charm of manner had flattered without convincing, had enchanted the mind without touching the heart. Besides, he had remained unknown to the mass of the people, at best a remote, vague figure; and it is among the obscure, the unpretentious, that loyal affection is usually to be found; Love, according to Virgil and Johnson, is a native of the rocks. The beau monde, therefore, acted, as it always acts, with decorous indifference, until something should occur which would rouse its passion for criticism.

As might be expected, the first stimulus to polite gossip was the publication of his will.[5] Though never the business of the public, who remain naturally uninformed of the motives and circumstances governing its provisions, a will straightway becomes public property; and it is amusing to note how seldom it pleases everybody. Just as the Earl himself had joined the hue and cry upon the will of Lord Bath some nine years earlier,[6] so now in turn he suffered a like fate. And this was all the more inevitable, because his will to a marked degree expressed his personality; and both by its phrasing and its provisions attracted notice.

To those who, unlike himself, were not, as he put it, "satisfied with the pompous follies of this life, of which he had had an uncommon share," the article directing that "he would have no posthumous follies displayed at his funeral," and that he should be interred at the nearest burying place after his death,* at no greater expense than £100, would seem beneath his dignity and his rank. To the friends of Lady Chesterfield, the bequest of £1000 a year and Chesterfield House during her life, together with his rose diamond ring, seemed unpardonably shabby; and they abused him in no measured terms. Even this pittance, including the ring, was to be held in trust for his godson, the next Earl, who inherited all his estates in Buckinghamshire, Bedfordshire, Hertfordshire, Derbyshire, and Nottinghamshire, the diamond ring of the Duchess of Marlborough, and £2500 annually until he came of age, when, it was reported, he would receive near upon £20,000 a year.[7] Surely Melusina deserved more. To the sentimental, a gift of fifty guineas to William Strickland, his "old and faithful servant," and of forty guineas to Jacob Ubret, his "old groom, who had lived with him above forty years," together with two years' wages in addition, would seem wholly inadequate, not to speak of the still meaner gift of £500 to his former mistress, Elizabeth du Bouchet. To the friends of Eugenia Stanhope, nee Peters, it would be an outrage that he omitted her from his will, though he provided £100 yearly for each of her sons during their minority, and the interest of £10,000 upon their coming of age. To the Dean and Chapter of Westminster, it must have seemed a gratuitous insult upon the clergy as a whole that he bequeathed them £5000, to be forfeited by his godson if the latter ever kept a race horse, a pack of hounds, spent a night at Newmarket, "that infamous seminary of iniquity and ill-manners," or lost on any one day at a bet £500; because, as he explained, "he felt sure that if the penalty should be incurred, they would not be remiss in claiming it."[8] Even to Philip Stanhope, the fortunate heir, this provision may well have appeared tyrannical, as also another stipulation, inspired perhaps by the memory of the earlier Philip, permitting him to travel in Europe north of the Alps, but not in Italy, which the Earl declared that he now looked upon as "the sink of illiberal manners and vices."[9]

---

*He was accordingly buried in Grosvenor Chapel, South Audley Street, London. His remains were subsequently moved to the family burying place at Shelford.

Mrs. Delany, a friend of Lady Chesterfield's, admitted that the latter's income was £4000 a year, "but chiefly her own money." "He even left away her jewels," she continued, "which were chiefly purchased with her own money, and presents of the Duchess of Kendal's, but the law restored them to her as her own paraphernalia. I did not hear that he left anything considerable to his sister, Lady Gertrude Hotham. . . . So, vanity . . . had taken possession of him, and drove out all gratitude and natural affection." [10] Mrs. Elizabeth Montagu, a chronic criticizer of wills * and also a friend of Lady Chesterfield's, recorded that, "People are so disgusted at Lord Chesterfield's will that they speak slightly of his character, of which indeed he scratched the varnish at last; which is a pity, for it was the best papier mâché character I ever knew, and with good management might have preserved its gloss a great while." [11] Horace Walpole had his flick at the testament, and pitied Lady Chesterfield. [12] Even the magazines voiced their disapproval. [13]

We need not join in the defense or censure of this document, but should note merely that it evoked the thinly veiled dislike, a result of envy, misunderstanding, and prejudice, with which Chesterfield had been regarded. It set people buzzing, and served as appetizer to the next incident that loosed the controversy which has been going on ever since. This, of course, was the publication in 1774 of the *Letters to his Son*. [14]

A good deal of wrangling and hard feeling preceded it. Eugenia Stanhope, who, fortunately for the world, but unfortunately for her father-in-law's, her husband's, and her own reputation, seems to have been an energetic business woman, felt aggrieved at her omission from the will, and determined to lay hands upon what money she could, regardless of sentimental objections. The well-preserved series of letters from the dead statesman to his son formed an obvious asset. She cared little that they had been written in confidence, or that they perpetuated her husband as a blockhead and a boor: they represented a handsome cash value. In addition, she had retained a copy of Chesterfield's "Characters of Contemporaries," which he had loaned Philip, and had demanded back from her, [15] a most succulent morsel to publishers. With a

* She equally criticized the wills of Lord Bath, Mr. Vesey, the Duchess of Portland, and the Archbishop of Armagh.

shrewd eye for the right sponsorship, she approached Horace Walpole through Lady Louisa Lennox, soliciting a preface.[16] But that fastidious gentleman declined on various grounds of delicacy. Most of all, he did not care to offend the Stanhope family, who were alarmed about the matter. They secured an injunction from the Lord Chancellor, forbidding publication, except at length on two conditions: "first that the family might expunge what passages they pleased"; and second, "that Mrs. Stanhope should give up to them, without reserving a copy, Lord Chesterfield's *Portraits of his Contemporaries*." Thus restrained, Eugenia sold the letters to Dodsley for £1575,[17] a very considerable sum at that time.

What letters the family suppressed, we do not know, but they were probably few. After all, it was not Lord Chesterfield's reputation, nor that of his son, which concerned them, but their own; and it is unlikely that they found much to object to from that standpoint. Perhaps, in the end, it was cheaper to content the voracious Eugenia by leaving her to Mr. Dodsley.

Immediately, the *Letters* became and long remained the book of the hour. There were five editions within a year; seven further editions followed them within the next thirty years.* There have been new editions, adaptations, imitations, and selections ever since. There was a German edition published in 1774–1776, a French edition in 1775, an American edition in 1779, an Italian edition in 1856. The book has become an especial favorite in Japan, where its author is frequently compared to the greatest Japanese and Chinese philosophers. † In brief, the world became mindful of Chesterfield as never before. There were contemporary parodies, lives, a new collection of letters, dialogues, anecdotes, reflections. And parallel with all this, ran the drumfire of attack. ‡

* For the eighteenth-century editions see Bibliography.

† Dr. Shio Sahaniki of the Congressional Library, to whom I am greatly indebted for this information, writes as follows in regard to Chesterfield: "Evidently he was first introduced in Japan around 1870. A small portion of his *Characters* was translated into Japanese soon afterward and had a wide vogue. I have no record as to when his letters came to be known in Japan, but it must have been not long after 1870. Any high school or college text-book in English has a few selections from him. Also the *Encyclopaedia japonica* has a column on Chesterfield. He is often compared with the greatest Japanese and Chinese philosophers. Popularity of Lord Chesterfield in Japan is not difficult to explain since Japanese philosophy is essentially based on common sense and everyday ethics."

‡ See Bibliography.

For now the renewed, the permanent Chesterfield had stepped out upon the world stage. He expressed frankly and eloquently that motive which governs the major part of mankind — the desire for success, power, and popularity — and had formulated the technique, the discipline and artifices by which these could be attained. No wonder that the editions have crowded upon each other, that he was read with avidity. He satisfied the curious, instructed the ambitious, and charmed the elegant. But no wonder also that he brought down upon himself a storm of indignation, in part sincere and in part conventional.

Few were bold enough to defend the *Letters*. Voltaire, who would have been amused at the English reaction, praised them warmly, to be sure, and observed, "I am not certain that it is not the best book on education which has ever been written" (*Je ne sais si ce n'est pas le meilleur livre d'éducation qu'on ait jamais fait*). In a letter to Frederick the Great, he remarked of Chesterfield that "among Englishmen, he was perhaps the one who has written most elegantly" (*De tous les Anglais c'est peut-être celui qui a écrit avec le plus de grâce*).[18] Lord Charlemont, in the letter to Lord Bruce which we have so often quoted, gave this new *enfant terrible* among books an impartial, lucid and, on the whole, favorable criticism. One or two reviews dared to praise it mildly. But such voices as these were negligible as against the prevailing tempest. Arguments in extenuation of the Chesterfieldian ethics as reflecting a morally laxer age are discredited by the blast of righteous disapproval which the *Letters* encountered. Victorian England could not have shown itself more scandalized; no dubious book of recent times has evoked so stern a condemnation. The editions were eagerly exhausted; men and women, worldlings and divines, aristocracy and bourgeoisie alike, devoured the shocking pages, and then decried them with all the zest of outraged respectability. It is a curious example of how unregenerate interest and orthodox morality may be equally gratified. But in the process, Chesterfield's character paid the price of this compromise.

"I believe, tho' many admired, no one ever esteem'd Lord Chesterfield," wrote Mrs. Montagu, and went on acidly to remark that, far from liking to kick a dead lion, she did not wish to insult even a dead ape — a metaphor which she then proceeded to elaborate in connection with the Earl, to whom she denied either a strong mind or an honest heart.[19] Horace Walpole began a parody of the *Letters*, and in the introduction to it observed that "as Chesterfield's appetite for fame and approbation was both intense and indefatigable, he would assuredly not have omitted all the virtues of the heart, had he not been convinced that virtue was never rewarded with public applause. He, who in forty years never uttered a word without stopping to search for a better, could not have been so indolent as not to cultivate the duties of humanity, had he discovered that they tended to recommend the possessor." [20] The *Town and Country Magazine* declared that "as a man, he was certainly solely actuated by pride, vanity, and ambition." [21] A rhymester, burlesquing the *Letters*, maintained that he would teach his son:

> In pleasing segments how to pare your nails,
> Segments must please as long as taste prevails,
> The conduct of your breeches there make known,
> How best to pull 'em up, and let 'em down,
> Teach thee to handle with peculiar grace,
> The snuff-box, toothpick, and the toothpick case,
> And how to cut and eat a currant tart,
> And let your napkin, or your chin have part.[22]

A satirist, in a skit entitled *Lord Chesterfield's Creed*, conceived the idea of a sort of Chesterfieldian baptism. It read in part:

> I believe that this world is the object of my hopes and morals, and that the little prettinesses of life will answer all the needs of human existence. I believe that . . . all women are children, and all men fools, except a few cunning people, who see through the rest, and make their use of them. I believe that hypocrisy, fornication, and adultery, are within the lines of morality; that a woman may be honourable when she has lost her honour and virtuous when she has lost her virtue, etc.
> *Q.* Wilt thou be initiated into these principles?
> *A.* That is my inclination.
> *Q.* Wilt thou keep up the rules of the Chesterfield morality?
> *A.* I will, Lord Chesterfield being my admonisher.
>   *Then the Officiator shall say:*
> Name this child.
> *A. A fine gentleman.*
>   *Then he shall say:*
> I introduce thee to the world, the flesh, and the devil, that thou mayest triumph over all awkwardness, and grow up in all

politeness; that thou mayest be acceptable to the ladies, celebrated for refined breeding, able to speak French, and read
Italian, invested with some public supernumerary character in
a foreign court, get into parliament, perhaps into the privy-
council; and that, when thou art dead, the letters written to
thy bastards may be published, in five editions, for the instruction of all sober families.[23]

A correspondent in one of the magazines discovered that
Chesterfield's letters prove the doctrine of original sin by the
picture they give of human degradation. "All I now intend," said
he, "is to refer the advocates for the present dignity and purity of
human nature to the picture Lord Chesterfield everywhere draws
of it. Let them answer him." [24]

Whatever we may think of the literary merit of these passages, or
however we may deplore their manifest injustice, they will suffice
as examples of an almost unanimous public opinion.

Fundamentally, the charges against Chesterfield derive from a
single misdeed, that of too frankly exposing the human heart. In
brief, he was guilty of indecency in the wider meaning of the word.
And just as other authors have been eagerly read and then condemned for too bold a treatment of physical matters, so has he
suffered for discarding conventional idealism. We may flatter and
court a certain great man in order to get something out of him, but
we despise the fellow who recommends flattery as a means of
success. We may use dissimulation, but we dislike calling it so.
We may, in practice, be utterly selfish, but it is more respectable
not to admit it. We may be hunters of women and exploit them for
one purpose or another, but woe to the scoundrel who suggests on
paper the advantages of such a policy. Most of us who live in the
world, and would succeed there, are ostriches on one count or
another. If Chesterfield had written with less force and frankness,
if he had concealed his worldliness under lip service to the Anglo-
Saxon code, if, indeed, he could have foreseen that the public
would ever sit in judgment on his letters, he would have been
more, rather than less, worldly by keeping silence. He would have
influenced his son in precisely the same way; but he would have
escaped most of his subsequent fame and obloquy.

And this holds true even of his sincerest critics, those who, by
the spiritual quality of their lives, are in a position to judge him.

Even they have been led to attack the man rather than that almost universal attitude of which he was merely the outspoken representative and distinguished product. Cowper's formerly well-known lines are the classical expression of this group, and, at the risk of triteness, are worth repeating here. Addressing him as the immortal *Arbiter Elegentiarum,* Cowper wrote:

Petronius! all the Muses weep for thee;
But every tear shall scald thy memory.
The Graces too, while Virtue at their shrine
Lay bleeding under that soft hand of thine,
Felt each a mortal stab in her own breast,
Abhorr'd the sacrifice, and cursed the priest.
Thou polish'd and high-finish'd foe to truth,
Greybeard corrupter of our listening youth,
To purge and skim away the filth of vice,
That, so refined, it might the more entice,
Then pour it on the morals of thy son,
To taint his heart, was worthy of thine own!
Now, while the poison all high life pervades,
Write, if thou canst, one letter from the shades,
One, and one only, charged with deep regret,
That thy worst part, thy principles, live yet;
One sad epistle thence may cure mankind
Of the plague spread by bundles left behind.[25]

The point of quoting this is that it expresses no more than the truth, if applied to the universal system of worldly standards and values; but that it is obviously unjust to single Chesterfield out as the scapegoat of this system, because he dared to voice its tenets clearly instead of bowdlerizing them.

He was so far from being a foe to truth, though perhaps in another sense than Cowper's, that he has suffered chiefly for stating it. And unless, in the shades mentioned by the poet, he has learned more completely the value of discretion and of hypocrisy, unless, in brief, he has become a liar there, it is hard to see how he could write differently from thence about the world as he knew it. In this connection the far truer estimate of Voltaire should be recalled — "never an impostor." As for the corruption of youth and the poison pervading high life, it is somewhat farfetched to hold Chesterfield accountable for the avidity of Mrs. Stanhope and the enterprise of Mr. Dodsley.

We may forgive, however, the unworldly Cowper or Wesley [26] or Johnson for their censure of Chesterfield. It is hard, on the other hand, to forgive or to avoid despising the long line of worldlings, headed by Walpole and Boswell, who have jeered at him while they followed a course of life which his more practical honesty would have scorned. In those government sinecures, for which he never did one stroke of work, it might have chastened Horace Walpole to remember that that was one form of corruption with which the more virile Chesterfield had never stained his hands. In his infinite self-indulgence, he might profitably have recalled that for long years Chesterfield had served England at home and abroad. As for Boswell's strictures, it would not have hurt him to bear in mind that, whereas he had provided £10 a year for the maintenance of his illegitimate son and had forthwith ignored him,[27] the Earl, for all his "glossy duplicity," had expended untold treasure and affection upon the equally illegitimate Philip Stanhope, had given him all he could give and had suffered with him. When we read in the correspondence of Johnson's biographer some of the moral treacle which he now and then served up, it is with relief that we turn to Chesterfield's frank realism.

Such treacle became, during the nineteenth century, the proper seasoning of judgment upon the wicked Earl. The Victorians, while commending his brilliant qualities, were constrained to deplore his lack of principles. Young Carlyle lamented "the pitiful disposition of this Lord," the flattery, dissimulation, and paltry cunning that he recommended.[28] Young Macaulay considered the letters "trash" and their fame due only to Chesterfield's position in society.[29] Others, more indulgent, expurgated them and brushed up the author to conform to the more refined taste of their own age. This process, in recent times, has called forth indignant and eloquent defenders.[30] And so the dispute goes on.

But in much of this there has been an essential confusion. It is the one that lies at the heart of the modern world. In one form or another, we profess a faith which is ignored in practice. And between that faith and that practice there can be no satisfactory compromise. To denounce Chesterfield is hypocrisy, as long as the critic himself is more or less governed by the motives that Chesterfield too frankly avowed. There is not much superiority in soiled over dirty linen. And, on the contrary, it does not clear Chesterfield's memory to maintain that, taking the world as it is, he was better, wiser, more gifted than most men of the world. Under the pagan dispensation, his rank would be high; judged by the Christian ideal, he would have no rank at all. In the preceding study, we have attempted to show what, at their best, the values, the implications, and rewards of life are on the conventional, the prevailing, level.

In conclusion, we can think of no more appropriate words than those with which Dr. Maty long ago brought his memoirs of the great Earl to an end. After briefly resuming the achievements of his career, his talents in public and private life, the biographer added: "These were his excellencies; — let those who surpass him speak of his defects."

Notes

Notes

1. E. B. Chancellor, *Eighteenth Century in London*, p. 6.
2. John Dryden, *Annus Mirabilis*, verse CCXCV.
3. Dedicatory Epistle to the opera *King Arthur*.
4. Cf. his phrase, "Our roses blasted and discoloured, whilst the lillies triumph and grow insolent," Halifax, *Miscellanies*, 1704, p. 177, "Character of a Trimmer."
5. Halifax, *op. cit.*, p. 341, "Letter to Charles Cotton."
6. Bishop Burnet, *History of My Own Time*, 1818, vol. i, p. 298.
7. Lord Hervey, *Memoirs*, 1931, vol. i, p. 71.
8. Halifax, *op. cit.*, pp. 17–22, "Advice to a Daughter."
9. Now Nos. 17 and 18. E. B. Chancellor, *History of the Squares of London*, p. 100.
10. H. C. Foxcroft, *Life and Letters of Halifax*, vol. ii, pp. 148 f. See his letter to Bates, Jan. 7, 1673.
11. To his son, Aug. 17, 1765.
12. W. H. Fitchett, *Wesley and his Century*, p. 139.
13. Halifax, *op. cit.*, p. 311, "Draught of a New Model at Sea," 1694.
14. Now known as London House, the town residence of the Bishops of London. Chancellor, *History of the Squares of London*. This house was vacated by Lord Stanhope in 1695. Willard Connely, *The True Chesterfield*, p. 9.
15. *Hist. MSS. Comm.*, MSS. of the Earl Cowper, vol. ii, pp. 439–440, second Earl of Chesterfield to Lady Mary Coke, Nov. 18, 1701: "I went yesterday to the Lady Halifax for her favour and the Lady Grace Pirpon's [Pierrepoint] to Mr. Coke in his elections."
16. On the extent of the original grants of property to Michael Stanhope in the reign of Henry VIII, see J. L. Sanford and M. Townsend, *Great Governing Families of England*, 1865, vol. i, p. 214. These were increased by purchase and marriage. Through the alliance with the Dormers came the large Buckinghamshire estates of that family. Lord Stanhope seems to have owned a house in Lichfield. *Hist. MSS. Comm.*, MSS. of the Earl Cowper, vol. ii, p. 416, "Lady Mary Coke to Thomas Coke at the Lord Stanhope's house, at the Palace at Lichfield." His father appears to have settled

the estate of Brisancoate on him. *Ibid.*, pp. 439–440, Earl of Chesterfield to Lady Mary Coke, Nov. 18, 1701, and W. H. Craig, *Life of Lord Chesterfield*, p. 37, and *Letters of 2nd Earl of Chesterfield*.

17. H. C. Foxcroft, *loc. cit.*
18. There is a letter from Lady Betty's mother-in-law complaining that "Darbysher [*sic*] is a dull place, and needs something to make it pleasint." Mrs. Jameson, *Beauties of the Court of Charles II*, 3rd ed., p. 200.
19. The *Epistolary Correspondence of Francis Atterbury, Bishop of Rochester*, 1783, vol. ii, p. 24. Even at this age, Stanhope complains of deafness. Also about his physical condition — Lord Stanhope to Thos. Coke, March 13, 1903. *Hist. MSS. Comm.*, MSS. of the Earl Cowper, vol. iii, p. 22.
20. Maty ed., *Miscellaneous Works of Chesterfield*, vol. i, p. 269.
21. To his son, Nov. 27, 1747.
22. To Mrs. Howard, Nov. 13, 1725.

CHAPTER II

1. Pope's *Dunciad*, iv, ll. 139–174; Maty, *op. cit.*, vol. i, p. 268.
2. Maty, *op. cit.*, vol. i, p. 7.
3. John Locke, "Some Thoughts Concerning Education," 1693 (*The Educational Writings of John Locke*, Cambridge, 1922), pp. 52–53. *Cf.* also pp. 69, 74, etc.
4. Maty, *op. cit.*, vol. i, p. 8.
5. To his godson, June 20, [1764].
6. Carnarvon, *Letters of Chesterfield to his Godson*, Introduction, p. lx.
7. To A. C. Stanhope, Feb. 16, 1764.
8. Carnarvon, *op. cit.*, p. lix.
9. Swift, "An Essay on Modern Education," *Works*, Bohn edition, vol. xi, p. 47 ff.
10. Ned Ward, *The London Spy*, 4th ed., pp. 159 f.
11. *Letters of 2nd Earl of Chesterfield*. A number of the Earl's love letters to this lady before 1660, when she was still the young and beautiful Barbara Villiers, are extant.
12. *Cf.* Earl of Halifax: Verses written for the Toasting-glasses of the Kit-Cat Club, 1703. *English Poets*, vol. xxvi, p. 305.
13. To Bubb Dodington, Aug. 20, 1716.
14. To his son, June 28, 1742.
15. To his godson, Oct. 3, 1763.
16. Maty, *op. cit.*, vol. i, p. 8.
17. Macky, *Characters*.
18. Maty, *op. cit.*, vol. i, p. 35.
19. See Edmund Lodge, *Portraits*.
20. "The Chequer Inn," *Poems on Affairs of State*, 1703.
21. Macky, *Characters*.
22. *Letters of 2nd Earl of Chesterfield*, p. 66.
23. Maty, *op. cit.*, vol. i, p. 35.

24. *Poems on Affairs of State*, 1716, IV, 90.
25. To the Hon. George Berkeley, May 29, 1714.
26. To his son, Nov. 18, 1748.
27. *Ibid.*
28. "I am old enough to have heard him [Bolingbroke] speak in parliament." To his son, Dec. 12, 1749.
29. *Cf.* Pope, "*Rape of the Lock*," I, 138, etc., and Montagu, "Countess Dowager of ——"
30. "To the Hon. Charles Montagu, Esq.," *English Poets*, vol. xxxii, p. 176.
31. Verses from Lord Halifax, *Hist. MSS. Comm.*, Dr. Z. Grey's MSS., p. 308.
32. Maty, *op. cit.*, vol. i, p. 9.
33. *Cf.* H. Walpole, *Letters*, vol. i, p. 115, 1741, "Cibber and Swiny have long had their freedom given them of this end of the town," etc.
34. *Cf. Tatler*, No. 50.
35. Horace Walpole: *Reminiscences*, p. 73 *n.*
36. *Cf.* Advertisement to the first edition of Joseph Butler, *Analogy of Religion*. . . .

CHAPTER III

1. Quoted by Christopher Wordsworth and R. Brimley Johnson: *The Undergraduate*, p. 289.
2. *Guardian*, No. 94.
3. To Jouneau, Aug. 22, 1712.
4. *Cf. Connoisseur*, No. 97.
5. Wordsworth and Johnson, *op. cit.*, p. 161.
6. *Warren's Book*, p. 353 (ed. A. W. W. Dale), 1911.
7. Wordsworth and Johnson, *op. cit.*, p. 45.
8. *Ibid.*, p. 81.
9. To his son, Feb. 28, 1751.
10. Wordsworth and Johnson, *op. cit.*, p. 134.
11. To his son, June 24, 1751.
12. To Jouneau, Aug. 22, 1712.
13. To his son, Oct. 12, 1748.
14. *Cf. Letters of 2nd Earl of Chesterfield*, p. 147 f. "To one who walked 4 whole nights with mee in St. Jeames Park, and yet I never knew who she was." See also the letters to Barbara Villiers, or to B. L., p. 153, and the letter to Bates, June 7, 1673(?).
15. Lord Hervey, *op. cit.*, vol. i, p. 72.
16. "As it may be of use to you, I am not unwilling, though at the same time ashamed to own, that the vices of my youth proceeded much more from my silly resolution of being what I heard called a man of pleasure than from my own inclinations, etc." To his son, Mar. 27, 1747.
17. For example, letter to his son, Nov. 16, 1752.
18. To his son, Feb. 12, 1745.

19. To Jouneau, Oct. 12, 1712.
20. Steele in the *Guardian,* No. 94.
21. To Jouneau, Oct. 12, 1712.
22. Earl of Bath's description in *The World,* No. 17, 1753.
23. Wordsworth and Johnson, *op. cit.,* p. 217.
24. To Jouneau, Aug. 22, 1712.
25. Wordsworth and Johnson, *op. cit.,* p. 81.
26. To his son, Feb. 28, 1751.
27. Wordsworth and Johnson, *op. cit.,* pp. 300–301.
28. "One of the company mentioned Chesterfield as a man who had no friend." Boswell, *Life of Johnson* (ed. George Birkbeck Hill), vol. iii, p. 387.

CHAPTER IV

1. Joseph Spence, *Anecdotes.* London, 1820, pp. xix f. and xxv f.; also the first volume of Walpole's *Letters.*
2. To his son, Feb. 13, 1748.
3. Cf. *Délices des Païs-Bas* quoted in introduction to Thomas Bowrey's *Diary of a Tour in Holland, 1698.* Hakluyt Society, 1925.
4. *Comme je ne faisois que passer, je n'ai pas eu le tems d'y faire aucune connoissance.* To Jouneau, Aug. 10, 1714.
5. "I was with them from morning to night while I stayed there." To George Berkeley, May 29, 1714.
6. Maty, *op. cit.,* vol. i, p. 15.
7. For a description of these celebrated ramparts, see Thomas Bowrey, *op. cit.,* pp. 59–61.
8. To his son, Nov. 18, 1748.
9. To his son, Nov. 11, 1752.
10. W. S. Sichel, *op. cit.,* vol. i, p. 219.
11. Pope, *Moral Essays,* ii, l. 123 ff.
12. For a defense of Bolingbroke's conduct as minister, see Sichel, *op. cit.,* vol. i. Whether or not that statesman plotted the return of the Pretender before his disgrace and exile need not concern us here.
13. William Coxe, *Memoirs of John, Duke of Marlborough,* vol. vi, p. 264 f. A letter to Robethon from Marlborough at Antwerp, Nov. 30, 1713.
14. Wordsworth and Johnson, *op. cit.,* p. 181.
15. See in this connection Maty, *op. cit.,* vol. i, p. 16: "Lord Chesterfield's sentiments . . . appear to have been at all times perfectly uniform. From these he never varied," etc.
16. To Jouneau, Aug. 10, 1714.
17. Duke of Argyll, *Intimate Society Letters,* p. 428, Dr. Moore to the Duchess of Argyll, July 11, 1776. "If the Duke is to remain another winter on the continent, I humbly imagine he ought to pass it in some capital where his usual company may be people of high rank or of eminent character, Paris, the Hague, or Vienna."
18. Diderot, *Voyage de Hollande.* 1821. P. 276.

19. To his son, March 15, 1745.
20. John Ashton, *Social Life in the Reign of Queen Anne*, pp. 97, 131.
21. Bowrey, *op. cit.*, p. 51. Possibly this may have been the prototype of that at Twickenham.
22. Diderot, *op. cit.* pp. 221–224.
23. Bowrey, *op. cit.*
24. To his son, Oct. 12, 1748.
25. Maty, *op. cit.*, vol. i, pp. 14, 272.
26. To his son, Oct. 17, 1749.
27. "Detached Thoughts," Chesterfield's *Works* (ed. Mahon), vol. v, p. 403.
28. *Imitations of Horace*, Second Epistle of the Second Book, ll. 274–275; *Satires of Dr. Donne Versified*, Satire iv, l. 177; *Epilogue to the Satires*, Dialogue i, l. 68, etc.
29. Walpole, *Letters* (ed. Toynbee), vol. xiii, p. 157.
30. To Dodington, Sept. 8, 1741.
31. *Common Sense*, No. 32.
32. Mahon, *op. cit.*, vol. v, p. 403.
33. Lord Hervey, *op. cit.*, vol. i, p. 435.
34. Maty, *loc. cit.*
35. To Jouneau, Aug. 10, 1714.
36. To his son, July 21, 1752.
37. To his son, Nov. 3, 1749.
38. Sichel, *op. cit.*, vol. i, p. 498.
39. To Jouneau from Paris, Dec. 7, 1714.

CHAPTER V

1. Maty, *op. cit.*, vol. i, p. 21.
2. Maty, *op. cit.*, vol. i, p. 22.
3. See letter, dated Paris, June 27, addressed by Stanhope to some unknown person; and Lord Mahon's apparently correct argument for the date, vol. iii, p. 13 of his edition of Chesterfield's *Works*.
4. V. du Bled, *Société française*, 5ᵉ Série, Paris, 1905, p. 171.
5. *Ibid.*, pp. 169, 170, 225.
6. To his son, Feb. 7, 1749.
7. For example, Roger Coxon, *Chesterfield and his Critics*, London, 1925, p. 57.
8. Boswell, *op. cit.*, vol. i, p. 265.
9. To his godson, Dec. 12, 1765. See also letter to son, May 2, 1751, as to the various postures and facial expressions he was to learn from his French dancing master, Marcel.
10. H. Taine, *The Ancient Régime*, trans. John Duroud, pp. 141–142.
11. Epistle III (*English Poets*, vol. 36, p. 175): "His minuet-step was fashioned by Marcel."
12. Chesterfield's *Works* (Mahon's ed.), vol. ii, p. 86 *n*.
13. Taine, *op. cit.*, p. 157.
14. To his son, Oct. 29, 1739 (in French).

15. "You know what high favour Voltaire and Montesquieu are in with the English; yesterday we drank their healths at the Earl of Chesterfield's, after a meal which was by no means philosophical, that is to say frugal: this learned Nobleman has the misfortune of having a French cook." Letter of Madame du Boccage, quoted by Coxon, *op. cit.*, p. 222 *n.*
16. Taine, *op. cit.*, p. 134.
17. From Madame de Tencin to Chesterfield, Oct. 22, 1742.
18. Sichel, *op. cit.*, vol. ii, p. 8.
19. Sichel, *op. cit.*, vol. ii, pp. 115, 146–147; Maty, vol. i, p. 4.
20. To his son, Dec. 12, 1749; Feb. 14, 1752; Feb. 20, 1752; Feb. 12, 1754.
21. Spence, *op. cit.*, pp. 143, 169.
22. Sir Leslie Stephen, *English Thought in the Eighteenth Century*, vol. ii, p. 169.
23. Sichel, *op. cit.*, vol. i, p. 162.
24. Du Bled, *op. cit.*, p. 232.
25. Sainte-Beuve, *Causeries*, vol. iii, p. 323.
26. To his son, March 9 and Oct. 19, 1748.
27. Louis Maigron, *Fontenelle*, p. 105.
28. Louis Maigron, *op. cit.*, pp. 88–89.
29. Du Bled, *op. cit.*, p. 245.
30. Sainte-Beuve, *op. cit.*, pp. 331–332.
31. Mahon, *op. cit.*, vol. v, pp. 440–441.
32. To his son, Dec. 24, 1750.
33. The Duchess of Montagu to the Duke of Montagu, May 28 [*circa* 1720]. Francis Bickley, *An English Letter Book*.
34. Saint-Simon, *Mémoires* (ed. 1857), vol. xiii, pp. 102, 131–134.
35. To his son, April 13, 1752.

CHAPTER VI

1. *Parliamentary History*, vol. vii, p. 371. The vote was 284 to 162.
2. "I look upon the rebellion in Scotland as crush'd," he writes to the Duke of Newcastle, "as soon as our army gets there; the Highlanders will return to their dens, and trust to their damn'd country for their security. But I hope they will not find it there. And were I to direct, I would have a short Act of Parliament for the transporting to the West Indies every man concern'd in the rebellion, and give a reward for every one that should be apprehended and brought to transportation. This, I think, would be a much better way than hanging some of the rascals and letting the others go home for another rebellion." *Private Correspondence of Chesterfield and Newcastle*, letter of Oct. 5, 1745. (See also letters of Dec. 6, 1745, and March 11, 1746.)
3. W. H. Wilkins, *Queen Caroline*, p. 235.
4. Lady Cowper's *Diary*, p. 140.
5. *Ibid.*, pp. xi–xii, note by Spencer Cowper. Also Lord Hervey, *op. cit.*, vol. iii, p. 666.

6. "Lord Stanhope (son of Lord Chesterfield) carried off a pretty many, by mentioning in the strongest terms the memory of the late lord of that name [Earl Stanhope]." *Parl. History*, vol. vii, p. 747*n*. This was on Feb. 28, 1721.
7. *Cf.* the debate on this bill in the Commons, *Parl. Hist.*, vol. vii, pp. 606–627.
8. "Character of George II," by Chesterfield. See also his "Character of Queen Caroline." Bradshaw's edition of Chesterfield's *Letters*, etc., vol. iii, pp. 1402 ff.
9. Pope, *Letters* (Elwin-Courthope ed.), vol. ix, p. 256.
10. Lady Cowper's *Diary*, p. 131.
11. Walpole, *Conversations with Lady Suffolk*, p. 116.
12. Lady Cowper's *Diary*, p. 161.
13. *Cf.* the two contrasting statements in Lady Cowper's *Diary*, Feb. 2, 1716, and in 1720, pp. 65 and 134.
14. Lady Cowper's *Diary*, p. 2 *n*.

CHAPTER VII

1. "The Mistresses of George the First," Mahon's edition of Chesterfield's *Works*, vol. ii, p. 458.
2. Edward and John Chamberlayne: *Angliae Notitia* and *Magnae Britanniae Notitia*, or Yearbooks, especially for 1715 and 1718; also the Yearbook of Guy Miege for 1718.
3. "I was ill from standing so long upon my feet, for which reason I did undress me as soon as I came home, and stayed within for two days, to recover myself." Lady Cowper's *Diary*, p. 21.
4. *Suffolk Correspondence* (ed. Croker), London, 1824, p. 111.
5. Lord Hervey, *op. cit.*, vol. i, p. 1.
6. Montagu, *Letters and Works* (ed. Wharncliffe-Thomas, Bohn series), vol. ii, pp. 302–303.
7. To his son, Jan. 15, 1753.
8. Robert Walpole to Charles [Townshend or Fielding], July 24, 1743. Bickley, *op. cit.*, pp. 139–140.
9. Walpole, *Conversations with Lady Suffolk*, pp. 121 *n*. and 132–133.
10. *Letter-books of John Hervey, 1st Earl of Bristol*, vol. ii, p. 268.
11. *Bruce's Weekly Journal*, Dec. 30, 1719, cited by Wilkins, *op. cit.*, pp. 256–257.
12. Montagu, *op. cit.*, vol. i, pp. 352–353.
13. Lady Cowper's *Diary*, p. 127.
14. *London Gazette*, Nov. 4, 1717, cited by Wilkins, *op. cit.*, p. 226.
15. Maty, *op. cit.*, vol. i, pp. 39–40, mentions some of these as Chesterfield's friends.
16. A fairly complete list of this cultured circle is to be found in Gay's *Epistle VI* addressed to Pope.
17. *Weekly Journal* or *British Gazetteer*, Apr. 18, 1719, cited by Wilkins, *op. cit.*

18. Montesquieu, *L'Esprit des lois*, bk. xiv, chaps. 12, 13; *Défense de l'esprit des lois*, Œuvres, vol. vi, p. 159; *Pensées diverses*, Œuvres, vol. vii, p. 467; *Notes*, Œuvres, vol. vii, p. 486.
19. John Churton Collins, *Voltaire . . . in England*, p. 13.
20. Césare de Saussure, *Letters*, pp. 197–199. Cf. also Karl Ludwig von Pöllnitz, *Memoirs*, vol. ii, pp. 454, 459, 466.
21. Pope, *Letters* (Elwin-Courthope ed.), vol. ix, p. 274.
22. Lord Hervey, *op. cit.*, vol. i, pp. 70–74.
23. To his son, Oct. 22, 1750. In 1767, Lady Hervey terms Chesterfield "the oldest friend I have now in the world." *Letters*, 1821, letter of Sept. 6, 1767. Her last letters contain frequent references to his calls.
24. Pope, *Letters* (Elwin-Courthope ed.), vol. ix, p. 295 *n.*
25. *Suffolk Correspondence*, vol. i, p. 89.
26. In regard to Lady Suffolk, see especially Wilkins, *op. cit.*, p. 255; Horace Walpole, *Reminiscences*, pp. 65–66; the *Suffolk Correspondence;* Hervey, *Memoirs*, e.g., vol. i, p. 42.
27. Pope, *Letters* (Elwin-Courthope ed.), vol. ix, pp. 319–320.
28. Walpole, *Conversations with Lady Suffolk*, p. 102.
29. Mahon, *op. cit.*, vol. ii, p. 460.

CHAPTER VIII

1. Lady Cowper's *Diary*, p. 136.
2. Pope, *Letters* (Elwin-Courthope ed.), vol. vii, p. 421. Cf. Chesterfield's "Character of Pope" (Mahon, *op. cit.*, vol. ii, p. 464) which gives an account of a conversation with Pope on the subject of Atterbury, from whom Pope had taken his leave the day before.
3. *Suffolk Correspondence*, vol. i, p. 192. Letter of July 30, 1725.
4. "His great fame, and no man had more in his time, arose from his wit. . . . For a series of years nothing was more talked of than Lord Chesterfield's bons mots." Horace Walpole, *Marginal Notes on Maty*, vol. i, p. 7.
5. Spence, *op. cit.*, pp. 377–378. This is presumably the source of the same episode quoted by Maty (vol. i, p. 281) as "in one of the magazines"; but in Maty the poet is Pope, not Young, and the scene is Lord Cobham's. It should be noted that the Young anecdote is contained in Spence's Fourth Memorandum Book, dated 1758, i.e., thirty-eight years after the event it chronicles, at which time Chesterfield's fame had been long established.
6. Cf. Maty, *op. cit.*, vol. i, p. 31. And Chesterfield calls the Commons "that numerous and noisy assembly." To his son, Feb. 11, 1751.
7. To his son, Mar. 18, 1751.
8. Maty, *op. cit.*, vol. i, pp. 30–31. See *Parl. History*, vol. viii, p. 46, for debate on Augmentation of the Army, Dec. 26, 1722.
9. Wm. J. Thoms, *Book of the Court*, second edition, 1844, pp. 368–369.
10. To Bubb Dodington, Aug. 20, 1716.
11. Chesterfield, *Poetical Works*, p. 9.

12. *Memoirs of Lady Sundon*, London, 1817, vol. i, p. 104.
13. *Hist. MSS. Comm.*, MSS. of the Earl Cowper, vol. iii, p. 179, George London to Thomas Coke, who is making a journey "to see gardens and plantations as my Lord Chesterfield's, Lord Ferrers', Duke of Devonshire's, etc." See also Carnarvon's edition of Chesterfield's *Letters* for a reproduction of the engraving.
14. Anthony Hamilton, *Mémoires de Gramont* (the Garnier edition) p. 247.
15. Walpole, *Marginal Notes on Maty*.
16. *Hist. MSS. Comm.*, MSS. of the Earl Cowper, vol. ii, pp. 439–440; second Earl of Chesterfield to his daughter, Lady Mary Coke, Nov. 18, 1701.
17. Swift, *Correspondence* (ed. Ball), vol. iii, p. 303 *n*. This was in March 1726. Also Bishop of Waterford to Maty. Maty, *op. cit.*, vol. i, p. 282.
18. Maty, *op. cit.*, vol. i, p. 42.
19. *Letter-books*, *first Earl of Bristol*, vol. iii, p. 5.
20. Chancellor, *History of the Squares of London*, pp. 80 ff.
21. *Complete Peerage* (ed. Vicary Gibbs).
22. Cf. Maty, *op. cit.*, vol. i, p. 32, and *Parl. Hist.*, vol. viii, pp. 518, 565. The occasions were on upholding the privilege of the House of Peers, April 20, 1726, and on the vote of credit, April 18, 1727.
23. Walpole, *Conversations with Lady Suffolk*, p. 108.
24. *Dictionary of National Biography*, "George II."
25. Walpole, *Conversations with Lady Suffolk*, p. 112.

CHAPTER IX

1. *Parl. Hist.*, vol. viii, p. 566.
2. *Hist. MSS. Comm.*, MSS. of the Marquess of Townshend, p. 332, Horatio Walpole to Sir Robert Walpole, Aug. 7/18, 1727.
3. *Hist. MSS. Comm.*, MSS. of the Earl of Egmont, vol. i, p. 10. Diary of the First Viscount Percival.
4. Lord Hervey, *op. cit.*, vol. i, p. 279.
5. Horatio Walpole's letter to Sir Robert Walpole already cited.
6. Lord Hervey, *op. cit.*, vol. i, p. 72; Maty, *op. cit.*, vol. i, p. 46.
7. Maty, *op. cit.*, vol. i, p. 49.
8. *Hist. MSS. Comm.*, Stopford-Sackville MSS., vol. i, p. 99.
9. *Ibid.*, MSS. of the Earl of Dartmouth, vol. iii, p. 192.
10. *Ibid.*, MSS. of the Earl of Egmont, vol. i, p. 370. Diary of Lord Percival.
11. Pope, *Letters* (Elwin-Courthope ed.), vol. viii, p. 72.
12. Dobrée edition of Chesterfield's *Letters*, vol. ii, p. 35.
13. *The Craftsman*, vol. v, p. 305 (ed. 1731).
14. In addition to this correspondence, see the learned and detailed essay by Th. Jorissen, *Lord Chesterfield en de Republiek der Nederlanden.* Hist. Studien, vol. v, 1894.
15. Horace Walpole, *Reminiscences*, p. 10.

16. Chesterfield's correspondence with Townshend, Dobrée, *op. cit.*, vol. ii.
17. Jan. 15, 1732. Dobrée, *op. cit.*
18. Oct. 30, 1731. Dobrée, *op. cit.*
19. To his son, Aug. 21, 1749.
20. *Cf.* Chesterfield's "Account of the Government of the Seven United Provinces," which was drawn up at The Hague. Mahon, *op. cit.*, vol. ii, p. 401 f.
21. Mahon, *op. cit.*, vol. ii, p. 403 *n.*
22. To his son, June 23, 1752.
23. Comte de Wassenaer *au* Comte de Chesterfield, Nov. 20, 1746. Mahon, *op. cit.*, vol. v, pp. 441–442.
24. Maty, *op. cit.*, vol. i, p. 50.
25. To Mrs. Howard, May 18, 1728.
26. To his son, March 30, 1759.
27. *Dictionary of National Biography*, "Chesterfield."
28. To the Duke of Richmond [Oct. (?), 1728]. Dobrée, *op. cit.*, Appendix I, No. 2.
29. To Mrs. Howard, Aug. 13, 1728.
30. Dobrée, *op. cit.*, vol. ii, No. 453, p. 214; also letter to Baron Torck, Jan. 2, 1733, where he mentions his *affaires délabrées*. Also the *Suffolk Correspondence*, vol. i, p. 328, Croker's note: "It appears by the periodical papers of the day that Lord Chesterfield's birthday entertainments were in the highest style of splendour, profusion, and magnificence."
31. To Baron Torck, July 17, 1731, Nov. 1731. Dobrée, *op. cit.*
32. To Baron Torck, Oct. 5, 1731. Maty, *op. cit.*, vol. i, p. 63.
33. To Baron Torck, Aug. 24, 1731. Dobrée, *op. cit.* Also Maty, *op. cit.*, vol. i, p. 62.
34. To Mrs. Howard, July 13, 1728.
35. *Wit à-la-mode, or Lord Chesterfield's Witticisms*. London, 1778. P. 36.
36. Dobrée, *op. cit.*, vol. ii, Nos. 147, 148, 153, 154.
37. To Lord Harrington, June 19, 1731. Dobrée, *op. cit.*
38. To Lord Harrington, Oct. 26, 1731. Dobrée, *op. cit.*

CHAPTER X

1. To Mrs. Howard, Oct. 21, 1728.
2. *Common Sense*, Sept. 10, 1737. *Cf.* Horace Walpole, *Marginal Notes on Maty*.
3. Lord Hervey, *op. cit.*, vol. i, p. 69.
4. To Mrs. Howard, Oct. 21, 1728.
5. Maty, *op. cit.*, vol. i, p. 292.
6. To Townshend, Aug. 31, 1728. Dobrée, *op. cit.*
7. To Townshend, March 25, 1729. Dobrée, *op. cit.*
8. To Townshend, May 24, 1729. Dobrée, *op. cit.*
9. Maty, *op. cit.*, vol. i, p. 60.

10. *Universal Spectator*, Saturday, Oct. 25, 1729. Cited by Collins, *op. cit.*, p. 134. Chesterfield's next letter from The Hague is dated Aug. 22, 1730; but he had probably returned a short while before that.

11. Maty, *op. cit.*, vol. i, pp. 291–292.

12. On the grounds for assigning this illness to the year 1729–30 rather than to 1732, *cf.* Coxon, *op. cit.*, pp. 36–37, who, I think, proves the point conclusively. For Palmer's treatment, *vide* letter to son, Nov. 15, 1766.

13. Lord Hervey, *op. cit.*, vol. i, 119.

14. *Cf.* Coxon, *op. cit.*, p. 34, where he quotes from *State Papers* (Russia).

15. *English Poets*, vol. 73, p. 258.

16. John and Edward Chamberlayne, *Magnae Britanniae Notitia* for 1718, Part II, p. 8.

17. Maty, *op. cit.*, vol. ii, pp. 568–572.

18. Mahon, *op. cit.*, vol. iv, p. 156.

19. This has unfortunately been lost. Maty, *op. cit.*, vol. i, p. 42.

20. *Correspondance de Montesquieu*, Paris, 1914, vol. ii, pp. 140, 157, 186, 195, 208, 407.

21. Collins, *op. cit.*

22. *Cf.* Chesterfield's tribute to Arbuthnot's proficiency in his profession, in his "Character" of him. Mahon, *op. cit.*, vol. ii, pp. 465 ff.

23. Maty, *op. cit.*, vol. i, p. 40.

24. *Suffolk Correspondence*, Mrs. Howard to Chesterfield, Aug. 1728.

25. *Ibid.*, Swift to Mrs. Howard, Oct. 26, 1731.

26. *Cf.* letter to Baron Torck, June 23, 1732 (Dobrée, *op. cit.*), where he calls "Mme. la Brigadière," with whom Elizabeth du Bouchet had been living, the future aunt of Torck. The latter married Mlle. Jacoba Maria van Wassenaer.

27. For Elizabeth du Bouchet's birth and family, see Connely, *op. cit.*, pp. 112 and 485.

28. To Harrington, Jan. 29, 1732. Dobrée, *op. cit.*

29. To Harrington, Feb. 20, 1732. Dobrée, *op. cit.*

30. Maty, *op. cit.*, vol. i, part ii, p. 260, dated Feb. 26 (New Style), 1732.

31. Apparently on Friday, Feb. 28 (New Style). See Coxon, *op. cit.*, pp. 39–40, for a discussion in regard to Chesterfield's departure from The Hague, where he proves, contrary to former biographers, that his recall was simply because he was tired of the work there.

32. To Baron Torck, no date [1732]. Dobrée, *op. cit.*, vol. ii, p. 258.

CHAPTER XI

1. Maty, *op. cit.*, vol. i, p. 63.

2. Carlyle, *History of Frederick the Great*, vol. ii, p. 226.

3. To Baron Torck, March 3, 1732; also undated letter to Torck [1732]. Dobrée, *op. cit.*

4. To Baron Torck, June 23, 1732. Dobrée, *op. cit.*
5. To Baron Torck, Sept. 12, 1732. Dobrée, *op. cit.*
6. To Baron Torck, Jan. 2, 1733. Dobrée, *op. cit.*
7. "The younger Mlle. Shulemberg, who came over with her [the Duchess of Kendal] and was created Countess of Walsingham, passed for her niece, but was so like to the King, that it is not very credible that the Duchess, who had affected to pass for cruel, had waited for the left-handed marriage." Walpole, *Reminiscences*, p. 28.
8. Maty, *op. cit.*, vol. i, p. 284.
9. Diaries of William Windham, *Hist. MSS. Comm.*, 12th Report, Appendix, Part IX, p. 209.
10. Walpole, *Marginal Notes on Maty*.
11. Lord Hervey, *op. cit.*, vol. i, p. 11. Also *Dictionary of National Biography*, "Saint-John."
12. To Baron Torck, Sept. 12, 1732. Dobrée, *op. cit.*
13. *Suffolk Correspondence*, vol. i, pp. 283–284.
14. Louis Melville, *Life and Letters of John Gay*, p. 140.
15. For a full and luminous account of this measure, see F. S. Oliver's life of Sir Robert Walpole, *The Endless Adventure*, vol. ii, pp. 234 ff.
16. *Parl. History*, vol. viii, p. 1235.
17. Maty, *op. cit.*, vol. i, p. 64.
18. *Parl. History*, vol. viii, pp. 1268 ff., and vol. ix, p. 8.
19. The classical description of this episode appears in Lord Hervey's *Memoirs*.
20. Maty, *op. cit.*, vol. i, p. 65.
21. Maty, *op. cit.*, vol. i, p. 66.
22. Lord Hervey, *op. cit.*, vol. i, p. 279.
23. *The Craftsman*, No. 354, April 14, 1733, and numbers following.
24. To Lady Suffolk, Aug. 1733.
25. To Baron Torck, Oct. 14, 1733. Dobrée, *op. cit.*
26. "Winter," ll. 656 ff. *English Poets*, vol. 54, pp. 183–184. Other verses addressed to Chesterfield are: "Taste and Beauty, an Epistle to the Earl of Chesterfield," 1732; "Boeotia," by the Rev. William Dunkin, D.D. (*Foundling Hospital for Wit*, No. V, p. 56); "An Epistle to Philip, Earl of Chesterfield," 1745; "An Ode to the Earl of Chesterfield Imploring His Majesty's Return," 1737; "An Essay on Happiness," by Mr. Nugent, dedicated to Lord Chesterfield, 1737; "Tar Water," a ballad inscribed to Philip, Earl of Chesterfield, 1747; "Seventeen Hundred and Thirty-nine, or the Modern P . . . s [Peers]: A Satire Inscribed to Philip, Earl of Chesterfield," 1739. This is not an exhaustive list. There were also very frequent book dedications.
27. Hammond, "Love Elegies," xiii. *English Poets*, vol. 39, p. 327.
28. Pope, *Epilogue to the Satires*, Dialogue II, l. 84.
29. One verse ran:

More changes, better times this isle
Demand, oh! Chesterfield, Argyle,
 To bleeding Britain bring 'em:
Unite all hearts, appease each storm,
'Tis yours such actions to perform,
My pride shall be to sing 'em.

See also Lord to Lady Orrery (*Orrery Papers*, vol. ii, pp. 179–180): "God preserve him [Chesterfield], and whenever he dies, may he die in the glory of his integrity."

30. To Baron Torck, Oct. 14, 1733. Dobrée, *op. cit.*
31. To Marchmont, June 15, 1734.
32. Maty, *op. cit.*, vol. i, p. 84; also *Hist. MSS. Comm.*, MSS. of the Earl of Carlisle, p. 177, Lady Irwin to Lord Carlisle: Cobham and Chesterfield considered the chief promoters.
33. Maty, *op. cit.*, vol. i, p. 92.
34. Maty, *op. cit.*, vol. i, p. 89.
35. To Baron Torck, Oct. 14, 1733. Dobrée, *op. cit.*
36. On this remarkable episode, *cf.* Lady Mary Wortley Montagu's *Letters*, vol. ii, pp. 38–39 and p. 39 *n.*; and Turberville, *House of Lords in the Eighteenth Century*, p. 238.
37. *Orrery Papers*, vol. ii, p. 256, Earl of Orrery to Earl of Barrymore, April 14, 1739: "The Duke of Argyle and the Earl of Chesterfield show'd to what an amazing height the Strength of Eloquence and the Spirit of Wit can rise," etc. Also Lady Mary Wortley Montagu, *loc. cit.*, who reports that Mrs. Delany said that "my Lord Chesterfield spoke exquisitely well."
38. *Cf. Marchmont Papers*, vol. ii, p. 90. Chesterfield is mentioned as a close adviser of the Prince. *Marchmont Papers*, vol. ii, p. 85.
39. To Chenevix, March 6, 1742.
40. *Hist. MSS. Comm.*, 4th Report, Part I, p. 414.
41. *Vide supra*, p. 135.
42. *Hist. MSS. Comm.*, 10th Report, p. 513, Hamilton to the Duke of Ormonde, Jan. 27, 1738.
43. *Hist. MSS. Comm.*, 12th Report, Appendix, Part IX, p. 191.
44. Maty, *op. cit.*, vol. i, part ii, p. 1, republished from *Fog's Journal*, Jan. 17, 1736.
45. *Ibid.*, p. 9, *Fog's Journal*, Jan. 24, 1736.
46. *Ibid.*, p. 14, *Fog's Journal*, April 10, 1736.
47. *Ibid.*, p. 26, *Common Sense*, Feb. 19, 1737.
48. *Ibid.*, p. 42, *Common Sense*, May 14, 1737.
49. Horace Walpole to Mann, Feb. 18, 1741/2.
50. Lord Hervey, *op. cit.*, vol. iii, pp. 652, 755.
51. Also *Old England*, Feb. 5, 1743; Maty, *op. cit.*, vol. i, part ii, pp. 111 ff.
52. Horace Walpole, *Marginal Notes on Maty*.
53. *Old England, loc. cit.*

54. On Samuel Johnson's relation to the existing text of this speech, see Boswell, *Life of Johnson* (ed. Birkbeck Hill), vol. iii, p. 351 and *n*.
55. Maty, *op. cit.*, vol. i, part ii.
56. *Hist. MSS. Comm.*, MSS. of the Marquess of Abergavenny, p. 257, March 3, 1742/3, John Pringle to Blayney Townley: "The thinking people speak against it with great warmth and I fear reason also; the Earl of Chesterfield calls it the Drinking Fund. . . ."
57. *Cf. The Case of the Hanover Forces in the pay of Great Britain examined*, etc., by the Earl of Chesterfield and E. Waller, 1743; *The Interest of Hanover steadily pursued*, etc., by a Broad-bottom [the Earl of Chesterfield?], 1743, and the governmental pamphlet in answer, *The Interest of Great Britain steadily pursued*, 1743; and *A Vindication of a late pamphlet entitled, the Case of the Hanover Troops considered*, etc. [by Chesterfield and Waller], 1743.
58. To Stair, Dec. 3, 1739.
59. To Lyttelton, June 19, 1742.
60. To Marchmont, Sept. 8, 1742.
61. Particularly in the letters to Lyttelton in 1741, but the same attitude is reflected here and there in his subsequent correspondence.

CHAPTER XII

1. The marriage took place early in September, as appears from a letter to Chesterfield from Alexander, Earl of Marchmont, Sept. 13, 1733. *Marchmont Papers*.
2. Maty, *op. cit.*, vol. i, p. 71. Mrs. Delany to Mrs. Dewes, Feb. 21, 1744. Mrs. Delany's *Letters* (ed. R. Brimley Johnson), London, 1925.
3. *Suffolk Correspondence*, vol. i, p. 195.
4. For this appraisal of Lady Chesterfield *cf.* the following: J. de Pesters to Lady Denbigh, *Hist. MSS. Comm.*, MSS. of the Earl of Denbigh, Part V, p. 185; John Stanhope to Lady Denbigh, *ibid.*, p. 222; Elizabeth Wyndham to Lady Denbigh, *ibid.*, p. 252; Diaries of William Windham, *ibid.*, Twelfth Report, Appendix, Part IX, p. 209; Hervey's *Memoirs*, vol. i, p. 13; Walpole, *Marginal Notes on Maty*. For her love of music, Chesterfield to Huntingdon, March 16, 1753.
5. *Orrery Papers*, vol. ii, pp. 205–206.
6. To Baron Torck, Oct. 14, 1733.
7. Maty, vol. i, p. 71.
8. *"The Mistresses of George I,"* Mahon, *op. cit.*, vol. ii, p. 458.
9. Daniel Lysons, *Environs of London*, 1798, vol. iii, p. 99.
10. *Hist. MSS. Comm.*, MSS. of the Earl of Denbigh, Part V, p. 126.
11. To Marchmont, Oct. 5, 1733.
12. To the Earl of Essex, Nov. 29, 1733.
13. To Irwine, April 25, 1752.
14. To A. C. Stanhope, Oct. 12, 1765.

15. Dobrée, *op. cit.*, p. 2942.
16. Pope, *Moral Essays*, Epistle ii, ll. 2–4, 113–114.
17. Diaries of William Windham, *Hist. MSS. Comm.*, 12th Report, Appendix, Part IX, p. 209.
18. Chesterfield, *Poetical Works*.
19. This trait of Chesterfield's is noted by Horace Walpole (*Memoirs of . . . George II*, vol. i, p. 45) and by Lord Hervey (*Memoirs*, vol. iii, p. 651), who speaks of the "avowing denial that he generally put on when verses were ascribed to him which he had not written, or mistresses that he had not lain with." As to the authorship of "Fanny," *cf.* Isaac Reed's very full note in Daniel Lysons, *Environs of London*, vol. iii, p. 599.
20. *Cf.* his poem, "On Receiving from the Lady Frances a Standish and Two Pens."
21. Lovel to Essex, Dec. 21, 1735. Add. MSS. 27735, *f.* 1. British Museum.
22. Lovel to Essex, Jan. 25, 1736. Add. MSS. 27735, *f.* 66. British Museum.
23. Lovel to Berkeley, July 23, 1735, *Suffolk Correspondence*, vol. ii, pp. 125–126.
24. *Circa* 1740.
25. Charles Hanbury Williams, *Works*, vol. i, pp. 86, 87.
26. Thomas Birch to the Earl of Orrery, *Orrery Papers*, vol. ii, p. 19.
27. Lady Bolingbroke to Lady Denbigh 1737, *Hist. MSS. Comm.*, MSS. of the Earl of Denbigh, Part V, p. 125.
28. To Nugent, Sept. 20, 1739. Dobrée, *op. cit.*, p. 376.
29. Mahon, *op. cit.*, vol. iv, p. 536. Aug. 13, 1773.
30. To Huntingdon, May 18, 1751.
31. Walpole, *Marginal Notes on Maty*, vol. i, p. 71.
32. Walpole to Mann, May 3, 1749.
33. Walpole to Mason, July 16, 1778.

CHAPTER XIII

1. *Cf. Marchmont Papers*, vol. ii, p. 19; *Hist. MSS. Comm.*, MSS. of the Earl of Egmont, vol. ii, p. 53, Diary of Lord Egmont, Monday, March 11 [1735].
2. Maty, *op. cit.*, vol. i, p. 329.
3. *Cf.* Hogarth, "The Rake's Progress," the scene at White's.
4. For an account of White's Club see John Timbs, *Clubs and Club Life in London*. On a membership list of the Old Club (there were Old and Young Clubs at White's) dated Oct. 30, 1736, Chesterfield's name appears together with those of the Duke of Devonshire, Earls of Cholmondeley and Rockingham, Sir John Cope, Major General Churchill, Bubb Dodington, and Colley Cibber, *inter alios;* p. 94.
5. Walpole, *Marginal Notes on Maty*, vol. i, p. 43; Walpole to Bentley, Oct. 31, 1755.
6. Maty, *op. cit.*, vol. i, p. 284.

7. *Ibid.*, p. 14.
8. *Ibid.*, p. 43.
9. *Ibid.*, p. 284.
10. Walpole to Mann, May 12, 1743.
11. *Cf.*, *inter alia*, Chesterfield's letter to his son, Oct. 12, 1748; and to his godson quoted by Dobrée, p. 2942.
12. To his son, Feb. 7, 1749.
13. Maty, *op. cit.*, vol. i, p. 43.
14. Walpole, *Marginal Notes on Maty*, vol. i, p. 43.
15. *Ibid.*
16. Cf. Lady Mary Wortley Montagu to the Countess of Bute, *Letters*, vol. ii, p. 182.
17. *Une société aimable est, à la longue, la plus grande douceur de la vie, et elle ne se trouve que dans les capitales.* To Madame de Monconseil, July 31, 1747. And: *Il n'y a pas d'autre bon quartier d'hiver que Paris et Londres. Ibid.*, Oct. 29, 1747.
18. To Dr. Cheyne, April 20, 1742.
19. To Dr. Chenevix, June 15, 1754.
20. "I am going to Cheltenham tomorrow less for my health, which is pretty good, than for the dissipation and amusement of the journey." To his son, July 1, 1748.
21. Cf. Sitwell, *Bath*, p. 145.
22. Pope to Marchmont, July or Aug. 1743. Pope, *Letters* (Elwin-Courthope ed.), vol. x, pp. 168–169.
23. Maty, *op. cit.*, vol. i, p. 88.
24. Lady Mary Wortley Montagu to the Countess of Pomfret, Oct. 1738. *Letters*, vol. ii, p. 30.
25. See letter to his son headed Tunbridge, July 15, 1739, and for a description of the life there, *cf.* Lewis Melville, *Society at Royal Tunbridge Wells*.
26. To Crébillon, Aug. 26, 1742.
27. To Lyttelton, June 6, 1741.
28. See the letters to Robert Nugent from Spa, June 20 and August 1741. Dobrée, *op. cit.*, Appendix I, Nos. 5 and 6.
29. Maty, *op. cit.*, vol. i, pp. 100–101.
30. To his son, Aug. 1741.
31. "I fancy my lord Chesterfield's journey is not merely to share the gaieties and diversions of Paris; he will find the shades and streams in its neighbourhood a more agreeable *séjour* at this season of the year, and therefore, I suppose, will retire to Argeville, and consult the oracle that inhabits those groves about what measures will be proper to be taken to serve his country, and perplex the schemes of those who have not put him at the head of its affairs, at the meeting of the next session of Parliament." *Correspondence between Frances, Countess of Hertford, and Henrietta Louisa, Countess of Pomfret,* London, 1805, vol. iii, pp. 375–376. Cf. also Lady Bolingbroke to Lady Denbigh, July 19 [1741], *Hist. MSS. Comm., MSS.* of the Earl of Denbigh, Part V, p. 133.

32. To his son, Sept. 1, 1741.
33. To Lyttelton, Aug. 1, 1741.
34. Walpole, *Marginal Notes on Maty*, vol. i, p. 101; also letters to Mann, Dec. 10, 1741, and July 5, 1745.
35. Walpole, *Marginal Notes on Maty*, *loc. cit.* Horace Walpole was at the same hotel with Chesterfield.
36. Pöllnitz, *Les Amusements des eaux de Spa.* Eng. trans., 3rd ed., 1745.
37. To Nugent, May 9, 1741. Dobrée, *op. cit.*
38. Pöllnitz, *Les Amusements des eaux de Spa*, vol. i, pp. 112–113.
39. E. Beresford Chancellor, *Pleasure Haunts of London*, pp. 233–234. The data in regard to Ranelagh are drawn from this excellent article.
40. Walpole to Montagu, May 26, 1748.
41. The above list is taken from one given by Horace Walpole to Conway, Oct. 31, 1741, six months before the opening of Ranelagh.
42. *Hist. MSS. Comm.*, MSS. of the Earl of Denbigh, Part V, p. 250, Lady Townshend to Lady Denbigh, June 22, 1744. Cf. also *ibid.*, July 2, 1744.
43. Walpole to Conway, June 29, 1744.
44. Tobias Smollett, *Humphry Clinker.* Quoted by Chancellor, *Pleasure Haunts of London*, pp. 231–232.

CHAPTER XIV

1. For this episode see Horace Walpole's *Reminiscences*, Lord Hervey's *Memoirs*, and the *Marchmont Papers*, vol. ii, pp. 55–56. In 1735, at the age of fifty-four, Lady Suffolk married Chesterfield's old college friend, George Berkeley, who was twelve years younger.
2. "Character of Dr. Arbuthnot," Mahon, *op. cit.*, vol. ii, p. 467.
3. Cf. Pope's description of his long and heroic death, Spence's *Anecdotes*, pp. 151 ff.
4. Walpole to Mann, May 12, 1743. To judge from this letter, it was upon the Duchess's death that Chesterfield and his wife began to live together.
5. For Chesterfield's relations to Pope and to Warburton, *cf.* "The Character of Mr. Pope" (Mahon, *op. cit.*, vol. ii, p. 463); *Hist. MSS. Comm.*, MSS. of the Earl of Denbigh, Part V, p. 171, De Pesters to Lady Denbigh; Chesterfield to Warburton, June 4, 1745, and Dec. 31, 1747, and Dobrée, *op. cit.*, p. 1078 *n.*; Pope to the Duchess of Marlborough, 1743 (*Letters*, Elwin-Courthope ed.); Pope to Marchmont, July or Aug. 1743 (*ibid.*, vol. x, pp. 168–169).
6. Pope, *Moral Essays*, Epistle II, ll. 239–248.
7. Horatio Walpole to Robert Trevor, Feb. 1, 1739/1740 (*Hist. MSS. Comm.*, 14th Report, Appendix, Part IX). Cf. also *ibid.*, 12th Report, Appendix, Part IX, p. 208, Diaries of William Windham; *ibid.*, 14th Report, Appendix, Part IX, p. 256; Francis Hare, Bishop of Chichester, to Francis Naylor, Feb. 23, 1739/1740; Mahon, *op. cit.*, vol. ii, pp. 477 ff., "Character of Scarborough."

8. Maty, *op. cit.*, vol. i, p. 95.
9. Cf. Leslie Stephen, *English Thought in the Eighteenth Century*, vol. ii, pp. 370 ff. and pp. 447–448.
10. Feb. 28, 1738, *Marchmont Papers*, vol. ii, p. 98.
11. Collins, *op. cit.*, p. 344.
12. Lord Hervey, *op. cit.*, vol. i, p. 92.
13. Aug. 24, 1744.
14. *Wesley's Standard Sermons* (ed. Edward H. Sugden), 1921, p. 110.
15. Pope, *Dunciad*, Book II, l. 258.
16. W. H. Fitchett, *Wesley and his Century*, p. 146.
17. Walpole to Mann, April 2, 1750.
18. Wesley, *Journal* (Everyman ed.), vol. i, pp. 198 f., June 5, 1739.
19. *Ibid.*, vol. i, p. 413.
20. *Ibid.*, Jan. 25, 1744.
21. Cf. letter to Crébillon, Aug. 26, 1742, in which he criticizes Voltaire for his attacks on the principles of morality.
22. To Huntingdon, Oct. 9, 1756.
23. Bolingbroke to Marchmont, Nov. 1, 1748. *Marchmont Papers*, vol. ii, p. 377.
24. To Huntingdon, Dec. 6, 1765.
25. Lady Mary Wortley Montagu, *Letters*, vol. ii, p. 88 and *n*.
26. Sitwell, *op. cit.*, p. 137; Horace Walpole, *Journal of the Reign of George the Third* (ed. John Doran), London, 1859, vol. i, p. 190; note by Doran; S. Tytler, *The Countess of Huntingdon and her Circle*, London, 1907, p. 84.
27. Bolingbroke to Marchmont, Nov. 1, 1748. *Marchmont Papers*, vol. ii, p. 377. Later on, however, Bolingbroke seems to have attended a sermon himself, and, like Chesterfield, to have treated Lady Huntingdon with the greatest politeness, asserting, "You may command my pen when you will: it shall be drawn in your service. For admitting the Bible to be true [which he did not], I shall have little apprehension of maintaining the doctrine of predestination and grace against all your revilers." Sitwell, *op. cit.*, p. 137.
28. Sitwell, *op. cit.*, p. 137. He remained in the good graces of Lady Huntingdon. Writing to Whitefield, she referred to him as "dear Lord Chesterfield." Tytler, *op. cit.*, p. 85.
29. To Mann, April 17, 1775. Doran, in his edition of Horace Walpole's *Journal of the Reign of George the Third*, vol. i, p. 190 *n.*, states, I know not upon what authority, that Lady Chesterfield, at the Earl's death, summoned the famous Methodist divine, Rowland Hill, but the Earl refused to see him.
30. Du Bled, *Société française*, 5ᵉ Série, p. 240.

CHAPTER XV

1. The fullest and clearest account of this period is unquestionably that of Sir Richard Lodge, *Studies in Eighteenth-Century Diplomacy, 1740–1748*, London, 1930. See also the same author's intro-

duction to the *Private Correspondence of Chesterfield and Newcastle, 1744–1746*, Royal Historical Society, 1930; also Dobrée's
introduction to Chesterfield's *Letters*. Both give excellent résumés
of Chesterfield's political career at this time.

2. Lord Hervey, *op. cit.*, vol. i, p. 119.
3. To Trevor [?], Aug. 13, 1745 (Dobrée, *op. cit.*), and *Marchmont
   Papers*, vol. i, p. 91.
4. *Cf.* Philip C. Yorke, *Life and Correspondence of Philip Yorke, Earl
   of Hardwicke*, vol. i, pp. 389–390, Andrew Stone to the Lord
   Chancellor: "An absolute negative put upon the proposal of Lord
   Chesterfield's going to Holland and a declaration that he should
   have nothing, a peremptory command not to trouble him with any
   more *such nonsense;* that he had been forced to part with those he
   liked, but would not on any account be prevailed on to take into
   his service those who were so disagreeable to him, with other strong
   expressions to the same effect."
5. *Cf. Hist. MSS. Comm.*, MSS. of the Earl of Denbigh, Part V,
   p. 186, J. de Pesters to Lady Denbigh, Nov. 29, 1744: ". . . *savoir
   si après cela* [the embassy to Holland] *on luy donnera cette lieu-
   tenance que vous savez qu'il ambitionne; c'est une question.*"
6. *Marchmont Papers, loc. cit.*
7. *Cf.* J. de Pesters to Lady Denbigh, *loc. cit.*: ". . . *on veut envoier un
   homme de poids en Hollande pour demander une réponse décisive,
   et cet homme-là sera, je crois, Lord Chesterfield.*" The Broad-
   Bottomed Ministry was not formed until a month after this.
8. To Weston, June 7 and June 28, 1745. Dobrée, *op. cit.*
9. To Newcastle, March 5, 1745.
10. To Huntingdon, May 18, 1751.
11. *Cf.* Dobrée, *op. cit.*, p. 1334 *n.*
12. To Huntingdon, *loc. cit.*
13. To Newcastle, April 13 and March 10, 1745.
14. To Newcastle, March 30, 1745.
15. To Newcastle, Nov. 29, 1745. Killaloe rated at £1200.
16. To Newcastle, March 23, 1745.
17. *Hist. MSS. Comm.*, 10th Report, pp. 293, 295, Stephen Poyntz to
    Edward Weston, June 22 and Dec. 4, 1746.
18. He set sail from Holland on May 19, 1745.
19. Maty, *op. cit.*, vol. i, p. 320.
20. Maty, *op. cit.*, vol. i, p. 156.
21. For the form of this oath see Maty, *op. cit.*, vol. i, p. 161.
22. *Cf., inter alia*, letter to Prior, July 15, 1746.
23. Maty, *op. cit.*, vol. i, p. 320. Walpole in his *Marginal Notes on Maty*
    asserts that the person was not Gardner, but Howth, Archbishop of
    Tuam.
24. *Ibid.*, vol. i, p. 322.
25. *Ibid.*, vol. i, p. 163.
26. *Ibid.*, vol. i, p. 320.

27. *Hist. MSS. Comm.*, MSS. of the Duke of Somerset, p. 333, Edmund Spencer to Francis Price, Dec. 7, 1745.
28. Chesterfield, *Poetical Works*, p. 38.
29. *Ibid.*, p. 46.
30. To Prior, Sept. 23, 1746.
31. Maty, *op. cit.*, vol. i, p. 160.
32. *Ibid.*, vol. i, p. 323. Cf. also "A Poem on His Excellency the Earl of Chesterfield's Being About to Leave Ireland," *Foundling Hospital for Wit*, No. III [1746], ed. 1763; "Merit, A Satire Humbly Addressed to His Excellency the Earl of Chesterfield," Dublin, 1746.
33. Maty, *op. cit.*, vol. i, pp. 151–152, quoting the Bishop of Waterford.
34. Cf. Maty, *op. cit.*, and General Charles Howard to Lord Carlisle, April 19, 1746: Chesterfield "though fond of play, has discontinued the Groom-porters" and settled £40 a year on the Keeper to make amends for profits that might arise from the table. *Hist. MSS. Comm.*, MSS. of the Earl of Carlisle, p. 200.
35. "Cicero, whom he had constantly before his eyes as an orator, became also the object of his imitation in his government." Maty, *op. cit.*, vol. i, p. 152.
36. Cf. especially the letters to Thomas Prior.
37. Dublin, May 29, 1746. *Hist. MSS. Comm.*, MSS. in Various Collections, vol. vi, p. 68.
38. To Prior, June 14, 1746.
39. Cf. the Prior, Madden, and Sexton letters.
40. To Newcastle, March 11, 1746.
41. To ——, July 23, 1745.
42. To Prior, June 14, 1746.
43. To Prior, Sept. 23, 1746.
44. To Newcastle, Jan. 11, 1745/1746.
45. Maty, *op. cit.*, vol. i, p. 152.
46. Maty, *op. cit.*, vol. i, p. 165.
47. To Newcastle, Sept. 29, 1745.
48. Newcastle to Chesterfield, Oct. 9, 1745. Lodge, *op. cit.*, pp. 73–74.
49. To Newcastle, March 20, 1746.
50. Cf. *Marchmont Papers*, vol. i, pp. 182–186.
51. Diary of Lord Marchmont, Aug. 31, 1747. *Marchmont Papers*, vol. i, p. 188.
52. Maty, *op. cit.*, vol. i, p. 322.
53. Cf. letters to Dayrolles, July 3 and 17, 1747.
54. To Madame de Monconseil, Feb. 25, 1751.
55. To Newcastle, Feb. 27, 1746, and Newcastle's reply, March 5, 1746. Lodge, *op. cit.*, p. 121.
56. To Newcastle, March 20, 1746.
57. To Newcastle, Sept. 12, 1745.
58. To Newcastle, Feb. 27, 1746.
59. To Newcastle, March 11, 1746.
60. To Newcastle, April 22, 1746.

61. *Cf.* such letters as General Howard to Lord Carlisle, May 31, 1746: "I heard this morning Lord Chesterfield was to go to Paris." *Hist. MSS. Comm.*, MSS. of the Earl of Carlisle, p. 200; Baron Bowes to George Dodington, already quoted; Earl of Orrery to Rev. Mr. Birch, May 26, 1747, *Orrery Papers*, p. 320 — wherein the assumption is that he will not return.
62. Maty, *op. cit.*, vol. i, pp. 167–168.
63. *Orrery Papers*, p. 320.
64. *Hist. MSS. Comm.*, MSS. of Mrs. Stopford-Sackville, vol. i, p. 226, Thomas Waite to Lord G. Sackville, Aug. 27, 1754.
65. *Cf.* particularly a letter from the Primate [?] to George Dodington, May 26, 1752. *Ibid.*, p. 183.
66. Lady Bolingbroke to Lady Denbigh, April 7, 1746: "My lord Chesterfield *revient à la fin de se mois; il a fort reussy d'où il vient icy.*" *Hist. MSS. Comm.*, MSS. of the Earl of Denbigh, Part V, p. 148.
67. *Cf.* James Henshaw to Vice-Admiral Medley, April 4, 1746, *Hist. MSS. Comm.*, MSS. of Lady du Cane, p. 113; and General Charles Howard to Lord Carlisle, May 31, 1746, *ibid.*, MSS. of the Earl of Carlisle, p. 200; letter to Robert Trevor, Aug. 5, 1746.
68. He was appointed on Oct. 29. *Cf. Marchmont Papers*, vol. i, pp. 182–186; Dobrée, *op. cit.*, Introduction, p. 143.

CHAPTER XVI

1. *Marchmont Papers*, vol. i, p. 182.
2. To Trevor, Aug. 5, 1746: "I can submit to the opinions of others, but I cannot act against my own," etc. — with his reasons for refusing the Breda appointment.
3. Newcastle to Hardwicke, Oct. 28, 1746, Lodge, *op. cit.*, Appendix C, p. 146: "The great events of this morning cannot surprise you more than they did me."
4. *Ibid.*
5. Chesterfield told Marchmont that he had had an interview with the King of the most cordial nature, wherein the King had emphatically expressed his belief in him. *Marchmont Papers*, vol. i, pp. 182–186.
6. "Character of the Duke of Newcastle," Mahon, *op. cit.*, vol. ii, p. 483.
7. To Madame de Monconseil, Dec. 2, 1746.
8. "Character of the Duke of Newcastle," Mahon, *loc. cit.*
9. To Sandwich, Nov. 28, 1746.
10. To Sandwich, Dec. 23, 1746.
11. *Marchmont Papers*, vol. i, p. 80 (cited by Dobrée).
12. To Dayrolles, June 16, 1747.
13. To Dayrolles, June 17, 1747.
14. *Ibid.*

15. Quoted by Coxon, *op. cit.*, p. 99.
16. Quoted by Dobrée, *op. cit.*, Introduction, p. 145. The date of this pamphlet is 1747. Cf. also *A critical, explanatory, and interesting address to a certain Right Hon. Apostate* [the Earl of Chesterfield], 1747.
17. Walpole, *Reminiscences*, pp. 78–79.
18. Maty, *op. cit.*, vol. i, p. 324.
19. To Dayrolles, May 3, 1748.
20. Cf. *Marchmont Papers*, vol. i, pp. 275–276, Sir George Rose's note drawn from Horace Walpole. Cf. also note of a conversation between Lord Hardwicke and his son on the events of this time, Feb. 14, 1748, Yorke, *Earl of Hardwicke*, vol. i, p. 630.
21. To Dayrolles, June 9, 1747.
22. Cf. also letter to Dayrolles, Sept. 11, 1747.
23. To Dayrolles, Sept. 22, 1747.
24. Yorke, *loc. cit.*
25. Cf. Boswell, *Life of Johnson* under date of 1772, March 27.
26. To Madame de Monconseil, July 31, 1747.
27. To Madame de Monconseil, July 30, 1748.
28. To Madame de Monconseil, Sept. 5, 1748.
29. To Madame de Monconseil, Dec. 26, 1748.
30. To Dayrolles, Nov. 4, 1748; Feb. 24, 1749; April 27, May 25, June 19, 1750; to his son, Nov. 18, 1748.
31. To his son, March 31, 1749.
32. To his son, Feb. 16, 1748.
33. Cf. E. Beresford Chancellor, *The Eighteenth Century in London*, pp. 148–149; and letter to Dayrolles, March 31, 1749.
34. In Burlington House (1724) and at Wilton.
35. To Dayrolles, June 10, 1748; *Marchmont Papers*, vol. i, p. 276 *n.* (Rose's note).
36. E. Beresford Chancellor, *Pleasure Haunts of London*, p. 346.
37. The first mention of the house is in a letter to Madame de Monconseil, July 31, 1747, where the building is spoken of as already advanced. The first letter dated in triumph from the house is on March 31, 1749. But on Dec. 28, 1749, Chesterfield wrote the Bishop of Waterford that he expected to have workmen in the house some months longer.
38. To Madame de Monconseil, June 24, 1745.
39. To Dayrolles, Oct. 23, 1747.
40. To Madame de Monconseil, April 13, 1747; July 26, 1745; July 31, 1747; Feb. 15, 1748; March 15, 1748.
41. E.g., his intervention in behalf of the Prince of Montbazon and other French naval officers, who had been taken prisoner (letter to Madame de Monconseil, March 15, 1748), and his protest to the Duke of Bedford regarding the treatment of French prisoners (letter to Bedford, 1745).
42. Cf. Argenson, *Journal et Mémoires*, Paris, 1867, vol. v, p. 205.

43. *Cf.* Lord Marchmont's Diary, Dec. 24, 1747. *Marchmont Papers,* vol. i, p. 262.
44. To Dayrolles, Jan. 26, 1748.
45. Lord Marchmont's Diary, Feb. 10, 1748. *Marchmont Papers,* vol. i, p. 272.
46. Maty, *op. cit.,* vol. i, p. 183; *Orrery Papers,* vol. ii, p. 19, Feb. 20, 1748.
47. *Marchmont Papers,* vol. i, pp. 275–276 (Rose's note).
48. Walpole, *Memoirs of . . . George II,* vol. i, pp. 44 ff.
49. To Dayrolles, Feb. 23, 1748, and to Waterford, March 1, 1748.
50. *Hist. MSS. Comm.,* Eighth Report, Part I, p. 569.
51. In spite of Chesterfield's assumed ignorance of the authorship of this pamphlet (letters to Dayrolles, April 8 and April 19, 1748) in letters that were presumably opened at the post office, there can be little doubt of his participation. *Cf.* Mahon, *op. cit.,* vol. v, pp. 60–90. The final paragraphs have a very personal ring, especially pp. 89–90.
52. Horace Walpole, *Memoirs of . . . George II,* vol. i, p. 44.
53. To Dayrolles, March 22, 1748.
54. To Dayrolles, May 13, 1748.
55. To Dayrolles, Feb. 23, 1748. On the subject of Chesterfield's resignation, consult in addition to the *Apology* and other sources already mentioned, *The Resignation discussed. In which many false facts are detected . . . in a pamphlet, entitled an Apology for a late Resignation,* etc., 1748; *An impartial Review of two pamphlets lately published: one intituled An apology for a late Resignation, the other the Resignation discussed,* 1748; *An Answer from a gentlemen at the Hague to a letter from his friend in London, in regard to a late Resignation,* 1748. The following comments may also be compared:

"Lord Chesterfield's conduct was probably the result in great part of personal pique, and showed a remarkable lack of political wisdom and firmness at this crisis. His foreign policy appears to have been nothing more than peace at any price, an immediate termination of the war at any cost or at any sacrifice, a yielding up of the struggle without any regard to future consequences." Lord Hardwicke, quoted in Yorke, *op. cit.,* vol. i, pp. 628–629.

On the other hand, Lady Hervey, writing to the Rev. Edmund Morris, Feb. 8, 1748, maintained that he had resigned out of the same worthy reasons for which he had entered the ministry, that is, love of his country. "His capacity, with his integrity, might have saved us." Lady Hervey's *Letters.*

CHAPTER XVII

1. To Dayrolles, March 22, 1748.
2. To Chenevix, Dec. 28, 1749.

3. To Dayrolles, June 19, 1750.
4. To Madame de Monconseil, July 8, 1749.
5. To Madame de Monconseil, May 23, 1751. *Cf.* also letter to Dayrolles, March 9, 1749.
6. Maty, *op. cit.*, vol. i, part ii, "Miscellaneous Pieces," p. 109.
7. To Dayrolles, June 10, 1748.
8. To Dayrolles, July 18, 174?.
9. Maty, *op. cit.*, vol. i, pp. 197–199.
10. *Ibid.*, p. 198.
11. *Cf.* Strachey-Calthrop edition of the *Letters*, vol. ii, p. 130 *n*.
12. *Cf. Parl. History*, vol. xiv, pp. 981 ff., where the Earl of Macclesfield's speech on the occasion has been reprinted.
13. To Dayrolles, March 9, 1749.
14. To Dayrolles, April 25, 1749; and to Madame du Boccage, May 20, 1751.
15. To Dayrolles, Oct. 5, 1751.
16. To Dayrolles, Jan. 12, 1748.
17. To Sexton, April 8, 1752; to Madden, Sept. 15, 1748, among others.
18. To Huntingdon, Sept. 24, 1750.
19. To Madame de Monconseil, Jan. 1, 1750. *Cf.* Dobrée, *op. cit.*, vol. vi, Appendix II; Horace Walpole to Mason, March 13, 1777; Mahon, *op. cit.*, vol. iii, p. 168 *n*.
20. To Madame de Monconseil, July 8, 1749.
21. To Madame de Monconseil, May 23, 1751.
22. To Madame de Monconseil, Sept. 22, 1748.
23. To Huntingdon, Sept. 24, 1750.
24. To his son, July 8, 1751.
25. To Madame de Monconseil, Aug. 1, 1751.
26. To Madame de Monconseil, Aug. 17, 1751.
27. To Madame de Monconseil, Feb. 15, 1748.
28. *Letters Concerning England, Holland, and Italy by the Celebrated Madame du Boccage*, London, 1770.
29. To Dayrolles, May 25, 1750.
30. Boccage, *op. cit.*, vol. i, p. 8 (quoted by Coxon, *op. cit.*).
31. *Hist. MSS. Comm.*, MSS. of the Earl of Denbigh, Part V, p. 266.
32. *Cf.* letter to Madame du Boccage, May 20, 1751; Walpole to Mann, April 2, 1750.
33. To Huntingdon, Sept. 29, 1750.
34. To Madame du Boccage, May 20, 1751; Sept. 30, 1750; Oct. 13, 1750.
35. To Madame du Boccage, May 20, 1751.
36. To Huntingdon, May 16, 1750.
37. To Huntingdon, Sept. 3, 1750.
38. "The Earl of Huntingdon, who, next to you, is the truest object of my affection and esteem." To his son, Oct. 22, 1750.
39. Feb. 7, 1768. *Hist. MSS. Comm.*, MSS. of the Earl of Carlisle, p. 239. Italics not in original text.

40. To Huntingdon, Nov. 18, 1756.
41. To Huntingdon, May 16, 1750; to his son, Oct. 22, 1750.
42. To Huntingdon, Sept. 29, 1750.
43. To Huntingdon, July 11, 1751. Dobrée, *op. cit.*, vol. vi, p. 2961.
44. To Huntingdon, Nov. 25, 1751.
45. To his son, June 6, 1751.
46. To Huntingdon, March 3, 1751.
47. To Huntingdon, April 8, 1751.
48. To Huntingdon, Sept. 16, 1751.
49. To Huntingdon, Nov. 15, 1750.
50. To Huntingdon, Aug. 10, 1752.
51. *Ibid.*
52. To Huntingdon, Dec. 31, 1750.
53. To Huntingdon, Nov. 18, 1756.
54. To his son, Nov. 16, 1752.
55. To Chenevix, March 12, 1755.
56. To Chenevix, June 18, 1747.
57. Walpole to Mann, May 19, 1747.
58. To Dayrolles, June 23, 1734.
59. *Cf. supra*, p. 241 f.
60. To Dayrolles, June 23, 1747.
61. To Dayrolles, March 9, 1749.
62. To Dayrolles, Aug. 25, 1747.
63. To Dayrolles, Jan. 1, 1748.
64. To Dayrolles, Aug. 16, 1753.
65. See article on Dayrolles in the *Dictionary of National Biography*, with the appended bibliography.
66. To Newcastle, March 11, 1746. Dobrée, *op. cit.*
67. To Dayrolles, Sept. 2, 1748.
68. To Dayrolles, Dec. 6, 1748.
69. To Dayrolles, Feb. 23, 1748.
70. Walpole, *Marginal Notes on Maty*, vol. ii, p. 345.
71. Spence, *Anecdotes*, p. 369.
72. To Madame de Monconseil, Dec. 30, 1751.
73. Walpole to Mann, July 25, 1750; Feb. 27, 1752.
74. To Dayrolles, April 17, May 19, 1752.
75. *Hist. MSS. Comm.*, MSS. of the Earl of Denbigh, Part V, p. 278.
76. To Dayrolles, May 19, 1752.
77. To Dayrolles, March 13, 1753.
78. To Dayrolles, Sept. 15, 1752.
79. To Huntingdon, Aug. 10, 1752.
80. To Madame de Monconseil, June 30, 1752.
81. To Dayrolles, June 30, 1752.
82. To Madame de Monconseil, Nov. 11, 1752.
83. Pope, *Imitations of Horace*, Second Epistle of the Second Book, ll. 322–327.

CHAPTER XVIII

1. *The World*, Nov. 28 and Dec. 5, 1754.
2. Walpole, *Marginal Notes on Maty*, vol. i, part ii, p. 166.
3. Boswell, *Life of Johnson* (ed. Birkbeck Hill), vol. i, p. 264.
4. To Dayrolles, Jan. 1, 1754.
5. *The World*, No. 18, May 3, 1753.
6. For criticism of these "Characters" by a contemporary who was in a position to judge them, see the remarks by the second Lord Hardwicke in a letter to Mrs. Montagu, Dec. 20, 1776. Mrs. Montagu's *Letters* (ed. R. Blunt), vol. i, pp. 344–347.
7. To Dayrolles, Jan. 1, 1754.
8. To his son, Dec. 14, 1756.
9. To his son, Feb. 8, 1750; Oct. 4, 1752; April 1, 1748; Feb. 8, 1750.
10. To his son, n.d., Strachey-Calthrop, *op. cit.*, vol. i, p. 113; Jan. 1, 1753; n.d., *ibid.*, p. 111; Jan. 6, 1752; to Huntingdon, March 16, 1753; to his son, Nov. 28, 1752; April 26, 1748.
11. To his son, Oct. 4, 1752; April 13, 1752.
12. "The late Earl of Corke . . . in a letter from Blackheath in 1760 says: 'Our neighbourhood, though lordly, is good. Lord Chesterfield, except deafness, is still Lord Chesterfield. He speaks and writes with all the Stanhope fire. Lady Chesterfield is goodness itself,' etc." *Gentleman's Magazine*, June 1774, p. 268.
13. To his son, Nov. 4, 1757.
14. *Cf.* Walpole to Montagu, July 7, 1770. The idea of Chesterfield, though still living, as belonging to the past, is evident here.
15. Jerningham, Aug. 12, 1763. Dobrée's note.
16. Walpole, *Marginal Notes on Maty*, vol. i, p. 223.
17. Walpole to the Countess of Upper Ossory, March 27, 1773.
18. To Lady Suffolk, Nov. 6 and Nov.?, 1766; Lady Suffolk to Chesterfield, Nov. 12, 1766.
19. Walpole to Conway, Sept. 2, 1757.
20. To Huntingdon, Aug. 2, 1757.
21. To his godson, Nov. 7, 1765.
22. To his godson, June 19, 1770.
23. Carnarvon's ed., facing p. 283.
24. Jan. 25 and April 22, 1771. Dobrée, *op. cit.*
25. To A. C. Stanhope, Jan. 26, 1764.
26. Contained in a letter to A. C. Stanhope, March 19, 1764.
27. Philip Stanhope to his father, Arthur Stanhope, April 14, 1767. Carnarvon, *op. cit.*
28. *Cf.* Dayrolles, Sept. 10 and 24, 1772. In his instructions to Georges Deyverdun, he wrote: *Faittes lui prendre le ton de la bonne compagnie, fut-ce meme au depens de sa chasteté.* Gulick, *op. cit.*, p. 67.
29. To Robinson, Jan. 15, 1757.
30. Mahon, *op. cit.*, vol. v, p. 410 ff.
31. To his son, May 17, 1750.

32. Carnarvon, *op. cit.*, Appendix, pp. 78 ff.
33. Carnarvon, *loc. cit.*
34. *Cf.* Yorke, *op. cit.*, vol. ii, pp. 310, 366, 398.
35. *Ibid.*, vol. ii, p. 310.
36. To General Irwine, Nov. 21, 1768.
37. *Cf.* letters to Kreunigen, May 8, 1753; Dayrolles, June 17, 1756; July 4, 1757; Newcastle, Oct. 13, 1757; Walpole to Ailesbury, March 5, 1762; Waterford, Oct. 7, 1762.
38. *Hist. MSS. Comm.*, Stopford-Sackville MSS., vol. i, p. 108, Lord Sackville to General Irwine; and Chesterfield to Lord Dartmouth, May 24, 1766, *ibid.*, MSS. of the Earl of Dartmouth, vol. iii, p. 182.
39. To his son, Dec. 25, 1753.
40. To A. C. Stanhope, Oct. 12, 1765.
41. Walpole to Mann, Sept. 1, 1763.
42. To his son, Sept. 30, 1763.
43. To his son, Sept. 1, 1763.
44. To A. C. Stanhope, Oct. 12 and 22, 1765.
45. To Waterford, March 12, 1767. Stanhope died in 1770.
46. To Waterford, Oct. 1, 1764.
47. To Dr. Monsey, Nov. 8, 1757. Dobrée, *op. cit.*
48. To his son, March 16, 1759.
49. *Cf.* Walpole to Conway, Dec. 5, 1765. "He [Richelieu] is an old piece of tawdry, worn out, but endeavouring to brush itself up; and put me in mind of Lord Chesterfield," etc.
50. To Waterford, Dec. 9, 1759.
51. To his godson, Nov. 3, 1761.
52. To Dayrolles, July 24, 1752.
53. To Dayrolles, April 6, 1752.
54. To Waterford, Nov. 14, 1754.
55. Walpole, *Marginal Notes on Maty*, vol. i, p. 220.
56. To Waterford, June 9 and Sept. 12, 1761.
57. To his son, Nov. 28, 1765; Nov. 15, 1766.
58. To his son, Aug. 17, 1765.
59. Oct. 24, 1771. Maty, *op. cit.*, vol. ii, p. 291.
60. To his son, April 22, 1765.
61. To his son, Nov. 4, 1757.

CHAPTER XIX

(All dates in Chapters XIX–XXII refer to letters from Chesterfield to his son, unless otherwise described.)

1. Jan. 21, 1751.
2. May 27, 1748.
3. *The Educational Writings of John Locke* (ed. John William Adamson), 1922.
4. Aug. 8, 1743; Dec. 6, 1748.

5. Locke, *op. cit.*, "Some Thoughts Concerning Education," sec. 216.
6. *Ibid.*, sec. 66.
7. To Madame du Boccage, Nov. 26, 1750.
8. Feb. 26, 1746; March 23, 1746; April 3, 1747; Jan. 15, 1748.
9. March 29, 1750; Oct. 29, 1748; n.d. [Nov. 1749]; July 30, 1748. On the entire subject of Chesterfield's educational views, consult Kurt Schumann, *Die pädagogischen Ansichten des Grafen Chesterfields*, Leipzig, 1917, which may be commended as the most thorough and scholarly article on Chesterfield yet published. In addition to the particular matter with which it deals, it contains an invaluable bibliography of editions, commentaries, and the like, up to the date of publication.
10. April 30, 1745.
11. *Cf.*, *inter alia*, letter to his son, Jan. 8, 1750, which is an excellent example of this sort of thing.
12. William Law, *Serious Call to a Devout and Holy Life*, Chap. xviii.
13. Sept. 29, 1752.
14. Pope's jibe at Maittaire was suppressed as a favor to the Earl of Oxford. *Cf.* note by Calthrop in the Strachey-Calthrop edition of the *Letters*, vol. i, p. 31; also Mahon, *op. cit.*, vol. i, p. 5 *n.*
15. April 16, 1739 (so dated by Dobrée).
16. Sept. 30, 1738.
17. Oct. 4, June 19, 1738.
18. Oct. 8, 1739.
19. July 8, 1739.
20. July 15, 1739.
21. Wednesday [July, 1739?].
22. Oct. 17, 1739.
23. Saturday [1740?]; June 25, 1740.
24. Oct. 14, 1740.
25. [Oct. 1740], Strachey, No. 63.
26. June 28, 1742.
27. *Sed, ut plane dicam; valde suspicor te, in ea scribenda, optimum et erudidissimum adjutorem habuisse.* Bath, 1740.
28. Feb. 8, 1746.
29. Friday Morning [June 1743?]. He was, no doubt, the Mr. Codere mentioned by Maty, *op. cit.*, vol. i, pp. 169, 324, as minister of the French chapel in Berwick Street. It was the same chapel of which Monsieur Jouneau had been minister.
30. Aug. 8, 1743; April 16, 1745.

CHAPTER XX

1. Maty, *op. cit.*, vol. i, pp. 170–171.
2. E.g., Sept. 22, 1749.
3. *Cf. English Poets*, Fenton, vol. 35, pp. 389–391, a lengthy note on Harte.
4. *Hist. MSS. Comm.*, MSS. of Lord Charlemont, pp. 326–330, Lord

Charlemont to Lord Bruce, July 17, 1744. Also reprinted in Bradshaw's edition of the *Letters,* vol. i, Introduction.
5. Maty, *loc. cit.*
6. *Cf.* "Outlines of a Plan," by Chesterfield in regard to his godson's education. Dobrée, *op. cit.,* pp. 2437 ff. Also Gulick, *op. cit.,* p. 8.
7. Oct. 4, 1746.
8. Oct. 9, 1746.
9. *Ibid.*
10. *Cf.* Dec. 2, 1746.
11. *Cf. infra,* p. 325, and note 21.
12. Through Lord Charlemont, *loc. cit.*
13. Feb. 24, 1747.
14. Dec. 2, 1746.
15. April 3, 1747.
16. *Cf.* letters to Madame de Monconseil, June 24, 1745; Dec. 4, 1749.
17. Charlemont, *loc. cit.* It will be recalled that Chesterfield was an international figure, and that, in boasting of such a father, Philip was not talking about someone unknown. J. Burnaby writes from Bern on Dec. 7, 1746, to Edward Weston that "all the foreign News Papers are filled with Encomiums upon my Lord Chesterfield." *Hist. MSS. Comm.,* 10th Report, p. 295.
18. March 6, 1747.
19. To Dayrolles, July 3 and July 31, 1747.
20. To Dayrolles, June 23, 1747.
21. Oct. 2, 1747: "I send you here a sketch of yourself drawn at Lausanne," etc. If this was all, the thunderbolt was pretty mild, but if we may judge by the letter described to Madame de Monconseil, Feb. 25, 1751, which has disappeared, the reproofs in question may have been suppressed.
22. *Cf., inter alia,* the letters of July 30, Nov. 6, Nov. 24, 1747; March 1 and 25, May 27, 1748; and the letter to Dayrolles, Dec. 1, 1747.
23. Dec. 29, 1747; March 25, 1748.
24. May 27, 1748.
25. Dec. 11, 1747.
26. Oct. 2, 1747.
27. Feb. 22, 1748.
28. To Dayrolles, Dec. 1, 1747.
29. Oct. 9, Oct. 16, 1747; March 9, May 10, 1748.
30. Sept. 5, 1748.
31. July 6, Aug. 2, 1748; Nov. 12, 1750; Dec. 20, 1748.
32. Oct. 30, 1747.
33. To Dayrolles, Feb. 23, 1748.
34. *Cf.* letters of July 30, 1747; Jan. 2 and Feb. 9, 1748.
35. Aug. 2, 1748.
36. *Cf., inter alia,* letter of Dec. 20, 1748; also 1st par., Jan. 15, 1748; 1st par., Jan. 2, 1748.
37. June 21, 1748.

38. Dec. 20, 1748.
39. Dec. 18, 1747.
40. *Cf.* May 17, 1748. As late as July 14, 1763, the Earl renews his admonitions on this subject. "Write to your mother often, if it be but three words, to prove your existence," etc.
41. Dodsley's *Collection*, 1755, vol. iv.
42. To Dayrolles, Sept. 23, 1748.
43. Sept. 5, 1748.
44. Sept. 5, 1748.
45. Sept. 20, 1748.
46. Sept. 27, 1748.
47. Oct. 12, 19, 29, Nov. 18, 1748; Jan. 10, 1749.
48. June 23, 1752.
49. *Cf., inter alia,* letters of Oct. 4, 1752; Jan. 15, 1754; Nov. 26, 1757; Maty, *op. cit.,* vol. i, pp. 100–101, 307.
50. To Huntingdon, May 10, 1756; and letters to his son, Oct. 4, 1752; also Feb. 26, 1754, where he refers to some of his letters to Berlin as "calculated for a supposed perusal previous to your opening them."
51. Maty, *loc. cit.*
52. Carlyle, *History of Frederick the Great,* vol. v, p. 244, quoting from Walpole's *George II*. Frederick knew of and admired Chesterfield before 1741. He quotes him to Voltaire in a letter dated Jan. 10, 1740. Elsewhere he called him *le plus spirituel* and *le plus beau génie de l'Angleterre et en même temps le plus éloquent.* R. Koser and H. Droysen, *Briefwechsel Friedrichs des Grossen mit Voltaire,* vol. i, p. 320; vol. ii, p. 239 *n.*
53. Jan. 24, 1749.
54. Maty, *loc. cit.*
55. Feb. 28, 1749.
56. April 19, 1749.
57. Nov. 18, 1748.
58. April 19, 1749. The original plan had been to spend a year in Turin.
59. *La semaine qui vient, je pars pour un endroit qu'on m'assure ne sera pas moins divertissant, je veux dire Turin, où je resterai jusqu'au Carnaval; puis j'irai à Venise, de-là à Rome,* etc. To Jouneau, Aug. 10, 1714.

CHAPTER XXI

1. July 6, 1749.
2. Nov. 26, 1749.
3. *Cf.* May 6, 1751; March 26, 1754.
4. Sept. 12, 1749.
5. To Madame de Monconseil, June 13, 1749.
6. Feb. 5, 1750.
7. Jan. 25, Jan. 11, March 8, 1750.

8. Jan. 25, 1750.
9. Charlemont, *loc. cit.*
10. "Mr. Harte . . . told me in his last a thing that pleases me extremely; which was, that at Rome you had constantly preferred the established Italian assemblies to the English conventicles set up against them by dissenting English ladies. That shows sense, and that you know what you are sent abroad for." April 30, 1750. *Cf.* also Jan. 11, 1750.
11. "When you meet with such sort of Englishmen abroad, who, either from their parts or their rank, are likely to make a figure at home, I would advise you to cultivate them," etc. Sept. 27, 1749.
12. "I heard with great satisfaction the other day from one who had been lately at Rome, that nobody was better received in the best companies than yourself." June 5, 1750.
13. March 29, 1750.
14. April 26, 1750.
15. To Madame de Monconseil, June 28, 1750.
16. Nov. 8, 1750. *Cf.* also Jan. 10, 1749.
17. May 24, 1750.
18. July 9, 1750.
19. Dec. 26, 1749.
20. "I long for your picture, which Mr. Harte tells me is now drawing." Jan. 11, 1750.
21. June 5, 1750.
22. Nov. 19, 1750.
23. To Edward Eliot, Nov. 29, 1750. Dobrée, *op. cit.*
24. *Cf., inter alia,* Jan. 8, 21, Feb. 4, 1751.
25. Jan. 14, 1751.
26. May 6, 1751 (in French).
27. See *supra*, p. 73; and letters of Feb. 11, 1751, May 2, 1751.
28. May 2, 1751.
29. Jan. 21, 1751.
30. June 10, May 23, 1751.
31. May 10, 1751.
32. "He shows, methinks, too much indifference for the fair sex, and does not endeavour sufficiently to make himself agreeable." Dayrolles to Chesterfield, Nov. 3, 1752; Mahon, *op. cit.*, vol. iv, p. 42 *n.*
33. Jan. 21, 1751.
34. Feb. 28, 1751.
35. April 15, 1751.
36. May 16, 1751.
37. May 10, 1751.
38. June 30, 1751.
39. June 10, 1751.
40. May 23, 1751 (in French).
41. June 30, 1751.
42. Jan. 1, 1759.

43. May 16, June 13, 1751.
44. July 15, 1751.
45. March 11, July 15, 1751.
46. July 8, 1751.
47. For Chesterfield's account of Philip in England see letters to Irwine, Sept. 1; Dayrolles, Oct. 5; Madame de Monconseil, Oct. 7; Dayrolles, Oct. 15, 1751; Lord Charlemont to Lord Bruce, *loc. cit.*
48. To Huntingdon, July 11, 1751. Dobrée, *op. cit.*, Appendix I, No. 10.
49. To Madame de Monconseil, Oct. 7, 1751.
50. June 1752 (ed. Strachey-Calthrop).

CHAPTER XXII

1. *Cf.* June 23, 26, July 21, and the preceding non-dated letter, 1752.
2. To Dayrolles, Sept. 15, 1752.
3. To Newcastle, Aug. 11, 1752. Dobrée, *op. cit.*
4. *Cf.* letters to Dayrolles, Sept. 15, Oct. 18 and 25, 1752.
5. Dayrolles to Chesterfield, Oct. 20, 1752. Mahon, *op. cit.*, vol. iv, p. 49 *n.*
6. To Dayrolles, Aug. 6, 1753.
7. To Newcastle, June 30, 1753.
8. To Dayrolles, June 22, 1753.
9. To Newcastle, Aug. 9, 1753.
10. To Dayrolles, Aug. 16, 1753.
11. To Madame de Monconseil, Sept. 13, 1753.
12. *Cf.* Oct. 3, Nov. 26, 1753; Jan. 15, 1754.
13. Feb. 12, 1754.
14. March 26, 1754.
15. Feb. 26, 1754.
16. To Dayrolles, April 2, 1754.
17. *Cf.* Maty, *op. cit.*, vol. i, p. 207; Walpole to Conway, Nov. 15, 1755; letter to son, Nov. 17, 1755.
18. To Waterford, Nov. 21, 1756: "And for the rest when my time comes, and the sooner the better for I am weary, I am ready and willing."
19. To Dayrolles, May 2, 1755. Lord Poulett had moved an address to the King not to visit his Electoral Dominions. This Chesterfield quashed on April 24, 1755, by moving the adjournment of the House.
20. "Take my word for it, twice your merit and knowledge, without the art of pleasing, would, at most, raise you to the *important post* of Resident at Hamburg or Ratisbon." June 6, 1751. Philip Stanhope occupied each of these in succession.
21. To Newcastle, Sept. 17, 1756 (Dobrée).
22. To Dayrolles, Oct. 5, 1756.
23. To Dayrolles, June 27, 1756.
24. Sept. 17, Nov. 26, Dec. 31, 1757; to Newcastle, Feb. 15, 1759; Nov. 28, 1760 (Dobrée, *op. cit.*).

25. Cf. Maty, *op. cit.*, vol. i, pp. 213–215; Boswell, *Life of Johnson* (ed. Birkbeck Hill), vol. i, p. 226 *n*.
26. Sept. 17, 1757.
27. Dec. 27, 1765.
28. Sept. 30, 1757.
29. Sept. 14, 1764.
30. Charlemont, *loc. cit.*
31. To Madame de Monconseil, June 5, 1764.
32. E.g., Sept. 30, 1766.
33. March 15, 1768.
34. Cf. G. Bayle, *Les Anglais à Vaucluse*, 1898.
35. To Eugenia Stanhope, March 16, 1769.

EPILOGUE

1. Cf. the particularly full memoirs of Chesterfield in the April number of the *Town and Country Magazine* for 1773.
2. Mrs. Montagu's *Letters* (ed. Reginald Blunt), Nov. 25, 1764; June 2, 1768.
3. Horace Walpole to the Countess of Upper Ossory, March 11 and 27, 1773.
4. *The New Foundling Hospital for Wit. A collection of . . . . pieces in verse and prose . . . by Lord Chesterfield and other eminent persons,* 1768; *The Humours of the Times, being a collection of several curious pieces, in verse and prose. By the most celebrated geniuses . . . particularly Lord Chesterfield, Lord Lyttelton, Mr. Wilkes, etc.,* 1771. The first edition of the *Witticisms* was published in 1773. Another appeared in 1778.
5. *Gentleman's Magazine*, July 1773.
6. On July 20, 1764, Chesterfield had written his son regarding Lord Bath: "The legacies he has left are trifling; for, in truth, he cared for nobody: the word *give* and *bequeath* were too shocking for him to repeat, and so he left all in one word to his brother. The public, which was long the dupe of his simulation and dissimulation, begins to explain upon him."
7. Mrs. Delany to Bernard Granville, Sept. 16, 1774. *Life and Correspondence of Mrs. Delany,* Boston, 1879.
8. Cf. Mahon, *op. cit.*, Preface; and Walpole to Countess of Upper Ossory, March 27, 1773.
9. Cf. also the longer and stronger statement in his instructions to Georges Deyverdun, his godson's governor while on the Continent. Gulick, *op. cit.*, p. 66.
10. *Life and Correspondence of Mrs. Delany,* vol. ii, p. 228.
11. Mrs. Montagu's *Letters*, Dec. 27, 1773.
12. Walpole, *Marginal Notes on Maty.*
13. Cf. *Gentleman's Magazine*, June 1774, p. 268.
14. *Letters written by the late right honourable Philip Dormer Stanhope, Earl of Chesterfield, to his son, Philip Stanhope, Esq., late*

envoy extraordinary to the Court of Dresden. Published by Mrs. Eugenia Stanhope, from the originals in her possession. [April?] 1774. 2 vols. The second edition was published in four volumes.

15. Walpole to Mason, April 7, 1774.
16. This was as early as Oct. 14, 1773. *Hist. MSS. Comm.*, MSS. of the Earl of Bathurst, p. 696. Walpole to Lady Lennox. The publisher Dodsley made a similar request of Edward Gibbon, but in vain. Birkbeck Hill, Introduction to *Eighteenth-Century Letters.*
17. Mahon, *op. cit.*, vol. i, p. xxvi, quoting from a trial on the copyright before the Court of Session in Scotland.
18. Voltaire, *Œuvres*, vol. xlix, pp. 56–57; Koser and Droysen, *op. cit.*, vol. iii, p. 303.
19. Mrs. Montagu's *Letters*, vol. i, pp. 284–285, July 18, 1774.
20. Horace Walpole, *Works*, 1798, vol. iv, pp. 355 ff.
21. *Town and Country Magazine*, October 1778.
22. *The Graces, a poetical epistle, etc.*, 1774.
23. *Gentleman's Magazine*, March 1775, p. 131.
24. *Ibid.*, December 1774, pp. 561–562. Cf. also Mrs. Carter to Mrs. Vesey, June 21, July 29, 1774. Mrs. Carter's *Letters*, London, 1809.
25. Cowper *Progress of Error*, 1781.
26. See Wesley's *Journal*, under date of 1775, vol. iv, p. 57, for a bitter comment on Chesterfield.
27. C. B. Tinker, *Young Boswell*, pp. 22, 24–25.
28. Carlyle, *Early Letters*, London, 1866, p. 34.
29. Trevelyan, *Life and Letters of Lord Macaulay*, 1876, vol. i, pp. 320–321.
30. E.g., Churton Collins and Roger Coxon.

Bibliography

Bibliography

Bibliography

A bibliography of Chesterfield, to be complete, would require a separate small volume. His social, political, and literary importance, the variety of his interests and connections both in England and on the Continent, brought him into touch with most of the leading personalities of his time; and it would serve no useful purpose to enumerate all the sources of contemporary reference. Similarly, the corpus of satire and criticism, the bowdlerized or fragmentary editions which reflect the fame of his *Letters* during the past hundred and fifty years, need not be detailed here. The following list will present, therefore, only the chief editions of Chesterfield's letters and miscellaneous writings, the chief biographical sources, and the principal works of criticism or biography which either have been concerned with, or are closely related to, him. A few titles indicative of the reception accorded his *Letters* have been added by way of illustration. Further casual items may be found in the notes. The reader would do well also to consult the bibliographical data contained in such works as Sir Sidney Lee's article on Chesterfield in the *Dictionary of National Biography*, Coxon's *Chesterfield and his Critics*, Schuman's *Paedagogische Ansichten des Grafen Chesterfields*, and Dobrée's Introduction to his recent edition of the *Letters*.

For foreign translations of the *Letters* and for the first Irish and American reprints, as well as for early fragmentary publications of the "Characters" and *Letters to his Godson*, the reader should turn to Sir Sidney Lee's article.

A. CHIEF EDITIONS OF CHESTERFIELD'S LETTERS AND MISCELLANEOUS WORKS

1774. *Letters written by the late right honourable Philip Dormer Stanhope, Earl of Chesterfield, to his son, Philip Stanhope, Esq., late envoy extraordinary to the Court of Dresden.* Published by Mrs. Eugenia Stanhope from the originals in her possession. [April?] 1774. 2 vols. [Subsequent eighteenth-century editions are as follows: 1st to 5th edition, 1774; 6th edition, 1775; 7th edition, 1776; 8th edition, 1777; 9th edition, 1787; 10th edition, 1789; 11th edition, 1800; 12th edition, 1803.]

1777. *Miscellaneous Works of . . . Chesterfield . . . to which are prefixed Memoirs of his Life by M. Maty, M.D.* London, 1777.
[This contains the first collection of Chesterfield's essays, which had previously appeared in *Fog's Journal, Common Sense, Old England,* and *The World.* It contains various political speeches more or less authentic; his letter on taking leave of the States-General; his "Characters" of Montesquieu and Scarborough; his letter of thanks to the Académie des Inscriptions et Belles-lettres; etc. It includes a large part of his letters to personal friends, such as Jouneau, Madame de Monconseil, Madame du Boccage, Dayrolles, and Chenevix.]

1845–53. *The Letters and Works of . . . Chesterfield.* Edited with an introduction and notes by Lord Mahon. London, 1845–53. 5 vols. Republished in 1892.
[This contains all the material of the above editions together with numerous additional letters, etc., such as fourteen letters to his godson, a few of his poems, and all of the "Characters."]

1890. *Letters of . . . Chesterfield to his Godson.* Edited with an introduction and notes by the Earl of Carnarvon.
[This is the first publication of the two hundred and thirty-six letters in question. The edition contains an appendix of ninety-four letters chiefly from Chesterfield to his godson's father, A. C. Stanhope.]

1892. *Letters of . . . Chesterfield.* Edited with an introduction and notes by John Bradshaw. London, 1892. 3 vols. Republished 1913.
[This is based on Lord Mahon's edition and adds little to it.]

1912. "Some Unpublished Letters of Lord Chesterfield." *Nineteenth Century,* August and September 1912.
[This contains the thirty-eight letters to Baron Torck (1731–47). They have never been printed in their entirety.]

1923. *Letters of Chesterfield to Lord Huntingdon.* Edited with introduction and notes by A. Francis Steuart. London, 1923.
[The first publication of this interesting collection.]

1927. *Poetical Works of Lord Chesterfield.* London, 1927.

1930. *Private Correspondence of Chesterfield and Newcastle, 1744–46.* Edited with an introduction and notes by Sir Richard Lodge. London, Royal Historical Society, 1930.
[The first publication of this important collection.]

1932. *The Letters of . . . Chesterfield.* Edited with an introduction and notes by Bonamy Dobrée. London, 1932. 6 vols.
[An inclusive edition containing all the letters hitherto published, and with many additional and valuable items. The editor restricts himself entirely to the letters, and does not republish the essays,

"Characters," poems, and the like. It is in every respect the best edition thus far published.]

1937. *Some unpublished letters of Lord Chesterfield* [to his godson]. Edited with an introduction by Sidney Lewis Gulick, Jr. University of California Press, Berkeley, 1937.
[Extremely valuable by reason both of the letters themselves and of Professor Gulick's scholarly introduction.]

B. BIOGRAPHICAL SOURCES

In addition to Chesterfield's letters and miscellaneous works, the following may be mentioned:

(An) Answer from a Gentleman at The Hague to a Letter from his Friend in London, in regard to a late Resignation. London, 1748.

(An) Apology for a late Resignation. London, 1748. Probably inspired by Chesterfield.

ARGENSON, RENÉ LOUIS DE VOYER DE PAULMY, MARQUIS D'
Journal et Mémoires. Paris, 1867. See especially vol. v, p. 205.

ATTERBURY, FRANCIS
The Epistolary Correspondence of Francis Atterbury, Bishop of Rochester. London, 1783–84. [Chesterfield's relations with his father.]

BICKLEY, FRANCIS
An English Letter Book. [Containing several letters from the third Earl of Chesterfield and other interesting letters reflecting the background of Chesterfield's early life.]

BOCCAGE, MARIE-ANNE DU
Letters Concerning England, Holland, and Italy by the celebrated Madame du Boccage. . . . London, 1770.

BOSWELL, JAMES
Life of Johnson (ed. George Birkbeck Hill). Oxford, 1887.

BOWREY, THOMAS
Diary of a Tour in Holland, 1698. Hakluyt Society, 1925. [As a background for Chesterfield's early visit to The Hague.]

BRISTOL, JOHN HERVEY, FIRST EARL OF
Letter-books. Wells, 1894.

BURNET, GILBERT (Bishop of Salisbury)
History of My Own Time. [In regard to Halifax.]

CARTER, ELIZABETH
Mrs. Carter's Letters. London, 1809.

CHAMBERLAYNE, EDWARD AND JOHN
Angliae Notitia and *Magnae Britanniae Notitia,* or Yearbooks for 1715 and 1718.

CHARLEMONT, JAMES CAULFEILD, FIRST EARL OF
Letter to Lord Bruce. [See Bradshaw's edition of Chesterfield's *Letters,* vol. i, p. xxix. This gives an interesting account of Chesterfield's son, Philip Stanhope.]

CHESTERFIELD, PHILIP STANHOPE, SECOND EARL OF
Letters of Philip, 2nd Earl of Chesterfield. London, 1829.

(Lord) Chesterfield's Witticisms. London, 1773.

CIBBER, COLLEY
Apology (ed. Lowe). London, 1889.

COWPER, MARY, COUNTESS
Diary of Mary, Countess Cowper. London, 1865.

(The) Craftsman
[See especially No. 354, April 14, 1733, and numbers following.]

(A) Critical, explanatory and interesting address to a certain Right Hon. Apostate. London, 1747.

DELANY, MARY
Mrs. Delany's Letters (ed. R. Brimley Johnson). London, 1925.
Life and Correspondence of Mrs. Delany. Boston, 1879.

DIDEROT, DENIS
Voyage de Hollande. Paris, 1821. [An interesting eighteenth-century account of Holland.]

Expostulatory Letter to a Certain Right Honourable Person upon his Late Promotion. London, 1747.

FOSTER, JOSEPH
London Marriage Licences. London, 1887.

Foundling Hospital for Wit (ed. 1763).

Gentleman's Magazine
[See Index for references to Chesterfield.]

HERTFORD, FRANCES, COUNTESS OF
Correspondence between Frances, Countess of Hertford and Henrietta Louisa, Countess of Pomfret. London, 1805.

HERVEY, LORD JOHN
Some Materials towards Memoirs of the Reign of King George II. London, 1931.

Lord Hervey and his Friends, 1726–1738 (ed. the Earl of Ilchester). London, 1950. [Based on letters from Holland House, Melbury, and Ickworth. Numerous references to Chesterfield, e.g., to his marriage, his speeches in Parliament, his gaming, his conversational power, and other topics.]

HERVEY, MARY LEPEL, BARONESS
Letters of Lady Hervey. London, 1821.

HILL, GEORGE BIRKBECK
Introduction to *Eighteenth-Century Letters*. London, 1898. [Contains some interesting data relative to the publication of the *Letters* in 1774.]

Historical Manuscripts Commission
[For the volumes of this series used in the foregoing study, see the notes.]

(*The*) *Humours of the Times, being a collection of several curious pieces, in verse and prose. By the most celebrated geniuses . . . particularly Lord Chesterfield, Lord Lyttelton, Mr. Wilkes, etc.* London, 1771.

(*An*) *Impartial Review of two Pamphlets lately published: one intituled An Apology for a late Resignation, the other the Resignation discussed*. London, 1748.

JOHNSON, SAMUEL
Plan [of the Dictionary] in his *Works*. Oxford, 1825. [See vol. v, pp. 1–22.]

KOSER, R., AND DROYSEN, H.
Briefwechsel Friedrichs des Grossen mit Voltaire. Leipzig, 1908–11.

LOCKE, JOHN
The Educational Writings of John Locke. Cambridge, 1922.

LODGE, EDMUND
Portraits. London, 1835.

LOVEL, THOMAS COKE, BARON
Letters to the Earl of Essex. British Museum. Add. MSS. 27735, f. 1 and f. 66. [For Chesterfield's relations with Lady Frances Shirley.]

MACKY, JOHN
Characters of the Court of Queen Anne. Swift's *Prose Works* (Bohn edition), vol. x, p. 279.

MARCHMONT, HUGH HUME, THIRD EARL OF
Marchmont Papers (ed. Sir George Henry Rose). London, 1831.

MATY, DR. M.
Memoirs of Lord Chesterfield in the edition of Chesterfield's *Miscellaneous Works* cited above under A. [This is the most important biographical source.]

MIEGE, GUY
  Yearbook for 1718.

MONTAGU, ELIZABETH
  Mrs. Montagu . . . Letters (ed. Reginald Blunt). Boston, 1923.

MONTAGU, LADY MARY WORTLEY
  Letters and Works (ed. Wharncliffe and Thomas in the Bohn series). London, 1887.

MONTESQUIEU, CHARLES LOUIS DE SECONDAT, BARON DE
  Correspondence. Paris, 1914.

NEWCASTLE, THOMAS PELHAM-HOLLES, DUKE OF
  Private Correspondence of Chesterfield and Newcastle, 1744–1746 (ed. Sir Richard Lodge). Royal Historical Society, 1930.

ORRERY, JOHN BOYLE, FIFTH EARL OF
  Orrery Papers. London, 1903.

Parliamentary History of England, compiled by William Cobbett. London, 1806–20.

PHILLIPS, TERESIA CONSTANTIA
  A Letter Humbly addressed to . . . Chesterfield by Mrs. Teresia Constantia Muilman. London, 1750.

PÖLLNITZ, KARL LUDWIG VON
  Les amusements des eaux de Spa. English translation, third edition. 1745. [As a background for Chesterfield's visit to Spa.]

POPE, ALEXANDER
  Letters. Elwin-Courthope edition.

(The) Resignation discussed. In which many false Facts are detected . . . in a Pamphlet, entitled an Apology for a late Resignation, etc. 1748.

SAUSSURE, CÉSAR DE
  A Foreign View of England in the Reigns of George I and George II. The Letters of Monsieur César de Saussure to his Family. London, 1902.

SMOLLETT, TOBIAS GEORGE
  History of England.

SPENCE, JOSEPH
  Anecdotes. London, 1820.

SUFFOLK, HENRIETTA HOWARD, COUNTESS OF
  Suffolk Correspondence (ed. Croker). London, 1824.

SUNDON, CHARLOTTE DYVE, BARONESS
  Memoirs. London, 1817.

SWIFT, JONATHAN
    Correspondence (ed. Ball), London, 1910–14.
    Observations on Macky's *Characters* (*Prose Works*, Bohn edition, vol. x).

THOMSON, JAMES
    The Seasons (Winter).

WALDEGRAVE, JAMES, SECOND EARL
    Memoirs. London, 1821.

WALPOLE, HORACE
    Letters of Horace Walpole (ed. Toynbee).
    Journal of the Reign of George the Third (ed. John Doran). London, 1859.
    Marginal notes on Maty (vols. x and xi of the *Miscellanies* of the Philobiblon Society).
    Memoirs of the Last Ten Years of the Reign of George II. London, 1822. *Reminiscences*, including *Conversations with Lady Suffolk* (ed. Paget Toynbee). Oxford, 1924.

WESLEY, JOHN
    Journal (Everyman edition).

WILLIAMS, SIR CHARLES HANBURY
    Works. London, 1822.

C. EIGHTEENTH-CENTURY OPINION OF THE LETTERS

Annual Register
    Vol. ii, pp. 19–24, 237–242. 1774.

(*An*) *Apology for the life and writings of David Hume, with a parallel between him and the late Lord Chesterfield.* London, 1777.

BOSWELL, JAMES
    [The *Life of Johnson* already cited.]

CHARLEMONT, JAMES CAULFEILD, FIRST EARL OF
    [His letter to Lord Bruce already cited.]

Chesterfield Travestie; or the School for Modern Manners. London, 1808.

COWPER, WILLIAM
    Progress of Error.

(*A*) *Dialogue* [in verse] *between the Earl of C——d and Mr. Garrick in the Elysian Shades.* 1785.

(*The*) *Fine Gentleman's Etiquette, or Lord Chesterfield's Advice to his Son Versified. By a Lady.* 1776.

Free and impartial remarks upon the Letters written by . . . *Chesterfield. By a man of the world.* 1774.

GORDON, REV. SIR A.
>The Contrast; or an antidote against the pernicious principles disseminated. 1791.

(*The*) *Graces, a poetical epistle from a gentleman to his son.* 1774.

HUNTER, THOMAS
>*Reflections on the Letters of the late Earl of Chesterfield.* London, 1776.

PRATT, SAMUEL J.
>*The Pupil of Pleasure.* [A satire.] London, 1777.
>*Curious . . . anecdotes respecting the late Lord Chesterfield and David Hume.* London, 1788.

THOMAS, A. L.
>*Lettre à M. Desenfans, pour servir à la défense de Fénelon contre Milord Chesterfield.* Paris, 1777.

Town and Country Magazine. April 1773; October 1778.

WALPOLE, HORACE
>*A Parody of Chesterfield's Letters* (*Works*, 1798, vol. iv, p. 355 ff.).

D. SUBSEQUENT BIOGRAPHY AND CRITICISM

BAYLE, G.
>*Les Anglais à Vaucluse.* Paris, 1898. [Some information about Philip Stanhope's death and burial.]

BRADSHAW, JOHN
>Introduction to the edition of the *Letters* already cited.

BROUGHAM, HENRY PETER, BARON
>*Quarterly Review*, 1845. Vol. 76, p. 459 ff.

CARLYLE, THOMAS
>*Early Letters.* 1866. [See p. 34.]
>*History of Frederick the Great.*

CARNARVON, HENRY HOWARD MOLYNEUX, FOURTH EARL OF
>Introduction to *Letters of Chesterfield to his Godson*, already cited. [A valuable criticism.]

CHANCELLOR, E. BERESFORD
>*The History of the Square of London.* London, 1907.
>*Pleasure Haunts of London.* London, 1925.
>*The Private Palaces of London.* London, 1908.
>*Eighteenth Century in London.* London, 1920.

COLLINS, JOHN CHURTON
>*Essays and Studies.* London, 1895.
>*Voltaire, Montesquieu, and Rousseau in England.* London, 1908.

CONNELY, WILLARD
> *The true Chesterfield; manners — women — education.* London, 1939.
> [A richly detailed biography. Valuable source material listed in the appended chapter notes.]

COXE, WILLIAM
> *Memoirs of John, Duke of Marlborough.* London, 1818.

COXON, ROGER
> *Chesterfield and his Critics.* London, 1925. [One of the most scholarly and valuable works on Chesterfield.]

CRAIG, W. H.
> *Life of Lord Chesterfield.* London, 1907.

Dictionary of National Biography

DOBRÉE, BONAMY
> Introduction to the edition of Chesterfield's *Letters* already cited. [This introduction is a long and excellent biography.]

DU BLED, VICTOR
> *Société française*, 5ᵉ Série. Paris, 1905.

ERNST, OR ERNST-BROWNING, W.
> *Life of . . . Chesterfield.* London, 1893.

FITCHETT, W. H.
> *Wesley and his Century.* London, 1906.

FOXCROFT, H. C.
> *Life and Letters of Halifax.* London, 1898. [The standard work on this subject.]

GULICK, SIDNEY LEWIS, JR.
> *A Chesterfield bibliography to 1800.* The University of Chicago Press. Chicago, 1935.
> Introduction to *Some unpublished letters of Lord Chesterfield* already cited. 1937.

HAYWARD, ABRAHAM
> *Life of Lord Chesterfield.* London, 1854.

JAMESON, ANNA M.
> *Beauties of the Court of Charles II.* London, 1851. [For the lives and portraits of some of Chesterfield's early contemporaries.]

JORISSEN, TH.
> *Lord Chesterfield en de Republiek der Nederlanden.* Hist. Studien, vol. v. 1894.

LEE, SIR SIDNEY
> Article on Chesterfield in the *Dictionary of National Biography.*

LODGE, SIR RICHARD
    Studies in Eighteenth-Century Diplomacy, 1740–1748. London, 1930.

MAHON, PHILIP HENRY STANHOPE, VISCOUNT
    Introduction to the edition of Chesterfield's *Works,* already cited. *History of England from the Peace of Utrecht to the Peace of Versailles.*

MELVILLE, LEWIS
    Life and Letters of John Gay. London, 1921.
    Society at Royal Tunbridge Wells. London, 1912.

OLIVER, F. S.
    The Endless Adventure. London, 1930–31.

SAINTE-BEUVE, C. A.
    Introductory Essay to *Letters, Sentences, and Maxims by Lord Chesterfield* (Bayard Series).

SANFORD, J. L., and TOWNSEND, M.
    Great Governing Families of England. London, 1865. [On the Stanhope family.]

SCHUMANN, KURT
    Die pädagogischen Ansichten des Grafen Chesterfields. Leipzig, 1917.

SICHEL, WALTER SYDNEY
    Bolingbroke and his Times. London, 1901–2.

SITWELL, EDITH
    Bath. London, 1932.

STEPHEN, SIR LESLIE
    English Thought in the Eighteenth Century. London, 1902.

STRACHEY, CHARLES
    Introduction to *Chesterfield's Letters to his Son.* London, 1901.

TIMBS, JOHN
    Clubs and Club Life in London. London, 1899.

TINKER, CHAUNCEY B.
    The Salon and English Letters. New York, 1915.

TREVELYAN, SIR GEORGE OTTO
    Life and Letters of Lord Macaulay. London, 1876. [See vol. i, pp. 320–321.]

TURBERVILLE, A. S.
    House of Lords in the Eighteenth Century. London, Oxford, 1927.

TYTLER, S. [pseud. of Henrietta Keddie]
    The Countess of Huntingdon and her Circle. London, 1907.

WILKINS, WILLIAM HENRY
  Queen Caroline. London, 1904.

WORDSWORTH, CHRISTOPHER, AND JOHNSON, R. BRIMLEY
  The Undergraduate. London, 1928.

YORKE, PHILIP C.
  Life and Correspondence of Philip Yorke, Earl of Hardwicke.
  Cambridge, 1913.

INDEX

Index